Mastering Git

Attain expert level proficiency with Git for enhanced
productivity and efficient collaboration

Jakub Narębski

PUBLISHING

BIRMINGHAM - MUMBAI

Mastering Git

First published: April 2016

Production reference: 1130416

Published by Packt Publishing Ltd.
Livery Place
35 Livery Street
Birmingham B3 2PB, UK.

ISBN 978-1-78355-375-4

www.packtpub.com

Credits

Author
Jakub Narębski

Reviewer
Markus Maiwald

Commissioning Editor
Dipika Gaonkar

Acquisition Editor
Vinay Argekar

Content Development Editor
Athira Laji

Technical Editor
Shivani Kiran Mistry

Copy Editor
Akshata Lobo

Project Coordinator
Bijal Patel

Proofreader
Safis Editing

Indexer
Hemangini Bari

Graphics
Disha Haria

Production Coordinator
Conidon Miranda

Cover Work
Conidon Miranda

About the Author

Jakub Narębski followed Git development from the very beginning of its creation. He is one of the main contributors to the gitweb subsystem (the original web interface for Git), and is an unofficial gitweb maintainer. He created, announced, and analyzed annual Git User's Surveys from 2007 till 2012 — all except the first one (you can find his analysis of those surveys on the Git Wiki). He shares his expertise with the technology on the StackOverflow question-and-answer website.

He was one of the proofreaders of the *Version Control by Example* by Eric Sink, and was the reason why it has chapter on Git.

He is an assistant professor in the faculty of mathematics and computer science at the Nicolaus Copernicus University in Toruń, Poland. He uses Git as a version control system of choice both for personal and professional work, teaching it to computer science students as a part of their coursework.

About the Reviewer

Markus Maiwald is an internet service provider, business webhoster, and domain provider. As an example, he offers agencies complete white labeling solutions for their customers (from registering a domain to deploying a webserver).

Therefore, his slogan is: *I build the systems your business runs on.*

Professionally, he is a consultant and systems administrator with over 15 years of Linux experience. He likes building high performance server systems and he develops usable and standard-compliant systems with focus on security.

As a true webworker 2.0, he runs his own international business with customers all over the world, from an insurance company in Europe to a web developer studio in Thailand.

This is the main reason why he was so passionate to work on this book. As a great team player and with a lot of experience in international teamwork, he brings in a great knowledge of tools such as Git.

I have to thank Bijal Patel, my project co-ordinator from Packt Publishing. I received outstanding support and had a great time.

I would also like to thank Sarah for her patience and encouragement while I finished this project.

www.PacktPub.com

Support files, eBooks, discount offers, and more

For support files and downloads related to your book, please visit www.PacktPub.com.

Did you know that Packt offers eBook versions of every book published, with PDF and ePub files available? You can upgrade to the eBook version at www.PacktPub.com and as a print book customer, you are entitled to a discount on the eBook copy. Get in touch with us at service@packtpub.com for more details.

At www.PacktPub.com, you can also read a collection of free technical articles, sign up for a range of free newsletters and receive exclusive discounts and offers on Packt books and eBooks.

https://www2.packtpub.com/books/subscription/packtlib

Do you need instant solutions to your IT questions? PacktLib is Packt's online digital book library. Here, you can search, access, and read Packt's entire library of books.

Why subscribe?

- Fully searchable across every book published by Packt
- Copy and paste, print, and bookmark content
- On demand and accessible via a web browser

Free access for Packt account holders

If you have an account with Packt at www.PacktPub.com, you can use this to access PacktLib today and view 9 entirely free books. Simply use your login credentials for immediate access.

Table of Contents

Preface

Mastering Git is meticulously designed to help you gain deeper insights into Git's architecture and its underlying concepts, behavior, and best practices.

Mastering Git starts with a quick implementation example of using Git for the collaborative development of a sample project to establish the foundation knowledge of Git's operational tasks and concepts. Furthermore, as you progress through the book, subsequent chapters provide detailed descriptions of the various areas of usage: from the source code archaeology, through managing your own work, to working with other developers. Version control topics are accompanied by in-detail description of relevant parts of Git architecture and behavior.

This book also helps augment your understanding to examine and explore your project's history, create and manage your contributions, set up repositories and branches for collaboration in centralized and distributed workflows, integrate work coming from other developers, customize and extend Git, and recover from repository errors. By exploring advanced Git practices, and getting to know details of Git workings, you will attain a deeper understanding of Git's behavior, allowing you to customize and extend existing recipes, and write your own.

What this book covers

Chapter 1, *Git Basics in Practice*, serves as a reminder of version control basics with Git. The focus will be on providing the practical aspects of the technology, showing and explaining basic version control operations for the development of an example project, and the collaboration between two developers.

Chapter 2, *Exploring Project History*, introduces the concept of the Directed Acyclic Graph (DAG) of revisions and explains how this concept relates to the ideas of branches, tags, and the current branch in Git. You will learn how to select, filter, and view the range of revisions in the history of a project, and how to find revisions using different criteria.

Chapter 3, Developing with Git, describes how to create such history and how to add to it. You will learn how to create new revisions and new lines of development. This chapter introduces the concept of the staging area for commits (the index), and explains how to view and read differences between the working directory, the index, and the current revision.

Chapter 4, Managing Your Worktree, focuses on explaining how to manage the working directory (the worktree) to prepare contents for a new commit. This chapter will teach the reader how to manage their files in detail. It will also show how to manage files that require special handling, introducing the concepts of ignored files and file attributes.

Chapter 5, Collaborative Development with Git, presents a bird's eye view of the various ways to collaborate, showing different centralized and distributed workflows. It will focus on the repository-level interactions in collaborative development. You will also learn here the concept of the chain of trust, and how to use signed tags, signed merges, and signed commits.

Chapter 6, Advanced Branching Techniques, goes deeper into the details of collaboration in a distributed development. It explores the relations between local branches and branches in remote repositories, and describes how to synchronize branches and tags. You will learn here branching techniques, getting to know various ways of utilizing different types of branches for distinct purposes (including topic branch workflow).

Chapter 7, Merging Changes Together, teaches you how to merge together changes from different parallel lines of development (that is, branches) using merge and rebase. This chapter will also explain the different types of merge conflicts, how to examine them, and how to resolve them. You will learn how to copy changes with cherry-pick, and how to apply a single patch and a patch series.

Chapter 8, Keeping History Clean, explains why one might want to keep clean history, when it can and should be done, and how it can be done. Here you will find step-by-step instructions on how to reorder, squash, and split commits. This chapter also demonstrates how can one recover from a history rewrite, and explains what to do if one cannot rewrite history: how to revert the effect of commit, how to add a note to it, and how to change the view of project's history.

Chapter 9, *Managing Subprojects – Building a Living Framework*, explains and shows different ways to connect different projects in the one single repository of the framework project, from the strong inclusion by embedding the code of one project in the other (subtrees), to the light connection between projects by nesting repositories (submodules). This chapter also presents various solutions to the problem of large repositories and of large files.

Chapter 10, *Customizing and Extending Git*, covers configuring and extending Git to fit one's needs. You will find here details on how to set up command line for easier use, and a short introduction to graphical interfaces. This chapter explains how to automate Git with hooks (focusing on client-side hooks), for example, how to make Git check whether the commit being created passes specified coding guidelines.

Chapter 11, *Git Administration*, is intended to help readers who are in a situation of having to take up the administrative side of Git. It briefly touches the topic of serving Git repositories. Here you will learn how to use server-side hooks for logging, access control, enforcing development policy, and other purposes.

Chapter 12, *Git Best Practices*, presents a collection of version control generic and Git-specific recommendations and best practice. Those cover issues of managing the working directory, creating commits and a series of commits (pull requests), submitting changes for inclusion, and the peer review of changes.

What you need for this book

To follow the examples used in this book and run the provided commands, you will need the Git software, preferably version 2.5.0 or later. Git is available for free on every platform (such as Linux, Windows, and Mac OS X). All examples use the textual Git interface, using the bash shell.

To compile and run sample program, which development is tracked in *Chapter 1*, *Git Basics in Practice*, as a demonstration of using version control, you would need working C compiler and the make program.

Who this book is for

If you are a Git user with reasonable knowledge of Git and you are familiar with basic concepts such as branching, merging, staging, and workflows, this is the book for you. If you have been using Git for a long time, this book will help you understand how Git works, make full use of its power, and learn about advanced tools, techniques, and workflows. The basic knowledge of installing Git and its software configuration management concepts is necessary.

Conventions

In this book, you will find a number of text styles that distinguish between different kinds of information. Here are some examples of these styles and an explanation of their meaning.

Code words in text, commands and their options, folder names, filenames, file extensions, pathnames, branch and tag names, dummy URLs, user input, environment variables, configuration options and their values are shown as follows: "For example, writing `git log -- foo` explicitly asks for the history of a path `foo`."

Additionally, the following convention is used: `<file>` denotes user input (here, the name of a file), `$HOME` denotes the value of environment variable, and tilde in a pathname is used to denote user's home directory (for example `~/.gitignore`).

A block of code, or a fragment of a configuration file, is set as follows:

```
void init_rand(void)
{
    srand(time(NULL));
}
```

When we wish to draw your attention to a particular part of a code block (which is quite rare), the relevant lines or items are set in bold:

```
void init_rand(void)
{
    srand(time(NULL));
}
```

Any command-line input or output is written as follows:

```
carol@server ~$ mkdir -p /srv/git
carol@server ~$ cd /srv/git
carol@server /srv/git$ git init --bare random.git
```

New terms and **important words** are shown in bold. Words that you see on the screen, for example, in menus or dialog boxes, appear in the text like this: "The default description that Git gives to a stash (**WIP on branch**)."

> Warnings or important notes appear in a box like this.

> Tips and tricks appear like this.

Reader feedback

Feedback from our readers is always welcome. Let us know what you think about this book—what you liked or disliked. Reader feedback is important for us as it helps us develop titles that you will really get the most out of.

To send us general feedback, simply e-mail feedback@packtpub.com, and mention the book's title in the subject of your message.

If there is a topic that you have expertise in and you are interested in either writing or contributing to a book, see our author guide at www.packtpub.com/authors.

Customer support

Now that you are the proud owner of a Packt book, we have a number of things to help you to get the most from your purchase.

Downloading the example code

You can download the example code files from your account at http://www. packtpub.com for all the Packt Publishing books you have purchased. If you purchased this book elsewhere, you can visit http://www.packtpub.com/support and register to have the files e-mailed directly to you.

Downloading the color images of this book

We also provide you with a PDF file that has color images of the screenshots/ diagrams used in this book. The color images will help you better understand the changes in the output. You can download this file from https://www.packtpub. com/sites/default/files/downloads/MasteringGit_ColorImages.pdf.

Errata

Although we have taken every care to ensure the accuracy of our content, mistakes do happen. If you find a mistake in one of our books—maybe a mistake in the text or the code—we would be grateful if you could report this to us. By doing so, you can save other readers from frustration and help us improve subsequent versions of this book. If you find any errata, please report them by visiting http://www.packtpub. com/submit-errata, selecting your book, clicking on the **Errata Submission Form** link, and entering the details of your errata. Once your errata are verified, your submission will be accepted and the errata will be uploaded to our website or added to any list of existing errata under the Errata section of that title.

To view the previously submitted errata, go to `https://www.packtpub.com/books/content/support` and enter the name of the book in the search field. The required information will appear under the **Errata** section.

Piracy

Piracy of copyrighted material on the Internet is an ongoing problem across all media. At Packt, we take the protection of our copyright and licenses very seriously. If you come across any illegal copies of our works in any form on the Internet, please provide us with the location address or website name immediately so that we can pursue a remedy.

Please contact us at `copyright@packtpub.com` with a link to the suspected pirated material.

We appreciate your help in protecting our authors and our ability to bring you valuable content.

Questions

If you have a problem with any aspect of this book, you can contact us at `questions@packtpub.com`, and we will do our best to address the problem.

1
Git Basics in Practice

This book is intended for novice and advanced Git users to help them on their road to mastering Git. Therefore the following chapters will assume that the reader knows the basics of Git, and has advanced past the beginner stage.

This chapter will serve as a reminder of version control basics with Git. The focus will be on providing practical aspects of the technology, showing and explaining basic version control operations in the example of the development of a sample project, and collaboration between two developers.

In this chapter we will recall:

- Setting up a Git environment and Git repository (`init`, `clone`)
- Adding files, checking status, creating commits, and examining the history
- Interacting with other Git repositories (`pull`, `push`)
- How to resolve a merge conflict
- Creating and listing branches, switching to a branch, and merging
- How to create a tag

An introduction to version control and Git

A **version control system** (sometimes called **revision control**) is a tool that lets you track the history and attribution of your project files over time (stored in a **repository**), and which helps the developers in the team to work together. Modern version control systems help them work simultaneously, in a non-blocking way, by giving each developer his or her own sandbox, preventing their work in progress from conflicting, and all the while providing a mechanism to merge changes and synchronize work.

Distributed version control systems such as Git give each developer his or her own copy of the project's history, a **clone** of a repository. This is what makes Git fast: nearly all operations are performed locally, and are flexible: you can set up repositories in many ways. Repositories meant for developing also provide a separate **working area** (or a **worktree**) with project files for each developer. The branching model used by Git enables cheap local branching and flexible branch publishing, allowing to use branches for context switching and for sandboxing different works in progress (making possible, among other things, a very flexible **topic branch** workflow).

The fact that the whole history is accessible allows for long-term undo, rewinding back to last working version, and so on. Tracking ownership of changes automatically makes it possible to find out who was responsible for any given area of code, and when each change was done. You can compare different revisions, go back to the revision a user is sending a bug report against, and even automatically find out which revision introduced a regression bug. The fact that Git is tracking changes to the tips of branches with **reflog** allows for easy undo and recovery.

A unique feature of Git is that it enables explicit access to the staging area for creating commits (new revisions of a project). This brings additional flexibility to managing your working area and deciding on the shape of a future commit.

All this flexibility and power comes at a cost. It is not easy to master using Git, even though it is quite easy to learn its basic use. This book will help you attain this expertise, but let's start with a reminder about basics with Git.

Git by example

Let's follow step by step a simple example of two developers using Git to work together on a simple project. You can download the example code files from `http://www.packtpub.com`. You can find there all three repositories (for two developers, and the bare server repository) with the example code files for this chapter, where you can examine code, history, and reflog..

Repository setup

A company has begun work on a new product. This product calculates a random number—an integer value of specified range.

The company has assigned two developers to work on this new project, Alice and Bob. Both developers are telecommuting to the company's corporate headquarters After a bit of discussion, they have decided to implement their product as a command-line app in C, and to use Git 2.5.0 (http://git-scm.com/) for version control. This project and the code are intended for demonstration purposes, and will be much simplified. The details of code are not important here—what's important is how the code changes:

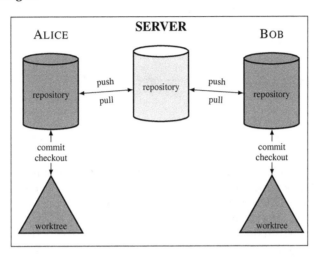

With a small team, they have decided on the setup shown in the preceding diagram.

> This is one possible setup, with the central *canonical* repository, and without a dedicated maintainer responsible for this repository (all developers are equal in this setup). It is not the only possibility; other ways of configuring repositories will be shown in *Chapter 5, Collaborative Development with Git*.

Creating a Git repository

Alice gets the project started by asking Carol, an administrator, to create a new repository specifically for collaborating on a project, to share work with all the team:

Command line examples follow the Unix convention of having `user@host` and directory in the command prompt, to know from the first glance who performs a command, on what computer, and in which directory. This is the usual setup on Unix (for example, on Linux).

You can configure your command prompt to show Git-specific information like the name of the repository name, the subdirectory within the repository, the current branch, and even the status of the working area, see *Chapter 10, Customizing and Extending Git*.

```
carol@server ~$ mkdir -p /srv/git
carol@server ~$ cd /srv/git
carol@server /srv/git$ git init --bare random.git
```

I consider the details of server configuration to be too much for this chapter. Just imagine that it happened, and nothing went wrong. Or take a look at *Chapter 11, Git Administration*.

You can also use a tool to manage Git repositories (for example Gitolite); creating a public repository on a server would then, of course, look different. Often though it involves creating a Git repository with `git init` (without `--bare`) and then pushing it with an explicit URI to the server, which then automatically creates the public repository.

Or perhaps the repository was created through the web interface of tools, such as GitHub, Bitbucket, or GitLab (either hosted or on-premise).

Cloning the repository and creating the first commit

Bob gets the information that the project repository is ready, and he can start coding.

Since this is Bob's first time using Git, he first sets up his `~/.gitconfig` file with information that will be used to identify his commits in the log:

```
[user]
   name = Bob Hacker
   email = bob@company.com
```

Now he needs to get his own repository instance:

```
bob@hostB ~$ git clone https://git.company.com/random
Cloning into random...
Warning: You appear to have cloned an empty repository.
```

```
done.

bob@hostB ~$ cd random

bob@hostB random$
```

 All examples in this chapter use the command-line interface. Those commands might be given using a Git GUI or IDE integration. The *Git: Version Control for Everyone* book, published by Packt Publishing, shows GUI equivalents for the command-line.

Bob notices that Git said that it is an empty repository, with no source code yet, and starts coding. He opens his text editor and creates the starting point for their product:

```c
#include <stdio.h>
#include <stdlib.h>

int random_int(int max)
{
  return rand() % max;
}

int main(int argc, char *argv[])
{
  if (argc != 2) {
    fprintf(stderr, "Usage: %s <number>\n", argv[0]);
    return EXIT_FAILURE;
  }

  int max = atoi(argv[1]);

  int result = random_int(max);
  printf("%d\n", result);

  return EXIT_SUCCESS;
}
```

Typically, like for most initial implementations, this version is missing a lot of features. But it's a good place to begin. Before committing his code, Bob wants to make sure that it compiles and runs:

```
bob@hostB random$ gcc -std=c99 random.c

bob@hostB random$ ls -l

total 43
```

```
-rwxr-xr-x  1 bob    staff   86139  May 29 17:36 a.out
-rw-r--r--  1 bob    staff     331  May 19 17:11 random.c
bob@hostB random$ ./a.out
Usage: ./a.out <number>
bob@hostB random$ ./a.out 10
1
```

Alright! It's time to add this file to the repository:

```
bob@hostB random$ git add random.c
```

Bob uses the status operation to make sure that the pending changeset (the future commit) looks proper:

> We use here a short form of the git status to reduce the amount of space taken by examples; you can find an example of full status output further in the chapter.

```
bob@hostB random$ git status -s
A   random.c
?? a.out
```

Git is complaining because it does not know what to do about the a.out file: it is neither tracked nor ignored. That's a compiled executable, which as a generated file should not be stored in a version control repository. Bob can just ignore that issue for the time being.

Now it's time to commit the file:

```
bob@hostB random$ git commit -a -m "Initial implementation"
[master (root-commit) 2b953b4] Initial implementation
 1 file changed, 22 insertions(+)
 Create mode 100644 random.c
```

> Normally, you would create a commit message not by using the -m <message> command-line option, but by letting Git open an editor. We use this form here to make examples more compact.
>
> The -a / --all option means to take all changes to the tracked files; you can separate manipulating the staging area from creating a commit — this is however a separate issue, left for *Chapter 4, Managing Your Worktree*.

Publishing changes

After finishing working on the initial version of the project, Bob decides that it is ready to be published (to be made available for other developers). He pushes the changes:

```
bob@hostB random$ git push
warning: push.default is unset; its implicit value has changed in
Git 2.0 from 'matching' to 'simple'. To squelch this message [...]
To https://git.company.com/random
 * [new branch]      master -> master
bob@hostB random$ git config --global push.default simple
```

 Note that, depending on the speed of network, Git could show progress information during remote operations such as `clone`, `push`, and `fetch`. Such information is omitted from examples in this book, except where that information is actually discussed while examining history and viewing changes.

Examining history and viewing changes

Since it is Alice's first time using Git on her desktop machine, she first tells Git how her commits should be identified:

```
alice@hostA ~$ git config --global user.name "Alice Developer"
alice@hostA ~$ git config --global user.email alice@company.com
```

Now Alice needs to set up her own repository instance:

```
alice@hostA ~$ git clone https://git.company.com/random
Cloning into random...
done.
```

Alice examines the working directory:

```
alice@hostA ~$ cd random
alice@hostA random$ ls -al
total 1
drwxr-xr-x    1 alice staff         0 May 30 16:44 .
drwxr-xr-x    4 alice staff         0 May 30 16:39 ..
drwxr-xr-x    1 alice staff         0 May 30 16:39 .git
-rw-r--r--    1 alice staff       353 May 30 16:39 random.c
```

The `.git` directory contains Alice's whole copy (clone) of the repository in Git internal format, and some repository-specific administrative information. See `gitrepository-layout`(5) manpage for details of the file layout, which can be done for example with `git help repository-layout` command.

She wants to check the `log` to see the details (to examine the project history):

```
alice@hostA random$ git log
commit 2b953b4e80abfb77bdcd94e74dedeeebf6aba870
Author: Bob Hacker <bob@company.com>
Date:   Thu May 29 19:53:54 2015 +0200

    Initial implementation
```

Naming revisions:

At the lowest level, a Git version identifier is a SHA-1 hash, for example `2b953b4e80`. Git supports various forms of referring to revisions, including the unambiguously shortened SHA-1 (with a minimum of four characters)—see *Chapter 2, Exploring Project History*, for more ways.

When Alice decides to take a look at the code, she immediately finds something horrifying. The random number generator is never initialized! A quick test shows that the program always generates the same number. Fortunately, it is only necessary to add one line to `main()`, and the appropriate `#include`:

```c
#include <stdio.h>
#include <stdlib.h>
#include <time.h>

int random_int(int max)
{
  return rand() % max;
}

int main(int argc, char *argv[])
{
  if (argc != 2) {
    fprintf(stderr, "Usage: %s <number>\n", argv[0]);
    return EXIT_FAILURE;
  }
```

```
    int max = atoi(argv[1]);

    srand(time(NULL));
    int result = random_int(max);
    printf("%d\n", result);

    return EXIT_SUCCESS;
}
```

She compiles the code, and runs it a few times to check that it really generates random numbers. Everything looks alright, so she uses the `status` operation to see the pending changes:

```
alice@hostA random$ git status -s
 M random.c
```

No surprise here. Git knows that `random.c` has been modified. She wants to double-check by reviewing the actual changes with the `diff` command:

 From here on, we will not show untracked files, unless they are relevant to the topic being discussed; let's assume that Alice set up an ignore file, as described in *Chapter 4, Managing Your Worktree*.

```
alice@hostA random$ git diff
diff --git a/random.c b/random.c
index cc09a47..5e095ce 100644
--- a/random.c
+++ b/random.c
@@ -1,5 +1,6 @@
 #include <stdio.h>
 #include <stdlib.h>
+#include <time.h>

 int random_int(int max)
 {
@@ -15,6 +16,7 @@ int main(int argc, char *argv[])

    int max = atoi(argv[1]);

+   srand(time(NULL));
    int result = random_int(max);
    printf("%d\n", result);
```

Now it's time to commit the changes and push them to the public repository:

```
alice@hostA random$ git commit -a -m "Initialize random number generator"
[master db23d0e] Initialize random number generator
 1 file changed, 2 insertions(+)
alice@hostA random$ git push
To https://git.company.com/random
   3b16f17..db23d0e master -> masterRenaming and moving files
```

Renaming and moving files

Bob moves on to his next task, which is to restructure the tree a bit. He doesn't want the top level of the repository to get too cluttered so he decides to move all their source code files into a src/ subdirectory:

```
bob@hostA random$ mkdir src
bob@hostA random$ git mv random.c src/
bob@hostA random$ git status -s
R  random.c -> src/random.c
bob@hostA random$ git commit -a -m "Directory structure"
[master 69e0d3d] Directory structure
 1 file changed, 0 insertions(+), 0 deletions(-)
 rename random.c => src/random.c (100%)
```

While at it, to minimize the impact of reorganization on the diff output, he configures Git to always use rename and copy detection:

```
bob@hostB random$ git config --global diff.renames copies
```

Bob then decides the time has come to create a proper Makefile, and to add a README for a project:

```
bob@hostA random$ git add README Makefile
bob@hostA random$ git status -s
A  Makefile
A  README
bob@hostA random$ git commit -a -m "Added Makefile and README"
[master abfeea4] Added Makefile and README
 2 files changed, 15 insertions(+)
 create mode 100644 Makefile
 create mode 100644 README
```

Bob decides to rename `random.c` to `rand.c`:

```
bob@hostA random$ git mv src/random.c src/rand.c
```

This of course also requires changes to the `Makefile`:

```
bob@hostA random$ git status -s
 M Makefile
R  src/random.c -> src/rand.c
```

He then commits those changes.

Updating your repository (with merge)

Reorganization done, now Bob tries to publish those changes:

```
bob@hostA random$ git push
$ git push
To https://git.company.com/random
 ! [rejected]        master -> master (fetch first)
error: failed to push some refs to 'https://git.company.com/random'
hint: Updates were rejected because the remote contains work that you do
hint: not have locally. This is usually caused by another repository
pushing
hint: to the same ref. You may want to first integrate the remote changes
hint: (e.g., 'git pull ...') before pushing again.
hint: See the 'Note about fast-forwards' in 'git push --help' for
details.
```

But Alice was working at the same time and she had her change ready to commit and push first. Git is not allowing Bob to publish his changes because Alice has already pushed something to the master branch, and Git is preserving her changes.

 Hints and advices in Git command output will be skipped from here on for the sake of brevity.

Bob uses `pull` to bring in changes (as described in `hint` in the command output):

```
bob@hostB random $ git pull
From https://git.company.com/random
 + 3b16f17...db23d0e master     -> origin/master
```

```
Auto-merging src/rand.c
Merge made by the 'recursive' strategy.
 src/rand.c | 2 ++
 1 file changed, 2 insertions(+)
```

Git `pull` fetched the changes, automatically merged them with Bob's changes, and committed the merge.

Everything now seems to be good:

```
bob@hostB random$ git show
commit ba5807e44d75285244e1d2eacb1c10cbc5cf3935
Merge: 3b16f17 db23d0e
Author: Bob Hacker <bob@company.com>
Date:    Sat May 31 20:43:42 2015 +0200


    Merge branch 'master' of https://git.company.com/random
```

The merge commit is done. Apparently, Git was able to merge Alice's changes directly into Bob's moved and renamed copy of a file without any problems. Marvelous!

Bob checks that it compiles (because *automatically merged* does not necessarily mean that the merge output is correct), and is ready to push the merge:

```
bob@hostB random$ git push
To https://git.company.com/random
   db23d0e..ba5807e  master -> master
```

Creating a tag

Alice and Bob decide that the project is ready for wider distribution. Bob creates a `tag` so they can more easily access/refer to the released version. He uses an **annotated tag** for this; an often used alternative is to use **signed tag**, where the annotation contains a PGP signature (which can later be verified):

```
bob@hostB random$ git tag -a -m "random v0.1" v0.1
bob@hostB random$ git tag --list
```

```
v0.1
bob@hostB random$ git log -1 --decorate --abbrev-commit
commit ba5807e (HEAD -> master, tag: v0.1, origin/master)
Merge: 3b16f17 db23d0e
Author: Bob Hacker <bob@company.com>
Date:   Sat May 31 20:43:42 2015 +0200

    Merge branch 'master' of https://git.company.com/random
```

Of course, the `v0.1` tag wouldn't help if it was only in Bob's local repository. He therefore pushes the just created `tag`:

```
bob@hostB random$ git push origin tag v0.1
Counting objects: 1, done.
Writing objects: 100% (1/1), 162 bytes, done.
Total 1 (delta 0), reused 0 (delta 0)
Unpacking objects: 100% (1/1), done.
To https://git.company.com/random
 * [new tag]         v0.1 -> v0.1
```

Alice updates her repository to get the `v0.1` tag, and to start with up-to-date work:

```
alice@hostA random$ git pull
From https://git.company.com/random
   f4d9753..be08dee  master     -> origin/master
 * [new tag]         v0.1       -> v0.1
Updating  f4d9753..be08dee
Fast-forward
 Makefile               | 11 +++++++++++
 README                 |  4 ++++
 random.c => src/rand.c |  0
 3 files changed, 15 insertions(+)
 create mode 100644 Makefile
 create mode 100644 README
 rename random.c => src/rand.c (100%)
```

Resolving a merge conflict

Alice decides that it would be a good idea to extract initialization of a pseudo-random numbers generator into a separate subroutine. This way, both initialization and generating random numbers are encapsulated, making future changes easier. She codes and adds `init_rand()`:

```
void init_rand(void)
{
    srand(time(NULL));
}
```

Grand! Let's see that it compiles.

```
alice@hostA random$ make
gcc -std=c99 -Wall -Wextra  -o rand src/rand.c
alice@hostA random$ ls -F
Makefile  rand*  README  src/
```

Good. Time to commit the change:

```
alice@hostA random$ git status -s
 M src/rand.c
alice@hostA random$ git commit -a -m "Abstract RNG initialization"
[master 26f8e35] Abstract RNG initialization
 1 files changed, 6 insertions(+), 1 deletion(-)
```

No problems here.

Meanwhile, Bob notices that the documentation for the `rand()` function used says that it is a weak pseudo-random generator. On the other hand, it is a standard function, and it might be enough for the planned use:

```
bob@hostB random$ git pull
Already up-to-date.
```

He decides to add a note about this issue in a comment:

```
bob@hostB random$ git status -s
 M src/rand.c
bob@hostB random$ git diff
diff --git a/src/rand.c b/src/rand.c
index 5e095ce..8fddf5d 100644
```

```
--- a/src/rand.c
+++ b/src/rand.c
@@ -2,6 +2,7 @@
 #include <stdlib.h>
 #include <time.h>

+// TODO: use a better random generator
 int random_int(int max)
 {
         return rand() % max;
```

He has his change ready to commit and push first:

```
bob@hostB random$ git commit -m 'Add TODO comment for random_int()'
[master 8c4ceca] Use Add TODO comment for random_int()
 1 files changed, 1 insertion(+)
bob@hostB random$ git push
To https://git.company.com/random
   ba5807e..8c4ceca  master -> master
```

So when Alice is ready to push her changes, Git rejects it:

```
alice@hostA random$ git push
To https://git.company.com/random
 ! [rejected]        master -> master (non-fast-forward)
error: failed to push some refs to 'https://git.company.com/random'
[...]
```

Ah. Bob must have pushed a new changeset already. Alice once again needs to pull and merge to combine Bob's changes with her own:

```
alice@hostA random$ git pull
From https://git.company.com/random
   ba5807e..8c4ceca  master       -> origin/master
Auto-merging src/rand.c
CONFLICT (content): Merge conflict in src/rand.c
Automatic merge failed; fix conflicts and then commit the result.
```

The merge didn't go quite as smoothly this time. Git wasn't able to automatically merge Alice's and Bob's changes. Apparently, there was a conflict. Alice decides to open the `src/rand.c` file in her editor to examine the situation (she could have used a graphical merge tool via `git mergetool` instead):

```
<<<<<<< HEAD
void init_rand(void)
{
        srand(time(NULL));
}


=======
// TODO: use a better random generator
>>>>>>> 8c4ceca59d7402fb24a672c624b7ad816cf04e08
int random_int(int max)
```

Git has included both Alice's code (between `<<<<<<<< HEAD` and `========` conflict markers) and Bob's code (between `========` and `>>>>>>>>`). What we want as a final result is to include both blocks of code. Git couldn't merge it automatically because those blocks were not separated. Alice's `init_rand()` function can be simply included right before Bob's added comment. After resolution, the changes look like this:

```
alice@hostA random$ git diff
diff --cc src/rand.c
index 17ad8ea,8fddf5d..0000000
--- a/src/rand.c
+++ b/src/rand.c
@@@ -2,11 -2,7 +2,12 @@@
  #include <stdlib.h>
  #include <time.h>

 +void init_rand(void)
 +{
 +        srand(time(NULL));
 +}
 +
```

```
+ // TODO: use a better random generator
  int random_int(int max)
  {
        return rand() % max;
```

That should take care of the problem. Alice compiles the code to make sure and then commits the merge:

```
alice@hostA random$ git status -s
UU src/rand.c
alice@hostA random$ git commit -a -m 'Merge: init_rand() + TODO'
[master 493e222] Merge: init_rand() + TODO
```

And then she retries the push:

```
alice@hostA random$ git push
To https://git.company.com/random
   8c4ceca..493e222  master -> master
```

And... done.

Adding files in bulk and removing files

Bob decides to add a COPYRIGHT file with a copyright notice for the project. There was also a NEWS file planned (but not created), so he uses a bulk add to add all the files:

```
bob@hostB random$ git add -v
add 'COPYRIGHT'
add 'COPYRIGHT~'
```

Oops. Because Bob didn't configure his **ignore patterns**, the backup file COPYRIGHT~ was caught too. Let's remove this file:

```
bob@hostB random$ git status -s
A  COPYRIGHT
A  COPYRIGHT~
bob@hostB random$ git rm COPYRIGHT~
error: 'COPYRIGHT~' has changes staged in the index
(use --cached to keep the file, or -f to force removal)
bob@hostB random$ git rm -f COPYRIGHT~
rm 'COPYRIGHT~'
```

Let's check the status and commit the changes:

```
bob@hostB random$ git status -s
A  COPYRIGHT
bob@hostB random$ git commit -a -m 'Added COPYRIGHT'
[master ca3cdd6] Added COPYRIGHT
 1 files changed, 2 insertions(+), 0 deletions(-)
 create mode 100644 COPYRIGHT
```

Undoing changes to a file

A bit bored, Bob decides to indent `rand.c` to make it follow a consistent coding style convention:

```
bob@hostB random$ indent src/rand.c
```

He checks how much source code it changed:

```
bob@hostB random$ git diff --stat
 src/rand.c |   40 +++++++++++++++++++++++-------------------
 1 files changed, 22 insertions(+), 18 deletions(-)
```

That's too much (for such a short file). It could cause problems with merging. Bob calms down and undoes the changes to `rand.c`:

```
bob@hostB random$ git status -s
 M src/rand.c
bob@hostB random$ git checkout -- src/rand.c
bob@hostB random$ git status -s
```

 If you don't remember how to revert a particular type of change, or to update what is to be committed (using `git commit` without `-a`), the output of `git status` (without `-s`) contains information about what commands to use. This is shown as follows:

```
bob@hostB random$ git status
# On branch master
# Your branch is ahead of 'origin/master' by 1 commit.
#
# Changed but not updated:
```

```
#    (use "git add <file>..." to update what will be committed)
#    (use "git checkout -- <file>..." to discard changes in working
directory)
#
#    modified:    src/rand.c
```

Creating a new branch

Alice notices that using a modulo operation to return random numbers within a given span does not generate uniformly distributed random numbers, since in most cases it makes lower numbers slightly more likely. She decides to try to fix this issue. To isolate this line of development from other changes, she decides to create her own named branch (see also *Chapter 6, Advanced Branching Techniques*), and switch to it:

```
alice@hostA random$ git checkout -b better-random
Switched to a new branch 'better-random'
alice@hostA random$ git branch
* better-random
  master
```

 Instead of using the git checkout -b better-random shortcut to create a new branch and switch to it in one command invocation, she could have first created a branch with git branch better-random, then switched to it with git checkout better-random.

She decides to shrink the range from RAND_MAX to the requested number by rescaling the output of rand(). The changes look like this:

```
alice@hostA random$ git diff
diff --git a/src/rand.c b/src/rand.c
index 2125b0d..5ded9bb 100644
--- a/src/rand.c
+++ b/src/rand.c
@@ -10,7 +10,7 @@ void init_rand(void)
 // TODO: use a better random generator
 int random_int(int max)
 {
```

```
-           return rand() % max;
+           return rand()*max / RAND_MAX;
 }


 int main(int argc, char *argv[])
```

She commits her changes, and pushes them, knowing that the push will succeed because she is working on her private branch:

```
alice@hostA random$ git commit -a -m 'random_int: use rescaling'
[better-random bb71a80]  random_int: use rescaling
 1 files changed, 1 insertion(+), 1 deletion(-)
alice@hostA random$ git push
fatal: The current branch better-random has no upstream branch.
To push the current branch and set the remote as upstream, use

    git push --set-upstream origin better-random
```

Alright! Git just wants Alice to set up a remote origin as the upstream for the newly created branch (it is using a simple `push` strategy); this will also push this branch explicitly.

```
alice@hostA random$ git push --set-upstream origin better-random
To https://git.company.com/random
 * [new branch]      better-random -> better-random
```

 If she wants to make her branch visible, but private (so nobody but her can push to it), she needs to configure the server with hooks, or use Git repository management software such as `Gitolite` to manage it for her.

Merging a branch (no conflicts)

Meanwhile, over in the default branch, Bob decides to push his changes by adding the COPYRIGHT file:

```
bob@hostB random$ git push
To https://git.company.com/random
 ! [rejected]        master -> master (non-fast-forward)
[...]
```

OK. Alice was busy working at extracting random number generator initialization into a subroutine (and resolving a merge conflict), and she pushed the changes first:

```
bob@hostB random$ git pull
From https://git.company.com/random
   8c4ceca..493e222  master       -> origin/master
 * [new branch]      better-random  -> origin/better-random
Merge made by 'recursive' strategy.
 src/rand.c | 7 ++++++-
 1 file changed, 6 insertions(+), 1 deletion(-)
```

Well, Git has merged Alice's changes cleanly, but there is a new branch present. Let's take a look at what is in it, showing only those changes exclusive to the `better-random` branch (the double dot syntax is described in *Chapter 2, Exploring Project History*):

```
bob@hostB random$ git log HEAD..origin/better-random
commit bb71a804f9686c4bada861b3fcd3cfb5600d2a47
Author: Alice Developer <alice@company.com>
Date:   Sun Jun 1 03:02:09 2015 +0200

    random_int: use rescaling
```

Interesting. Bob decides he wants that. So he asks Git to merge stuff from Alice's branch (which is available in the respective remote-tracking branch) into the default branch:

```
bob@hostB random$ git merge origin/better-random
Merge made by the 'recursive' strategy.
 src/rand.c | 2 +-
 1 file changed, 1 insertion(+), 1 deletion(-)
```

Undoing an unpublished merge

Bob realizes that it should be up to Alice to decide when the feature is ready for inclusion. He decides to undo a merge. Because it is not published, it is as simple as rewinding to the previous state of the current branch:

```
bob@hostB random$ $ git reset --hard @{1}
HEAD is now at 3915cef Merge branch 'master' of https://git.company.com/
random
```

> This example demonstrates the use of reflog for undoing operations; another solution would be to go to a previous (pre-merge) commit following the first parent, with HEAD^ instead of @{1}.

Summary

This chapter walked us through the process of working on a simple example project by a small development team.

We have recalled how to start working with Git, either by creating a new repository or by cloning an existing one. We have seen how to prepare a commit by adding, editing, moving, and renaming files, how to revert changes to file, how to examine the current status and view changes to be committed, and how to tag a new release.

We have recalled how to use Git to work at the same time on the same project, how to make our work public, and how to get changes from other developers. Though using a version control system helps with simultaneous work, sometimes Git needs user input to resolve conflicts in work done by different developers. We have seen how to resolve a merge conflict.

We have recalled how to create a tag marking a release, and how to create a branch starting an independent line of development. Git requires tags and new branches to be pushed explicitly, but it fetches them automatically. We have seen how to merge a branch.

2
Exploring Project History

One of the most important parts of mastering a version control system is exploring project history, making use of the fact that with version control systems we have an archive of every version that has ever existed. Here, the reader will learn how to select, filter, and view the range of revisions; how to refer to the revisions (revision selection); and how to find revisions using different criteria.

This chapter will introduce the concept of **Directed Acyclic Graph** (**DAG**) of revisions and explain how this concept relates to the ideas of branches, tags, and of the current branch in Git.

Here is the list of topics we will cover in this chapter:

- Revision selection
- Revision range selection, limiting history, history simplification
- Searching history with "pickaxe" tool and diff search
- Finding bugs with `git bisect`
- Line-wise history of file contents with `git blame`, and rename detection
- Selecting and formatting output (the `pretty` formats)
- Summarizing contribution with shortlog
- Specifying canonical author name and e-mail with `.mailmap`
- Viewing specific revision, diff output options, and viewing file at revision

Directed Acyclic Graphs

What makes version control systems different from backup applications is, among others, the ability to represent more than linear history. This is necessary, both to support the simultaneous parallel development by different developers (each developer in his or her own clone of repository), and to allow independent parallel lines of development—branches. For example, one might want to keep the ongoing development and work on bug fixes for the stable version isolated; this is possible by using individual branches for the separate lines of development. **Version control system (VCS)** thus needs to be able to model such a (non-linear) way of development and to have some structure to represent multiple revisions.

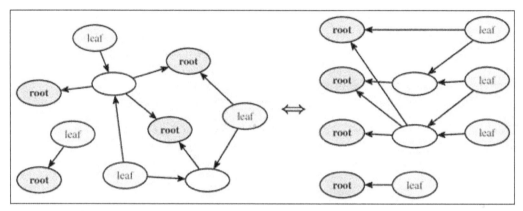

Fig 1. A generic example of the Directed Acyclic Graph (DAG). The same graph is represented on both sides: in free-form on the left, left-to-right order on the right.

The structure that Git uses (on the abstract level) to represent the possible non-linear history of a project is called a Directed Acyclic Graph (DAG).

A *directed graph* is a data structure from computer science (and mathematics) composed of nodes (vertices) that are connected with directed edges (arrows). A directed graph is *acyclic* if it doesn't contain any cycles, which means that there is no way to start at some node and follow a sequence of the directed edges to end up back at the starting node.

In concrete examples of graphs, each node represents some object or a piece of data, and each edge from one node to another represents some kind of relationship between objects or data, represented by the nodes this edge connects.

The DAG of revisions in **distributed version control systems (DVCS)** uses the following representation:

- **Nodes**: In DVCS, each node represents one revision (one version) of a project (of the entire tree). These objects are called **commits**.
- **Directed edges**: In DVCS, each edge is based on the relationship between two revisions. The arrow goes from a later **child** revision to an earlier **parent** revision it was based on or created from.

As directed edges' representation is based on a causal relationship between revisions, the arrows in the DAG of revisions may not form a cycle. Usually, the DAG of revisions is laid out left-to-right (root nodes on the left, leaves on the right) or bottom-to-top (the most recent revisions on top). Figures in this book and ASCII-art examples in Git documentation use the left-to-right convention, while the Git command line use bottom-to-top, that is, the most recent first convention.

There are two special type of nodes in any DAG (see *Fig 1*):

- **Root nodes**: These are the nodes (revisions) that have no parents (no outgoing edges). There is at least one root node in the DAG of revisions, which represents the initial (starting) version of a project.

> There can be more than one root node in Git's DAG of revisions. Additional root nodes can be created when joining two formerly originally independent projects together; each joined project brings its own root node.
>
> Another source of root nodes are **orphan branches**, that is, disconnected branches having no history in common. They are, for example, used by GitHub to manage a project's web pages together in one repository with code, and by Git project to store the pregenerated documentation (the man and html branches) or related projects (todo).

- **Leaf nodes (or leaves)**: These are the nodes that have no children (no incoming edges); there is at least one such node. They represent the most recent versions of the project, not having any work based on them. Usually, each leaf in the DAG of revisions has a branch head pointing to it.

The fact that the DAG can have more than one leaf node means that there is no inherent notion of the latest version, as it was in the linear history paradigm.

Whole-tree commits

In DVCS, each node of the DAG of revisions (a model of history) represents a version of the project as a whole single entity: of all the files and all the directories, and of the whole directory tree of a project.

This means that each developer will always get the history of all the files in his or her clone of the repository. He or she can choose to get only a part of the history (shallow clone and/or cloning only selected branches) and checkout only the selected files (sparse checkout), but to date, there is no way to get only the history of the selected files in the clone of the repository. *Chapter 9, Managing Subprojects - Building a Living Framework* will show some workarounds for when you want to have the equivalent of the partial clone, for example, when working with large media files that are needed only for a selected subset of your developers.

Branches and tags

A **branch operation** is what you use when you want your development process to fork into two different directions to create another line of development. For example, you might want to create a separate branch to keep managing bug fixes to the released stable version, isolating this activity from the rest of the development.

A **tag operation** is a way to associate a meaningful symbolic name with the specific revision in the repository. For example, you might want to create v1.3-rc3 with the third release candidate before releasing version 1.3 of your project . This makes it possible to go back to this specific version, for example, to check the validity of the bug report.

Both branches and tags, sometimes called **references** (**refs**) together, have the same meaning (the same representation) within the DAG of revisions. They are the external references (pointers) to the graph of revisions, as shown in *Fig 2*.

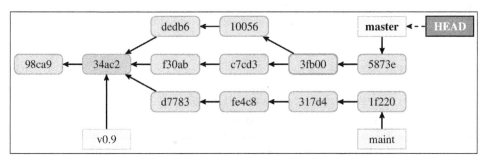

Fig 2. Example graph of revisions in a version control system, with two branches "master" (current branch) and "maint", single tag "v0.9", one branching point with shortened identifier 34ac2, and one merge commit: 3fb00.

A **tag** is a symbolic name (for example, `v1.3-rc3`) for a given revision. It always points to the same object; it does not change. The idea behind having tags is, for every project's developer, to be able to refer to the given revision with a symbolic name, and to have this symbolic name mean the same for each and every developer. Checking out or viewing the given tag should have the same results for everyone.

A **branch** is a symbolic name for the line of development. The most recent commit (leaf revision) on such a line of development is referred to as the top or tip of the branch, or branch head, or just a branch. Creating a new commit will generate a new node in the DAG, and advance the appropriate branch ref.

The branch in the DAG is, as a line of development, the subgraph of the revisions composed of those revisions that are reachable from the tip of the branch (the branch head); in other words, revisions that you can walk to by following the *parent* edges starting from the branch head.

Git, of course, needs to know which branch tip to advance when creating a new commit. It needs to know which branch is the current one and is checked out into the working directory. Git uses the **HEAD** pointer for this, as shown in *Fig 2* of this chapter. Usually, this points to one of branch tips, which, in turn, points to some node in the DAG of revisions, but not always—see *Chapter 3, Developing with Git*, for an explanation of the **detached HEAD** situation; that is, when HEAD points directly to a node in the DAG.

Full names of references (branches and tags)

Originally, Git stored branches and tags in files inside `.git` administrative area, in the `.git/refs/heads/` and `.git/refs/tags/` directories, respectively. Modern Git can store information about tags and branches inside the `.git/packed-refs` file to avoid handling a very large number of small files. Nevertheless, active references use original *loose* format — one file per reference.

The `HEAD` pointer (usually a symbolic reference, for example `ref: refs/heads/master`) is stored in `.git/HEAD`.

The `master` branch is stored in `.git/refs/heads/master`, and has `refs/heads/master` as full name (in other words, branches reside in the `refs/heads/` namespace). The tip of the branch is referred to as *head* of a branch, hence the name of a namespace. In *loose* format, the file content is an SHA-1 identifier of the most current revision on the branch (the *branch tip*), in plain text as hexadecimal digit. It is sometimes required to use the full name if there is ambiguity among refs.

The remote-tracking branch, `origin/master`, which remembers the last seen position of the `master` branch in the remote repository, `origin`, is stored in `.git/refs/remotes/origin/master`, and has `refs/remotes/origin/master` as its full name. The concept of **remotes** will be explained in *Chapter 5, Collaborative Development with Git*, and that of **remote-tracking branches** in *Chapter 6, Advanced Branching Techniques*.

The `v1.3-rc3` tag has `refs/tags/v1.3-rc3` as the full name (tags reside in the `refs/tags/` namespace). To be more precise, in the case of **annotated** and **signed tags**, this file stores references to the **tag object**, which, in turn, points to the node in the DAG, and not directly to a commit. This is the only type of ref that can point to any type of object.

These full names (fully qualified names) can be seen when using commands is intended for scripts, for example, `git show-ref`.

Branch points

When you create a new branch starting at a given version, the lines of development usually diverge. The act of creating a divergent branch is denoted in the DAG by a commit, which has more than one child, that is a node pointed to by more than one arrow.

Git does not track information about creating (forking) a branch, and does not mark branch points in any way that is preserved across clones and pushes. There is information about this event in the reflog (*branch created from HEAD*), but this is local to the repository where branching occurred, and is temporary. However, if you know that the B branch started from the A branch, you can find a branching point with `git merge-base A B`; in modern Git you can use `--fork-point` option to make it also use the reflog.

In *Fig 2*, the commit **34ac2** is a branching point for the **master** and **maint** branches.

Merge commits

Typically, when you have used branches to enable independent parallel development, you will later want to join them. For example, you would want bug fixes applied to the stable (maintenance) branch to be included in the main line of development as well (if they are applicable and were not fixed accidentally during the main-line development).

You would also want to merge changes created in parallel by different developers working simultaneously on the same project, each using their own clone of repository and creating their own lines of commits.

Such a merge operation will create a new revision, joining two lines of development. The result of this operation will be based on more than one commit. A node in the DAG representing the said revision will have more than one parent. Such an object is called a merge commit.

You can see a merge commit, **3fb00**, in *Fig 2*.

Single revision selection

During development, many times you want to select a single revision in the history of a project, to examine it, or to compare with the current version. The ability to a select revision is also the basis for selecting a revision range, for example a subsection of history to examine.

Many Git commands take revision parameters as arguments, which is typically denoted by <rev> in Git reference documentation. Git allows you to specify specific commits or a range of commits in several ways.

HEAD – the implicit revision

Most, but not all, Git commands that require the revision parameter, default to using HEAD. For example, git log and git log HEAD will show the same information.

The HEAD denotes the *current branch*, or in other words the commit that was checked out into the working directory, and forms a base of a current work.

There are a few other references which are similar to HEAD:

- FETCH_HEAD: This records the information about the remote branches that were fetched from a remote repository with your last git fetch or git pull invocation. It is very useful for one-off fetch, with the repository to fetch from given by a URL, unlike when fetching from a named repository such as origin, where we can use the remote-tracking branch instead, for example, origin/master. Moreover, with named repositories, we can use the reflog for remote-tracking branch, for example, origin/master@{1}, to get the position before the fetch. Note that FETCH_HEAD is overwritten by each fetch from any repository.

- ORIG_HEAD: This records the previous position of the current branch; this reference is created by commands that move the current branch in a drastic way (creating a new commit doesn't set ORIG_HEAD) to record the position of the HEAD command before the operation. It is very useful if you want to undo or abort such operations; though nowadays the same can be done using reflogs, which store additional information that can be examined in their use.

You can also stumble upon the short-lived temporary references used during specific operations:

- During a merge, before creating a merge commit, the MERGE_HEAD records the commit(s) that you are merging into your branch. It vanishes after creating a merge commit.

- During a cherry-pick, before creating a commit that copies picked changes into another branch, the CHERRY_PICK_HEAD records the commit that you have selected for cherry-picking.

Branch and tag references

The most straightforward and commonly used way to specify a revision is to use symbolic names: branches, naming the line of development, pointing to the tip of said line, and tags, naming specific revision. This way of specifying revisions can be used to view the history of a line of development, examine the most current revision (current work) on a given branch, or compare the branch or tag with the current work.

You can use any refs (external references to the DAG of revisions) to select a commit. You can use a branch name, tag name, and remote-tracking branch in any Git command that requires revision as a parameter.

Usually, it is enough to give a *short* name to a branch or tag, for example, `git log master`, to view the history of a `master` branch, or `git log v1.3-rc3` to see how version `v1.3-rc1` came about. It can, however, happen that there are different types of refs with the same name, for example, both branch and tag named `dev` (though it is recommended to avoid such situations). Or, you could have created (usually by accident) the local branch, `origin/master`, when there was a remote-tracking branch with the short name, `origin/master`, tracking where the `master` branch was in the remote repository, `origin`.

In such a situation, when ref name is ambiguous, it is disambiguated by taking the first match in the following rules (this is a shortened and simplified version; for the full list, see the *gitrevisions(7)* manpage):

1. The top level symbolic name, for example, HEAD.
2. Otherwise, the name of the tag (`refs/tags/` namespace).
3. Otherwise, the name of the local branch (`refs/heads/` namespace).
4. Otherwise, the name of the remote-tracking branch (`refs/remotes/` namespace).
5. Otherwise, the name of the remote if there exists a default branch for it; the revision is said default branch (example `refs/remotes/origin/HEAD` for `origin` as a parameter).

SHA-1 and the shortened SHA-1 identifier

In Git, each revision is given a unique identifier (object name), which is a SHA-1 hash function, based on the contents of the revision. You can select a commit by using its SHA-1 identifier as a 40-character long hexadecimal number (120 bits). Git shows full SHA-1 identifiers in many places, for example, you can find them in the full `git log` output:

```
$ git log
commit 50f84e34a1b0bb893327043cb0c491e02ced9ff5
Author: Junio C Hamano <gitster@pobox.com>
Date:   Mon Jun 9 11:39:43 2014 -0700

    Update draft release notes to 2.1
```

```
Signed-off-by: Junio C Hamano <gitster@pobox.com>


commit 07768e03b5a5efc9d768d6afc6246d2ec345cace
Merge: 251cb96 eb07774
Author: Junio C Hamano <gitster@pobox.com>
Date:    Mon Jun 9 11:30:12 2014 -0700


    Merge branch 'jc/shortlog-ref-exclude'
```

It is not necessary to give a full 40 characters of the SHA-1 identifier. Git is smart enough to figure out what you meant if you provide it with the first few characters of the SHA-1 revision identifier, as long as the partial SHA-1 is at least four characters long. To be able to use a shortened SHA-1 to select revision, it must be long enough to be unambiguous, that is, there is one and only one commit object which SHA-1 identifier begins with given characters.

For example, both `dae86e1950b1277e545cee180551750029cfe735` and `dae86e` name the same commit object, assuming, of course, that there is no other object in your repository whose object name starts with `dae86e`.

In many places, Git shows unambiguous shortened SHA-1 identifiers in its command output. For example, in the preceding example of the `git log` output, we can see the shortened SHA-1 identifiers in the `Merge:` line.

You can also request that Git use the shortened SHA-1 in place of the full SHA-1 revision identifiers with the `--abbrev-commit` option. By default, Git will use at least seven characters for the shortened SHA-1; you can change it with the optional parameter, for example, `--abbrev-commit=12`.

Note that Git would use as many characters as required for the shortened SHA-1 to be unique at the time the command was issued. The parameter `--abbrev-commit` (and the similar `--abbrev` option) is the minimal length.

HA short note about the shortened SHA-1:

Generally, 8 to 10 characters are more than enough to be unique within a project. One of the largest Git projects, the Linux kernel, is beginning to need 12 characters out of the possible 40 to stay unique. While a hash collision, which means having two revisions (two objects) that have the same full SHA-1 identifier, is extremely unlikely (with $1/2^{80} \approx 1/1.2 \times 10^{24}$ probability), it is possible that formerly unique shortened SHA-1 identifier will stop to be unique due to the repository growth.

The SHA-1 and the shortened SHA-1 are most often copied from the command output and pasted as a revision parameter in another command. They can also be used to communicate between developers in case of doubt or ambiguity, as SHA-1 identifiers are the same in any clone of the repository. *Fig 2* uses a five-character shortened SHA-1 to identify revisions in the DAG.

Ancestry references

The other main way to specify a revision is via its ancestry. One can specify a commit by starting from some child of it (for example from the current commit i.e. HEAD, a branch head, or a tag), and then follow through parent relationships to the commit in question. There is a special suffix syntax to specify such ancestry paths.

If you place ^ at the end of a revision name, Git resolves it to mean a (first) parent of that revision. For example, HEAD^ means the parent of the HEAD, that is, the previous commit.

This is actually a shortcut syntax. For merge commits, which have more than one parent, you might want to follow any of the parents. To select a parent, put its number after the ^ character; using the ^<n> suffix means the *n*th parent of a revision. We can see that ^ is actually a short version of ^1.

As a special case, ^0 means the commit itself; it is important only when a command behaves differently when using the branch name as a parameter and when using other revision specifier. It can be also used to get the commit an annotated (or a signed) tag points to; compare git show v0.9 and git show v0.9^0.

This suffix syntax is composable. You can use HEAD^^ to mean grandparent of HEAD, and parent of HEAD^.

There is another shortcut syntax for specifying a chain of first parents. Instead of writing *n* times the ^ suffix, that is, ^^...^ or ^1^1...^1, you can simply use ~<n>. As a special case, ~ is equivalent to ~1, so, for example, HEAD~ and HEAD^ are equivalent. And, HEAD~2 means *the first parent of the first parent*, or *the grandparent*, and is equivalent to HEAD^^.

You can also combine it all together, for example, you can get the second parent of the great grandparent of HEAD (assuming it was a merge commit) by using HEAD~3^2 and so on. You can use git name-rev or git describe --contains to find out how a revision is related to local refs, for example, via:

```
$ git log | git name-rev --stdin
```

Reverse ancestry references: the git describe output

The ancestry reference describes how a historic version relates to the current branches and tags. It depends on the position of the starting revision. For example, HEAD^ would usually mean completely different commit next month.

Sometimes, we want to describe how the current version relates to prior named version. For example, we might want to have a human-readable name of the current version to store in the generated binary application. And, we want this name to refer to the same revision for everybody. This is the task of git describe.

The git describe finds the most recent tag that is reachable from a given revision (by default, HEAD) and uses it to describe that version. If the found tag points to the given commit, then (by default) only the tag is shown. Otherwise, git describe suffixes the tag name with the number of additional commits on top of the tagged object, and the abbreviated SHA-1 identifier of the given revision. For example, v1.0.4-14-g2414721 means that the current commit was based on named (tagged) version v1.0.4, which was 14 commits ago, and that it has 2414721 as a shortened SHA-1.

Git understands this output format as a revision specifier.

Reflog shortnames

To help you recover from some of types of mistakes, and to be able to undo changes (to go back to the state before the change), Git keeps a **reflog**—a *temporary* log of where your HEAD and branch references have been for the last few months, and how they got there. The default is to keep reflog entries up to 90 days, 30 days for revisions which are reachable only through reflog (for example, amended commits). This can be, of course, configured, even on a ref-by-ref basis.

You can examine and manipulate your reflog with the git reflog command and its subcommands. You can also display reflog like a history with git log -g (or git log --walk-reflog):

```
$ git reflog
ba5807e HEAD@{0}: pull: Merge made by the 'recursive' strategy.
3b16f17 HEAD@{1}: reset: moving to HEAD@{2}
2b953b4 HEAD@{2}: reset: moving to HEAD^
69e0d3d HEAD@{3}: reset: moving to HEAD^^
3b16f17 HEAD@{4}: commit: random.c was too long to type
```

Every time your HEAD and your branch head are updated for any reason, Git stores that information for you in this local temporary log of ref history. The data from reflog can be used to specify references (and therefore, to specify revisions):

- To specify the *n*th prior value of HEAD in your local repository, you can use the HEAD@{n} notation that you see in the git reflog output. It's same with the *n*th prior value of the given branch, for example, master@{n}. The special syntax, @{n}, means the *n*th prior value of the current branch, which can be different from HEAD@{n}.

- You can also use this syntax to see where a branch was some specific amount of time ago. For instance, to denote where your master branch was yesterday in your local repository, you can use master@{yesterday}.

- You can use the @{-n} syntax to refer to the *n*th branch checked out (used) before the current one. In some places, you can use - in place of @{-1}, for example, git checkout - will switch to the previous branch.

Upstream of remote-tracking branches

The local repository which you use to work on a project does not usually live in the isolation. It interacts with other repositories, usually at least with the origin repository it was cloned from. For these remote repositories with which you interact often, Git will track where their branches were at the time of last contact.

To follow the movement of branches in the remote repository, Git uses remote-tracking branches. You cannot create new commits on remote-tracking branches as they would be overwritten on the next contact with remote. If you want to create your own work based on some branch in remote repository, you need to create a local branch based on the respective remote-tracking branch.

For example, when working on a line of development that is to be ultimately published to the next branch in the origin repository, which is tracked by the remote-tracking branch, origin/next, one would create a local next branch. We say that origin/next is upstream of the next branch and we can refer to it as next@{upstream}.

The suffix, @{upstream} (short form <refname>@{u}), which can be applied only to a local branch name, selects the branch that the ref is set to build on top of. A missing ref defaults to the current branch, that is, @{u} is upstream for the current branch.

You can find more about remote repositories, the concept of the upstream, and remote tracking branches in *Chapter 5, Collaborative Development with Git* and *Chapter 6, Advanced Branching Techniques*.

Selecting revision by the commit message

You can specify the revision a by matching its commit message with a regular expression. The `:/<pattern>` notation (for example, `:/^Bugfix`) specifies the youngest matching commit, which is reachable from any ref, while `<rev>^{/<pattern>}` (for example, `next^{/fix bug}`) specifies the youngest matching commit which is reachable from `<rev>`:

```
$ git log 'origin/pu^{/^Merge branch .rs/ref-transactions}'
```

This revision specifier gives similar results to the `--grep=<pattern>` option to `git log`, but is composable. On the other hand, it returns the first (youngest) matching revision, while the `--grep` option returns all matching revisions.

Selecting the revision range

Now that you can specify individual revisions in multiple ways, let's see how to specify ranges of revisions, a subset of the DAG we want to examine. Revision ranges are particularly useful for viewing selected parts of history of a project.

For example, you can use range specifications to answer questions such as, "What work is on this branch that I haven't yet merged into my main branch?" and "What work is on my main branch I haven't yet published?", or simply "What was done on this branch since its creation?".

Single revision as a revision range

History traversing commands such as `git log` operate on a set of commits, walking down a chain of revisions from child to parent. These kind of commands, given a single revision as an argument (as described in the *Single revision selection* section of this chapter), will show the set of commits reachable from that revision, following the commit ancestry chain, all the way down to the root commits.

For example, `git log master` would show all the commits reachable from the tip of a `master` branch (all the revisions that are or were based on the current work on the said branch), which means that it would show the whole `master` branch, the whole line of development.

Double dot notation

The most common range specification is the double-dot syntax, A..B. For a linear history, it means all the revisions between A and B, or to be more exact, all the commits that are in B but not in A, as shown in *Fig 3*. For example, the range, HEAD~4..HEAD, means four commits: HEAD, HEAD^, HEAD^^, and HEAD^^^ or in other words, HEAD~0, HEAD~1, HEAD~2, and HEAD~3, assuming that there are no merge commits starting between the current branch and its fourth ancestor.

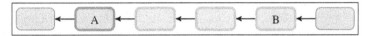

Fig 3. A double dot notation A..B for linear history; the selected revision range is shown in orange

 If you want to include a starting commit (in general case: boundary commits), which Git considers uninteresting, you can use the --boundary option to git log.

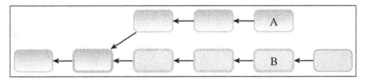

Fig 4. A double dot notation A..B for a non-linear history (revision A is not an ancestor of revision B); where, the selected revision range is orange, while the excluded revisions are shaded, and boundary revision is marked with a thick outline

The situation is more complicated for history that is not a straight line. One such case is when A is not the ancestor of B (there is no path in the DAG of revisions leading from B to A) but both have a common ancestor, like in Fig 4. Another situation with non-linear history is when there are merge commits between A and B, as shown in *Fig 5*. Precisely in view of nonlinear history the double-dot notation A..B, or "between A and B", is defined as reachable from A and not reachable from B.

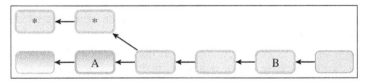

Fig 5 A double dot notation for a non-linear history, with merge commits between A and B. To exclude commits marked with star "*" use --strict-ancestor.

Git A..B means a range of all the commits that are reachable from one revision (B) but are not reachable from another revision (A), following the ancestry chain. In the case of divergent A and B, like in *Fig 4*, this is simply all commits in B from the branch point of A.

For example, say your branches `master` and `experiment` diverge. You want to see what is in your `experiment` branch that hasn't yet been merged into your `master` branch. You can ask Git to show you a log of just those commits with `master..experiment`.

If, on the other hand, you want to see the opposite—all the commits in `master` that aren't in `experiment`—you can reverse the branch names. The `experiment..master` notation shows you everything in `master` not reachable from `experiment`.

 Another example, `origin/master..HEAD`, shows what you're about to push to the remote (commits in your current branch that are not yet present in the `master` branch in the remote repository `origin`), while `HEAD..origin/master` shows what you have fetched but not yet merged in. You can also leave off one side of the syntax to have Git assume HEAD: `origin/master..` is `origin/master..HEAD` and `..origin/master` is `HEAD..origin/master`; Git substitutes HEAD if one side is missing.

Git uses double-dot notation in many places, for example in `git fetch` and `git push` output for an ordinary fast-forward case, so you can just copy and paste a fragment of output as parameters to `git log`. In this case, the beginning of the range is the ancestor of the end of the range; the range is linear:

```
$ git push
To https://git.company.com/random
   8c4ceca..493e222  master -> master
```

Multiple points – including and excluding revisions

The double-dot `A..B` syntax is very useful and quite intuitive, but it is really a shorthand notation. Usually it is enough, but sometimes you might want more than it provides. Perhaps, you want to specify more than two branches to indicate your revision, such as seeing what commits are in any of the several branches that aren't in the branch you're currently on. Perhaps you want to see only those changes on the `master` branch that are not in any of the other long-lived branches.

Git allows you to exclude the commits that are reachable from a given revision by prefixing the said revision with a `^`. For example, to view all the revisions which are on `maint` or `master` but are not in `next`, you can use `git log maint master ^next`. This means that the `A..B` notation is just a shorthand for `B ^A`.

Instead of having to use ^ character as a prefix for each of the revisions we want to exclude, Git allows you to use the --not option, which *negates* all the following revisions. For example, B ^A ^C might be written as B --not A C. This is useful, for example, when generating those excluded revisions programmatically.

Thus, these three commands are equivalent:

```
$ git log A..B
$ git log B ^A
$ git log B --not A
```

The revision range for a single revision

There is another useful shortcut, namely A^!, which is a range composed of a single commit. For non-merge commits, it is simply A^..A.

For merge commits, the A^!, of course, excludes all the parents. With the help of yet another special notation, namely A^@, denoting all the parents of A (A^1, A^2,..., A^n), we can say that A^! is a shortcut for A --not A^@.

Triple-dot notation

The last major syntax for specifying revision ranges is the triple-dot syntax, A...B. It selects all the commits that are reachable by either of the two references, but not by both of them, see *Fig 6*. This notation is called the symmetric difference of A and B.

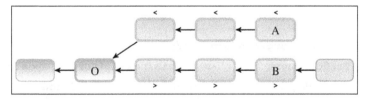

Fig 6. A triple-dot notation A...B for a non-linear history, where the selected range
is shown in orange color, boundary commit O is marked with a bold outline, and the
characters below and above the nodes show --left-right markers

It is a shortcut notation for A B --not $(git merge-base --all A B), where $ (...) denotes shell **command substitution** (using POSIX shell syntax). Here, it means that the shell will first run the git merge-base command to find out all the best common ancestors (all merge bases), and then paste back its output on the command line, to be negated.

A common switch to use with the `git log` command with triple dot notation is
`--left-right`. This option makes it show which side of the range each commit is in
by prefixing commits from the left side (A in A...B) with `<`, and those from the right
(B in A...B) with `>`, as shown in *Fig 6* and the following example. This helps make
the data more useful:

```
$ git log --oneline --left-right 37ec5ed...8cd8cf8
>8cd8cf8 Merge branch 'fc/remote-helper-refmap' into next
>efcd02e Merge branch 'rs/more-starts-with' into next
>831aa30 Merge branch 'jm/api-strbuf-doc' into next
>1aeca19 Merge branch 'jc/revision-dash-count-parsing' into next
<1a7e8e8 Revert "replace: add --graft option"
<7a30690 t9001: avoid non-portable '\n' with sed
>5cc3268 fetch doc: remove "short-cut" section
```

If the `--left-right` option is combined with `--boundary`,
these normally uninteresting boundary commits are prefixed
with `-`.

In the case of using a triple-dot A...B revision range, these
boundary commits are `git merge-base --all A B`.

Git uses triple-dot notation in the `git fetch` and `git push` output when there
was a *forced update*, in cases where the old version (left-hand side) and the updated
version (right-hand side) diverged, and the new version was forced to overwrite the
old version:

```
$ git fetch
From git://git.kernel.org/pub/scm/git/git
 + 37ec5ed...8cd8cf8 next         -> origin/next  (forced update)
 + 9478935...16067c9 pu           -> origin/pu  (forced update)
   d0b0081..1f58507  todo         -> origin/todo
```

Using revision range notation in diff

To make it easier to copy and paste revisions between log and diff commands, Git allows us to use *revision range* double-dot notation A..B and triple-dot A...B to denote a *set of revisions (endpoints)* in the git diff command.

For Git, using git diff A..B is the same as git diff A B, which means the difference between revision A and revision B. If the revision on either side of double dot is omitted, it will have the same effect as using HEAD instead. For example, git diff A.. is equivalent to git diff A HEAD.

 The git diff A...B notation is intended to show the incoming changes on the branch B. Incoming changes mean revisions up to B, starting at a common ancestor, that is, a merge base of both A and B. Thus, writing git diff A...B is equivalent to git diff $(git merge-base A B) B; note that git merge-base is without --all here. The result of this convention makes it so that a copy and paste of the git fetch output (whether with double-dot or triple-dot) as an argument to git diff will always show fetched changes. Note, however, that it does not include the changes that were made on A since divergence!

Additionally, this feature makes it possible to use a git diff A^! command to view how revision A differs from its parent (it is a shortcut for git diff A^ A).

Searching history

A huge number and variety of useful options to the git log command are limiting options — that is, options that let you show only a subset of commits. This complements selecting commits to view by passing the appropriate revision range, and allows us to search the history for the specific versions, utilizing information other than the shape of the DAG of revisions.

Limiting the number of revisions

The most basic way of limiting the git log output, the simplest limiting option, is to show only then most recent commits. This is done using the -<n> option (where n is any integer); this can be also written as -n <n>, or in long form as --max-count=<n>. For example, git log -2 would show the two last (most recent) commits in the current line of development, starting from the implicit HEAD revision.

You can skip the first few commits shown with --skip=<n>.

Matching revision metadata

History limiting options can be divided into those that check information stored in the commit object itself (the revision metadata), and those that filter commits based on changeset (on changes from parent commit(s)).

Time-limiting options

If you are interested in commits created within some date range that you're interested in, you can use a number of options such as `--since` and `--until`, or `--before` and `--after`. For example, the following command gets the list of commits made in the last two weeks:

```
$ git log --since=2.weeks
```

These options work with lots of formats. You can specify a specific date such as "2008-04-21" or a relative date such as "2 years, 3 months, and 3 days ago"; you can use a dot in place of a space.

When using a specific date, one must remember that these dates are interpreted to be in the local time zone, if the date does not include the time zone. It is important because, in such a situation, Git will not yield identical results when run by different colleagues, who may be situated in other time zones around the world. For example, `--since="2014-04-29 12:00:00"` would catch an additional 6 hours, worth of commits when issued in Birmingham, England, United Kingdom (where it means 2014-04-29Z11:00:00 universal time) than when issued in Birmingham, Alabama, USA. (where it means 2014-04-29Z17:00:00). To have everyone get the same results, you need to include the time zone in the time limit, for example, `--after="2013-04-29T17:07:22+0200"`.

Note that Git stores not one but two dates describing the version: author date and committer date. Time-limiting options described here examine the committer date, which means the date and time when the revision object was created. This might be different from author date, which means the date and time when a changeset was created (the change was made).

The date of authorship can be different from the date of committership in a few cases. One is when the commit was created in one repository, converted to e-mail, and then applied by other person in an other repository. Another way to have these two dates differ is to have the commit recreated while rebasing; by default, it keeps the author date and gets a new committer date (refer to *Chapter 8, Keeping History Clean*).

Matching commit contents

If you want to filter your commit history to only show those done by a specific author or committer, you can use the `--author` or `--committer` options, respectively. For example, let's say you're looking for all the commits in the Git source code authored by Linus. You could use something like `git log --author=Linus`. The search is, by default, case-sensitive, and uses regular expressions. Git will search both the name and the e-mail address of the commit author; to match first name only use `--author=^Linus`.

The `--grep` option lets you search commit messages (which should contain descriptions of the changes). Let's say that you want to find all the security bug fixes that mention the Common Vulnerabilities and Exposures (CVE) identifier in the commit message. You could generate a list of such commits with `git log --grep=CVE`.

If you specify both `--author` and `--grep` options, or more than one `--author` or `--grep` option, Git will show commits that match either query. In other words, Git will logically OR all the commit matching options. If you want to find commits that match all the queries, with matching options logically AND, you need to use the `--all-match` option.

There is also a set of options to modify the meaning of matching patterns, similar to the ones used by the `grep` program. To make the search case-insensitive, use the `-i` / `--regexp-ignore-case` option. If you want to match simply a substring, you can use `-F` / `--fixed-strings` (you might want to do it to avoid having to escape regular expression metacharacters such as "." and "?"). To write more powerful search terms, you can use `--extended-regexp` or `--perl-regexp` (use the last one only if Git was compiled linked with the PCRE library).

Commit parents

Git, by default, will follow all the parents of each merge commit, when walking down the ancestry chain. To make it follow only the first parent, you can use the aptly named `--first-parent` option. This will show you the main line of the history (sometimes called the trunk), assuming that you follow the specific practices with respect to merging changes; you will learn more about this in *Chapter 7, Merging Changes Together*.

Compare (this example uses the very nice `--graph` option that makes an ASCII-art diagram of the history) the following code...

```
$ git log -5 --graph --oneline
* 50f84e3 Update draft release notes to 2.1
*   07768e0 Merge branch 'jc/shortlog-ref-exclude'
```

```
| \
| * eb07774 shortlog: allow --exclude=<glob> to be passed
* |   251cb96 Merge branch 'mn/sideband-no-ansi'
| \ \
| * | 38de156 sideband.c: do not use ANSI control sequence
```

...with this:

```
$ git log -5 --graph --oneline --first-parent
* 50f84e3 Update draft release notes to 2.1
* 07768e0 Merge branch 'jc/shortlog-ref-exclude'
* 251cb96 Merge branch 'mn/sideband-no-ansi'
* d37e8c5 Merge branch 'rs/mailinfo-header-cmp'
* 53b4d83 Merge branch 'pb/trim-trailing-spaces'
```

You can filter the list to show only the merge commits, or show only the non-merge commits, with the `--merges` and `--no-merges` options, respectively. These options can be considered just a shortcut for a more generic options: `--min-parents=<number>` (`--merges` is `--min-parents=2`) and `--max-parents=<number>` (`--no-merges` is `--max-parents=1`).

Let's say that you want to find the starting point(s) of your project. You can do this with the help of `--max-parents=0`, which would give you all the root commits:

```
$ git log --max-parents=0 --oneline
0ca71b3 basic options parsing and whatnot.
16d6b8a Initial import of a python script…
cb07fc2 git-gui: Initial revision.
161332a first working version
1db95b0 Add initial version of gitk to the CVS repository
2744b23 Start of early patch applicator tools for git.
e83c516 Initial revision of "git", the information manager from hell
```

Searching changes in revisions

Sometimes, searching through commit messages and other revision metadata is not enough. Perhaps, descriptions of the changes were not detailed enough. Or, what if you are looking for a revision when a function was introduced, or where variables started to be used?

Git allows you to look through the changes that each revision brought (the difference between commit and its parent). The faster option is called a `pickaxe` search.

With the `-S<string>` option, Git will look for differences that introduce or remove an instance of a given string. Note that this is different from the string simply appearing in diff output. (You can do a match using a regular expression with the `--pickaxe-regex` option.) Git checks for each revision if there are files whose *current* side and whose *parent* side have a different number of specified strings, and shows the revisions that match.

As a side effect, `git log` with the `-S` option would also show the changes that each revision made (as if the `--patch` option were used), but only those differences that match the query. To show differences for all the files, and not only those diffs where the change in number occurred, you need to use the `--pickaxe-all` option:

```
$ git log -S'sub href'
commit 06a9d86b49b826562e2b12b5c7e831e20b8f7dce
Author: Martin Waitz <tali@admingilde.org>
Date:    Wed Aug 16 00:23:50 2006 +0200

    gitweb: provide function to format the URL for an action link.

    Provide a new function which can be used to generate an URL for the
CGI.
    This makes it possible to consolidate the URL generation in order to
make
    it easier to change the encoding of actions into URLs.

    Signed-off-by: Martin Waitz <tali@admingilde.org>
    Signed-off-by: Junio C Hamano <junkio@cox.net>
```

With `-G<regex>`, Git will literally look for differences whose added or removed line matches the given regular expression. Note that the unified diff format (that Git uses) considers changing line as removing the old version and adding a new one; refer to *Chapter 3, Developing with Git* for an explanation of how Git describes changes.

To illustrate the difference between `-S<regex>` `--pickaxe-regex` and `-G<regex>`, consider a commit with the following `diff` in the same file:

```
    if (lstat(path, &st))
-        return error("cannot stat '%s': %s", path,
+        ret = error("cannot stat '%s': %s", path,
                    strerror(errno));
```

While `git log -G"error\("` will show this commit (because the query matches both changed lines), `git log -S"error\(" --pickaxe-regex` will not (because the number of occurrences of that string did not change).

> If we are interested in a single file, it is easier to use `git blame` (perhaps in a graphical blame browser, like with `git gui blame`) to check when the given change was introduced. However, `git blame` can't be used to find a commit that deleted a line—you need a `pickaxe` search for that.

Selecting types of change

Sometimes, you might want to see only those changes that added or renamed files. With Git, you can do this with `git log --diff-filter=AM`. You can select any combination of types of changes; see the `git-log(1)` manpage for details.

History of a file

As described in the *Whole-tree commits* section at the beginning of this chapter, in Git revisions are about the state of the whole project as one single entity.

In many cases, especially with larger projects, we are interested only in the history of a single file, or in the history limited to the changes in the given directory (in the given subsystem).

Path limiting

To examine the history of a single file, you can simply use use `git log <pathname>`. Git will then only show all those revisions that affected the pathname (a file or a directory) given, which means those revisions where there was a change to the given file, or a change to a file inside the given subdirectory.

Disambiguation between branch names and path names

Git usually guesses what you meant by writing `git log foo`; did you meant to ask for the history of branch `foo` (line of development), or for the history of the file `foo`. However, sometimes Git can get confused. To prevent confusion between pathnames and branch names, you can use `--` to separate filename arguments from other options. Everything after `--` will be taken to be a pathname, everything before it will be taken to be the branch name or other option.

For example, writing `git log -- foo` explicitly asks for the history of a path `foo`.

One of the common situations where it is needed, besides having the same name for a branch and for a file, is examining the history of a deleted file, which is no longer present in a project.

You can specify more than one path; you can even look for the changes that affect the given type of file with the help of wildcards (pattern matching). For example, to find only changes to Perl scripts (to files with the `*.pl` extension), you can use `git log -- '*.pl'`. Note that you need to protect the `*.pl` wildcard from being expanded by the shell, before Git sees it, for example via single quotes as shown here.

However, as Git uses pathname parameters as limiters in showing the history of a project, querying for a history of a single file doesn't automatically *follow renames*. You need to use `git log --follow <file>` to continue listing the history of a file beyond renames. Unfortunately, it doesn't work in all the cases. Sometimes, you need to use either the blame command (see the next section), or examine boundary commits with rename detection turned on (`git show -M -C --raw --abbrev <rev>`) and follow renames and file moving *manually*.

In modern Git, you can also trace the evolution of the line range within the file using `git log -L`, which is currently limited to walk starting from a single revision (zero or one positive revision arguments) and a single file. The range is given either by denoting the start and end of the range with `-L <start>,<end>:<file>` (where either `<start>` or `<end>` can be the line number or `/regexp/`), or a function to track with `-L :<funcname regexp>:<file>`. This cannot be used together with the ordinary spec-based path limiting.

History simplification

By default, when requested for the history of a path, Git would simplify the history, showing only those commits that are required (that are enough) to explain how the files that match the specified paths came to be. Git would exclude those revisions that do not change the given file. Additionally, for non-excluded merge commits, Git would exclude those parents that do not change the file (thereby excluding lines of development).

You can control this kind of history simplification with the `git log` options such as `--full-history` or `--simplify-merges`. Check the Git documentation for more details, like the "History Simplification" section in git-log(1) manpage.

Blame – the line-wise history of a file

The `blame` command is a version control feature designed to help you determine who made changes to a file. This command shows for each line in the file when this line was created, who authored given line, and so on. It does that by finding the latest commit in which the current shape of each line was introduced. A revision introducing given shape is the one where the given line has its current form, but where the line is different in this revision parent. The default output of `git blame` annotates each line with appropriate line-authorship information.

Git can start annotating from the given revision (useful when browsing the history of a file or examining how older version of a file came to be) or even limit the search to a given revision range. You can also limit the range of lines annotated to make blame faster — for example to check only the history of an `esc_html` function in `gitweb/gitweb.perl` file you can use:

```
$ git blame -L '/^sub esc_html {/,/}/' gitweb/gitweb.perl
```

What makes blame so useful is that it follows the history of file across whole-file renames. It can optionally follow lines as they were moved from one file to another (with the `-M` option), and even follow lines that were copied and pasted from another file (with the `-C` option); this includes internal code movement.

When following code movement, it is useful to ignore changes in whitespace, to find out when given fragment of code was truly introduced and avoid finding when it was just re-indented (for example, due to refactoring repeated code into a function — code movement). This can be done by passing the `diff` formatting option `-w` or `--ignore-all-space`.

Rename detection

Good version control systems should be able to deal with renaming files and other ways of changing the directory structure of a project. There are two ways to deal with this problem. The first is the **rename tracking**, which means that the information about the fact that a file was renamed is saved at the commit time; the version control system marks renames. This usually requires using the `rename` and `move` commands to rename files (no use of non-version control aware file managers), or it can be done by detecting the rename at the time of creating the revision. It can involve some kind of **file identity** surviving across renames.

The second method, and the one used by Git, is the **rename detection**. In this case, the `mv` command is only a shortcut for deleting a file with the old name and adding a file with the same contents and a new name. Rename detection means that the fact that file was renamed is detected at the time it is needed: when doing a merge, viewing the line-wise history of a file (if requested), or showing a diff (if requested or configured). This has the advantage that the rename detection algorithm can be improved, and is not frozen at the time of commit. It is a more generic solution, allowing to handle not only the whole-file renames, but also the code movement and copying within a single file and across different files, as can be seen in the description of `git blame`.

The disadvantage of the rename detection, which in Git is based on the heuristic similarity of the file contents and pathname, is that it takes resources to run, and that in rare cases it can fail, not detecting renames or detecting a rename where there isn't one.

Note that, in Git, rename detection is not turned on for diffs by default.

Many graphical interfaces for Git include a graphical version of blame. The git gui blame command is an example of such a graphical interface to blame operation (it is a part of git gui, a Tcl/Tk-based graphical interface). Such graphical interfaces can show the full description of changes and simultaneously show the history with and without considering renames. From such a GUI, it is usually possible to go to a specified commit, browsing the history of lines of a file interactively. In addition, the GUI blame tool makes it very easy to follow files across renames.

Fig 7. The GUI blame in action, showing the detection of copying or moving fragments of code

Finding bugs with git bisect

Git provides a couple of tools to help you debug issues in your projects. These tools can be extremely useful, especially in the case of a software regression, a software bug which makes a feature stop functioning as intended after a certain revision. If you don't know where the bug is, and there have been dozens or hundreds of commits since the last state where you know the code worked, you'll likely turn to git bisect for help.

The `bisect` command searches semi-automatically step by step through the project history, trying to find the revision that introduced the bug. In each step, it bisects the history into roughly equal parts, and asks whether there is a bug in the dividing commit. It then uses the answer to eliminate one of the two sections, and reduces the size of the revision range where there can be a commit that introduced the bug.

Suppose version 1.14 of your project worked, but the release candidate, 1.15-rc0, for the new version crashes. You go back to the 1.15-rc0 version, and it turns out that you can *reproduce the issue* (this is very important!), but you can't figure out what is going wrong.

You can bisect the code history to find out. You need to start the bisection process with `git bisect start`, and then tell Git which version is broken with `git bisect bad`. Then, you must tell bisect the last-known good state (or set of states) with `git bisect good`:

```
$ git bisect start
$ git bisect bad   v1.15-rc0
$ git bisect good v1.14
Bisecting: 159 revisions left to test after this (roughly 7 steps)
[7ea60c15cc98ab586aea77c256934acd438c7f95] Merge branch 'mergetool'
```

Git figured out that about 300 commits came between the commit you marked as the last good commit (`v1.14`) and the bad version (`v1.15-rc0`), and it checked out the middle one (`7ea60c15`) for you. If you run `git branch` at this point, you'll see that git has temporarily moved you to `(no branch)`:

```
$ git branch
* (no branch, bisect started on master)
  master
```

At this point, you need to run your test to check whether the issue is present in the commit currently checked out by the bisect operation. If the program crashes, mark this commit as bad with `git bisect bad`. If the issue is not present, mark it as correct with `git bisect good`. After about seven steps, Git would show the suspect commit:

```
$ git bisect good
b047b02ea83310a70fd603dc8cd7a6cd13d15c04 is first bad commit
commit b047b02ea83310a70fd603dc8cd7a6cd13d15c04
Author: PJ Hyett <pjhyett@example.com>
Date:   Tue Jan 27 14:48:32 2009 -0800

    secure this thing

:040000 040000 40ee3e7… f24d3c6… M  config
```

The last line in the preceding example output is in so called *raw* diff output, showing which files changed in a commit. You can then examine the suspected commit with `git show`. From there, you can find the author of the said commit, and ask them for clarification, or to fix it (or to send them a bug report). If the good practice of creating small incremental changes was followed during the development of the project, the amount of code to examine after finding the bad commit should be small.

If at any point, you land on a commit that broke something unrelated, and is not a good one to test, you can skip such a commit with `git bisect skip`. You can even skip a range of commits by giving the revision range to the `skip` subcommand.

When you're finished, you should run `git bisect reset` to return you to the branch you started from:

```
$ git bisect reset
Previous HEAD position was b047b02... secure this thing
Switched to branch 'master'
```

To finish bisection while staying on located bad commit, you can use `git bisect reset HEAD`.

You can even fully automate finding bad revision with `git bisect run`. For this, you need to have a script that will test for the presence of bug, and exit the value of `0` if the project works all right, or non-0 if there is a bug. The special exit code, `125`, should be used when the currently checked out code cannot be tested. First, you again tell it the scope of the `bisect` by providing the known bad and good commits. You can do this by listing them with the `bisect start` command if you want, listing the known bad commit first and the known good commit(s) second. You can even cut down the number of trials, if you know what part of the tree is involved in the problem you are tracking down, by specifying path parameters:

```
$ git bisect start v1.5-rc0 v1.4 -- arch/i386
$ git bisect run ./test-error.sh
```

Doing so automatically runs `test-error.sh` on each checked-out commit until Git finds the first broken commit. Here, we have provided the scope of the `bisect` by putting known bad and good commits with the `bisect start` command, listing the known bad commit first and the known good commit(s) second.

If the bug is that the project stopped compiling (a broken build), you can use `make` as a test script (`git bisect run make`).

Selecting and formatting the git log output

Now that you know how to select revisions to examine and to limit which revisions are shown (selecting those that are interesting), it is time to see how to select which part of information associated with the queried revisions to show, and how to format this output. There is a huge number and variety of options of the `git log` command available for this.

Predefined and user defined output formats

A very useful `git log` option is `--pretty`. This option changes the format of log output. There are a few prebuilt formats available for you to use. The `oneline` format prints each commit on a single line, which is useful if you're looking at a lot of commits; there exists `--oneline`, shorthand for `--pretty=oneline --abbrev-commit` used together. In addition, the `short`, `medium` (the default), `full`, and `fuller` formats show the output in roughly the same format, but with less or more information, respectively. The `raw` format shows commits in the internal Git representation. It is possible to change the format of dates shown in those verbose pretty formats with an appropriate `--date` option: make Git show relative dates, like for example *2 hours ago*, with `--date=relative`, dates in your local time zone with `--date=local`, and so on.

You can also specify your own log format with `--pretty=format:"<string>"` (and its `tformat` variant). This is especially useful when you're generating output for machine parsing, for use in scripts, because when you specify the format explicitly you know it won't change with updates to Git. The format string works a little bit like in `printf`:

```
$ git log --pretty="%h - %an, %ar : %s"
50f84e3 - Junio C Hamano, 7 days ago : Update draft release notes
0953113 - Junio C Hamano, 10 days ago : Second batch for 2.1
afa53fe - Nick Alcock, 2 weeks ago : t5538: move http push tests out
```

There is a very large number of placeholders selected of those are listed in the following table:

Placeholder	Description of output
%H	Commit hash (full SHA-1 identifier of revision)
%h	Abbreviated commit hash
%an	Author name

Placeholder	Description of output
%ae	Author e-mail
%ar	Author date, relative
%cn	Committer name
%ce	Committer email
%cr	Committer date, relative
%s	Subject (first line of a commit message, describing revision)
%%	A raw %

Author versus committer

The *author* is the person who originally wrote the patch (authored the changes), whereas the *committer* is the person who last applied the patch (created a commit object with those changes, representing the revision in the DAG). So, if you send a patch to a project and one of the core members applies the patch, both of you get credit—you as the author and the core member as the committer.

The --oneline format option is especially useful together with another git log option called --graph; though it can be used with any format. The latter option adds a nice little ASCII graph showing your branch and merge history. To see where tags and branches are, you can use an option named --decorate:

```
$ git log --graph --decorate --oneline origin/maint
*   bce14aa (origin/maint) Sync with 1.9.4
|\
| * 34d5217 (tag: v1.9.4) Git 1.9.4
| *   12188a8 Merge branch 'rh/prompt' into maint
| |\
| * \   64d8c31 Merge branch 'mw/symlinks' into maint
| |\ \
* | | | d717282 t5537: re-drop http tests
* | | | e156455 (tag: v2.0.0) Git 2.0
```

You might want to use a graphical tool to visualize your commit history. One such tool is a Tcl/Tk program called gitk that is distributed with Git. You can find more information about various types of graphical tools in *Chapter 10, Customizing and Extending Git*.

Including, formatting, and summing up changes

You can examine single revision with the `git show` command, which, in addition to the commit metadata, shows changes in the unified `diff` format. Sometimes, however, you might want to display changes alongside the selected part of the history in the `git log` output. You can do this with the help of the `-p` option. This is very helpful for code review, or to quickly browse what happened during a series of commits that a collaborator has added.

Ordinarily, Git would not show the changes for a merge commit. To show changes from all parents, you need to use the `-c` option (or `-cc` for compressed output), and to show changes from each parent individually, use `-m`.

The `git log` accepts various options to change the format of diff output. Sometimes, it's easier to review changes on the word level rather than on the line level. The `git log` command accepts various options to change the format of diff output. One of those options is `--word-diff`. This way of viewing differences is useful for examining changes in documents (for example, documentation):

```
commit 06ab60c06606613f238f3154cb27cb22d9723967
Author: Jason St. John <jstjohn@purdue.edu>
Date:    Wed May 21 14:52:26 2014 -0400

    Documentation: use "command-line" when used as a compound adjective,
and fix

    Signed-off-by: Jason St. John <jstjohn@purdue.edu>
    Signed-off-by: Junio C Hamano <gitster@pobox.com>

diff --git a/Documentation/config.txt b/Documentation/config.txt
index 1932e9b..553b300 100644
--- a/Documentation/config.txt
+++ b/Documentation/config.txt
@@ -381,7 +381,7 @@
        Set the path to the root of the working tree.
        This can be overridden by the GIT_WORK_TREE environment
        variable and the '--work-tree' [-command line-]{+command-line+}
option.
        The value can be an absolute path or relative to the path to
        the .git directory, which is either specified by --git-dir
        or GIT_DIR, or automatically discovered.
```

Another useful set of options are about ignoring changes in whitespace, including `-w` / `--ignore-all-space` to ignore all whitespace changes, and `-b` / `--ignore-space-change` to ignore changes in the amount of whitespace.

Sometimes, you are interested only in the summary of changes, and not the details. There is a series of `diff` summarizing options that you can use. If you want to know only which files changed, use `--names-only` (or `--raw --abbrev`). If you also want to know how much those files changed, you can use the `--stat` option (or perhaps its machine-parse friendly version, `--numstat`) to see some abbreviated stats. If you are interested only in short summary of changes, use `--shortstat` or `--summary`.

Summarizing contributions

Ever wondered how many commits you've contributed to a project? Or perhaps, who is the most active developer during the last month (with respect to the number of commits)? Well, wonder no more, because this is what `git shortlog` is good for:

```
$ git shortlog -s -n
 13885   Junio C Hamano
  1399   Shawn O. Pearce
  1384   Jeff King
  1108   Linus Torvalds
   743   Jonathan Nieder
```

The `-s` option squashes all of the commit messages into the number of commits; without it, `git shortlog` would list summary of all the commits, grouped by developer (its output can be configured to some extent with `pretty` like the `--format` option.) The `-n` option sorts the list of developers by the number of commits; otherwise, it is sorted alphabetically. You can add an `-e` option to show also an e-mail address; note that, however, with this option, Git will separate contributions made by the same author under different e-mail.

The `git shortlog` command accepts a revision range, and other revision limiting options such as `--since=1.month.ago`; almost options that `git log` command accepts makes sense for `shortlog`. For example, to see who contributed to the last release candidate you can use the following command:

```
$ git shortlog -e v2.0.0-rc2..v2.0.0-rc3
Jonathan Nieder <jrnieder@gmail.com> (1):
      shell doc: remove stray "+" in example


Junio C Hamano <gitster@pobox.com> (14):
```

```
Merge branch 'cl/p4-use-diff-tree'
Update draft release notes for 2.0
Merge branch 'km/avoid-cp-a' into maint
```

> One needs to remember that the number of revisions authored is only one way of measuring contribution. For example, somebody, who creates buggy commits only to fix them later, would have a larger number of commits than the developer who doesn't make mistakes (or cleans the history before publishing changes).

There are other measures of programmer productivity, for example, the number of changed lines in authored commits, or the number of *surviving* lines — these can be calculated with the help of Git, but there is no built-in command to calculate them.

Mapping authors

One problem with running git shortlog -s -n -e or git blame in Git repositories of long running projects is that authors may change their name or e-mail, or both during the course of the project, due to many reasons: changing work (and work e-mail), misconfiguration, spelling mistakes, and others:

Bob Hacker <bob@example.com>

Bob <bob@example.com>

When that happens, you can't get proper attribution. Git allows you to coalesce author/e-mail pairs with the help of the .mailmap file in the top directory of your project. It allows us to specify *canonical* names for contributors, for example:

Bob Hacker <bob@example.com>

(Actually it allows us to specify the canonical name, canonical e-mail, or both name and email, matching by email or name and email.)

By default, those corrections are applied to git blame and to git shortlog, but not to the git log output. With custom output, you can, however, use placeholders that output corrected name, or corrected e-mail; or you can use the --use-mailmap option, or the log.mailmap configuration variable.

Viewing a revision and a file at revision

Sometimes, you might want to examine a single revision (for example, a commit suspected to be buggy, found with `git bisect`) in more detail, examining together changes with their description. Or perhaps, you want to examine the tag message of an annotated tag together with the commit it points to. Git provides a generic `git show` command for this; it can be used for any type of object.

For example, to examine the grandparent of the current version, use the following command:

```
$ git show HEAD^^
commit ca3cdd6bb3fcd0c162a690d5383bdb8e8144b0d2
Author: Bob Hacker <bob@virtech.com>
Date:   Sun Jun 1 02:36:32 2014 +0200

    Added COPYRIGHT

diff --git a/COPYRIGHT b/COPYRIGHT
new file mode 100644
index 0000000..862aafd
--- /dev/null
+++ b/COPYRIGHT
@@ -0,0 +1,2 @@
+Copyright (c) 2014 VirTech Inc.
+All Rights Reserved
```

The `git show` command can also be used to display directories (trees) and file contents (blobs). To view a file (or a directory), you need to specify where it is from (from which revision) and the path to the file, using `:` to connect them. For example, to view the contents of the `src/rand.c` file as it was in the version tagged `v0.1` use:

```
$ git show v0.1:src/rand.c
```

This might be more convenient than checking out the required version of the file into the working directory with `git checkout v0.1 -- src/rand.c`. Before the colon may be anything that names a commit (`v0.1` here), and after that, it may be any path to a file tracked by Git (`src/rand.c` here). The pathname here is the full path from the top of the project directory, but you can use `./` after the colon for relative paths, for example, `v0.1:./rand.c` if you are in the `src/` subdirectory.

You can use the same trick to compare arbitrary files at arbitrary revisions.

Summary

This chapter showed us the various ways of exploring project history: finding relevant revisions, selecting and filtering revisions to display, and formatting the output.

We started with the description of the conceptual model of project history: the Directed Acyclic Graph (DAG) of revisions. Understanding this concept is very important because many selection tools refer directly or indirectly to the DAG.

Then, you learnt how to select a single revision and the range of revisions. We can use this knowledge to see what changes were made on a branch since its divergence from the base branch, and to find all the revisions which were made by the given developer.

We can even try to find bugs in the code by exploring the history: finding when a function was deleted from the code with a `pickaxe` search, examining a file for how its code came to be and who wrote it with `git blame`, and utilizing semi-automatic or automatic searches through the project history to find which version introduced regression with `git bisect`.

When examining a revision, we can select the format in which the information is shown, even to the point of user-defined formats. There are various ways of summarizing the information, from the statistics of the changed files to the statistics of the number of commits per author.

3
Developing with Git

The previous chapter explained how to examine the project history. This chapter will describe how to create such history and how to add to it. We will learn how to create new revisions and new lines of development. Now it's time to show how to develop with Git.

Here we will focus on committing one's own work, on the solo development. The description of working as one of the contributors is left for *Chapter 5, Collaborative Development with Git*, while *Chapter 7, Merging Changes Together*, shows how Git can help in maintainer duties.

This chapter will introduce the very important Git concept of the staging area (the index). It will also explain, in more detail, the idea of a detached HEAD, that is, an anonymous unnamed branch. Here you can also find a detailed description of the extended unified diff format that Git uses to describe changes.

The following is the list of the topics we will cover in this chapter:

- The index – a staging area for commits
- Examining the status of the working area and changes in it
- How to read the extended unified diff that is used to describe changes
- Selective and interactive commit, and amending a commit
- Creating, listing, and selecting (switching to) branches
- What can prevent switching branch, and what you can do then
- Rewinding a branch with `git reset`
- Detached HEAD, that is, the unnamed branch (checking out tag and so on)

Creating a new commit

Before starting to develop with Git, you should introduce yourself with a name and an e-mail, as shown in *Chapter 1, Git Basics in Practice*. This information will be used to identify your work, either as an author or as a committer. The setup can be global for all your repositories (with `git config --global`, or by editing the `~/.gitconfig` file directly), or local to a repository (with `git config`, or by editing `.git/config`). The per-repository configuration overrides the per-user one (you will learn more about it in *Chapter 10, Customizing and Extending Git*). You might want to use your company e-mail for work repositories, but your own non-work e-mail for public repositories you work on.

A relevant fragment of the appropriate `config` file could look similar to this:

```
[user]
  name = Joe R. Hacker
  email = joe@company.com
```

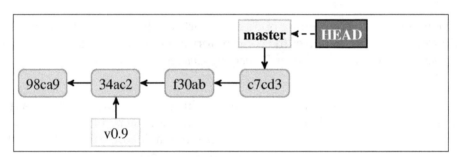

Fig 1. The graph of revisions (the DAG) for a starting point of an example project, before creating a new commit. The current branch is master, and its tip is at revision c7cd3; this is also currently checked out revision, which can be referred to as HEAD.

The DAG view of creating a new commit

Chapter 2, Exploring Project History, introduced the concept of *Directed Acyclic Graph* (DAG) of revisions. Contributing to the development of a project usually consists of creating new revisions of the said project, and adding them as commit nodes to the graph of revisions.

Let's assume that we are on the `master` branch, as shown in *Fig 1* of the preceding section, and that we want to create a new version (the details of this operation will be described in more detail later). The `git commit` command will create a new commit object—a new revision node. This commit will have as a patent the checked out revision (`c7cd3` in the example). That revision is found by following refs starting from HEAD; here, it is HEAD to master to c7cd3 chain.

Then Git will move the `master` pointer to the new node, creating a situation as in *Fig 2*. In it, the new commit is marked with a thick red outline, and the old position of the `master` branch is shown semi-transparent. Note that the HEAD pointer doesn't change; all the time it points to `master`:

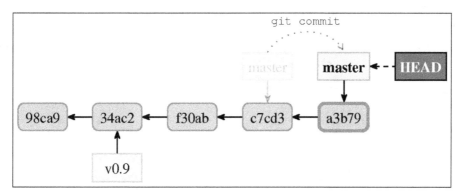

Fig 2: The graph of revisions (the DAG) for an example project just after creating a new commit, starting from the state given by Fig 1

The new commit, `a3b79`, is marked with the thick red outline. The tip of the `master` branch changes from pointing to commit `c7cd3` to pointing to commit `a3b79`, as shown with the dotted line.

The index – a staging area for commits

Each of your files inside the working area of the Git repository can be either known or unknown to Git (be a **tracked file**). The files unknown to Git can be either untracked or ignored (you can find more information about ignoring files in *Chapter 4, Managing Your Worktree*).

Files tracked by Git are usually in either of the two states: committed (or unchanged) or modified. The committed state means that the file contents in the working directory is the same as in the last release, which is safely stored in the repository. The file is modified if it has changed compared to the last committed version.

But, in Git, there is another state. Let's consider what happens when we use the `git add` command to add a file, but did not yet create a new commit adding it. A version control system needs to store such information somewhere. Git uses something called the **index** for this; it is the *staging area* that stores information that will go into the next commit. The `git add <file>` command *stages* the current contents (current version) of the file, adding it to the index.

If you want to only mark a file for addition, you can use `git add -N <file>`; this stages empty contents for a file.

The index is a third section storing copy of a project, after a working directory (which contains your own copy of the project files, used as a private isolated workspace to make changes), and a local repository (which stores your own copy of a project history, and is used to synchronize changes with other developers):

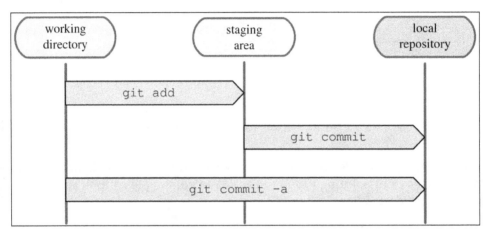

Fig 3. Working directory, staging area, and the local git repository; creating a new commit

The *arrows* show how the Git commands copy contents, for example, `git add` takes the content of the file from the working directory and puts it into the staging area.

Creating a new commit requires the following steps:

1. You make changes to files in your *working directory*, usually modifying them using your favorite editor.

2. You stage the files, adding snapshots of them (their current contents) to your *staging area*, usually with the `git add` command.

3. You create a new revision with the `git commit` command, which takes the files as they are in the staging area and stores that snapshot permanently to your *local repository*.

At the beginning (and just after the commit), the tracked files in the working directory, in the staging area, and in the last commit (the committed version) are identical.

Usually, however, one would use a special shortcut, the `git commit -a` command (which is `git commit --all`), which will take *all the changed tracked files*, add them to the staging area (as if with `git add -u`, at least in modern Git), and create a new commit (see *Fig 3* of this section). Note that the new files still need to be explicitly `git add` to be tracked, and to be included in the new commit.

Examining the changes to be committed

Before committing the changes and creating a new revision (a new commit), you would want to see what you have done.

Git shows information about the pending changes to be committed in the commit message template, which is passed to the editor, unless you specify the commit message on the command line, for example, with `git commit -m "Short description"`. This template is configurable (refer to *Chapter 10, Customizing and Extending Git* for more information).

 You can always abort creating a commit by exiting editor without any changes or with an empty commit message (comment lines, that is, lines beginning with #, do not count).

In most cases, you would want to examine changes for correctness before creating a commit.

The status of the working directory

The main tool you use to examine which files are in which state: which files have changes, whether there are any new files, and so on, is the `git status` command.

The default output is explanatory and quite verbose. If there are no changes, for example, directly after clone, you could see something like this:

```
$ git status
On branch master
nothing to commit, working directory clean
```

If the branch (you are on the `master` branch in this example) is a local branch intended to create changes that are to be published and to appear in the public repository, and is configured to track its upstream branch, `origin/master`, you would also see the information about the tracked branch:

```
Your branch is up-to-date with 'origin/master'.
```

In further examples, we will ignore it and not include this information.

Let's say you add two new files to your project, a COPYING file with the copyright and license, and a NEWS file, which is currently empty. In order to begin tracking a new COPYING file, you use git add COPYING. Accidentally, you remove the README file from the working directory with rm README. You modify Makefile and rename rand.c to random.c with git mv (without modifying it).

The default, long format, is designed to be human-readable, verbose, and descriptive:

```
$ git status
On branch master
Changes to be committed:
  (use "git reset HEAD <file>..." to unstage)


        new file:   COPYING
        renamed:    src/rand.c -> src/random.c


Changes not staged for commit:
  (use "git add <file>..." to update what will be committed)
  (use "git checkout -- <file>..." to discard changes in working
directory)


        modified:   Makefile
        deleted:    README


Untracked files:
  (use "git add <file>..." to include in what will be committed)


        NEWS
```

As you can see, Git does not only describe which files have changed, but also explains how to change their status—either include in the commit, or remove from the set of pending changes (more information about commands in use in git status output can be found in *Chapter 4, Managing Your Worktree*). There are up to three sections present in the output:

- **Changes to be committed**: This is about the staged changes that would be committed with git commit (without the -a option). It lists files whose snapshot in the staging area is different from the version from the last commit (HEAD).

- **Changes not staged for commit**: This lists the files whose working area contents are different from their snapshot in the staging area. Those changes would not be committed with `git commit`, but would be committed with `git commit -a` as changes in the tracked files.

- **Untracked files**: This lists the files, unknown to Git, which are not ignored (refer to *Chapter 4, Managing Your Worktree* for how to use `gitignores` to make files to be ignored). These files would be added with the bulk `add` command, `git add .`, in top directory. You can skip this section with `--untracked-files=no` (`-uno` for short).

One does not need to make use of the flexibility that the explicit staging area gives; one can simply use `git add` just to add new files, and `git commit -a` to create the commit from changes to all tracked files. In this case, you would create commit from both the *Changes to be committed* and *Changes not staged for commit* sections.

There is also a terse `--short` output format. Its `--porcelain` version is suitable for scripting because it is promised to remain stable, while `--short` is intended for user output and could change. For the same set of changes, this output format would look something like this:

```
$ git status --short
A  COPYING
 M Makefile
 D README
R  src/rand.c -> src/random.c
?? NEWS
```

In this format, the status of each path is shown using a two-letter status code. The first letter shows the status of the index (the difference between the staging area and the last commit), and the second letter shows the status of the worktree (the difference between the working area and the staging area):

Symbol	Meaning
	Not updated / unchanged
M	Modified (updated)
A	Added
D	Deleted
R	Renamed
C	Copied

Not all the combinations are possible. Status letters A, R, and C are possible only in the first column, for the status of the index.

A special case, ??, is used for the unknown (untracked) files and !! for ignored files (when using git status --short --ignored). Note that not all the possible outputs are described here; the case where we have just done a merge that resulted in merge conflicts is not shown in this table, but is left to be described in *Chapter 7, Merging Changes Together*.

Examining differences from the last revision

If you want to know not only which files were changed (which you get with git status), but also what exactly you have changed, use the git diff command:

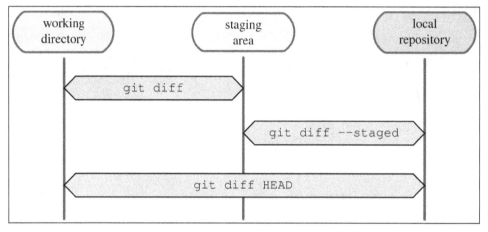

Fig 4. Examining the differences between the working directory, staging area, and local git repository

In the last section, we learned that in Git there are three stages: the working directory, the staging area, and the repository (usually the last commit). Therefore, we have not one set of differences but three, as shown in *Fig 4*. You can ask Git the following questions:

- What have you changed but not yet staged, that is, what are the differences between the staging area and working directory?
- What have you staged that you are about to commit, that is, what are the differences between the last commit (HEAD) and staging area?

To see what you've changed but not yet staged, type git diff with no other arguments. This command compares what is in your working directory with what is in your staging area. These are the changes that *could* be added, but wouldn't be present if we create commit with git commit (without -a): *Changes not staged for commit* in the git status output.

To see what you've staged that will go into your next commit, use `git diff --staged` (or `git diff --cached`). This command compares what is in your staging area to the content of your last commit. These are the changes that *would* be added with `git commit` (without `-a`): *Changes to be committed* in the `git status` output. You can compare your staging area to any commit with `git diff --staged <commit>`; HEAD (the last commit) is just the default.

You can use `git diff HEAD` to compare what is in your working directory with the last commit (or arbitrary commit with `git diff <commit>`). These are the changes that would be added with the `git commit -a` shortcut.

If you are using `git commit -a`, and not making use of the staging area, usually it is enough to use `git diff` to check the changes which will be in the next commit. The only issue is the new files that are added with bare `git add`; they won't show in the `git diff` output unless you use `git add --intent-to-add` (or its equivalent `git add -N`) to add new files.

Unified Git diff format

Git, by default and in most cases, will show the changes in **unified diff output format**. Understanding this output is very important, not only when examining changes to be committed, but also when reviewing and examining changes (for example, in code review, or in finding bugs after `git bisect` has found the suspected commit).

You can request only statistics of changes with the `--stat` or `--dirstat` option, or just names of the changed files with `--name-only`, or file names with type of changes with `--name-status`, or tree-level view of changes with `--raw`, or a condensed summary of extended header information with `--summary` (see later for an explanation of what extended header means and what information it contains). You can also request *word diff*, rather than line diff, with `--word-diff`; though this changes only the formatting of chunks of changes, headers and chunk headers remain similar.

Diff generation can also be configured for specific files or types of files with appropriate **gitattributes**. You can specify external diff helper, that is, the command that describes the changes, or you can specify text conversion filter for binary files (you will learn more about this in *Chapter 4, Managing Your Worktree*).

If you prefer to examine the changes in a graphical tool (which usually provides side-by-side diff), you can do it by using `git difftool` in place of `git diff`. This may require some configuration, and will be explained in *Chapter 10, Customizing and Extending Git*.

Let's take a look at an example of advanced diff from Git project history . Let's use the diff from the commit 1088261f from the git.git repository. You can view these changes in a web browser, for example, on GitHub; this is the third patch in this commit:

```
diff --git a/builtin-http-fetch.c b/http-fetch.c
similarity index 95%
rename from builtin-http-fetch.c
rename to http-fetch.c
index f3e63d7..e8f44ba 100644
--- a/builtin-http-fetch.c
+++ b/http-fetch.c
@@ -1,8 +1,9 @@
 #include "cache.h"
 #include "walker.h"

-int cmd_http_fetch(int argc, const char **argv, const char *prefix)
+int main(int argc, const char **argv)
 {
+       const char *prefix;
        struct walker *walker;
        int commits_on_stdin = 0;
        int commits;
@@ -18,6 +19,8 @@ int cmd_http_fetch(int argc, const char **argv,
        int get_verbosely = 0;
        int get_recover = 0;

+       prefix = setup_git_directory();
+
        git_config(git_default_config, NULL);

        while (arg < argc && argv[arg][0] == '-') {
```

Let's analyze this patch line after line:

- The first line, diff --git a/builtin-http-fetch.c b/http-fetch.c, is a *git* diff header in the form diff --git a/file1 b/file2. The a/ and b/ filenames are the same unless rename or copy is involved (such as in our case), even if the file is added or deleted. The --git option means that diff is in the git diff output format.

- The next lines are one or more extended header lines. The first three lines in this example tell us that the file was renamed from `builtin-http-fetch.c` to `http-fetch.c` and that these two files are `95%` identical (which information was used to detect this rename):

```
similarity index 95%
rename from builtin-http-fetch.c
Rename to http-fetch.c
```

> Extended header lines describe information that cannot be represented in an ordinary unified diff (except for information that file was renamed). Besides similarity (or dissimilarity) score like in example they can describe the changes in file type (example from non-executable to executable).

- The last line in extended diff header, which, in this example is `index f3e63d7..e8f44ba 100644` tells us about the mode of given file (`100644` means that it is an ordinary file and not a symbolic link, and that it doesn't have executable permission bit; these three are only file permissions tracked by Git), and about shortened hash of pre-image (the version of the file before the given change) and post-image (the version of the file after the change). This line is used by `git am --3way` to try to do a three-way merge if the patch cannot be applied itself. For the new files, pre-image hash is `0000000`, the same for the deleted files with post-image hash.

- Next is the unified diff header, which consists of two lines:

```
--- a/builtin-http-fetch.c
+++ b/http-fetch.c
```

- Compared to the `diff -U` result, it doesn't have from-file-modification-time or to-file-modification-time after source (pre-image) and destination or target (post-image) filenames. If the file was created, the source would be `/dev/null`; if the file was deleted, the target would be `/dev/null`.

> If you set the `diff.mnemonicPrefix` configuration variable to `true`, in place of the a/ prefix for pre-image and b/ for post-image in this two-line header, you can instead have the c/ prefix for commit, i/ for index, w/ for worktree, and o/ for object, respectively, to show what you compare.

- Next comes one or more hunk of differences; each hunk shows one area where the files differ. Unified format hunks start with the line describing where the changes were in the file:

```
@@ -1,8 +1,9 @@
```

This line is in the format `@@ from-file-range to-file-range @@`. The from-file-range is in the form `-<start line>,<number of lines>`, and to-file-range is `+<start line>,<number of lines>`. Both start-line and number-of-lines refer to the position and length of hunk in pre-image and post-image, respectively. If number-of-lines is not shown, it means that it is `0`. In this example, the changes, both in pre-image (file before the changes) and post-image (file after the changes) begin at the first line of the file, and the fragment of code corresponding to this hunk of diff has `8` lines in pre-image, and `9` lines in post-image (one line is added). By default, Git will also show three unchanged lines surrounding changes (three context lines). Git will also show the function where each change occurs (or equivalent, if any, for other types of files; this can be configured with `.gitattributes`); it is like the `-p` option in GNU diff:

```
@@ -18,6 +19,8 @@ int cmd_http_fetch(int argc, const char
```

- Next is the description of where and how files differ. The lines common to both the files begin with a space (" ") indicator character. The lines that actually differ between the two files have one of the following indicator characters in the left print column:

    ○ +: A line was added here to the second file

    ○ -: A line was removed here from the first file

> Note that the changed line is denoted as removing the old version and adding the new version of the line.
>
> In the plain word-diff format, instead of comparing file contents line by line, added words are surrounded by {+ and +}, while removed by [- and -].

- If the last hunk includes, among its lines, the very last line of either version of the file, and that last line is incomplete, (which means that the file does not end with the end-of-line character at the end of hunk) you would find:

```
\ No newline at end of file
```

This situation is not present in the presented example.

So, for the example used here, first chunk means that `cmd_http_fetch` was replaced by `main` and the `const char *prefix;` line was added:

```
#include "cache.h"
#include "walker.h"

-int cmd_http_fetch(int argc, const char **argv, const char *prefix)
+int main(int argc, const char **argv)
 {
+       const char *prefix;
        struct walker *walker;
        int commits_on_stdin = 0;
        int commits;
```

See how for the replaced line, the old version of the line appears as removed (-) and the new version as added (+).

In other words, before the change, the appropriate fragment of the file, that was then named `builtin-http-fetch.c`, looked similar to the following:

```
#include "cache.h"
#include "walker.h"

int cmd_http_fetch(int argc, const char **argv, const char *prefix)
{
        struct walker *walker;
        int commits_on_stdin = 0;
        int commits;
```

After the change, this fragment of the file that is now named `http-fetch.c`, looks similar to this instead:

```
#include "cache.h"
#include "walker.h"

int main(int argc, const char **argv)
{
        const char *prefix;
        struct walker *walker;
        int commits_on_stdin = 0;
        int commits;
```

Selective commit

Sometimes, after examining the pending changes as explained, you realize that you have two (or more) unrelated changes in your working directory that should belong to two different logical changes; it is the tangled working copy problem. You need to put those unrelated changes into separate commits, as separate changesets. This is the type of situation that can occur even when trying to follow the best practices.

One solution is to create commit as-is, and fix it later (split it in two). You can read how to do this in *Chapter 8, Keeping History Clean*.

Sometimes, however, some of the changes are needed now, and shipped immediately (for example bug fix to a live website), while the rest of the changes are work in progress, not ready. You need to tease those changes apart into two separate commits.

Selecting files to commit

The simplest situation is when these unrelated changes touch different files. For example, if the bug was in the `view/entry.tmpl` file and only in this file, and there were no other changes to this file, you can create a bug fix commit with the following command:

```
$ git commit view/entry.tmpl
```

This command will ignore changes staged in the index (what was in the staging area), and instead record the current contents of a given file or files (what is in the working directory).

Interactively selecting changes

Sometimes, however, the changes cannot be separated in this way. The changes to the file are tangled together. You can try to tease them apart by giving the `--interactive` option to `git commit`:

```
$ git commit --interactive
           staged      unstaged path
  1:     unchanged        +3/-2 Makefile
  2:     unchanged       +64/-1 src/rand.c

*** Commands ***
  1: status      2: update      3: revert      4: add untracked
  5: patch       6: diff        7: quit        8: help
What now>
```

Here, Git shows us the status and the summary of changes to the working area (unstaged) and to the staging area / the index (staged) — the output of the status subcommand. The changes are described by the number of added and deleted files (similar to what the git diff --numstat command shows):

```
What now> h
status          - show paths with changes
update          - add working tree state to the staged set of changes
revert          - revert staged set of changes back to the HEAD version
patch           - pick hunks and update selectively
diff            - view diff between HEAD and index
add untracked - add contents of untracked files to the staged set of
changes
*** Commands ***
  1: status        2: update        3: revert        4: add untracked
  5: patch         6: diff          7: quit          8: help
```

To tease apart changes, you need to choose the patch subcommand (for example, with 5 or s). Git will then ask for the files with the Update>> prompt; you then need to select the files to selectively update with their numeric identifiers, as shown in the status, and type return. You can say * to select all the files possible. After making the selection, end it by answering with an empty line. (You can skip directly to patching files with the --patch option.)

Git will then display all the changes to the specified files on a hunk-by-hunk basis, and let you choose, among others, one of the following options for each hunk:

```
        y - stage this hunk
        n - do not stage this hunk
        q - quit; do not stage this hunk or any of the remaining ones

        s - split the current hunk into smaller hunks
        e - manually edit the current hunk
        ? - print help
```

The hunk output and the prompt look similar to this:

```
@@ -16,7 +15,6 @@ int main(int argc, char *argv[])

        int max = atoi(argv[1]);
```

```
+           srand(time(NULL));
            int result = random_int(max);
            printf("%d\n", result);
```

```
Stage this hunk [y,n,q,a,d,/,j,J,g,e,?]? y
```

In many cases, it is enough to simply select which of those hunks of changes you want to have in the commit. In extreme cases, you can split a chunk into smaller pieces, or even manually edit the diff.

Creating a commit step by step

Interactively selecting changes to commit with `git commit --interactive` doesn't unfortunately allow to test the changes to be committed. You can always check that everything works after creating a commit (compile and/or run tests), and then amend it if there are any errors. There is, however, an alternative solution.

You can prepare commit by putting the pending changes into the staging area with `git add --interactive`, or an equivalent solution (like graphical Git commit tool for Git, for example, `git gui`). The interactive commit is just a shortcut for interactive add followed by commit, anyway. Then you should examine these changes with `git diff --cached`, modifying them as appropriate with `git add <file>`, `git checkout <file>`, and `git reset <file>`.

In theory, you should also test these changes whether they are correct, checking that at least they do not break the build. To do this, first use `git stash save --keep-index` to save the current state and bring the working directory to the state prepared in the staging area (the index). After this command, you can run tests (or at least check whether the program compiles and doesn't crash). If tests pass, you can then run `git commit` to create a new revision. If tests fail, you should restore the working directory while keeping the staging area state with the `git stash pop --index` command; it might be required to precede it with `git reset --hard`. The latter might be needed because Git is overly conservative when preserving your work, and does not know that you have just stashed. First, there are uncommitted changes in the index prevent Git from applying the stash, and second, the changes to the working directory are the same as stashed, so of course they would conflict.

You can find more information about stashes, including how they work, in *Chapter 4, Managing Your Worktree*.

Amending a commit

One of the better things in Git is that you can undo almost anything; you only need to know how. No matter how carefully you craft your commits, sooner or later, you'll forget to add a change, or mistype the commit message. That's when the `--amend` flag of the `git commit` command comes in handy; it allows you to change the very last commit really easily. Note that you can also amend the merge commits (for example, fix a merging error).

> If you want to change a commit deeper in history (assuming that it was not published, or at least, there isn't anyone who based their work on the old version of the said commit), you need to use **interactive rebase** or some specialized tool, such as **StGit** (a *patch stack management interface* on top of Git). Refer to *Chapter 8, Keeping History Clean*, for more information.

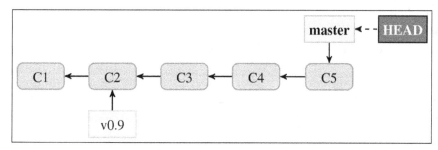

Fig 5. The DAG of revisions, C1 to C2, before amending a topmost (most recent) and currently checked out commit, which is named C5. Here, we have used numbers instead of SHA-1 to be able to indicate related commits.

If you just want to correct the commit message, you simply *commit again*, without any staged changes, and fix it (note that we use `git commit` without the `-a` / `--all` flag):

```
$ git commit --amend
```

If you want to add some more changes to that last commit, you can simply stage them as normal with `git add` and then commit again as shown in the preceding example, or make the changes and use `git commit -a --amend`:

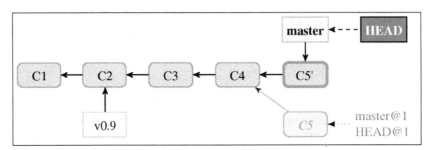

Fig 6. The DAG of revisions after amending the last commit (revision C5) on Fig 5. Here, the new commit C5 is old commit C5 with changes (amended); it replaces old commit place in history.

There is a very important caveat: you should *never* amend a commit that has already been published! This is because amend effectively produces a completely new commit object that replaces the old one, as can be seen on *Fig 6*. If you're the only person who had this commit, doing this is safe. However, after publishing the original commit to a remote repository, other people might already have based their new work on that version of the commit. Replacing the original with an amended version will cause problems downstream. You will find more about this issue in *Chapter 8, Keeping History Clean*.

If you try to push (publish) a branch with the published commit amended, Git would prevent overwriting the published history, and ask to force push if you really want to replace the old version (unless you configure it to force push by default). The old version of commit before amending would be available in the branch reflog and in the HEAD reflog; for example, just after *amend*, it would be available as `@{1}`. Git would keep the old version for a month, by default, unless manually purged.

Working with branches

Branches are symbolic names for lines of development. In Git, each branch is realized as a named *pointer* (reference) to some commit in the DAG of revisions, so it is called **branch head**.

The representation of branches in Git

Git uses currently two different on-disk representations of branches: the *loose* format and the *packed* format.

Take, for example, the master branch (which is the default name of a branch in Git; you start on this branch in the newly-created repository). In *loose* format (which takes precedence), it is represented as the one-line file, .git/refs/heads/master with textual hexadecimal representation of SHA-1 tip of the branch. In the *packed* format, it is represented as a line in the .git/packed-refs file, connecting SHA-1 identifier of top commit with the fully qualified branch name.

The (named) line of development is the set of all revisions that are reachable from the branch head. It is not necessarily a straight line of revisions, it can fork and join.

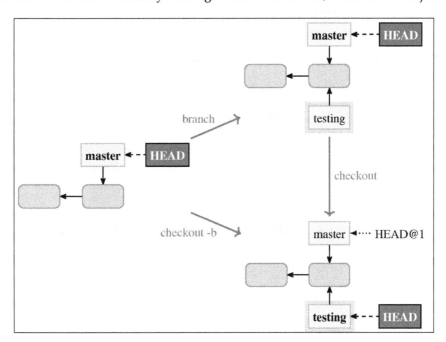

Fig 7. Creating a new testing branch and switching to it, or creating a new branch and switching to it at once (with one command)

Creating a new branch

You can create a new branch with the `git branch` command; for example, to create a new branch `testing` starting from the current branch (see the top right part of *Fig 7*), run:

```
$ git branch testing
```

What happens here? Well, this command creates a new pointer (a new reference) for you to move around. You can give an optional parameter to this command if you want to create the new branch pointing to some other commit.

Note, however, that the `git branch` command would not change the position of the HEAD (the symbolic reference pointing to current branch), and would not change the contents of the working directory.

If you want to create a new branch and switch to it (to start working on new branch immediately), you can use the following shortcut:

```
$ git checkout -b testing
```

If we create a new branch at the current state of repository, the `checkout -b` command differs only in that it also moves the HEAD pointer; see transition from left-hand side to the bottom-right in *Fig 7*.

Creating orphan branches

Sometimes you might want to create a new unconnected *orphan* branch in your repository. Perhaps you want to store the generated documentation for each release to make it easy for users to get readable documentation (for example, as man pages or HTML help) without requiring to install conversion tools or renderers (for example, AsciiDoc parser). Or, you might want to store web pages for a project in the same repository as project; that is what GitHub project pages use. Perhaps you want to open source your code, but you need to clean up the code first (for example, because of copyrights and licensing).

One solution is to create a separate repository for the contents of an orphan branch, and fetch from it into some remote-tracking branch. You can then create a local branch based on it.

You can also do this with:

```
$ git checkout --orphan gh-pages
Switched to a new branch 'gh-pages'
```

This reproduces somewhat the state just after `git init`: the HEAD symref points to the `gh-pages` branch, which does not exist yet; it will be created on the first commit.

If you want to start with clean state, like with GitHub Pages, you would also need to remove the contents of the start point of branch (which defaults to HEAD, that is, to current branch and to the current state of the working directory), for example with:

```
$ git rm -rf .
```

In the case of open sourcing code with proprietary parts to be excluded (*orphan* branch is not to bring this proprietary code accidentally to the open source version on merging), you would want to carefully edit the working directory instead.

Selecting and switching to a branch

To switch to an existing local branch, you need to run the `git checkout` command. For example, after creating the `testing` branch, you can switch to it with the following command:

```
$ git checkout testing
```

It is shown in *Fig 7* as the vertical transition from the top-right to bottom-right state.

Obstacles to switching to a branch

When switching to a branch, Git also checks out its contents into the working directory. What happens then if you have uncommitted changes (which are not considered by Git to be on any branch)?

> It is a good practice to switch branch in a clean state, stashing away changes or creating a commit, if necessary. Checking out a branch with uncommitted changes is useful only in a few rare cases, some of which are described in the following section.

If the difference between the current branch and the branch you want to switch to does not touch the changed files, the uncommitted changes are moved to the new branch. This is very useful if you started working on something, and only later realized that it would be better to do this work in a separate feature branch.

If uncommitted changes conflict with changes on the given branch, Git will refuse to switch to the said branch, to prevent you from losing your work:

```
$ git checkout other-branch
error: Your local changes to the following files would be overwritten by
checkout:
        file-with-local-changes
Please, commit your changes or stash them before you can switch branches.
```

In such situation you have a few possible different solutions:

- You can *stash away* your changes, and restore them when you come back to the branch you were on (this is usually the preferred solution). Or you can simply create a temporary commit of the work in progress with those changes, and then either amend the commit or rewind the branch when you get back to it.

- You can try to move your changes to the new branch by *merging*, either with `git branch --merge` (which would do the three-way merge between the current branch, the contents of your working directory with unsaved changes, and the new branch), or by stashing away your changes before checkout and then unstashing them after a switch.

- You can also *throw away* your changes with `git checkout --force`.

Anonymous branches

What happens if you try to check out something that is not a local branch: for example an arbitrary revision (like HEAD^), or a tag (like v0.9), or a remote-tracking branch (for example, `origin/master`)? Git assumes that you need to be able create commits on top of the current state of the working directory.

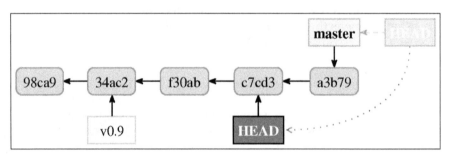

Fig 8. The result of checking out non-branch, the state after Git checkout HEAD command, detached HEAD, or anonymous branch

Older Git refused to switch to non-branch. Nowadays, Git will create an anonymous branch by detaching HEAD pointer and making it refer directly to a commit, rather than being a symbolic reference to a branch, see *Fig 8* for an example. To create an anonymous branch at the current position explicitly, you can use the `--detach` option to the checkout command. The detached HEAD state is shown in branch listing as *(no branch)* in older versions of Git, or *(detached from HEAD)* or *(HEAD detached at ...)* in newer.

If you did detach HEAD by mistake, you can always go back to the previous branch with (here "-" means the name of previous branch):

```
$ git checkout -
```

As Git informs you when creating a detached branch, you can always give a name to the anonymous branch with `git checkout -b <new-name>`.

Git checkout DWIM-mery

There is a special case of checking out something that is not a branch. If you check out remote-tracking branch (for example, `origin/next`) by its short name (in this case, `next`), as if it was a local branch, Git would assume that you meant to create new contents on top of the remote-tracking branch state, and will do what it thinks you need. **Do What I Mean** (**DWIM**) will create a new local branch, tracking the remote-tracking branch.

This means that:

```
$ git checkout next
```

Is equivalent to:

```
$ git checkout -b next --track origin/next
```

Git will do it only if there are no ambiguities: the local branch must not exist (otherwise the command would simply switch to local branch given), and there can be only one remote-tracking branch that matches. This can be checked by running `git show-ref next` (using the short name) and verifying that it returns only one line, with remote-tracking branch info (the last can be recognized by the `refs/remotes/` prefix in ref name).

Listing branches

If you use the `git branch` commands without any other arguments, it would list all the branches, marking the current branch with asterisk, that is, `*`.

This command is intended for the end user; its output may change in the future version of Git. To find out programmatically, in a shell script:

- To get the name of the current branch, use `git symbolic-ref HEAD`.
- To find SHA-1 of the current commit, use `git rev-parse HEAD`.
- To list all the branches, use `git show-ref` or `git for-each-ref`.

They are all **plumbing**, that is, commands intended for use in scripts.

You can request more information with `-v` (`--verbose`) or `-vv`. You can also limit branches shown to only those matching given shell wildcard with `git branch --list <pattern>` (quoting pattern to prevent its expansion by shell, if necessary).

Querying information about remotes, which includes the list of remote branches, by using `git remote show`, is described in *Chapter 6, Advanced Branching Techniques*.

Rewinding or resetting a branch

What to do if you want to abandon the last commit, and rewind (reset) the current branch to its previous position? For this, you need to use the `reset` command. It would change where the current branch points to. Note that unlike the `checkout` command, the `reset` command does not change the working directory by default; you need to use instead `git reset --keep` (to try to keep the uncommitted changes) or `git reset --hard` (to drop them).

The reset command, and its effects on the working area, will be explained in more detail in *Chapter 4, Managing Your Worktree*.

Fig 9 shows the differences between the `checkout` and `reset` commands, when given the branch and non-branch argument. In short, `reset` always changes where the current branch points to (moves the ref), while `checkout` either switches branch, or detaches HEAD at a given revision if it is given non-branch:

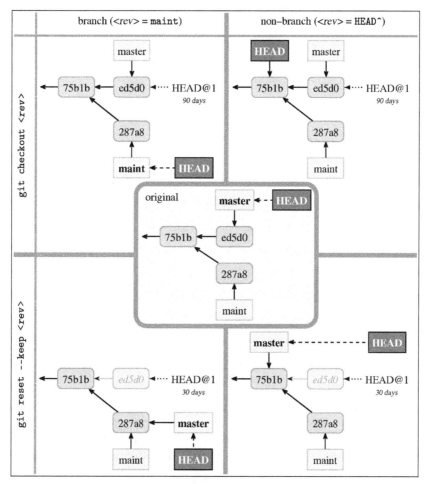

Fig 9. A table comparing the checkout and reset commands with either branch (for example, maint) and non-branch revision (for example, HEAD^) as arguments.

In the preceding figure, for example, the left-top graph of the revision shows the result of running of the Git checkout maint command, starting from the state given by the graphs in the centre.

Deleting a branch

As in Git, a branch is just a pointer, and an external reference to the node in the DAG of revisions, deleting a branch is just deleting a pointer:

 Actually deleting a branch also removes, irretrievably, (at least, in the current Git version) the reflog for the branch being deleted, that is, the log of its local history.

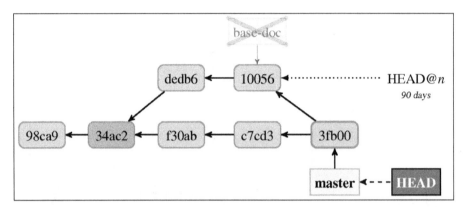

Fig 10. Deleting just merged in base-doc branch with git branch -d base-doc, when we are on a branch (master here) that includes it

You can do this with `git branch -d`. There is, however, one issue to consider — what happens if you delete a branch, and there is no other reference to the part of project history it pointed to? Those revisions will become unreachable and Git would delete them after the HEAD reflog expires (which, with default configuration, is after 30 days).

That is why Git would allow you to delete only the completely merged-in branch, whose all commits are reachable from HEAD as in *Fig 10* (or is reachable from its upstream branch, if it exists).

To delete a branch that was not merged in, risking parts of the DAG becoming unreachable, you need a stronger command, namely, `git branch -D` (Git will suggest this operation when refusing to delete a branch); see *Fig 11*:

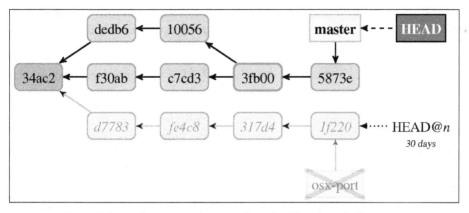

Fig 11. Deleting the unmerged osx-port branch with git branch -D osx-port

You can check if the branch was merged in into any other branch, by checking whether `git branch --contains <branch>` shows anything.
You cannot delete the current branch.

Changing the branch name

Sometimes the name chosen for a branch needs to be changed. This can happen, for example, if the scope of the feature branch changed during the development.

You can rename a branch with `git branch -m` (use `-M` if target name exists and you want to overwrite it); it will rename a branch and move the corresponding reflog (and add rename operation to the reflog), and change the branch in all of its configuration (its description, its upstream, and so on).

Summary

In this chapter, we learnt how to develop with Git and add to the project history by creating new commits and new lines of development (branches). We know what it means to create a commit, to amend a commit, to create a branch, to switch a branch, to rewind a branch, and to delete a branch from the point of view of the Directed Acyclic Graph of revisions.

This chapter shown a very important Git feature—the staging area for creating commits, also known as the index. This is what makes it possible to untangle the changes to the working directory by selectively and interactively choosing what to commit.

We learnt how to examine the changes to the working area before creating a commit. This chapter described, in detail, the extended unified diff format that Git uses to describe the changes.

We also learnt about the concept of detached HEAD (or anonymous branch) and of orphan branches.

In the next chapter, *Managing Your Worktree*, we will learn how to use Git to prepare new commits and how to configure it to make our work easier. We will also learn how to examine, search, and study the contents of the working directory, the staging area, and the project history. We will also see how to use Git to deal with interruptions and recover from mistakes.

4
Managing Your Worktree

The previous chapter, *Developing with Git*, described how to use Git for development, including how to create new revisions. Now we will focus on learning how to manage your working directory (worktree) to prepare contents for a new commit. This chapter will teach you how to manage your files, in detail. It will show how to care for files that require special handling, introducing the concepts of ignored files and file attributes.

You will also learn how to fix mistakes in handling files, both in the working directory and in the staging area; and how to fix the latest commit. You will find out how to safely handle interruptions in the workflow with stash and multiple working directories.

The previous chapter taught you how to examine changes. Here you will learn how to undo and redo those changes selectively, and how to view different versions of a file.

This chapter will cover the following topics:

- Ignoring files: marking files as intentionally not under version control
- File attributes: path-specific configuration
- Handling text and binary files
- End of line conversion of text files, for repository portability
- Using various modes of the `git reset` command
- Stashing away your changes to handle interruptions
- Searching and examining files in any place
- Resetting files and reverting file changes interactively
- Cleaning the working area by removing untracked files

Ignoring files

Your files inside your working area (also known as the **worktree**) can be either *tracked* or *untracked* by Git. Tracked files, as the name suggests, are whose changes Git will follow. For Git, if a file is present in the *staging area* (also known as **the index**), it will be tracked and — unless specified otherwise — it will be a part of the next revision. You **add** files to be tracked so as to have them as a part of the project history.

> The index, or the staging area, is used not only for Git to know which files to track, but also as a kind of a scratchpad to create new commits, as described in *Chapter 3, Developing with Git*, and to help resolve merge conflicts, as shown in *Chapter 7, Merging Changes Together*.

Often you will have some individual files or a class of files that you never want to be a part of the project history, and never want to track. These can be your editor backup files, or automatically generated files produced by the project's build system.

You don't want Git to automatically add such files, for example, when doing *bulk add* with `git add :/` (adding the entire working tree), `git add .` (adding the current directory), or when updating the index to the worktree state with `git add --all`. Quite the opposite: you want Git to actively prevent from accidentally adding them. You also want such files to be absent from the `git status` output, as there can be quite a number of them. They could drown out legitimate new *unknown* files there otherwise. You want such files to be intentionally untracked: *ignored*.

> **Un-tracking and re-tracking files**
>
> If you want to start ignoring a file that was formerly tracked, for example when moving from hand-generated HTML file to using a lightweight markup language such as Markdown instead, you usually need to **un-track** the file without removing it from the working directory, while adding it to the list of ignored files. You can do this with `git rm --cached <file>`.
>
> To add (start tracking) an intentionally untracked (that is, ignored) file, you need to use `git add -f`.

Marking files as intentionally untracked

In such case, you can add a shell glob pattern to match files that you want to have ignored by Git to one of the **gitignore** files, one pattern per line:

- The per-user file that can be specified by the configuration variable core. excludesFile, which by default is $XDG_CONFIG_HOME/git/ignore. This in turn defaults to the $HOME/.config/git/ignore if $XDG_CONFIG_HOME environment variable is not set or empty.

- The per-local repository $GIT_DIR/info/exclude file in the administrative area of the local clone of the repository.

- The .gitignore files in the working directories of a project; these are usually tracked and thus shared among developers.

Some commands, such as git clean, also allow us to specify ignore patterns from a command line.

When deciding whether to ignore a path, Git checks all those sources in the order specified on preceding list, with the last matching pattern deciding the outcome. The .gitignore files are checked in order, starting from the top directory of the project down to the directory of files to be examined.

To make gitignore files more readable you can use blank lines to separate groups of files (a blank line matches no files). You can also describe patterns or groups of patterns with comments; a line starting with # serves as one (to ignore a pattern beginning with the hash character, #, escape the first hash character with a backslash \, for example, \#*#). Trailing spaces (at the end of the line) are ignored unless escaped with a backslash \.

Each line in the gitignore file specifies a Unix glob pattern, a shell wildcard. The * wildcard matches zero or more characters (any string), while the ? wildcard matches any single character. You can also use character classes with brackets [...]. Take for example the following list of patterns:

```
*.[oa]
*~
```

Here the first line tells Git to ignore all files with the .a or .o extension — archive (for example, a static library) and object files that may be the products of compiling your code. The second line tells Git to ignore all files ending with a tilde, ~; this is used by many Unix text editors to mark temporary backup files.

If the pattern does not contain a slash /, which is a directory (path component) separator, Git treats it as a shell glob and checks file name or directory name for a match, starting at appropriate depth, for example the `.gitignore` file location, or the top level of the repository. The exception is patterns ending with slash / — which is used to have the pattern matched against directories only — but otherwise the trailing slash is removed. A leading slash matches the beginning of the path name. This means the following:

- Patterns not containing a slash match everywhere in the repository; one can say that the pattern is recursive.

  For example, the `*.o` pattern matches object files anywhere, both in the `gitignore` file level and in subdirectories: `file.o`, `obj/file.o`, and so on.

- Patterns ending with a slash match only directories, but are otherwise recursive (unless they contain other slashes).

  For example, the `auto/` pattern will match the top-level `auto` directory and for example `src/auto`, but will not match the `auto` file (or a symbolic link either).

- To *anchor* a pattern and make it non-recursive, add a leading slash.

  For example the `/TODO` file will ignore the current-level `TODO` file, but not files in subdirectories, for example `src/TODO`.

- Patterns containing a slash are anchored and non-recursive, and wildcard characters (`*`, `?`, a character class such as `[ao]`) do not match the directory separator that is slash. If you want to match any number of directories, use two consecutive asterisks `**` in place of the path component (which means `**/foo`, `foo/**`, and `foo/**/bar`).

  For example, `doc/*.html` matches `doc/index.html` file but not `doc/api/index.html`; to match HTML files anywhere inside the `doc` directory you can use the `doc/**/*.html` pattern (or put the `*.html` pattern in the `doc/.gitignore` file).

You can also negate a pattern by prefixing it with an exclamation mark !; any matching file excluded by the earlier rule is then included (non-ignored) again. For example to ignore all generated HTML files, but include one generated by hand, you can put the following in the gitignore file:

```
# ignore html files, generated from AsciiDoc sources
*.html
# except for the files below which are generated by hand
!welcome.html
```

Note however that for performance reasons Git doesn't go into excluded directories, and (up till Git 2.7) this meant that you cannot re-include a file if a parent directory is excluded. This means that to ignore everything except for the subdirectory, you need to write the following:

```
# exclude everything except directory t0001/bin
/*
!/t0001
/t0001/*
!/t0001/bin
```

To match a pattern beginning with `!`, escape it with a backslash — for example, `\!important!.md` to match `!important!.md`.

Which types of file should be ignored?

Now that we know *how* to mark files as intentionally untracked (ignored), there is the question of *which* files (or classes of files) should be marked as such. Another issue is *where*, in which of the three gitignore files, should we add a pattern for ignoring specific types of file?

First, you should never track automatically generated files (usually generated by the build system of a project). If you add them to the repository, there is a high chance that they will get out of sync with their source. Besides, they are not necessary, as you can always re-generate them. The only possible exception is generated files where the source changes rarely, and generating them requires extra tools that developers might not have (if the source changes more often, you can use an orphan branch to store these generated files, and refresh this branch only at release time).

Those are the files that all developers will want to ignore. Therefore they should go into a tracked `.gitignore` file. The list of patterns will be version-controlled and distributed to other developers via a clone. You can find a collection of useful `.gitignore` templates for different programming languages at `https://github.com/github/gitignore`.

Second, there are temporary files and by-products specific to one user's toolchain; those should usually not be shared with other developers. If the pattern is specific to both the repository and the user, for example, auxiliary files that live inside the repository but are specific to the workflow of a user (for example, to the IDE used for the project), it should go into the per-clone `$GIT_DIR/info/exclude` file.

Patterns which the user wants to ignore in all situations, not specific to the repository (or to the project), should generally go into a file specified by the `core.excludesFile` config variable, set in the per-user (global) config file `~/.gitconfig` (or `~/.config/git/config`). This is usually by default `~/.config/git/ignore`.

> The per-user ignore file cannot be `~/.gitignore`, as this would be the in-repository `.gitignore` file for the versioned user's home directory, if the user wants to keep the `~/` directory (`$HOME`) under version control.

This is the place where you can put patterns matching the backup or temporary files generated by your editor or IDE of choice.

> **Ignored files are considered expendable**
>
> Warning: Do not add precious files, that is those which you do not want to track in a given repository but whose contents are important, to the list of ignored files! The types of file that are ignored (excluded) by Git are either easy to re-generate (build products and other generated files), or not important to the user (temporary files, backup files).
>
> Therefore Git considers ignored files expendable and will remove them without warning when required to do a requested command, for example, if the ignored file conflicts with the contents of the revision being checked out.

Listing ignored files

You can list untracked ignored files with the `--ignored` option to the status command:

```
$ git status --ignored
On branch master
Ignored files:
  (use "git add -f <file>..." to include in what will be committed)

        rand.c~

no changes added to commit (use "git add" and/or "git commit -a")

$ git status --short --branch --ignored
## master
!! rand.c~
```

You could instead use the dry-run option of cleaning ignored files: `git clean -Xnd`, or the low-level (plumbing) command `git ls-files`:

```
$ git ls-files --others --ignored --exclude-standard
rand.c~
```

The latter command can also be used to list tracked files that match ignore patterns. Having such files might mean that some files need to be un-tracked (perhaps because what was once a source file is now generated), or that ignore patterns are too broad. As Git uses the existence of a file in the staging area (cache) to know which files to track, this can be done with the following command:

```
$ git ls-files --cached --ignored --exclude-standard
```

Plumbing versus porcelain commands

Git commands are divided into two sets: high-level **porcelain** commands intended for interactive usage by the user, and low-level **plumbing** commands intended mainly for shell scripting. The major difference is that high-level commands have output that can change and that is constantly improving, for example, going from (no branch) to (detached from HEAD) in the `git branch` output in the detached from HEAD case; though some porcelain commands have the option (usually `--porcelain`) to switch to unchanging output. Their output and behavior are subject to configuration.

Another important difference is that plumbing commands try to guess what you meant, have default parameters, use the default configuration, and so on. Not so with plumbing commands. In particular you need to pass the `--exclude-standard` option to the `git ls-files` command to make it respect the default set of ignore files.

You can find more on this topic in *Chapter 10, Customizing and Extending Git*.

Ignoring changes in tracked files

You might have files in the repository that are changed, but rarely committed. These can be various local configuration files that are edited to match the local setup, but should never be committed upstream. This can be a file containing the proposed name for a new release, to be committed when tagging the next released version.

You would want to keep such files in the *dirty* state most of the time, but you would like Git not to tell you about their changes all the time, in case you miss other changes because you are used to ignore such messages.

Git can be configured to skip checking the worktree (to assume that it is always up to date), and to use instead the staged version of the file, by setting the aptly named `skip-worktree` flag for a file. For this you would need to use the low-level `git update-index` command, the plumbing equivalent of the user-facing `git add` porcelain (you can check file status and flags with `git ls-files`):

```
$ git update-index --skip-worktree GIT-VERSION-NAME
$ git ls-files -v
S GIT-VERSION-NAME
H Makefile
```

Note however that this elision of worktree also includes the `git stash` command; to stash away your changes and make the working directory clean, you need to disable this flag (at least temporarily). To make Git again look at the working directory version, and start tracking changes to the file, use the following command:

```
$ git update-index --no-assume-unchanged GIT-VERSION-NAME
```

There is a similar `assume-unchanged` flag that can be used to make Git completely ignore any changes to the file, or rather assume that it is unchanged. Files marked with this flag never show as changed in the output of the `git status` or `git diff` command. The changes to it will not be staged nor committed.

This is sometimes useful when working with a big project on a filesystem with very slow checking for changes. *Do not use assume-unchanged for ignoring changes to tracked files.* You are promising that the file didn't change; lying to Git with, for example, `git stash save` believing what you stated, would lose your local changes.

File attributes

There are some settings and options in Git that can be specified on a per-path basis; similar to how ignoring files (marking files as intentionally untracked) works. These path-specific settings are called attributes.

To specify attributes for files matching a given pattern, you need to add a line with a pattern followed by a whitespace-separated list of attributes to one of the gitattribute files (similarly to how the gitignore files work):

- The per-user file, for attributes that should affect all repositories for a single user, specified by the configuration variable `core.attributesFile`, by default `~/.config/git/attributes`

- The per repository `.git/info/attributes` file in the administrative area of the local clone of the repository, for attributes that should affect only a single specific clone of the repository (for one user's workflow)

- The `.gitattributes` files in the working directories of a project, for those attributes that should be shared among developers

The rules for how patterns are used to match files are the same as for the gitignore files, described in an earlier section, except that there is no support for negative patterns.

Each attribute can be in one of the following states for a given path: *set* (special value `true`), *unset* (special value `false`), and set to given value, or *unspecified*:

```
pattern*   set -unset set-to=value !unspecified
```

Note that there can be no whitespace around the equals sign = when setting an attribute to a string value!

When more than one pattern matches the path, a later line overrides an earlier line on a per-attribute basis. Gitattribute files are used in order, from the per-user to the `.gitattributes` file in a given directory, like for gitignore files.

Identifying binary files and end-of-line conversions

Different operating systems and different applications can differ in how they represent newline in text files. Unix and Unix-like systems (including MacOS X) use a single control character LF (\n), while MS Windows uses CR followed by LF (\n\r); MacOS up to version 9 used CR alone (\r).

That might be a problem for developing portable applications if different developers use different operating systems. We don't want to have spurious changes because of different end of line conventions. Therefore Git makes it possible to automatically normalize **end of line** (**eol**) characters to be LF in the repository on commit (check-in), and optionally to convert them to *CR + LF* in the working directory on checkout.

You can control whether a file should be considered for end of line conversion with the `text` attribute. Setting it enables end-of-line conversion, unsetting it disables it. Setting it to the `auto` value makes Git guess if given file is a text file; if it is, end-of-line conversion is enabled. For files where the `text` attribute is unspecified, Git uses `core.autocrlf` to decide whether to treat them as `text=auto` case.

How Git detects if a file contains binary data

To decide whether a file contains binary data, Git examines the beginning of the file for an occurrence of a zero byte (the null character or \0). When deciding about converting a file (as in end-of-line conversion), the criterion is more strict: for a file to be considered text it must have no nulls, and no more than around 1% of it should be non-printable characters.

This means that Git usually considers files saved in the UTF-16 encoding to be binary.

To decide what line ending type Git should use in the working directory for text files, you need to set up the core.eol configuration variable. This can be set to crlf, lf, or native (the last is the default). You can also force a specific line ending for a given file with the eol=lf or eol=crlf attribute.

Old crlf attribute	New text and eol attributes
crlf	text
-crlf	-text
crlf=input	eol=lf

Table 1. Backward compatibility with the crlf attribute

End of line conversion bears a slight chance of corrupting data. If you want Git to warn or prevent conversion for files with a mixture of LF and CRLF line endings, use the core.safecrlf configuration variable.

Sometimes Git might not detect that a file is binary correctly, or there may be some file that is nominally text, but which is opaque to a human reader. Examples include PostScript documents (*.ps) and Xcode build settings (*.pbxproj). Such files should be not normalized and textual diff for them doesn't make sense. You can mark such files explicitly as binary with the binary attribute macro (which is equivalent to -text -diff):

```
*.ps       binary
*.pbxproj  binary
```

Forcing end-of-line conversion when turning it on

When normalization of line endings is turned on in the repository (by editing the .gitattributes file) one should also force normalization of files. Otherwise the change in newline representation will be misattributed to the next change to the file:

```
$ rm .git/index
$ git reset
$ git add -u
$ git add .gitattributes
```

You can check which files will be normalized (for example, with git status) after git resetstep, but before git add -u.

Diff and merge configuration

In Git, you can use the attributes functionality to configure how to show differences between different versions of a file, and how to do a 3-way merge of its contents. This can be used to enhance those operation, making diff more attractive and merge less likely to conflict. It can be even used to make it possible to effectively diff binary files.

In both cases we would usually need to set up the diff and/or merge driver. The attributes file only tells us which driver to use; the rest of the information is contained in the configuration file, and the configuration is not automatically shared among developers unlike the .gitattributes file (though you can create a shared configuration fragment, add it to the repository, and have developers include it in their local per-repository config, via the relative include.path). This is easy to understand — the tool configuration may be different on different computers, and some tools may be not available for the developer's operating system of choice. But this means that some information needs to be distributed out-of-band.

There are however a few built-in diff drivers and merge drivers that you can use.

Generating diffs and binary files

Generating diffs for particular files is affected by the diff attribute. If this attribute is unset, Git will treat files as binary with respect to generating diffs, and show just *binary files differ* (or a binary diff). Setting it will force Git to treat a file as text, even if it contains byte sequences that normally mark the file as binary, such as the null (\0) character.

You can use the `diff` attribute to make Git effectively describe the differences between two versions of a binary file. In this you have two options: the easier one is to tell Git how to convert a binary file to a text format, or how to extract text information (for example metadata) from binary data. This text representation is then compared using the ordinary textual diff command. Even though conversion to text usually loses some information, the resulting diff is useful for human viewing (even though it is not information about all the changes).

This can be done with the `textconv` config key for a diff driver, where you specify a program that takes the name of the file as an argument and returns a text representation on its output.

For example, you might want to see the diff of the contents of MS Word documents, and see the difference in metadata for JPEG images. First you need to put something like this in your `.gitattributes` file:

```
*.doc   diff=word
*.jpg   diff=exif
```

You can for example use the `catdoc` program to extract text from binary MS Word documents, and the `exiftool` to extract `EXIF` metadata from JPEG images. Because conversion can be slow, Git provides a mechanism to cache the output in the form of the Boolean `cachetextconv` attribute; the cached data is stored using *notes* (this mechanism will be explained in *Chapter 8, Keeping History Clean*). The part of the configuration file responsible for this setup looks like this:

```
[diff "word"]
  textconv = catdoc

# cached data stored in refs/notes/textconv/exif
[diff "exif"]
  textconv = exiftool
  cachetextconv = true
```

You can see how the output of the `textconv` filter looks with `git show` or `git cat-file -p` with the `--textconv` option.

The more complicated but also more powerful option is to use an *external diff driver* (an attribute version of the global driver that can be specified with the `GIT_EXTERNAL_DIFF` environment variable or the `diff.external` configuration variable) with the `command` option of the diff driver. On the other hand, you lose some options that Git diff gives: colorization, word diff, and combined diff for merges.

Such a program will be called with seven parameters: `path`, `old-file`, `old-hex`, `old-mode`, `new-file`, `new-hex`, and `new-mode`. Here `old-file` and `new-file` are files that the diff driver can use to read the contents of two versions of the differing file, `old-hex` and `new-hex` are SHA-1 identifiers of file contents, and `old-mode` and `new-mode` are octal representations of file modes. The command is expected to generate diff-like output. For example, you might want to use the XML-aware diff tool to compare XML files:

```
$ echo "*.xml diff=xmldiff" >>.gitattributes
$ git config diff.xmldiff.command xmldiff-wrapper.sh
```

This example assumes that you have written the `xmldiff-wrapper.sh` shell script to reorder options to fit the XML diff tool.

Configuring diff output

The diff format that Git uses to show changes for users was described in detail in *Chapter 3*, *Developing with Git*. Each group of changes (called a **chunk**) in textual diff output is preceded by the chunk header line, for example:

```
@@ -18,6 +19,8 @@ int cmd_http_fetch(int argc, const char **argv,
```

The text after the second `@@` is meant to describe the section of file where the chunk is; for C source files it is the start of the function. Decision on how to detect the description of such a section depends of course on the type of file. Git allows you to configure this by setting the `xfuncname` configuration option of the `diff` driver to the regular expression which match the description of the section of the file. For example, for LaTeX documents you might want to use the following configuration for the `tex` diff driver (but you don't need to, as `tex` is one of the pre-defined, built-in diff drivers).

```
[diff "tex"]
    xfuncname = "^(\\\\(sub)*section\\{.*)$"
    wordRegex = "\\\\[a-zA-Z]+|[{}]|\\\\.|[^\\{}[:space:]]+"
```

The `wordRegex` configuration defines what word is in LaTeX documents for `git diff --word-diff`.

Performing a 3-way merge

You can also use the `merge` attribute to tell Git to use specific merge strategies for specific files or classes of files in your project. Git by default will use the 3-way merge driver (similar to `rcsmerge`) for text files, and it will take our (being merged) version and mark the result as a conflicted merge for binary files. You can force a 3-way merge by setting the `merge` attribute (or by using `merge=text`); you can force binary-like merging by unsetting this attribute (with `-merge`, which is equivalent to `merge=binary`).

You can also write your own merge driver, or configure Git to use a third-party external merge driver. For example, if you keep a GNU-style `ChangeLog` file in your repository (with a curated list of changes with their description), you can use the `git-merge-changelog` command from the GNU Portability Library (Gnulib). You need to add the following to the appropriate Git `config` file:

```
[merge "merge-changelog"]
    name = GNU-style ChangeLog merge driver
    driver = git-merge-changelog %O %A %B
```

Here the token `%O` in `merge.merge-changelog.driver` will be expanded to the name of the temporary file holding the contents of the merge ancestor's (old) version. Tokens `%A` and `%B` expand to the names of temporary files holding contents being merged, respectively the current (ours, merged into) version and the other branches' (theirs, merged) version. The merge driver is expected to leave the merged version in the `%A` file, exiting with non-zero status if there is a merge conflict.

Note that you can use a different driver for an internal merge between common ancestors (when there is more than one). This is done with `merge.*.recursive` — for example using the predefined `binary` driver.

Of course you will also need to tell Git to use this driver for `ChangeLog` files, adding the following line to `.gitattributes`:

```
ChangeLog merge=merge-changelog
```

Transforming files (content filtering)

Sometimes you might want to massage the content into a shape that is more convenient for Git, the platform (operating system), the file system, and the user to use. End of line conversion can be considered a special case for such an operation.

To do this, you need to set the `filter` attribute for appropriate paths, and to configure the `clean` and `smudge` commands of specified filter driver (either command can be left unspecified for a pass-through filter). When checking out the file matching given pattern, the `smudge` command is fed file contents from the repository in its standard input, and its standard output is used to update the file in the working directory:

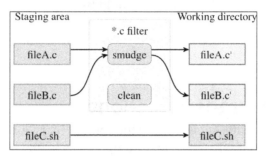

Fig 1. The "smudge" filter is run on checkout
(when writing files to the working directory).

Similarly, the `clean` command of a filter is used to convert the contents of the worktree file to a shape suitable to be stored in the repository:

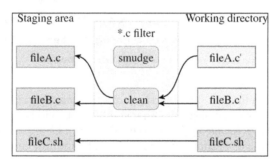

Fig 2. The "clean" filter is run when files are staged
(added to the index—the staging area).

When specifying a command, you can use the `%f` token, which will be replaced by the name of the file the filter is working on.

One simple example is to use `rezip` script for **OpenDocument Format (ODF)** files. ODF documents are ZIP archives of mainly XML files. Git uses compression itself and also does deltification (but cannot do it on already compressed files); the idea is to store uncompressed files in the repository, but to checkout compressed files:

```
[filter "opendocument"]
    clean = "rezip -p ODF_UNCOMPRESS"
    smudge = "rezip -p ODF_COMPRESS"
```

Of course you also need to tell Git to use this filter for all kinds of ODF files:

```
*.odt filter=opendocument
*.ods filter=opendocument
*.odp filter=opendocument
```

Another example of an *advisory* filter is to use the indent program to force a code formatting convention; a similar example would be to replace tabs with spaces on check-in:

```
[filter "indent"]
    clean = indent
```

Obligatory file transformations

Another use of content filtering is to store the content that cannot be directly used in the repository and turn it into a usable form upon checkout.

One such example might be use gitattributes to store large binary files, used only by a subset of developers, outside the Git repository; inside the repository there is only an identifier that allows us to get file contents from external storage. That's how git-media works:

```
$ git config filter.media.clean  "git-media filter-clean"
$ git config filter.media.smudge "git-media filter-smudge"
$ echo "*.mov filter=media -crlf" >> .gitattributes
```

> You can find the git-media tool at https://github.com/
> schacon/git-media. Other similar tools will be mentioned in
> *Chapter 9, Managing Subprojects - Building a Living Framework*, as
> alternative solutions to the problem of handling large files.

Another example would be encrypting sensitive content, or replacing a local sensitive program configuration that is required for an application to work (for example, a database password) with a placeholder. Because running such a filter is required to get useful contents, you can mark it as such:

```
[filter "clean-password"]
    clean  = sed -e 's/^pass = .*$/pass = @PASSWORD@/'
    smudge = sed -e 's/^pass = @PASSWORD@/pass = passw0rd/'
    required
```

Note that this is only a simplified example; in real use you would have to consider the security of the config file itself if you do this, or store the real password in an external smudge script. In such case you'd better also set up a pre-commit, pre-push, and update hook to ensure that the password won't make it to the public repository (see *Chapter 10, Customizing and Extending Git* for details).

Keyword expansion and substitution

Sometimes there is a need to have a piece of dynamic information about the versioned file in the contents of the file itself. To keep such information up to date you can request the version control system to do the *keyword expansion*: replace the *keyword anchor* in the form of a string of text (in the file contents) formatted like the following: $Keyword$, with the keyword inside dollar characters (keyword anchor), which is usually replaced by VCS with $Keyword: value$, that is keyword followed by its expansion.

The main problem with this in Git is that you cannot modify the file contents stored in the repository with information about the commit after you've committed because of the way Git works (more information about this can be found in *Chapter 8, Keeping History Clean*). This means that keyword anchors must be stored in the repository as-is, and only expanded in the worktree on checkout. However, this is also an advantage; you would get no spurious differences due to keyword expansion when examining the history.

The only built-in keyword that Git supports is Id: its value is the SHA-1 identifier of the file contents (the SHA-1 checksum of the blob object representing the file contents, which is not the same as the SHA-1 of the file; see *Chapter 8, Keeping History Clean*, for how objects are constructed). You need to request this keyword expansion by setting the ident attribute for a file.

You can however write your own keyword expansion support with an appropriate filter, defining the smudge command that would expand the keyword, and the clean command that would replace the expanded keyword with its keyword anchor.

With this mechanism you can, for example, implement support for the $Date$ keyword, expanding it on checkout to the date when the file was last modified:

```
[filter "dater"]
    clean  = sed -e 's/\\\$Date[^\\\$]*\\\$/\\\$Date\\\$/'
    smudge = expand_date %f
```

The expand_date script, which is passed the name of file as an argument, could for example run the git log --pretty=format:"%ad" "$1" command to get the substitution value.

You need however to remember another limitation. Namely, for a better performance, Git does not touch files that did not change, be it on commit, on switching the branch (on checkout), or on rewinding the branch (on reset). This means that this trick cannot support the keyword expansion for date of the last revision of a project (as opposed to the last revision that changed the file).

If you need to have such information in distributed sources (for example, the description of the current commit, how long since the tagged release), you can either make it a part of build system, or use *keyword substitution* for the `git archive` command. The latter is quite a generic feature: if the `export-subst` attribute is set for a file, Git will expand the `$Format:<PLACEHOLDERS>$` generalized keyword when adding the file to an archive.

The expansion of the `$Format$` meta-keyword depends on the availability of the revision identifier; it cannot be done if you, for example, pass the SHA-1 identifier of a tree object to the `git archive` command.

The placeholders are the same as for the `--pretty=format:` custom formats for `git log`, which are described in *Chapter 2*, *Exploring Project History*. For example, the string `$Format:%H$` will be *replaced* (not expanded) by the commit hash. It is an irreversible keyword substitution; there is no trace of the keyword in the result of the archive (export) operation.

Other built-in attributes

You can also tell Git not to add certain files or directories when generating an archive. For example, you might want to not include in the user-facing archive the directory with distribution tests, which are useful for the developer but not for end users (they may require additional tools, or check the quality of the program and process rather than the correctness of the application behavior). This can be done by setting the `export-ignore` attribute, for example, by adding the following line to `.gitattributes`:

```
xt/    export-ignore
```

Another thing that can be configured with file attributes is defining what `diff` and `apply` should consider a whitespace error for specific types of file; this is a fine-grained version of the `core.whitespace` configuration variable. Note that the list of common whitespace problems to take notice of should use commas as an element separator, without any surrounding whitespace, when put in the `.gitattributes` file. See the following example (taken from the Git project):

```
*          whitespace=!indent,trail,space
*.[ch]     whitespace=indent,trail,space
*.sh       whitespace=indent,trail,space
```

With file attributes you can also specify the character encoding that is used by a particular file, by providing it as a value of the encoding attribute. Git can use it to select how to display the file in GUI tools (for example, `gitk` and `git gui`). This is a fine-grained version of the `gui.encoding` configuration variable, and is used only when explicitly asked for due to performance considerations. For example, GNU gettext Portable Object (`.po`) files holding translations should use the UTF-8 encoding:

```
/po/*.po    encoding=UTF-8
```

Defining attribute macros

In the *Identifying binary files and end-of-line conversions* section of this chapter, we learned to mark binary files with the `binary` attribute. This is actually the attribute macro expanding to `-diff -merge -text` (unsetting three file attributes). It would be nice to define such macros to avoid unnecessary duplication; there can be more than one pattern matching given type of files, but one `gitattribute` line can contain only one file pattern. Git allows defining such macros, but only in top-level gitattributes files: `core.attributesFile`, `.git/info/attributes`, or `.gitattributes` in the main (top level) directory of a project. The built-in `binary` macro could have been defined as follows:

```
[attr]binary -diff -merge -text
```

You can also define your own attributes. You can then programmatically check which attributes are set for a given file, or what the value is of an attribute for a set of files, with the `git check-attr` command.

Fixing mistakes with the reset command

At any stage during development, you might want to undo something, to fix mistakes, or to abandon the current work. There is no `git undo` command in core Git, and neither is there support for the `--undo` option in Git commands, though many commands have an `--abort` option to abandon current work in progress. One of the reasons why there is no such command or option yet is the ambiguity on what needs to be undone (especially for multi-step operations).

Many mistakes can be fixed with the help of the `git reset` command. It can be used for various purposes and in various ways; understanding how this command works will help you in using it in many situation, not limited to provided example usage.

Note that this section covers only the full-tree mode of `git reset`; resetting the state of a file, that is the description of what `git reset -- <file>` does, is left for the *Managing worktree and staging area* section at the end of this chapter.

Rewinding the branch head, softly

The `git reset` command in its full-tree mode affects the current branch head, and can also affect the index (the staging area) and the working directory. Note that **reset** does not change which branch is current, as opposed to checkout — the difference is described in *Chapter 3, Developing with Git*.

To reset only the current branch head, and not touch the index or the working tree, you use `git reset --soft [<revision>]`.

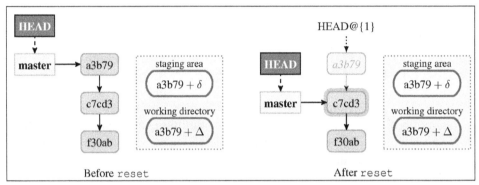

Fig 3. Before and after hard reset

Effectively, we are just changing the pointer of the current branch (`master` in the example shown in *Fig 3*) to point to a given revision (`HEAD^` — the previous commit in the example). Neither the staging area nor the working directory are affected. This leaves all your changed files (and all files that differ between the old and new revision pointed by branch) in the *Changes to be committed* state, as `git status` would put it.

Removing or amending a commit

The way the command works means that a *soft reset* can be used to undo the act of creating a commit. This can be used for example to amend a commit, though it is far easier to simply use the `--amend` option of `git commit`. In fact, running the following command:

```
$ git commit --amend [<options>]
```

is equivalent to:

```
$ git reset --soft HEAD^
$ git commit --reedit-message=ORIG_HEAD [<options>]
```

The `git commit --amend` command also works for merge commits as opposed to using soft reset. When amending commit, if you want to just fix the commit message there will be no additional options. If you want to include a fix from the working directory without changing the commit message, you can use `-a --no-edit`. If you want to fix the authorship information after correcting Git configuration, use `--reset-author --no-edit`.

Squashing commits with reset

You are not limited to rewinding the branch head to just the previous commit. Using a soft reset, you can squash a few earlier commits (for example, `commit` and `bugfix`, or introducing new functionality and using it), making one commit out of two (or more); alternatively, you can instead use the `squash` instruction of **interactive rebase**, as described in *Chapter 8, Keeping History Clean*. With the latter, you can actually `squash` any series of commits, not just most recent ones.

Resetting the branch head and the index

The default mode of reset command, so called **mixed reset** (because it is between the soft and hard forms), changes the current branch head to point to a given revision, and also resets the index, putting the contents of that revision into the staging area:

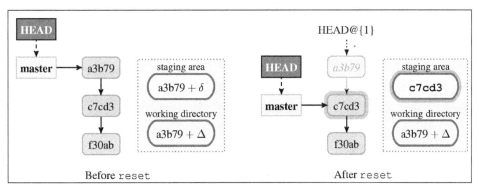

Fig 4. Before and after hard reset

This leaves all your changed files (and all files that differ between the old and new revision pointed by branch) in the *Changes not staged for commit* state, as `git status` would put it. The `git reset --mixed` command will report what has not been updated, using the short status format.

This version of reset command can be used, for example, to undo all additions of new files. This can be done by running `git reset`, assuming that you didn't stage any changes (or that you can put up with losing them). If you want to un-add a particular file, use `git rm --cached <file>`.

Splitting a commit with reset

You can use a mixed reset to split a commit in two. First, run `git reset HEAD^` to reset the branch head and the index to the previous revision. Then interactively add changes that you want to have in the first commit, and then create this first commit from the index (`git add -i` and `git commit`). A second commit can then be created from the working directory state (`git commit -a`).

If it is easier to interactively remove changes, you can do this too. Use `git reset --soft HEAD^`, interactively un-stage changes with an interactive per-file reset, create the first commit from the constructed state in the index, and create the second commit from the working directory.

Here again you can instead use the interactive rebase to split commits further in the history. The rebase operation will switch to the appropriate commit, and the actual splitting would probably be done as described here.

Saving and restoring state with the WIP commit

Suppose you are interrupted by an urgent fix request while you are in the middle of work on the development branch. You don't want to lose your changes, but the worktree is a bit of a mess. One possible solution is to save the current state of the working area by creating a temporary commit:

```
$ git commit -a -m 'snapshot WIP (Work In Progress)'
```

Then you handle the interruption, switching to the maintenance branch and creating a commit to fix the issue. Then you need to go back to the previous branch (by using checkout), remove the WIP commit from the history (using a soft reset), and go back to the un-staged starting state (with a mixed reset):

```
$ git checkout -
$ git reset --soft HEAD^
$ git reset
```

Though it is much easier to just use `git stash` instead to handle interruptions, see the *Stashing away your changes* section in this chapter. On the other hand, such temporary commits (or similar proof-of-concept work) can be shared with other developers, as opposed to stash.

Discarding changes and rewinding branch

Sometimes your files will get in such a mess that you want to discard all changes, and to return the working directory and the staging area (the index) to the last committed state (the last good version). Or you might want to rewind the state of the repository to an earlier version. A *hard reset* will change the current branch head and reset the index and the working tree. Any changes to tracked files are discarded.

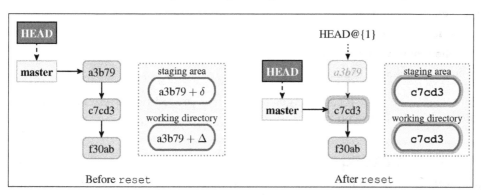

Fig 5. Before and after hard reset

This command can be used to undo (remove) a commit as if it had never happened. Running `git reset --hard HEAD^` will effectively discard the last commit (though it will be available for a limited time via reflog), unless it is reachable from some other branch.

Another common usage is to discard changes to the working directory with `git reset --hard`.

It is very important to remember that a hard reset would irrecoverably remove all changes from the staging area and working directory. You cannot undo this part of the operation! Changes are lost forever!

Moving commits to a feature branch

Say that you were working on something on the `master` branch, and you have already created a sequence of commits. You realize that the feature you are working on is more involved, and you want to continue polishing it on a topic branch, as described in *Chapter 6, Advanced Branching Techniques*. You want to move all those commits that are in `master` (let's say, the last three revisions) to the aforementioned feature branch.

You need to create the feature branch, save uncommitted changes (if any), rewind `master` removing those *topical* commits from it, and finally switch to the feature branch to continue working (or you can use rebase instead):

```
$ git branch feature/topic
$ git stash
No local changes to save
$ git reset --hard HEAD~3
HEAD is now at f82887f before
$ git checkout feature/topic
Switched to branch 'feature/topic'
```

Of course, if there were local changes to save, this preceding series of commands would have to be followed by `git stash pop`.

Undoing a merge or a pull

Hard resets can also be used to abort a failed merge with `git reset --hard HEAD` (the `HEAD` is the default value for revision and can be omitted), for example, if you decide that you don't want to resolve the merge conflict at this time (though with modern Git you can use `git merge --abort` instead).

You can also remove a successful fast-forward pull or undo a rebase (and many other operations moving the branch head) with `git reset --hard ORIG_HEAD`. (You can here use `HEAD@{1}` instead of `ORIG_HEAD`).

Safer reset – keeping your changes

A hard reset will discard your local changes, similarly to the way `git checkout -f` would. Sometimes you might want to rewind the current branch while keeping local changes: that's what `git reset --keep` is for.

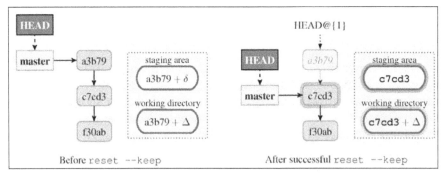

Fig 6. Before and after successful git reset --keep HEAD^.

This mode resets the staging area (index entries), but retains the unstaged (local) changes that are currently in the working directory. If it is not possible, the reset is aborted. This means that local changes in the worktree are preserved and *moved* to the new commit, in a similar way to how `git checkout <branch>` works with uncommitted changes. The successful case is a bit like stashing changes away, hard resetting, then unstashing.

 The way `git reset --keep <revision>` works is by updating the version (in the working directory) of only those files that are different between the revision we rewind to and the HEAD. The reset is aborted if there is any file that is different between HEAD and `<revision>` (and thus should be updated) and has local uncommitted changes.

Rebase changes to an earlier revision

Suppose that you are working on something, but now you realize that what you have in your working directory should be in another branch, unrelated to a previous commit. For example, you might have started to work on a bug while on the `master` branch, and only then realized that it also affects the maintenance branch `maint`. This means that the fix should therefore be put earlier in a branch, starting from the common ancestor of those branches (or a place where the bug was introduced). This would make it possible to merge the same fix both into `master` and `maint`, as described in *Chapter 12, Git Best Practices*:

```
$ edit
$ git checkout -b bugfix-127
$ git reset --keep start
```

An alternate solution would be to simply use `git stash`:

```
$ edit
$ git stash
$ git checkout -b bugfix-127 start
$ git stash pop
```

Stashing away your changes

Often, when you've been working on a project, and things are in a messy state not suitable for a permanent conflict, you want to temporarily save the current state and go to work on something else. The answer to this problem is the `git stash` command.

Stashing takes the dirty state of your working area—that is, your modified tracked files in your worktree (though you can also stash untracked files with the `--include-untracked` option), and the state of the staging area, then saves this state, and resets both the working directory and the index to the last committed version (to match the HEAD commit), effectively running `git reset --hard HEAD`. You can then reapply the stashed changes at any time.

Stashes are saved on a stack: by default you apply the last stashed changes (`stash@{0}`), though you can list stashed changes (with `git stash list`), and explicitly select any of the stashes.

Using git stash

If you don't expect for the interruption to last long, you can simply stash away your changes, handle the interruption, then unstash them:

```
$ git stash
$ ... handle interruption ...
$ git stash pop
```

By default `git stash pop` will apply the last stashed changes, and delete the stash if applied successfully. To see what stashes you have stored, you can use `git stash list`:

```
$ git stash list
stash@{0}: WIP on master: 049d078 Use strtol(), atoi() is deprecated
stash@{1}: WIP on master: c264051 Error checking for <number>
```

You can use any of the older stashes by specifying the stash name as an argument. For example, you can run `git stash apply stash@{1}` to apply it, and you can drop it (remove it from the list of stashes) with `git stash drop stash@{1}`; the `git stash pop` command is just a shortcut for `apply + drop`.

The default description that Git gives to a stash (*WIP on branch*) is useful for remembering where you were when stashing the changes (giving branch and commit), but doesn't help you remember what you were working on, and what is stashed away. However, you can examine the changes recorded in the stash as a diff with `git stash show -p`. But if you expect that the interruption might be more involved, you should better save the current state to a stash with a description of what you were working on:

```
$ git stash save 'Add <count>'
Saved working directory and index state On master: Add <count>
HEAD is now at 049d078 Use strtol(), atoi() is deprecated
```

Git would then use the provided message to describe stashed changes:

```
$ git stash list
stash@{0}: On master: Add <count>
stash@{1}: WIP on master: c264051 Error checking for <number>
```

Sometimes the branch you were working on when you ran `git stash save` has changed enough that `git stash pop` fails, because there are new revisions past the commit you were on when stashing the changes. If you want to create a regular commit out of the stashed changes, or just test stashed changes, you can use `git stash branch <branch name>`. This will create a new branch at the revision you were at when saving the changes, switch to this branch, reapply your work there, and drop stashed changes.

Stash and the staging area

By default, stashing resets both the working directory and the staging area to the HEAD version. You can make `git stash` keep the state of the index, and reset the working area to the staged state, with the `--keep-index` option.

This is very useful if you used the staging area to untangle changes in the working directory, as described in the section about interactive commits in *Chapter 3, Developing with Git*, or if you want to split the commit in two as described in *Splitting a commit with reset* section in this chapter. In both cases you would want to test each change before committing. The workflow would look like the following:

```
$ git add --interactive
$ git stash --keep-index
$ make test
$ git commit -m 'First part'
$ git stash pop
```

You can also use `git stash --patch` to select how the working area should look after stashing away the changes.

When restoring stashed changes, Git will ordinarily try to apply only saved worktree changes, adding them to the current state of the working directory (which must match the staging area). If there are conflicts while applying the state, they are stored in the index as usual—Git won't drop the stash if there were conflicts.

You can also try to restore the saved state of the staging area with the `--index` option; this will fail if there are conflicts when applying working tree changes (because there is no place to store conflicts; the staging area is busy).

Stash internals

Perhaps you applied stashed changes, did some work, and then for some reason want to un-apply those changes that originally came from the stash. Or you have mistakenly dropped the stash, or cleared all stashes (which you can do with `git stash clear`), and would like to recover them. Or perhaps you want to see how the file looked when you stashed away changes. For this, you need to know what Git does when creating a stash.

To stash away your changes, Git creates two automatic commits: one for the index (staging area), and one for the working directory. With `git stash --include-untracked`, Git creates an additional third automatic commit for untracked files.

The commit containing the work in progress in the working directory (the state of files tracked from there) is the stash, and has the commit with the contents of the staging area as its second parent. This commit is stored in a special ref: `refs/stash`. Both WIP (stash) and index commits have the revision you were on when saving changes as its first (and only for the `index` commit) parent.

We can see this with `git log --graph` or `gitk`:

```
$ git stash save --quiet 'Add <count>'
$ git log --oneline --graph --decorate --boundary stash ^HEAD
*   81ef667 (refs/stash) On master: Add <count>
|\
| * ed95050 index on master: 765b095 Added .gitignore
|/
o 765b095 (HEAD, master) Added .gitignore
$ git show-ref --abbrev
765b095 refs/heads/master
81ef667 refs/stash
```

We had to use `git show-ref` here (we could have used `git for-each-ref` instead), because `git branch -a` shows only branches, not arbitrary refs.

When saving untracked changes, the situation is similar:

```
$ git stash --include-untracked
Saved working directory and index state WIP on master: 765b095 Added\
  .gitignore
HEAD is now at 765b095 Added .gitignore
$ git log --oneline --graph --decorate --boundary stash ^HEAD
```

```
*-.    bb76632 (refs/stash) WIP on master: 765b095 Added .gitignore
|\ \
| | * 1ae1716 untracked files on master: 765b095 Added .gitignore
| * d093b52 index on master: 765b095 Added .gitignore
|/
o 765b095 (HEAD, B) Added .gitignore
```

We see that the untracked file commit is the third parent of the `WIP` commit, and that it doesn't have any parents.

Well, that's how stashing works, but how does Git maintain the stack of stashes? If you have noticed that the `git stash list` output and the `stash@{<n>}` notation therein looks like reflog, you have guessed right; Git finds older stashes in the reflog for the `refs/stash` reference:

```
$ git reflog stash
81ef667 stash@{0}: On master: Add <count>
bb76632 stash@{1}: WIP on master: Added .gitignore
```

Un-applying a stash

Let's take the first example from the beginning of the section: un-applying changes from the earlier `git stash apply`. One possible solution to achieve the required effect is to retrieve the patch associated with working directory changes from a stash, and apply it in reverse:

```
$ git stash show -p stash@{0} | git apply -R -
```

Note the -p option to the `git stash show` command — it forces patch output instead of a summary of changes. We could use `git show -m stash@{0}` (the -m option is necessary because a `WIP` commit representing the `stash` is a merge commit), or even simply `git diff stash@{0}^1 stash@{0}`, in place of `git stash show -p`.

Recovering stashes that were dropped erroneously

Let's try the second example: recovering stashes that were accidentally dropped or cleared. If they are still in your repository, you can search all commit objects that are unreachable from other refs and look like stashes (that is, they are merge commits and have a commit message using a strict pattern).

A simplified solution might look like this:

```
$ git fsck --unreachable |
grep "unreachable commit " | cut -d" " -f3 |
git log --stdin --merges --no-walk --grep="WIP on "
```

The first line finds all unreachable (lost) objects, the second one filters out everything but commits and extracts their SHA-1 identifiers, and third line filters out even more, showing only merge commits with a commit message containing the `"WIP on "` string.

This solution would not, however, find stashes with a custom message (those created with `git stash save "message"`).

Managing worktrees and the staging area

In *Chapter 3, Developing with Git*, we learned that, besides the working directory where you work on changes, and the local repository where you store those changes as revisions, there is also a third section between them: the staging area, sometimes called the index.

In the same chapter, we also learned how to examine the status of the working directory, and how to view the differences. We saw how to create a new commit out of the working directory, or out of the staging area.

Now it is time to learn how to examine and modify the state of individual files.

Examining files and directories

It is easy to examine the contents of the working directory: just use the standard tools for viewing files (for example, an editor or a pager) and examining directories (for example, a file manager or the `dir` command). But how do we view the staged contents of a file, or the last committed version?

One possible solution is to use the `git show` command with the appropriate selector. *Chapter 2, Exploring Project History*, gave us the `<revision>:<pathname>` syntax to examine the contents of a file at a given revision. Similar syntax can be used to retrieve the staged contents, namely `:<pathname>` (or `:<stage>:<pathname>` if the file is in a merge conflict; `:<pathname>` on itself is equivalent to `:0:<pathname>`).

Let's assume that we are in the `src/` subdirectory, and want to see the contents of the `rand.c` file there as it is in the working directory, in the staging area (using the absolute and relative path), and in the last commit:

```
src $ less -FRX rand.c
src $ git show :src/rand.c
src $ git show :./rand.c
src $ git show HEAD:src/rand.c
src $ git show HEAD:./rand.c
```

To see what files are staged in the index, there is the `git ls-files` command. By default it operates on the staging area contents, but can also be used to examine the working directory (which, as we have seen in this chapter, can be used to list ignored files). This command lists all files in the specified directory, or the current directory (because the index is a flat list of files, similar to MANIFEST files); you can use `:/` to denote the top-level directory of a project. Without using the `--full-name` option, it would show filenames relative to the current directory (or the one specified as parameter). In all examples it is assumed that we are in the `src/` subdirectory, as seen in command prompt.

```
src $ git ls-files
rand.c
src $ git ls-files --full-name :/
COPYRIGHT
Makefile
README
src/rand.c
```

What about committed changes? How can we examine which files were in a given revision? Here `git ls-tree` comes to the rescue (note that it is a plumbing command and does not default to the HEAD revision):

```
src $ git ls-tree --name-only HEAD
rand.c
src $ git ls-tree --abbrev --full-tree -r -t HEAD
100644 blob 862aafd      COPYRIGHT
100644 blob 25c3d1b      Makefile
100644 blob bdf2c76      README
040000 tree 7e44d2e      src
100644 blob b2c087f      src/rand.c
```

Searching file contents

Let's assume that you were reviewing code in the project and noticed an erroneous doubled semicolon '`;;`' in the C source code. Or perhaps you were editing the file and noticed a bug nearby. You fix it, but you wonder: "How many of those mistakes are there?" — you would like to create a commit to fix every and each such errors.

Or perhaps you want to search the version scheduled for the next commit? Or maybe examine how it looks in the `next` branch?

With Git, you can use the `git grep` command:

```
$ git grep -e ';;'
```

This will only search tracked files in the working directory, from the current directory downwards. We will get many false positives, for example, from shell scripts—let's limit the search space to C source files:

```
$ git grep -e ';;' -- '*.c'
```

The quotes are necessary for Git to do expansion (path limiting), instead of `git grep` getting the list of files expanded by the shell. We still have many false matches from the *forever loop* C idiom:

```
    for (;;) {
```

With `git grep` you can construct complex conditions, excluding false positives. Say that we want to search the whole project, not only the current directory:

```
$ git grep -e ';;' --and --not 'for *(.*;;' -- '**/*.c'
```

To search the staging area, use `git grep --cached` (or the equivalent, and perhaps easier to remember, `git grep --staged`). To search the `next` branch, use `git grep next --`; similar command can be used to search any version, actually.

Un-tracking, un-staging, and un-modifying files

If you want to undo some file-level operation (if for example you have changed your mind about tracking files, or about staging changes)—look no further than `git status` hints:

```
$ git status --ignored
On branch master
Changes to be committed:
   (use "git reset HEAD <file>..." to unstage)


Changes not staged for commit:
   (use "git add <file>..." to update what will be committed)
   (use "git checkout -- <file>..." to discard changes in working\
  directory)


Untracked files:
   (use "git add <file>..." to include in what will be committed)


Ignored files:
   (use "git add -f <file>..." to include in what will be committed)
```

You need to remember that only the contents of the working directory and the staging area can be changed. Committed changes are immutable.

If you want to undo adding a previously untracked file to the index — or remove a formerly tracked file from the staging area so that it would be *deleted* (not present) in the next commit, while keeping it in the working directory — use `git rm --cached <file>`.

Difference between the --cached (--staged) and --index options

Many Git commands, among others `git diff`, `git grep`, and `git rm`, support the `--cached` option (or its alias `--staged`). Others, such as `git stash`, have the `--index` option (the index is an alternate name for the staging area). These are *not* synonyms (as we will later see with `git apply` command, which supports both).

The `--cached` option is used to ask the command that usually works on files in the working directory to *only* work on the staged contents *instead*. For example, `git grep --cached` will search the staging area instead of the working directory, and `git rm --cached` will only remove a file from the index, leaving it in the worktree.

The `--index` option is used to ask the command that usually works on files in the working directory to *also* affect the index, *additionally*. For example, `git stash apply --index` not only restores stashed working directory changes, but also restores the index.

If you asked Git to record a state of the path in the staging area, but changed your mind, you can reset the staged contents of the file to the committed version with `git reset HEAD -- <file>`.

If you mis-edited a file, so that the working directory version is a mess, and you want to restore it to the version from the index, use `git checkout -- <file>`. If you staged some of this mess, and would like to reset to the last committed version, use `git checkout HEAD -- <file>` instead.

Actually these commands *do not really undo* operations; they restore the previous state based on a backup that is the worktree, the index, or the committed version. For example, if you staged some changes, modified a file, then added modifications to the staging area, you can reset the index to the committed version, but not to the state after the first and before the second `git add`.

Resetting a file to the old version

Of course, you can use any revision with a per-file `reset` and per-file `checkout`. For example, to replace the current worktree version of the `src/rand.c` file with the one from the previous commit, you can use `git checkout HEAD^ -- src/rand.c` (or redirect the output of `git show HEAD^:src/rand.c` to a file). To put the version from the `next` branch into the staging area, run `git reset next -- src/rand.c`.

Note: `git add <file>`, `git reset <file>`, and `git checkout <file>` all enter interactive mode for a given file with the `--patch` option. This can be used to hand-craft a staged or worktree version of a file by selecting which changes should be applied (or un-applied).

 You might need to put a double dash `--` before the file name here, if for example, you have a file with the same name as a branch.

Cleaning the working area

Untracked files and directories may pile up in your working directory. They can be left overs from merges, or be temporary files, proof of concept work, or perhaps mistakenly put there. Whatever the case, often there really is no pattern to them, and you don't need to make Git ignore them (see the *Ignoring files* section of this chapter); you just want to remove them. You can use `git clean` for this.

Because untracked files do not have a backup in the repository, and you cannot undo their removal (unless the operating system or file system supports undo), it's advisable to first check which files would be removed with `--dry-run` / `-n`. Actual removal by default requires the `--force` / `-f` option.

```
$ git clean --dry-run
Would remove patch-1.diff
```

Git will clean all untracked files recursively, starting from the current directory. You can select which paths are affected by listing them as an argument; you can also exclude additional types of file with the `--exclude=<pattern>` option. You can also interactively select which untracked files to delete with the `--interactive` option.

```
$ git clean --interactive
Would remove the following items:
  src/rand.c~
  screenlog.0
*** Commands ***
```

```
1: clean        2: filter by pattern    3: select by numbers
4: ask each     5: quit                 6: help
What now>
```

The clean command also allows us to only remove ignored files, for example, to remove build products but keep manually tracked files with the -x option (though usually it is better to leave removing build byproducts to the build system, so that cleaning the project files works even without having to clone the repository).

You can also use git clean -x in conjunction with git reset --hard, to create a pristine working directory to test a clean build, by removing both ignored and not-ignored untracked files, and resetting tracked files to the committed version.

> **Dirty working directory**
>
> The working directory is considered clean if it is the same as the committed and staged version, and dirty if there are modifications.

Multiple working directories

Git for a long time allowed to specify where to find the administrative area of the repository (the .git directory) with the git --git-dir=<path> <command>, or the GIT_DIR environment variable, making it possible to work from the detached working directory.

To be able to reliably use multiple working directories sharing a single repository, we had to wait until version 2.5 of Git. With it, you can create a new linked work tree by using git worktree add <path> <branch>, allowing us to have more than one branch checked out. For convenience, if you omit the <branch> argument, then a new branch will be created based on the name of the created worktree.

> If you use an older Git version, there is always the git-new-workdir script, which can be found in the contrib/ area of the Git project repository. It is however, Unix-only (it relies on symbolic links), and is somewhat fragile.

This mechanism can be used instead of git stash if you need to switch to a different branch (for example, to urgently fix a security bug), but your current working directory, and possibly also the staging area, is in a state of high disarray. Instead of disturbing it, you create a temporary linked working tree to make a fix, and remove it when done.

This is an evolving area — consult the Git documentation for more information.

Summary

In this chapter we have learned how to better manage the contents of the working directory, and the contents of the staging area, preparing to create a new commit.

We know how to undo the last commit, how to drop changes to the working area, how to retroactively change the branch we are working on, and other uses of the `git reset` command. We now understand the three (and a half) forms of the reset.

We have learned how to examine and search the contents of the working directory, the staging area, and committed changes. We know how to use Git to copy the file version from the worktree, the index, or the HEAD into the worktree or the index. We can use Git to clean (remove) untracked files.

This chapter showed how to configure the handling of files in the working directory; how to make Git ignore files (by making them intentionally untracked) and why. It described how to handle the differences between line ending formats between operating systems. It explained how to enable (and write) keyword expansion, how to configure the handling of binary files, and enhance viewing the diff and merging specific classes of files.

We learned to stash away changes to handle interruptions, and to make it possible to test interactively prepared commits, before creating a commit. This chapter explained how Git manages stashes, enabling us to go beyond built-in operations.

This chapter, together with *Chapter 3, Developing with Git,* taught how to create your contribution to a project; together with *Chapter 2, Exploring Project History,* it also taught how to examine your clone of a project's repository.

The following chapters will teach you how to collaborate with other people, how to send what you contributed, and how to merge changes from other developers.

5

Collaborative Development with Git

Previous chapters, *Chapter 3, Developing with Git*, and *Chapter 4, Managing Your Worktree*, taught you how to make a new contributions to a project, but limited it to affecting only your own clone of the project's repository. The former chapter described how to commit new revisions, while the latter showed how Git can help you prepare it.

This chapter will present a *bird's-eye view* of various ways to collaborate, showing centralized and distributed workflows. It will focus on the repository-level interactions in collaborative development, while the set-up of branches will be covered in the next chapter, *Chapter 6, Advanced Branching Techniques*.

This chapter will describe different collaborative workflows, explaining the advantages and disadvantages of each. You will also learn here the *chain of trust* concept, and how to use signed tags, signed merges, and signed commits.

The following topics will be covered in this chapter:

- Centralized and distributed workflows, and bare repositories
- Managing remotes and one-off single-shot collaboration
- Push, pull requests, and exchanging patches
- Using bundles for off-line transfer (sneakernet)
- How versions are addressed — the chain of trust
- Tagging, lightweight tags versus signed tags
- Signed tags, signed merges, and signed commits

Collaborative workflows

There are various *levels of engagement* when using a version control system. One might only be interested in using it for archaeology. *Chapter 2, Exploring Project History,* will help with this. Of course, examining project's history is an important part of development, too.

One might use version control for your private development, for a single developer project, on a single machine. *Chapter 3, Developing with Git,* and *Chapter 4, Managing Your Worktree,* show how to do this with Git. Of course, your own development is usually part of a collaboration.

But one of the main goals of version control systems is to help multiple developers work together on a project, collaboratively. Version control makes it possible to work simultaneously on a given piece of software in an effective way, ensuring that their changes do not conflict with each other, and helps with merging those changes together.

One might work on a project together with a few other developers, or with many. One might be a contributor, or a project maintainer; perhaps the project is so large that it needs subsystem maintainers. One might work in tight software teams, or might want to make it easy for external contributors to provide proposed changes (for example, to fix bugs, or an error in the documentation). There are various different workflows that are best suited for those situations:

- Centralized workflow
- Peer-to-peer workflow
- Maintainer workflow
- Hierarchical workflow

Bare repositories

There are two types of repositories: an ordinary non-bare one, with a working directory and a staging area, and a **bare repository**, bereft of the working directory. The former type is meant for private solo development, for creating new history, while the latter type is intended for collaboration and synchronizing development results.

By convention, bare repositories use the `.git` extension—for example, `project.git`—while non-bare repositories don't have it—for example, `project` (with the administrative area and the local repository in `project/.git`). You can usually omit this extension when cloning, pushing to, or fetching from the repository; using either `http://git.example.com/project.git` or `http://git.example.com/project` as the repository URL will work.

To create the bare repository, you need to add the `--bare` option to the `init` or the `clone` command:

```
$ git init --bare project.git
Initialized empty Git repository in /home/user/project.git/
```

Interacting with other repositories

After creating a set of revisions, an extension to the project's history, you usually need to share it with other developers. You need to synchronize with other repository instances, publish your changes, and get changes from others.

From the perspective of the local repository instance, of your own clone of repository, you need to *push* your changes to other repositories (either the repository you cloned from, or your public repository), and *fetch* changes from other repositories (usually the repository you cloned from). After fetching changes, you sometimes need to incorporate them into your work, *merging* two lines of development (or *rebasing*) — you can do it in one operation with *pull*.

Usually you don't want your local repository to be visible to the public, as such repository is intended for private work (keeping work not ready yet from being visible). This means that there is an additional step required to make your finished work available; you need to publish your changes, for example with `git push`. The following diagram demonstrates creating and publishing commits, an extension of the one in *Chapter 3, Developing with Git*. The *arrows* show Git commands to copy contents from one place to another, including to and from the remote repository.

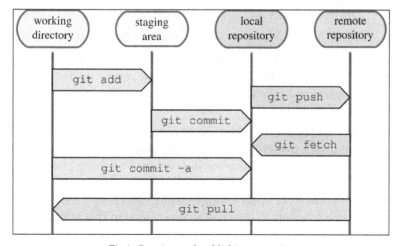

Fig 1: Creating and publishing commits.

The centralized workflow

With distributed version control systems you can use different collaboration models, more distributed or less distributed. In a centralized workflow, there is one central hub, usually a bare repository, that everyone uses to synchronize their work:

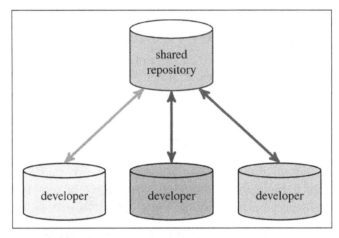

Fig 2: Centralized workflow. The shared repository is bare. The color of the line represents from which repository the transport is initiated; for example, a green line means that the command was invoked from within green repository, by its developer.

Each developer has his or her own non-bare clone of the central repository, which is used to develop new revisions of software. When changes are ready, they push those changes to the central repository, and fetch (or pull) changes from other developers from the central shared repository, so integration is distributed. This workflow is shown in *Fig 2*. The advantages and disadvantages of a centralized workflow are as follows:

- The advantage is its simple setup; it is a familiar paradigm for people coming from centralized version control systems and centralized management, and provides centralized access control and backup. It might be a good setup for a private project with a small team.

- The disadvantages are that the shared repository is a single point of failure (if there are problems with the central repository, then there is no way to synchronize changes), and that each developer pushing changes (making them available for other developers) might require updating one's own repository first and merging changes from others. You need also to trust developers with access to the shared repository in this setup.

The peer-to-peer or forking workflow

The opposite of a centralized workflow is a **peer-to-peer** or **forking workflow**. Instead of using a single shared repository, each developer has a public repository (which is bare), in addition to a private working repository (with a working directory), like in the following figure:

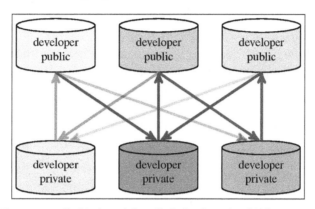

Fig 3: Peer-to-peer (forking) workflow. Each developer has his/her own private non-bare and their own public bare repository. The line color represents who did the transfer (who ran the command). Lines pointing up are push, lines pointing down are fetch.

When changes are ready, developers push to their own public repositories. To incorporate changes from other developers, one needs to fetch them from the public repositories of other developers. The advantages and disadvantages of the peer-to-peer or forking workflow are as follows:

- One advantage of the forking workflow is that contributions can be integrated without the need for a central repository; it is a fully distributed workflow. Another advantage is that you are not forced to integrate if you want to publish your changes; you can merge at your leisure. It is a good workflow for organic teams without requiring much setup.

- The disadvantages are a lack of the *canonical* version, no centralized management, and the fact that in this workflow base form you need to interact with many repositories (though `git remote update` can help here, doing multiple fetches with a single command.). Setup requires that developer public repositories need to be *reachable* from other developers' workstations; this might not be as easy as using one's own machine as a server for one's own public repositories. Also, as can be seen in *Fig 3*, collaboration gets more complicated with the growing number of developers.

The maintainer or integration manager workflow

One of the problems with peer-to-peer workflow was that there was no canonical version of a project, something that non-developers can use. Another was that each developer had to do his or her own integration. If we promote one of the public repositories in *Fig 3* to be canonical (official), and make one of the developers responsible for integration, we arrive at the **integration manager workflow** (or **maintainer workflow**). The following diagram shows this workflow, with bare repositories at the top and non-bare at the bottom:

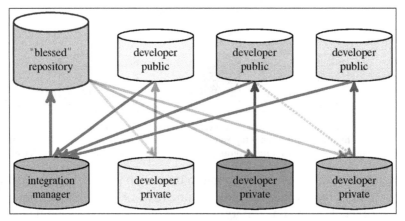

Fig 4: Integration-manager (maintainer) workflow. One of the developers has the role of integration manager, and his or her public repository is "blessed" as the official repository for a project. Incoming lines of the same color denote fetching; outgoing lines denote push. Dotted lines show the possibility of fetching from a non-official repository (for example, collaboration within a smaller group of developers).

In this workflow, when changes are ready, the developer pushes them to his or her own public repository, and tells the maintainer (for example via a pull request) that they are ready. The maintainer pulls changes from the developer's repository into own working repository and integrates the changes. Then the maintainer pushes merged changes to the blessed repository, for all to see. The advantages and disadvantages are as follows:

- The advantages are having an official version of a project, and that developers can continue to work without doing or waiting for integration, as maintainers can pull their changes at any time. It is a good workflow for a large organic team, like in open source projects. The fact that the blessed repository is decided by social consensus allows an easy switch to other maintainers, either temporarily (for example, time off) or permanently (forking a project).

- The disadvantage is that for large teams and large projects the ability of the maintainer to integrate changes is a bottleneck. Thus, for very large organic teams, such as in Linux kernel development, it is better to use a hierarchical workflow.

The hierarchical or dictator and lieutenants workflows

The **hierarchical workflow** is a variant of the blessed repository workflow, generally used by huge projects with hundreds of collaborators. In this workflow, the project maintainer (sometimes called the **benevolent dictator**) is accompanied by additional integration managers, usually in charge of certain parts of the repository (subsystems); they're called **lieutenants**. The benevolent dictator's public repository serves as the blessed reference repository from which all the collaborators need to pull. Lieutenants pull from developers, the maintainer pulls from lieutenants, as shown in the following figure:

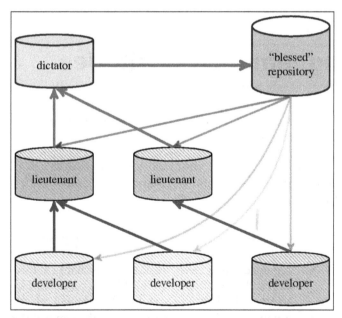

Fig 5. Dictator and lieutenants (hierarchical) workflow. There is an overall maintainer for the whole project, called dictator (whose public repository is official, "blessed" repository of a project), and subsystem integration managers, called lieutenants. Dashed pattern repositories are actually a pair of private and public repositories of a developer or a lieutenant. The person that initiates transfer is shown via line color.

In dictator and lieutenant workflows, there is a hierarchy (a network) of repositories. Before starting work: either development or merging, one would usually pull updates from the canonical (blessed) repository for a project. Developers prepare changes in their own private repository, then send changes to an appropriate subsystem maintainer (lieutenant). Changes can be sent as patches in email, or by pushing them to the developer's public repository and sending a pull request.

Lieutenants are responsible for merging changes in their respective area of responsibility. The master maintainer (dictator) pulls from lieutenants (and occasionally directly from developers). The dictator is also responsible for pushing merged changes to the reference (canonical) repository, and usually also for release management (for example, creating tags for releases). The advantages and disadvantages are as follows:

- The advantage of this workflow is that it allows the project leader (the dictator) to delegate much of the integration work. This can be useful in very big projects (with respect to the number of developers and/or changes), or in highly hierarchical environments. Such workflow is used to develop Linux kernel.

- Its complicated setup is a disadvantage of this workflow. It is usually overkill for an ordinary project.

Managing remote repositories

When collaborating on any project managed with Git, you will interact often with a constant set of other repositories; for example, in an integration-manager workflow it would be (at least) the canonical blessed repository of a project. In many cases, you will interact with more than one remote repository.

Git allows us to save the information about a remote repository (in short: **remote**) in the `config` file, giving it a nickname (a shorthand name). Such information can be managed with the `git remote` command.

> There are also two legacy mechanisms to store repository shorthand:
>
> - A named file in `.git/remotes` — the name of this file will be shorthand for remote. This file can contain information about the URL or URLs, and fetch and push refspecs.
> - A named file in `.git/branches` — the name of this file will be shorthand for remote. The contents of this file are just an URL for the repository, optionally followed by # and the branch name.
>
> Neither of those mechanisms is likely to be found in modern repositories. See the *Remotes* section in the `git-fetch(1)` manpage for more details.

The origin remote

When cloning a repository, Git will create one remote for you—**the origin remote**, storing information about where you cloned from—that is the origin of your copy of the repository (hence the name). You can use this remote to fetch updates.

This is the default remote; for example `git fetch` without the remote name will use the origin remote; unless it is specified otherwise by the `remote.default` configuration variable, or unless the configuration for the current branch (`branch.<branchname>.remote`) specifies otherwise.

Listing and examining remotes

To see which remote repositories you have configured, you can run the `git remote` command. It lists the shortnames of each remote you've got. In a cloned repository you will have at least one remote: `origin`.

```
$ git remote
origin
```

To see the URL together with remotes, you can use -v / --verbose option:

```
$ git remote --verbose
origin git://git.kernel.org/pub/scm/git/git.git (fetch)
origin git://git.kernel.org/pub/scm/git/git.git (push)
```

If you want to inspect remotes to see more information about a particular remote, you can use the `git remote show <remote>` subcommand:

```
$ git remote show origin
* remote origin
  Fetch URL: git://git.kernel.org/pub/scm/git/git.git
  Push  URL: git://git.kernel.org/pub/scm/git/git.git
  HEAD branch: master
  Remote branches:
    maint   tracked
    master  tracked
    next    tracked
    pu      tracked
    todo    tracked
  Local branch configured for 'git pull':
    master merges with remote master
  Local ref configured for 'git push':
    master pushes to master (up-to-date)
```

Git will consult the remote configuration, the branch configuration, and the remote repository (for an up-to-date status). If you want to skip contacting the remote repository and use cached information instead, add the `-n` option to `git remote show`.

As the information about remotes is stored in the repository configuration file, you can simply examine `.git/config`:

```
[remote "origin"]
    fetch = +refs/heads/*:refs/remotes/origin/*
    url = git://git.kernel.org/pub/scm/git/git.git
```

The difference between local and remote branches (and remote tracking branches: local representations of remote branches) will be described in *Chapter 6*, *Advanced Branching Techniques*, together with an explanation of **refspecs**, as in `+refs/heads/*:refs/remotes/origin/*` in the preceding example.

Adding a new remote

To add a new remote Git repository and to store its information under a shortname, run `git remote add <shortname> <URL>`:

```
$ git remote add alice https://git.company.com/alice/random.git
```

Adding remote doesn't fetch from it automatically — you need to use the `-f` option for that (or run `git fetch <shortname>`).

This command has a few options that affect how Git creates a new remote. You can select which branches in the remote repository you are interested in with the `-t <branch>` option. You can change which branch is the default one in the remote repository (and which you can refer to by the remote name), using the `-m <branch>` option. Or you can configure the remote repository for mirroring rather than for collaboration with `--mirror=push` or `--mirror=fetch`.

For example, running the command:

```
$ git remote add -t master -t next -t maint github \ https://github.com/
jnareb/git.git
```

will result in the following configuration of the remote:

```
[remote "github"]
  url = https://github.com/jnareb/git.git
  fetch = +refs/heads/master:refs/remotes/github/master
  fetch = +refs/heads/next:refs/remotes/github/next
  fetch = +refs/heads/maint:refs/remotes/github/maint
```

Updating information about remotes

The information about the remote repository is stored in three places: in the remote configuration: `remote.<remote name>`, in remote-tracking branches, in remote-HEAD (`refs/remotes/<remote name>/HEAD` is a `symref` that denotes the default remote-tracking branch; that is, the remote tracking branch that `<remote name>` used as a branch expands to), and optionally the per-branch configuration: `branch.<branch name>`.

You could manipulate this information directly – either by editing the appropriate files or using manipulation commands such as `git config` and `git symbolic-ref` – but Git provides various `git remote` subcommands for this.

Renaming remotes

Renaming remote – that is, changing its nickname – is quite a complicated operation. Running `git remote rename <old> <new>` would not only change the section name in `remote.<old>`, but also the remote-tracking branches and accompanying refspec, their reflogs (if there are any – see the `core.logAllRefUpdates` configuration variable), and the respective branch configuration.

Changing the remote URLs

You can add or replace the URL for a remote with `git remote set-url`, but it is also quite easy to simply directly edit the configuration.

You can also use the `insteadOf` (and `pushInsteadOf`) configuration variables. This can be useful if you want to temporarily use another server, for example if the canonical repository is temporarily down. Say that you want to fetch Git from the repository on GitHub, because `https://www.kernel.org/` is down; you can do this by adding the following text to the `config` file:

```
[url "https://github.com/git/git.git"]
    insteadOf = git://git.kernel.org/pub/scm/git/git.git
```

Another use case for this feature is handling repository migration; you can use `insteadOf` rewriting in the per-user configuration file `~/.gitconfig` (or `~/.config/git/config`) without having to change the URL in each and every per-repository `.git/config` file. In the case of more than one match, the longest match is used.

> **Multiple URLs for a remote**
>
> You can set multiple URLs for a remote. Git will try all those URLs sequentially when fetching, and use the first one that works; when pushing, Git will publish to all URLs (all servers) simultaneously.

Changing the list of branches tracked by remote

A similar situation to changing the URL is with changing the list of branches tracked by a remote (that is, the contents of `fetch` lines): you can use `git remote set-branches` (with a sufficiently modern Git), or edit the config file directly.

Note that freeing a branch in a remote repository from being tracked does not remove the remote tracking branch—the latter is simply no longer updated.

Setting the default branch of remote

Having a default branch on remote is not required, but it lets us use the remote name (for example, `origin`) to be specified in lieu of a specific remote-tracking branch (for example, `origin/master`). This information is stored in the symbolic ref `<remote name>/HEAD` (for example, `origin/HEAD`).

You can set it with `git remote set-head`; the `--auto` option does that based on what is the current branch in the remote repository:

```
$ git remote set-head origin master
$ git branch -r
  origin/HEAD -> origin/master
  origin/master
```

You can delete the default branch on the remote with the `--delete` option.

Deleting remote-tracking branches

When a public branch is deleted in the remote repository, Git nevertheless keeps the corresponding remote-tracking branch. It does that because you might want to do, or might have done, your own work on top of it. You can however delete the remote tracking branch with `git branch -r -d`, or you can ask Git to prune all stale remote tracking branches under the remote with `git remote prune`. Or you can configure Git to do it automatically on fetch, as if `git fetch` were run with the `--prune` option, by setting the `fetch.prune` and `remote.<name>.prune` configuration variables.

You can check which remote tracking branches are stale with the `--dry-run` option to `git remote prune`, or with the `git remote show` command.

Deleting remote as a whole is as simple as running `git remote delete` (or its alias `git remote rm`). It also removes remote-tracking branches for the deleted remote.

Support for triangular workflows

In many collaborative workflows, like for example the maintainer (or integration manager) workflow, you fetch from one URL (from the blessed repository) but push to another URL (to your own public repository). See *Fig 4*: the developer interacts with three repositories—he or she fetches from the blessed repository (light red) into the developer private repository (darker), then pushes his or her work into the developer public repository (lighter).

In such a **triangular workflow** (three repositories), the remote you fetch or pull from is usually the default `origin` remote (or `remote.default`). One option for configuring which repository you push to is to add this repository as a separate remote, and perhaps also set it up as the default with `remote.pushDefault`.

```
[remote "origin"]
    url = https://git.company.com/project
    fetch = +refs/heads/*:refs/remotes/origin/*
[remote "myown"]
    url = git@work.company.com:user/project
    fetch = +refs/heads/*:refs/remotes/myown/*
[remote]
    pushdefault = myown
```

You could also set it as `pushremote` in the per-branch configuration:

```
[branch "master"]
    remote = origin
    pushremote = myown
    merge = refs/heads/master
```

Another option is to use a single remote (perhaps even `origin`), but set it up with a separate `pushurl`. This solution however has the slight disadvantage that you don't have separate remote-tracking branches for the push repository (and thus there is no support `@{push}` notation in addition to having `@{upstream}` as a shortcut for specifying the appropriate remote-tracking branches; however, the former has only been available since Git 2.5.0):

```
[remote "origin"]
    url = https://git.company.com/project
    pushurl = git@work.company.com:user/project
    fetch = +refs/heads/*:refs/remotes/origin/*
```

Transport protocols

In general, URLs in the configuration of remote contain information about the transport protocol, the address of the remote server (if any), and the path to the repository. Sometimes, the server that provides access to the remote repository supports various transport protocols; you need to select which one to use. This section is intended to help with this choice.

Local transport

If the other repository is on the same local filesystem, you can use the following syntaxes for specifying the URL:

```
/path/to/repo.git/
file:///path/to/repo.git/
```

The former implies the `--local` option to the Git clone, which bypasses the smart Git-aware mechanism and simply makes a copy (or a hardlink for immutable files under `.git/objects`, though you can avoid this with the `--no-hardlinks` option); the latter is slower but can be used to get a clean copy of a repository.

This is a nice option for quickly grabbing work from someone else's working repository, or for sharing work using a shared filesystem with the appropriate permissions.

As a special case, a single dot "." denotes the current repository. This means that

```
$ git pull . next
```

is roughly equivalent to

```
$ git merge next
```

Legacy (dumb) transports

Some transports do not require any Git-aware smart server – they don't need Git installed on the server (for smart transports at least `git-upload-pack` and/or `git-receive-pack` is needed), though most of them do need extra information generated by `git update-server-info` alongside the repository refs, objects, and packfiles (copied in some way).

Rsync protocol transport – the unsafe one

One of the old protocols that Git supported from the very beginning, allowing us to fetch and push, read and write to the remote repository, is the `rsync` protocol, using the following URL type:

```
rsync://host.example.com/path/to/repo.git/
```

The `rsync` protocol is deprecated, because it does not ensure proper ordering when getting data; if you fetch from a non-quescient repository, you can get *invalid data*. On the other hand it is quite fast and actually resumable. However, if you have a problem doing the initial clone on an unreliable network, it is better to use bundles rather than rsync protocol,as described next in the part about dumb HTTP.

FTP(S) and dumb HTTP(S) protocol transports – the ineffective ones

These transports need only the appropriate stock server (an FTP server or a web server), and up-to-date data from `git update-server-info`. When fetching from such a server, Git uses the so-called **commit walker** downloader: going down from fetched branches and tags, Git walks down the commit chain, and downloads objects or packs containing missing revisions and other data (for example, file contents at revision).

This transport is inefficient (in terms of bandwidth, but especially in terms of latency), but on the other hand it can be resumed if interrupted. Nevertheless there are better solutions than using dumb protocols, namely involving bundles (see the *Offline transport with bundles* section in this chapter), when the network connection to the server is unreliable enough that you can't get the clone.

Pushing to a dumb server is possible only via the HTTP and HTTPS protocols, requires the web server to support WebDAV, and Git has to be built with the expat library linked. The FTP and FTPS protocols are read-only (supporting only `clone`, `fetch`, and `pull`).

Smart transports

When the repository you want to fetch from is on another machine, you need to access the Git server. Nowadays most commonly encountered are Git-aware smart servers. The smart downloader negotiates which revisions are necessary, and creates a customized packfile to send to a client. Similarly, during the push the Git on the server talks to the Git on the user's machine (to the client) to find which revisions to upload.

Git-aware smart servers use the `git upload-pack` downloader for fetching and the `git receive-pack` for pushing. You can tell Git where to find them if they are not in PATH (but for example are installed in one's home directory) with the `--upload-pack` and `--receive-pack` options for fetch and push, or the `uploadpack` and `receivepack` remote configuration.

With very few exceptions (such as the repository using submodules accessed by an ancient Git that does not understand them), Git transport is backward- and forward-compatible— the client and server negotiate what capabilities they can both use.

Native Git protocol

The native transport, using `git://` URLs, provides read-only anonymous access (though you could in principle configure Git to allow pushing by enabling the receive-pack service, either from the command line or via the `daemon.receivePack` boolean-valued configuration variable; using this mechanism is not recommended at all, even in a closed local network).

Git protocol does no authentication, including no server authentication, and should be used with caution on unsecured networks. The `git daemon` TCP server for this protocol normally listens on port 9418; you need to be able to access this port (through the firewall) to be able to use the native Git protocol.

SSH protocol

The **Secure SHell** (**SSH**) transport protocol provides authenticated read-write access. Git simply runs `git upload-pack` or `git receive-pack` on the server, using SSH to execute the remote command. There is no possibility for anonymous, unauthenticated access, though you could as workaround set up a `guest` account for it (password-less or with an empty password).

Using public-private key authentication allows access without requiring you to provide a password on every connection, with the only possible exception of providing it once: to unlock a password-protected private key. You can read more about authentication in the *Credentials/password management* section.

For SSH protocol you can use the URL syntax with `ssh://` as the protocol part:

`ssh://[user@]host.example.com[:port]/path/to/repo.git/`

Alternatively you can use the `scp`-like syntax:

`[user@]host.example.com:path/to/repo.git/`

The SSH protocol additionally supports the `~username` expansion, just like the native Git transport (`~` is the home directory of the user you log in as, `~user` is the home directory of `user`), in both syntax forms:

`ssh://[user@]host.example.com[:port]/~[user]/path/to/repo.git/`

`[user@]host.example.com:~[user]/path/to/repo.git/`

SSH uses the first contact authentication for servers—it remembers the key that the server side previously used, and warns the user if it has changed, asking then for confirmation (the server key could have been changed legitimately, for example due to a SSH server reinstall). You can check the server key fingerprint on the first connection.

Smart HTTP(S) protocol

Git also supports the smart HTTP(S) protocol, which requires a Git-aware CGI or server module—for example, `git-http-backend` (itself a CGI module). As a design feature, Git can automatically upgrade dumb protocol URLs to smart URLs. Conversely, a Git-aware HTTP server can downgrade to the backward-compatible dumb protocol (at least for fetching: it doesn't support WebDAV-based dumb HTTP push). This feature allows to use the same HTTP(S) URL for both dumb and smart access:

`http[s]://[user@]host.example.com[:port]/path/to/repo.git/`

By default, without any other configuration, Git allows anonymous downloads (`git fetch`, `git pull`, `git clone`, and `git ls-remote`), but requires that the client is authenticated for upload (`git push`).

Standard HTTP authentication is used if authentication is required to access a repository, which is done by the HTTP server software. Using SSL/TLS with HTTPS ensures that if the password is sent (for example, if the server uses Basic HTTP authentication), it is sent encrypted, and that the server identity is verified (using server CA certificates).

Offline transport with bundles

Sometimes there is no direct connection between your machine and the server holding the Git repository that you want to fetch from. Or perhaps there is no server running, and you want to copy changes to another machine anyway. Maybe your network is down. Perhaps you're working somewhere on-site and don't have access to the local network for security reasons. Maybe your wireless/Ethernet card just broke.

Enter the `git bundle` command. This command will package up everything that would normally be transferred over the wire, putting objects and references into a special binary archive file called **bundle** (like packfile, only with branches and so on). You need to specify which commits are to be packed—something that network protocols do automatically for you for online transport.

> When you are using one of the smart transports, a want/have negotiation phase takes place, where the client tells the server what it has in its repository and which advertised references on the server it wants, to find common revisions. This is then used by the server to create a packfile and send the client only what's necessary, minimizing the bandwidth use.

Next you move this archive by some means (for example, by so called sneakernet, which means saving bundle to a removable storage and physically moving the media) to your machine. You can then incorporate the bundle contents by using `git clone` or `git fetch` with the filename of bundle in place of the repository URL.

Proxies for Git transports

When direct access to the server is not possible, for example, from within a firewalled LAN, sometimes you can connect via a proxy.

For the native Git protocol (`git://`), you can use the `core.gitProxy` configuration variable, or the `GIT_PROXY_COMMAND` environment variable to specify a proxy command—for example, `ssh`. This can be set on a per-remote basis with this special syntax for the `core.gitProxy` value: `<command> for <remote>`.

You can use the `http.proxy` configuration variable or curl environment variables to specify the HTTP proxy server to use for the HTTP(S) protocol (`http(s)://`). This can be set on a per-remote basis with the `remote.<remote name>.proxy` configuration variable.

You can configure SSH (using its configuration files, for example, `~/.ssh/config`) to use tunneling (port forwarding) or a proxy command (for example, the `netcat/nc`, or netcat mode of `ssh`). It is a recommended solution for the SSH proxy; if neither tunneling nor proxy is possible, you can use the `ext::` transport helper, as shown later in this chapter.

Cloning and updating with bundle

Let's assume that you want to transfer the history of a project (say, limited to the master branch for simplicity) from machineA (for example, your work computer) to machineB (for example, an onsite computer). There is however no direct connection between those two machines.

First, we create a bundle that contains the whole history of the master branch (see *Chapter 2, Exploring Project History*), and tag this point of history to know what we bundled, for later:

```
user@machineA ~$ cd repo
user@machineA repo$ git bundle create ../repo.bundle master
user@machineA repo$ git tag -f lastbundle master
```

Here the bundle file was created outside the working directory. This is a matter of choice; storing it out of the repository means that you don't have to worry about accidentally adding it to your project history, or having to add a new ignore rule. The *.bundle file extension is also a matter of the naming convention used.

> For security reasons, to avoid information disclosure about the parts of history that was deleted but not purged (for example, an accidentally committed file with a password), Git only allows fetching from git show-ref-compatible references: branches, remote-tracking branches, and tags.
>
> The same restrictions apply when creating a bundle. This means for example that (for implementation reasons) you cannot run git bundle create master^1. Though of course, because you control the server end, as a workaround you can create a new branch for master^, (temporarily) rewind master, or check out the detached HEAD at master^.

Then you transfer the just created repo.bundle file to machineB (via email, on a USB pen drive, on CD-R, and so on.). Because this bundle consists of a self-contained, whole subset of the history, down to the first (parent-less) root commit, you can create a new repository by cloning from it, putting the bundle filename in place of the repository URL:

```
user@machineB ~$ git clone repo.bundle repo
Initialized empty Git repository in /home/user/repo/.git/
warning: remote HEAD refers to non-existent ref, unable to checkout.

user@machineB ~$ cd repo
user@machineB repo$ git branch -a
  remotes/origin/master
```

Oops. We didn't bundle HEAD, so git clone didn't know which branch is current and therefore should be checked out.

```
user@machineB repo$ git bundle list-heads ../repo.bundle
5d2584867fe4e94ab7d211a206bc0bc3804d37a9 refs/heads/master
```

 Because bundle can be treated as a remote repository, we could simply use git ls-remote ../repo.bundle here instead of git bundle list-heads ../repo.bundle.

Therefore, with this bundle being as it were, we need to specify which branch to check out (this would not be necessary if we had bundled HEAD too):

```
user@machineB ~$ git clone repo.bundle --branch master repo
```

Let's fix the problem with the lack of checkout (assuming that you use a modern enough Git):

```
user@machineB repo$ git checkout master
Branch master set up to track remote branch master from origin.
Already on 'master'
```

 Here we used a special case of git checkout <branch>—because the master branch does not exist, but there is a remote-tracking branch with the same name for exactly one remote (origin/master here), Git will assume that we meant to create a local branch for the development that is to be published to the master branch in the origin repository. With an older Git, we would need to specify this explicitly:

```
user@machineB repo$ git checkout -b master --track
origin/master
```

This will define a remote called origin, with the following configuration:

```
[remote "origin"]
    url = /home/user/repo.bundle
    fetch = +refs/heads/*:refs/remotes/origin/*
[branch "master"]
    remote = origin
    merge = refs/heads/master
```

To update the repository on machineB cloned from the bundle, you can fetch or pull after replacing the original bundle stored at /home/user/repo.bundle with the one with incremental updates.

To create a bundle containing changes since the last transfer in our example, go to `machineA` and run the following command:

```
user@machineA repo$ git bundle create ../repo.bundle \
   lastbundle..master
user@machineA repo$ git tag -f lastbundle master
```

This will bundle all changes since the `lastbundle` tag; this tag denotes what was copied with the previous bundle (see *Chapter 2, Exploring Project History,* for an explanation of double-dot syntax). After creating a bundle, this will update the tag (using `-f` to replace it), like it was done the first time when creating a bundle, so that the next bundle can also be created incrementally from the now current point.

Then you need to copy the bundle to `machineB`, replacing the old one. At this point one can simply pull to update the repository:

```
user@machineB repo$ git pull
From /home/user/repo.bundle
   ba5807e..5d25848  master       -> origin/master
Updating ba5807e..5d25848
Fast-forward
```

Using bundle to update an existing repository

Sometimes you might have a repository cloned already, only for the network to fail. Or perhaps you moved outside the local area network (LAN), and now you have no access to the server. End result: you have an existing repository, but no direct connection to the upstream (to the repository we cloned from).

Now if you don't want to bundle up the whole repository, like in the *Cloning and updating with bundle* section, you need to find some way to specify the cut-off point (base) in such a way that it is included in the target repository (on your machine). You can specify the range of revisions to pack into the bundle using almost any technique from *Chapter 2, Exploring Project History*. The only limitation is that the history must start at a branch or tag (anything that `git show-ref` accepts). You can of course check the range with the `git log` command.

Commonly used solutions for specifying the range of revisions to pack into bundle are as follows:

- Use the tag that is present in both repositories:

    ```
    machineA repo$ git bundle create ../repo.bundle v0.1..master
    ```

- Create a cut-off based on the time of commit creation:

```
machineA repo$ git bundle create ../repo.bundle --since=1.week
master
```

- Bundle just the last few revisions, limiting the revision range by the number of commits:

```
machineA repo$ git bundle create ../repo.bundle -5 master
```

>
> Better to pack too much, than too little. Otherwise you get something like this:
>
> ```
> user@machineB repo$ git pull ../repo.bundle master
> error: Repository lacks these prerequisite commits:
> error: ca3cdd6bb3fcd0c162a690d5383bdb8e8144b0d2
> ```
>
> You can check if the repository has the requisite commits to fetch from bundle with `git bundle verify`.

Then, after transporting it to `machineB`, you can use the bundle file just like a regular repository to do a one-off pull (putting bundle filename in place of URL or remote name):

```
user@machineB repo$ git pull ../repo.bundle master
From ../repo.bundle
 * branch            master       -> FETCH_HEAD
Updating ba5807e..5d25848
```

If you don't want to deal with the merge, you can fetch into the remote-tracking branch (the `<remote branch>:<remote-tracking branch>` notation used here, which is known as refspec, will be explained in *Chapter 6, Advanced Branching Techniques*):

```
user@machineB repo$ git fetch ../repo.bundle \
   refs/heads/master:refs/remotes/origin/master
From ../repo.bundle
   ba5807e..5d25848  master       -> origin/master
Updating ba5807e..5d25848
```

Alternatively, you can use `git remote add` to create a new shortcut, using the path to the bundle file in place of the repository URL. Then you can simply deal with bundles as described in the previous section.

Utilizing bundle to help with the initial clone

Smart transports provide much more effective transport than dumb ones. On the other hand, the concept of a resumable clone using smart transport remains elusive to this day (it is not available in Git version 2.7.0, though perhaps somebody will implement it in the future). For large projects with a long history and with a large number of files, the initial clone might be quite large (for example, linux-next is more than 800 MB) and take pretty long time. This might be a problem if the network is unreliable.

You can create a bundle from the source repository, for example with the following command:

```
user@server ~$ git --git-dir=/dir/repo.git bundle create --all HEAD
```

Some servers may offer such bundles to help with the initial clone. There is an emerging practice (a convention) that the repository with given URL has a bundle available at the same URL but with the .bundle suffix. For example, https://git.example.com/git/repo.git can have its bundle available at https://git.example.com/git/repo.bundle.

You can then download such a bundle, which is an ordinary static file, using any resumable transport: HTTP(S), FTP(S), rsync, or even BitTorrent (with the appropriate client that supports resuming the download).

Remote transport helpers

When Git doesn't know how to handle a certain transport protocol (which doesn't have built-in support), it attempts to use the appropriate remote helper for a protocol, if one exists. That's why an error within the protocol part of the repository URL looks like it does:

```
$ git clone shh://git@example.com:repo
Cloning into 'repo'...
fatal: Unable to find remote helper for 'shh'
```

This error message means that Git tried to find git-remote-shh to handle the shh protocol (actually a typo for ssh), but didn't find an executable with such a name.

You can explicitly request a specific remote helper with the <transport>::<address> syntax, where <transport> defines the helper (git remote-<transport>), and <address> is a string that the helper uses to find the repository.

Modern Git implements support for the dumb HTTP, HTTPS, FTP, and FTPS protocols with a curl family of remote helpers: git-remote-http, git-remote-https, git-remote-ftp, and git-remote-ftps, respectively.

Transport relay with remote helpers

Git includes two generic remote helpers that can be used to proxy smart transports: the `git-remote-fd` helper to connect to remote server via either a bidirectional socket or a pair of pipes, and the `git-remote-ext` helper to use an external command to connect to the remote server.

In the case of the latter, which uses the `"ext::<command>[ <arguments>...]>"` syntax for the repository URL, Git runs the specified command to connect to the server, passing data for the server to the standard input of the command, and receiving a response on its standard output. This data is assumed to be passed to a `git://` server, `git-upload-pack`, `git-receive-pack`, or `git-upload-archive` (depending on the situation).

For example, let's assume that you have your repository on a LAN host where you can log in using SSH. However, for security reasons this host is not visible on the Internet, and you need to go through the gateway host: `login.example.com`.

```
user@home ~$ ssh user@login.example.com
user@login ~$ ssh work
user@work ~$ find . -name .git -type d -print
./repo/.git
```

The trouble is that, also for security reasons, this gateway host either doesn't have Git installed (reducing the attack surface), or doesn't have your repository present (it uses a different filesystem). This means that you cannot use the ordinary SSH protocol. But the SSH transport is just `git-receive-pack` / `git-upload-pack` accessed remotely via SSH, with the path to the repository as a parameter. This means that you can use the `ext::` remote helper:

```
user@home ~$ git clone \
    "ext::ssh -t user@login.example.com ssh work %S 'repo'" repo
Cloning into 'repo'...
Checking connectivity... done.
```

Here, `%S` will be expanded by Git into the full name of the appropriate service—`git-upload-pack` for fetching and `git-receive-pack` for the push. The `-t` option is needed if logging to the internal host uses interactive authentication (for example, a password). Note that you need to give the name (`repo`, here) to the result of cloning; otherwise, Git will use the command (`ssh`) as the repository name.

You can also use `"ext::ssh [<parameters>...]`
`%S '<repository>'"` to use specific options for SSH
transport—for example, selecting the keypair to use -
without needing to edit `.ssh/config`.

This is not the only possible solution—though there is no built-in support for
sending the SSH transport through a proxy, like there is for native `git://` protocol
(among others, `core.gitProxy`) and for HTTP (among others, `http.proxy`), you can
however do it via configuring the SSH example in `.ssh/config` (see `ProxyCommand`),
or by creating a SSH tunnel.

On the other hand, you can use the `ext::` remote helper also to proxy the `git://`
protocol—for example, with the help of `socat`—including using a single proxy for
multiple servers. See the `git-remote-ext(1)` manpage for details and examples.

Using foreign SCM repositories as remotes

The remote helper mechanism is very powerful. It can be used to interact with
other version control systems, transparently using their repositories as if they were
native Git repositories. Though there is no such built-in helper (unless you count the
`contrib/` area in the Git sources), you can find `git-remote-hg` (or `gitifyhg`) helper
to access Mercurial repositories, and `git-remote-bzr` to access Bazaar repositories.

Once installed, those remote helper bridges will allow you to `clone`, `fetch`, and
`push` to and from the Mercurial or Bazaar repositories as if they were Git ones,
using the `<helper>::<URL>` syntax. For example, to clone Mercurial repository
you can simply run the following command:

```
$ git clone "hg::http://hg.example.com/repo"
```

There is also the `remote.<remote name>.vcs` configuration variable, if you don't
like using the `<helper>::` prefix in the repository URL. With this method you can
use the same URL for Git like for the original VCS (version control system).

Of course one needs to remember about impedance mismatches between different
version control systems, and the limitations of the remote helper mechanism.
There are some features that do not translate at all, or do not translate well—for
example, *octopus* merges (with more than two parent commits) in Git, or multiple
anonymous branches (heads) in Mercurial. With remote helpers there is also no place
to fix mistakes, replace references to other revisions with target native syntax, and
otherwise clean up artifacts created by repository conversions—as can and should
be done with a one-time conversion when changing version control systems. (Such
a clean-up can be done with, for example, the help of the `reposurgeon` third-party
tool).

With remote helpers, you can even use things that are not version control repositories in the strict sense; for example, with the Git-Mediawiki project you can use Git to view and edit a MediaWiki-based wiki (for example, Wikipedia), treating the history of pages as a Git repository:

```
$ git clone mediawiki::http://wiki.example.com
```

Beside that, there are remote helpers that allow additional transport protocols, or storage options—such as the `git-remote-s3bundle` to store the repository as a bundle file on Amazon S3.

Credentials/password management

In most cases, with the exception of the local protocol, publishing changes to the remote repository requires authentication (the user identifies itself) and authorization (the given user has permission to push) provided by Git. Sometimes, fetching the repository also requires authentication.

Commonly used **credentials** for authentication are username and password. You can put the username in the HTTP and SSH repository URLs, if you are not concerned about information leakage (in respect of valid usernames), or you can use the credential helper mechanism. You should *never* put passwords in URLs, even though it is technically possible for HTTP ones — the password can be visible to other people, for example when they are listing processes.

Besides the mechanism inherent in the underlying transport engine, be it SSH_ASKPASS for ssh, or the ~/.netrc file for curl-based transport, Git provides its own integrated solution.

Asking for passwords

Some Git commands that interactively ask for a password (and a username if it is not known)—such as `git svn`, the HTTP interface, or IMAP authentication—can be told to use an external program. The program is invoked with a suitable prompt (a so-called domain, describing what the password is for), and Git reads the password from the standard output of this program.

Git will try the following places to ask the user for usernames and passwords; see the `gitcredentials(7)` manpage:

- The program specified by environment variable GIT_ASKPASS, if set (Git-specific environment variables always have higher precedence than configuration variables)
- Otherwise, the core.askpass configuration variable is used, if set

- Otherwise, the `SSH_ASKPASS` environment variable is used, if set (not Git-specific)
- Otherwise, user is prompted on the terminal

This "askpass" external program is usually selected according to the desktop environment of the user (after installing it, if necessary). For example (x11-)ssh-askpass provides a plain X-Window dialog asking for the username and password; there is `ssh-askpass-gnome` for GNOME, `ksshaskpass` for KDE, `mac-ssh-askpass` can be used for MacOS X, and `win-ssh-askpass` can be used for MS Windows. Git comes with a cross-platform password dialog in Tcl/Tk—`git-gui--askpass`—to accompany the `git gui` graphical interface and the `gitk` history viewer.

Git configuration precedence

Commands in Git have many ways to configure their behavior. They are applied in this order: the first existing specification wins, from the most specific to the least specific:

- Command line option, example, `--pager`,
- Git-specific environment variable, for example, `GIT_PAGER`, or `GIT_ASKPASS` (such variables usually use the `GIT_` prefix)
- Configuration option (in one of the config files, with its own precedence), for example, `core.pager` or `core.askpass`
- A generic environment variable, for example, `PAGER` or `SSH_ASKPASS`
- The built-in default, for example, the `less` pager or terminal prompt.

Public key authentication for SSH

For the SSH transport protocol there are additional authentication mechanisms besides passwords. One of them is **public key authentication**. It is very useful to avoid being asked for a password over and over. Also, the repository hosting service providing the SSH access may require using it, possibly because identifying a user based on his or her public key doesn't require an individual account (that's what, for example, `gitolite` uses).

The idea is that the user creates a public/private key pair by running, for example, `ssh-keygen`. The public key is then sent to the server, for example, using `ssh-copy-id` (which adds the public key `*.pub` at the end of the `~/.ssh/authorized_keys` file on the remote server). You can then log in with your private key that is on your local machine, for example, as `~/.ssh/id_dsa`. You might need to configure `ssh` (in `~/.ssh/config` on Linux) to use a specific identity file for a given connection (hostname), if it is not the default identity key.

Another convenient way to use public key authentication is with an authentication agent such as `ssh-agent` (or Pageant from PuTTY on MS Windows). Utilizing an agent also makes it more convenient to work with passphrase-protected private keys — you need to provide the password only once, to the agent, at the time of adding the key (which might require user action, for example running `ssh-add` for `ssh-agent`).

Credential helpers

It can be cumbersome to input the same credentials over and over. For SSH, you can use public key authentication; there is no true equivalent for other transports. Git credential configuration provides two methods to at least reduce the number of questions.

The first is the static configuration of default usernames (if one is not provided in the URL) for a given **authentication context**, for example `hostname`:

```
[credential "https://git.example.com"]
        username = user
```

It helps if you don't have secure storage for credentials.

The second is to use external programs from which Git can request both usernames and passwords — **credential helpers**. These programs usually interface with secure storage (a keychain, keyring, wallet, credentials manager, and so on) provided by the desktop environment or the operating system.

Git by default includes at least the `cache` and `store` helpers. The `cache` helper (`git-credential-cache`) stores credentials in memory for a short period of time; by default it caches usernames and passwords for 15 minutes. The `store` helper (`git-credential-store`) stores *unencrypted* credentials for indefinitely long time on disk, in files readable only by the user (similar to `~/.netrc`); there is also a third-party `netrc` helper (`git-credential-netrc`) for GPG-encrypted `netrc/authinfo` files.

Selecting a credential helper to use and its options, can be configured either globally or per-authentication context, as in the previous example. Global credentials configuration looks like this:

```
[credential]
        helper = cache --timeout=300
```

This will create Git cache credentials for 300 seconds (five minutes). If the credential helper name is not an absolute path (for example, `/usr/local/bin/git-kde-credentials-helper`), Git will prepend the `git credential-` prefix to the helper name. You can check what types of helper are available with `git help -a | grep credential-` (excluding those with a double dash `--` in the name — those are internal implementations).

There exist credential helpers that are using secure storage of the desktop environment. When you are using them, you need to provide the password only once, to unlock the storage (some helpers can be found in the contrib/ area in Git sources). There is git-credential-gnome-keyring and git-credential-gnomekeyring for the Gnome Keyring, git-credential-osxkeychain for the MacOS X Keychain, and git-credential-wincred and git-credential-winstore for MS Windows' Credential Manager/Store.

Git will use credential configuration for the most specific authentication context, though if you want distinguish the HTTP URL by pathname (for example, providing different usernames to different repositories on the same host) you need to set the useHttpPath configuration variable to true. If there are multiple helpers configured for context, each will be tried in turn, until Git acquires both a username and a password.

> Before the introduction of credential helpers, one could use askpass programs that interface with the desktop environment keychain, for example, kwalletaskpass (for KDE Wallet) or git-password (for the MacOS X Keychain).

Publishing your changes upstream

Now that the *Collaborative workflows* section has explained various repository setups, we'll learn about a few common patterns for contributing to a project. We'll see what our (main) options for publishing changes are.

Before starting work on new changes, you should usually sync to the main development, merging the official version into your repository. This, and the work of the maintainer, is left to be described in *Chapter 7, Merging Changes Together*.

Pushing to a public repository

In a **centralized workflow**, publishing your changes consists simply of **pushing** them to the central server, as shown in *Fig 2*. Because you share this central repository with other developers, it can happen that somebody has already pushed to the branch you are trying to update (the non-fast-forward case). In this scenario, you need to pull (fetch and merge, or fetch and rebase) others' changes, before being able to push yours.

Another possible system with similar workflow is when your team submits each set of changes to the code review system, for example, Gerrit. One available option is to push to a special ref (which is named after a target branch, for example to refs/for/<branchname>) in a special repository. Then change review server makes each set of changes land automatically on a separate per-set ref (for example, refs/changes/<change-id> for commits belonging to a series with given Change-ID).

> In both peer-to-peer (see *Fig 3*), and in maintainer workflows
> or its hierarchical workflow variant (*Fig 4* and *Fig 5*), the first
> step in getting your changes included in the project is also to
> push, but to push to your own public repository. Then you
> need to ask your co-developers, or the project maintainer,
> to merge in your changes. You can do this for example by
> generating a `pull request`.

Generating a pull request

In workflows with personal public repositories, one needs to send the notification
that the changes are available to co-developers, or to the maintainer, or to integration
managers. The `git request-pull` command can help with this step. Given the
starting point (the bottom of the revision range of interest) and the URL or the name
of remote public repository, it will generate a summary of changes:

```
$ git request-pull origin/master publish

The following changes since commit
ba5807e44d75285244e1d2eacb1c10cbc5cf3935:

  Merge: strtol() + checks (2014-05-31 20:43:42 +0200)

are available in the git repository at:

  https://git.example.com/random master

Alice Developer (1):
      Support optional <count> parameter

 src/rand.c |   26 +++++++++++++++++++++-----
 1 files changed, 21 insertions(+), 5 deletions(-)
```

The pull request contains the SHA-1 of the base of the changes (which is the revision
just before the first commit, in series proposed for pull), the title of the base commit,
the URL and the branch of the public repository (suitable as `git pull` parameters),
and the `shortlog` and `diffstat` of changes. This output can be sent to the
maintainer, for example, by email.

Many Git hosting software and services include a built-in equivalent for `git
request-pull` (for example, the `Create pull request` action in GitHub).

Exchanging patches

Many larger projects (and many open-source projects) have established procedures for accepting changes in the form of patches, for example, to lower the barrier to entry for contributing. If you want to send a one-off code proposal to a project, but you do not plan to be a regular contributor, sending patches might be easier than a full collaboration setup (acquiring the permission to commit in the centralized workflow, setting up a personal public repository for the forking workflow and for similar workflows). Besides, one can generate patches with any compatible tool, and the project can accept patches no matter which version control setup they're using.

> Nowadays, with the proliferation of various free Git hosting services, it might be more difficult to set up an e-mail client for sending properly formatted patch emails—though services such as `submitGit` (for submitting patches to the Git project mailing list) could help.

Additionally, patches, being a text representation of changes, can be easily understood by computers and humans alike. This makes them universally appealing, and very useful for code review purposes. Many open-source projects use the public mailing list for that purpose: you can email a patch to this list, and the public can review and comment on your changes.

To generate e-mail versions of each commit series, turning them into mbox-formatted patches, you can use the `git format-patch` command, as follows:

```
$ git format-patch -M -1
0001-Support-optional-count-parameter.patch
```

You can use any revision range specifier with this command, most commonly used is limiting by the number of commits, as in the preceding example, or by using the double-dot revision range syntax—for example, `@{u}..` (see *Chapter 2, Exploring Project History*). When generating a larger number of patches, it is often useful to select a directory where to save generated patches. This can be done with the `-o <directory>` option. The `-M` option for `git format-patch` (passed to `git diff`) turns on rename detection; this can make patches smaller and easier to review.

The patch files end up looking like this:

```
From db23d0eb16f553dd17ed476bec731d65cf37cbdc Mon Sep 17 00:00:00 2001
From: Alice Developer <alice@company.com>
Date: Sat, 31 May 2014 20:25:40 +0200
Subject: [PATCH] Initialize random number generator
```

```
Signed-off-by: Alice Developer <alice@company.com>
---
 random.c |    2 ++
 1 files changed, 2 insertions(+), 0 deletions(-)

diff --git a/random.c b/random.c
index cc09a47..5e095ce 100644
--- a/random.c
+++ b/random.c
@@ -1,5 +1,6 @@
 #include <stdio.h>
 #include <stdlib.h>
+#include <time.h>

 int random_int(int max)
@@ -15,6 +16,7 @@ int main(int argc, char *argv[])

   int max = atoi(argv[1]);

+  srand(time(NULL));
   int result = random_int(max);
   printf("%d\n", result);
--
2.5.0
```

It is actually a complete email in the mbox format. The subject (after stripping the [PATCH] prefix) and everything up to the three-dash line --- forms the commit message—the description of the change. To email this to a mailing list or a developer, you can use either git send-email or git imap-send. The maintainer can then use git am to apply the patch series, creating commits automatically; there's more about this in *Chapter 7, Merging Changes Together*.

> The [PATCH] prefix is here to make it easier to distinguish patches from other emails. The prefix can—and often does—include additional information, such as the number in the series (set) of patches, revision of series, information about it being a work-in-progress, or the request-for-comments status, for example: [RFC/PATCHv4 3/8].

You can also edit these patch files to add more information for prospective reviewers—for example, information about alternative approaches, about the differences between previous revisions of the patch (previous attempts), or a summary and/or references to the discussion on implementing the patch (for example, on a mailing list). You add such text between the --- line and the beginning of the patch, before the summary of changes (diffstat); it will be ignored by git am.

Chain of trust

An important part of collaborative efforts during the development of a project is ensuring the quality of its code. This includes protection against the accidental corruption of the repository, and unfortunately also from malicious intent—a task that the version control system can help with. Git needs to ensure trust in the repository contents: your own and other developers' (including especially the canonical repository of the project).

Content-addressed storage

In *Chapter 2, Exploring Project History*, we learned that Git uses SHA-1 hashes as a native identifier of commit objects (which represent revisions of the project, and form its history). This mechanism makes it possible to generate commit identifiers in a distributed way, taking the SHA-1 cryptographic hash function of the commit object link to the previous commit (the SHA-1 identifier of the parent commit) included.

Moreover, all other data stored in the repository (including the file contents in the revision represented by the blob objects, and the file hierarchy represented by the tree objects) also use the same mechanism. All types of object are addressed by their contents, or to be more accurate, the hash function of the object. You can say that the base of a Git repository is the content-addressed object database.

Thus Git provides a built-in **trust chain** through secure SHA-1 hashes. In one dimension, the SHA-1 of a commit depends on its contents, which includes the SHA-1 of the parent commit, which depends on the contents of the parent commit, and so forth down to the initial root commit. In the other dimension, the content of a commit object includes the SHA-1 of the tree representing the top directory of a project, which in turn depends on its contents, and these contents includes the SHA-1 of subdirectory trees and blobs of file contents, and so forth down to the individual files.

All of this allows SHA-1 hashes to be used to verify whether objects obtained from a (potentially untrusted) source are correct, and that they have not been modified since they have been created.

Lightweight, annotated, and signed tags

The trust chain allows us to verify contents, but does not verify the identity of the person that created this contents (the author and committer name are fully configurable). This is the task for GPG/PGP signatures: signed tags, signed commits, and signed merges.

Lightweight tags

Git uses two types of tags: lightweight and annotated. A **lightweight tag** is very much like a branch that doesn't change – it's just a pointer (reference) to a specific commit in the graph of revisions, though in `refs/tags/` namespace rather than in `refs/heads/` one.

Annotated tags

Annotated tags, however, involve **tag objects**. Here the tag reference (in `refs/tags/`) points to a tag object, which in turn points to a commit. Tag objects contain a creation date, the tagger identity (name and e-mail), and a tagging message. You create an annotated tag with `git tag -a` (or `--annotate`). If you don't specify a message for an annotated tag on the command line (for example, with `-m "<message>"`), Git will launch your editor so you can enter it.

You can view the tag data along with the tagged commit with the `git show` command as follows, (commit skipped):

```
$ git show v0.2
tag v0.2
Tagger: Joe R Hacker <joe@company.com>
Date:   Sun Jun 1 03:10:07 2014 -0700

random v0.2

commit 5d2584867fe4e94ab7d211a206bc0bc3804d37a9
```

Signed tags

Signed tags are annotated tags with a clear text GnuPG signature of the tag data attached. You can create it with `git tag -s` (which uses your committer identity to select the signing key, or `user.signingKey` if set), or with `git tag -u <key-id>`; both versions assume that you have a private GPG key (created, for example, with `gpg --gen-key`).

 Annotated or signed tags are meant for marking a release, while lightweight tags are meant for private or temporary revision labels. For this reason, some Git commands (such as `git describe`) will ignore lightweight tags by default.

Of course in collaborative workflows it is important that the signed tag is made public, and that there is a way to verify it.

Publishing tags

Git does not push tags by default: you need to do it explicitly. One solution is to individually push a tag with `git push <remote> tag <tag-name>` (here `tag <tag>` is equivalent to the longer refspec `refs/tags/<tag>:refs/tags/<tag>`); however, you can skip `tag` in most cases, here. Another solution is to push tags in mass either all the tags—both lightweight and annotated—with the use of the `--tags` option, or just all annotated tags that point to pushed commits with `--follow-tags`. This explicitness allows you to re-tag (using `git tag -f`) with impunity, if it turns out that you tagged the wrong commit, or there is a need for a last-minute fix—but only if the tag was not made public.

When fetching changes, Git automatically follows tags, downloading annotated tags that point to fetched commits. This means that downstream developers will automatically get signed tags, and will be able to verify releases.

Tag verification

To verify a signed tag, you use `git tag -v <tag-name>`. You need the signer's public GPG key in your keyring for this (imported using for example `gpg --import` or `gpg --keyserver <key-server> --recv-key <key-id>`), and of course the tagger's key needs to be vetted in your chain of trust.

```
$ git tag -v v0.2
object 1085f3360e148e4b290ea1477143e25cae995fdd
type commit
tag signed
tagger Joe Random <jrandom@example.com> 1411122206 +0200

project v0.2
gpg: Signature made Fri Jul 19 12:23:33 2014 CEST using RSA key ID
A0218851
gpg: Good signature from "Joe Random <jrandom@example.com>"
```

Signed commits

Signed tags are a good solution for users and developers to verify that the tagged release was created by the maintainer. But how do we make sure that a commit purporting to be by a somebody named Jane Doe, with the `jane@company.com` e-mail, is *actually* a commit from her? How to make it so anybody can check it?

One possible solution, available since Git version 1.7.9, is to GPG-sign individual commits. You can do this with `git commit --gpg-sign[=<keyid>]` (or `-S` in short form). The key identifier is optional—without this, Git would use your identity as the author. Note that `-S` (capital *S*) is different from `-s` (small *s*); the latter adds a *Signed-off-by* line at the end of the commit message for the Digital Certificate of Ownership.

```
$ git commit -a --gpg-sign
```

```
You need a passphrase to unlock the secret key for
user: "Jane Doe <jane@company.com>"
2048-bit RSA key, ID A0218851, created 2014-03-19
```

```
[master 1085f33] README: eol at eof
 1 file changed, 1 insertion(+), 1 deletion(-)
```

To make commits available for verification, just push them. Anyone can then verify them with the `--show-signature` option to `git log` (or `git show`), or with one of the `%Gx` placeholders in `git log --format=<format>`.

```
$ git log -1 --show-signature
commit 1085f3360e148e4b290ea1477143e25cae995fdd
gpg: Signature made Wed Mar 19 11:53:49 2014 CEST using RSA key ID
A0218851
gpg: Good signature from "Jane Doe <jane@company.com>"
Author: Jane Doe <jane@company.com>
Date:   Wed Mar 19 11:53:48 2014 +0200

    README: eol at eof
```

Since Git version 2.1.0, you can also use the `git verify-commit` command for this.

Merging signed tags (merge tags)

The **signed commit** mechanism, described in the previous section, may be useful in some workflows, but it is inconvenient in an environment where you push commits out early—for example, to your own public repository—and only after a while do you decide whether they are worth including in the upstream (worth sending to the main repository). This situation can happen if you follow the recommendations of *Chapter 8, Keeping History Clean*; you know only after the fact (long after the commit was created), that the given iteration of the commit series passes code review.

You can deal with this issue by rewriting the whole commit series after its shape is finalized (after passing the review), signing each rewritten commit; or just amending and signing only the top commit. Both of those solutions would require forced push to replace old not signed history. Or you can create an empty commit (with `--allow-empty`), sign it, and push it on top of the series. But there is a better solution: requesting the pull of a signed tag (available since Git version 1.7.9).

In this workflow, you work on changes and, when they are ready, you create and push a signed tag (tagging the last commit in the series). You don't have to push your working branch—pushing the tag is enough. If the workflow involves sending a pull request to the integrator, you create it using a tag as the end commit:

```
$ git tag -s for-maintainer
$ git request-pull origin/master public-repo 1253-for-maintainer \
  >msg.txt
```

The signed tag message is shown between the dashed lines in the pull request, which means that you may want to explain your work in the tag message when creating the signed tag. The maintainer, after receiving such pull request, can copy the repository line from it, fetching and integrating the named tag. When recording the merge result of pulling the named tag, Git will open an editor and ask for a commit message. The integrator will see the template starting with:

```
Merge tag '1252-for-maintainer'

Work on task tsk-1252

# gpg: Signature made Wed Mar 19 12:23:33 2014 CEST using RSA key ID
A0218851
# gpg: Good signature from "Jane Doe <jane@company.com>"
```

This commit template includes the commented out output of the GPG verification of the signed tag object being merged (so it won't be in the final merge commit message). The tag message helps describe the merge better.

The signed tag being pulled is *not* stored in the integrator's repository, not as a tag object. Its content is stored, hidden, in a merge commit. This is done so as to not pollute the tag namespace with a large number of such working tags. The developer can safely delete the tag (`git push public-repo --delete 1252-for-maintainer`) after it gets integrated.

Recording the signature inside the merge commit allows for after-the-fact verification with the `--show-signature` option:

```
$ git log -1 --show-signature
commit 0507c804e0e297cd163481d4cb20f3f48ceb87cb
merged tag '1252-for-maintainer'
gpg: Signature made Wed Mar 19 12:23:33 2014 CEST using RSA key ID
A0218851
gpg: Good signature from "Jane Doe <jane@company.com>"
Merge: 5d25848 1085f33
Author: Jane Doe <jane@company.com>
Date:   Wed Mar 19 12:25:08 2014 +0200

    Merge tag 'for-maintainer'


    Work on task tsk-1252
```

Summary

We have learnt how to use Git for collaborative development, how to work together on a project in a team. We got to know different collaborative workflows, different ways of setting up repositories for collaboration. Which one to use depends on circumstances: how large the team is, how diverse, and so on. This chapter focuses on repository-to-repository interaction; the interplay between branches and remote-tracking branches in those repositories is left for *Chapter 6, Advanced Branching Techniques*.

We have learnt how Git can help manage information about remote repositories (remotes) involved in the chosen workflow. We were shown how to store, view, and update this information. This chapter explains how one can manage triangular workflows, in which you fetch from one repository (canonical), and push to the other (public).

We have learnt how to choose a transport protocol if the remote server offers such choice, and a few tricks such as using foreign repositories as if they were native Git repositories.

Contact with remote repositories can require providing credentials, usually the username and password, to be able to, for example, push to the repository. This chapter describes how Git can help make this part easier to use thanks to credential helpers.

Publishing your changes, sending them upstream, may involve different mechanisms, depending on the workflow. This chapter describes the push, pull request and patch-based techniques.

We have learned about the chain of trust: how to verify that a release comes from the maintainer, how to sign your work so that the maintainer can verify that it comes from you, and how the Git architecture helps with this.

The two following chapters will expand the topic of collaboration: *Chapter 6, Advanced Branching Techniques,* will explore relations between local branches and branches in a remote repository, and how to set up branches for collaboration, while *Chapter 7, Merging Changes Together,* will talk about the opposite issue—how to join the results of parallel work.

6

Advanced Branching
Techniques

The previous chapter, *Collaborative Development with Git*, described how to arrange teamwork, focusing on repository-level interactions. In that chapter, you learned about various centralized and distributed workflows, and their advantages and disadvantages.

This chapter will go deeper into the details of collaboration in a distributed development. It would explore the relations between local branches and branches in remote repositories. It will introduce the concept of remote tracking branches, branch *tracking*, and *upstream*. This chapter will also teach us how to specify the synchronization of branches between repositories, using refspecs and push modes.

You will also learn branching techniques: how branches can be used to prepare new releases and to fix bugs. You will learn how to use branches in such way so that it makes it easy to select which features go into the next version of the project.

In this chapter, we will cover the following topics:

- Different kinds of branches, both long-lived and short-lived, and their purpose
- Various branching models, including topic branch-based workflow
- Release engineering for different branching models
- Using branches to fix a security issue in more than one released version
- Remote-tracking branches and refspecs, the default remote configuration
- Rules for fetching and pushing branches and tags
- Selecting a push mode to fit chosen collaboration workflow

Types and purposes of branches

A **branch** in a version control system is a active parallel line of development. They are useful, as we will see, to isolate and separate different types of work. For example, branches can be used to prevent your current work on a feature in progress from interfering with the management of bug fixes.

A single Git repository can have an arbitrary number of branches. Moreover, with a distributed version control system, such as Git, there could be many repositories (forks) for a single project, some public and some private; each repository will have its own local branches.

Before examining how the collaboration between repositories looks like at the branch level, we need to know what types of branches we would encounter in local and remote repositories. Let's now talk about how these branches are used and examine why people would want to use multiple branches in a single repository.

> **A bit of history: a note on the evolution of branch management**
>
> Early distributed version control systems used one branch per repository model. Both **Bazaar** (then Bazaar-NG) and **Mercurial** documentation, at the time when they begin their existence, recommended to clone the repository to create a new branch.
>
>
>
> Git, on the other hand, had good support for multiple branches in a single repository almost from the start. However, at the beginning, it was assumed that there would be one central multibranch repository interacting with many single-branch repositories (see, for example, the legacy .git/branches directory to specify URLs and fetch branches, described in the gitrepository-layout(7) man page), though with Git it was more about defaults than capabilities.
>
> Because branching is cheap in Git (and merging is easy), and collaboration is quite flexible, people started using branches more and more, even for solitary work. This led to the wide use of extremely useful topic branch workflow.

There are many reasons for keeping a separate line of development, thus there are many kinds of branches. Different types of branches have different purposes. Some branches are long-lived or even permanent, while some branches are short-lived and expected to be deleted after their usefulness ends. Some branches are intended for publishing, some are not.

Long-running, perpetual branches

Long-lived or permanent branches are intended to last (indefinitely or, at least, for a very long time).

From the collaboration point of view, a long-lived branch can be expected to be there when you are next updating data or publishing changes. This means that one can safely start their own work basing it on (forking it from) any of the long-lived branches in the remote repository, and be assured that there should be no problems with integrating that work.

Also, what you can find in public repositories are usually only long-lived branches. In most cases, these branches should never rewind (the new version is always a descendant of the old versions). There are some special cases here though; there can be branches that are rebuilt after each new release (requiring forced fetch at that time), and there can be branches that do not fast forward. Each such case should be explicitly mentioned in the developer documentation to help avoiding unpleasant surprises.

Integration, graduation, or progressive-stability branches

One of the uses of branches is to separate ongoing development (which can include temporarily some unstable code) from maintenance work (where you are accepting only bug fixes). There are usually a few of such branches. The intent of each of these branches is to *integrate* the development work of the respective degree of stability, from maintenance work, through stable, to unstable or development work.

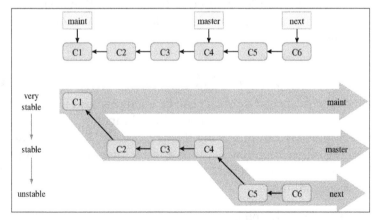

Fig 1. A linear view and a "silo" view of the progressive-stability branches. In the linear view, the stable revisions are further down the line in your commit history, and the cutting-edge unstable work is further up the history. Alternatively, we can think of branches as work silos, where work goes depending on the level of the stability (graduation) of changes.

These branches form a hierarchy with a decreasing level of graduation or stability of work, as shown in *Fig 1*. Note that, in real development, progressive-stability branches would not keep this simple image exactly as it is shown. There would be new revisions on the branches after the forking points. Nevertheless, the overall shape would be kept the same, even in the presence of merging.

The rule is to always merge more stable branches into less stable ones, that is, *merge upwards*, which will preserve the overall shape of branch *silos* (see also *Fig 2* in the *Graduation, or progressive-stability branches workflow* section of this chapter). This is because merging means including all the changes from the merged branch. Therefore, merging a less stable branch into a more stable one would bring unstable work to the stable branch, violating the purpose and the contract of a stable branch.

Often, we see the graduation branches of the following levels of stability:

- `maint` or `maintenance` of the `fixes` branch, containing only bug fixes to the last major release; minor releases are done with the help of this branch.

- The `master` or `trunk`, or `stable` branch, with the development intended for the next major release; the tip of this branch should be always in the production-ready state.

- `next` or `devel`, `development`, or `unstable`, where the new development goes to test whether it is ready for the next release; the tip can be used for nightly builds.

- `pu` or `proposed` for the proposed updates, which is the integration testing branch meant for checking compatibility between different new features.

Having multiple long-running branches is not necessary, but it's often helpful, especially in very large or complex projects. Often in operations, each of levels of stability corresponds to its own platform or deployment environment; giving a branch per platform.

Per-release branches and per-release maintenance

Preparing for the new release of a project can be a lengthy and involved process. Per-release branches can help with this. The release branch is meant for separating the ongoing development from preparing the new release. It allows other developers to continue working on writing new features and on integration testing, while the quality assurance team with the help of the release manager takes time to test and stabilize the release candidate.

After creating a new release, keeping such per-release branches allows us to support and maintain older released versions of the software. At these times, such branches work as a place to gather bug fixes (for their software versions) and create minor releases.

Not all the projects find utilizing per-release branches necessary. You can prepare a new release on the stable-work graduation branch, or use a separate repository in place of using a separate branch. Also, not all the projects require providing support for more than the latest version.

This type of branches is often named after the release it is intended for, for example, having names such as `release-v1.4`, or `v1.4.x` (it better not have the same name as tag for release, though).

Hotfix branches for security fixes

Hotfix branches are like release branches, but for unplanned releases. Their purpose is to act upon the undesired state of a live production or a widely deployed version, usually to resolve some critical bug in the production (usually a severe security bug). This type of branches can be considered a longer lived equivalent of the bugfix topic branches (see the *Bugfix branches* section of this chapter).

Per-customer or per-deployment branches

Let's say that some of your project's customers require a few customization tweaks, since they do things differently. Or perhaps, there are some deployment sites that have special requirements. Suppose that these customizations cannot be done by simply changing the configuration. You would then need to create separate the lines of development for these customers or customizations.

But you don't want these lines of development to remain separate. You expect that there will be changes that apply to all of them. One solution is to use one branch for each customization set, per customer or per deployment. Another would be to use separate repositories. Both solutions help maintain parallel lines of development and transfer changes from one line to another.

Automation branches

Say that you are working on a web application and you want to automate its deployment using a version control system. One solution would be to set up a daemon to watch a specific branch (for example the one named 'deploy') for changes. Updating such branch would automatically update and reload the application.

This is, of course, not the only possible solution. Another possibility would be to use a separate deploy repository and set up hooks there, so push would trigger refreshing of the web application. Or, you could configure a hook in a public repository so that push to a specific branch triggers redeployment (this mechanism is described in *Chapter 11, Git Administration*).

These techniques can be used also for **continuous integration** (**CI**); instead of deploying the application, pushing it into a specific branch would trigger the running of test suite (the trigger could be creating a new commit on this branch or merging into it).

Mob branches for anonymous push access

Having a branch in a remote repository (on server) with special treatment on push, is a technique that has many uses, including helping to collaborate. It can be used to enable *controlled* anonymous push access for a project.

Let's assume that you want to allow random contributors to push into the central repository. You would want, however, to do this in a managed way: one solution is to create a special mob branch or a mob/* namespace (set of branches) with relaxed access control.

You can find how to set this up in *Chapter 11, Git Administration.*

The orphan branch trick

All the types of branches described up to this point differed in their purpose and management. However, from the technical point of view (from the point of view of the graph of commits), they all look the same. This is not the case with the so-called *orphan* branches.

The orphan branch is a parallel disconnected (orphaned) line of development, sharing no revisions with the main history of a project. It is a reference to a disjoint subgraph in the DAG of revisions, without any intersection with the main DAG graph. In most cases, their checkout is also composed of different files.

Such branches are sometimes used as a trick to store tangentially related contents in a single repository, instead of using separate repositories. (When using separate repositories to store related contents, one might want to use some naming convention to denote this fact, for example a common prefix.) They can be used to:

- Store the project's web page files. For example, GitHub uses a branch named gh-pages for the project's pages.
- Store generated files, when the process of creating them requires some nonstandard toolchain. For example, the project documentation can be stored in html, man, and pdf orphan branches (the html branch can be also used to deploy the documentation). This way the user can get it without needing to install its toolchain.
- Store the project TODO notes (for example in the todo branch), perhaps together with storing there some specialized maintainer tools (scripts).

You can create such branch with `git checkout --orphan <new branch>`, or by pushing into (or fetching into) a specific branch from a separate repository, as follows:

```
$ git fetch repo-htmldocs master:html
```

> Creating an orphan branch with `git checkout --orphan` does not technically create a branch, that is, it does not make a new branch reference. What it does is point the symbolic reference HEAD to an unborn branch. The reference is created after the first commit on a new orphan branch.
>
> That is why there is no option to create an orphan branch for `git branch` command.

Short-lived branches

While long-lived branches stay forever, short-lived or temporary branches are created to deal with single issues, and are usually removed after dealing with said issue. They are intended to last only as long as the issue is present. Their purpose is time-limited.

Because of their provisional nature, they are usually present only in the local private repository of a developer or integration manager (maintainer), and are not pushed to public distribution repositories. If they appear in public repositories, they are there only in a public repository of an individual contributor (see the blessed repository workflow in *Chapter 5, Collaborative Development with Git*), as a target for a pull request.

Topic or feature branches

Branches are used to separate and gather together different subsets of development efforts. With easy branching and merging, we can go further than creating a branch for each stability level, as described earlier. We can create a separate branch for each separate issue.

The idea is to make a new branch for each topic, that is, a feature or a bug fix. The intent of this type of branch is both to gather together subsequent development steps of a feature (where each step – a commit – should be a self contained piece, easy to review) and to isolate the work on one feature from the work on other topics. Using a feature branch allows topical changes to be kept together and not mixed with other commits. It also makes it possible for a whole topic to be dropped (or reverted) as a unit, be reviewed as a unit, and be accepted (integrated) as a unit.

The end goal for the commits on a topic branch is to be included in a released version of a product. This means that, ultimately, the short-lived topic branch is to be merged into the long-lived branch which is gathering stable work, and to be deleted. To make it easier to integrate topic branches, the recommended practice is to create such branches by forking off the oldest, the most stable integration branch that you will eventually merge it into. Usually, this means creating a branch from the stable-work graduation branch. However, if a given feature does depend on a topic not yet in the stable line, you need to fork off the appropriate topic branch containing the dependency you need.

Note that if it turns out that you forked off the wrong branch, you can always fix it by rebasing (see *Chapter 7, Merging Changes Together*, and *Chapter 8, Keeping History Clean*), as topic branches are not public.

Bugfix branches

We can distinguish a special case of a topic branch whose purpose is fixing a bug. Such branch should be created starting from the oldest integration branch it applies to (the most stable branch that contains the bug). This usually means forking off the maintenance branch, or off the divergence point of all the integration branches, rather than the tip of the stable branch. A bugfix branch's goal is to be merged into relevant long-lived integration branches.

Bugfix branches can be thought of as a short-lived equivalent of a long-lived hotfix branch.

Using them is a better alternative to simply committing fixes on the maintenance branch (or another appropriate integration branch).

Detached HEAD – the anonymous branch

You can think of the detached HEAD state (described in *Chapter 3, Developing with Git*) as the ultimate in temporary branches—so temporary that it even doesn't have a name. Git uses such anonymous branches automatically in a few situations, for example, during bisection and rebasing.

Because, in Git, there is only one anonymous branch and it must always be the current branch, It is usually better to create a true temporary branch with a temporary name; you can always change the name of the branch later.

One possible use of the detached HEAD is for proof of concept work. You, however, need to remember to set the name of the branch if the changes turn out to be worthwhile (or if you need to switch branches). It is easy to go from an anonymous branch to a named branch. You simply need to create a new branch from the current detached HEAD state.

Branching workflows and release engineering

Now that we know what types of branches are there and what their purposes are, let's examine how branches are used. Note that different situations call for different use of branches. For example, smaller projects are better suited for simpler branching workflows, while larger projects might need more advanced ones.

We will now describe here how to use different standard workflows. Each workflow is distinguished by the various types of branches it uses (the types described earlier in this chapter). In addition to getting to know how the ongoing development looks like for a given workflow, we would also see what to do at the time of the new release (major and minor, where relevant). Among others, we will find out what happens then to branches used in the chosen workflow.

The release and trunk branches workflow

One of the simplest workflows is to use just a single integration branch. Such branches are sometimes called **the trunk**; in Git, it would usually be the `master` branch (it is the default branch when creating a repository). In a pure version of this workflow, one would commit everything on the said branch, at least, during the normal development stage. This way of working comes from the times of centralized version control, when branching and especially merging was more expensive and people avoided branch-heavy workflows.

 In more advanced versions of this workflow, one would also use topic branches, one short-lived branch per feature, and merge them into the trunk, instead of committing directly on it (see *Fig 3*).

In this workflow, we create the new release branch out of trunk when deciding to cut the new major release. This is done to avoid the interference between stabilizing for release and ongoing development work. The rule is that all the stabilization work goes on the release branch, while all the ongoing development goes to the trunk. **Release candidates** are cut (tagged) from the release branch, as is the final version of a release.

The release branch for a given version can be later used to gather bug fixes, and to cut minor releases from it.

The disadvantage of such simple workflow is that during development, we often get in an unstable state. In this case, it could be hard to come up with a good starting point, stable enough to start working on creating a new release. An alternative solution is to create revert commits on the release branch, undoing the work that is not ready. But it can be a lot of work and it would make the history of a project hard to follow.

Another difficulty with this workflow is that the feature that looks good at the first glance might show problems later in use. This is something this workflow has trouble dealing with. If it turns out during development that some feature created in multiple commits feature is not a good idea, reverting it can be difficult. This is true especially if its commits are spread across the timeline (across the history).

Moreover, the trunk and release branch workflow does not provide any inherent mechanism for finding bad interactions between different features, that is, for the integration testing.

In spite of these problems, this simple workflow can be a good fit for a small team.

The graduation, or progressive-stability branches workflow

To be able to provide the stable line of the product and to be able to test it in practice as a kind of floating beta version, one needs to separate work that is stable from the work that is ongoing and might destabilize code. That's what graduation branches are for: to integrate revisions with different degrees of maturation and stability (this type of long-running branches is also called **integration** branches or **progressive-stability** branches). See *Fig 1* of the *Integration, or graduation, or progressive-stability branches* section in this chapter, which shows a graph view and a silo view of a simple case with progressive-stability branches and linear history. Let's call the technique that utilizes mainly (or only) this type of branches **the graduation branches workflow**.

Besides keeping stable and unstable development separate sometimes, there is also a need for an ongoing maintenance. If there is only one version of the product to support, and the process of creating a new release is simple enough, one can also use the graduation-type branch for this.

 Here, *simple enough* means that one can just create the next major release out of the stable branch.

In such situation, one would have at least three integration branches. There would be one branch for the ongoing maintenance work (containing only bug fixes to the last version), to create minor releases. One branch for stable work to create major releases; this branch can also be used for nightly stable builds. And last, one branch for ongoing development, possibly unstable.

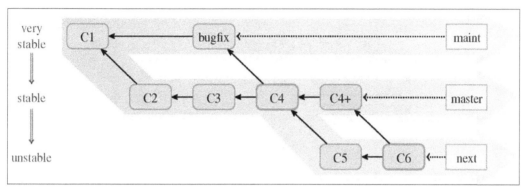

Fig 2. The graduation or progressive-stability branches workflow. You should never merge a less stable branch into more stable one, as merging would bring all the unstable history.

You can use this workflow as it is, with only graduation branches, and no other types of branches. You commit bug fixes on the maintenance branch and merge it into the stable branch and development branch, if necessary. You create revisions with the well-tested work on the stable branch, merging it into the development branch when needed (for example, if the new work depends on them). You put the work in progress, possibly unstable, on the development branch. During normal development, you never merge less stable into more stable branches, otherwise you would decrease their stability. It is always more stable into less stable, as represented in *Fig 2*.

This, of course, requires that you know upfront whether the feature that you are working on should be considered stable or unstable. There is also an underlying assumption that different features work well together from the start. One would expect in practice, however, that each piece of the development matures from the proof of concept, through being a work in progress during possibly several iterations, before it stabilizes. This problem can be solved with the workflow involving use of topic branches, which will be described next.

In the pure graduation branches workflow, one would create minor releases (with bug fixes) out of the maintenance branch. Major releases (with new features) are created out of the stable-work branch. After a major release, the stable-work branch is merged into the maintenance branch to begin supporting the new release that was just created. At this point also, an unstable (development) branch can be merged into a stable one. This is the only time when merging upstream, which means merging less stable branches into more stable branches, should be done.

The topic branches workflow

The idea behind the topic branches workflow is to create a separate short-lived branch for each topic, so that all the commits belonging to a given topic (all the steps in its development) are kept together. The purpose of each topic branch is a development of the new feature, or a creation of a bug fix.

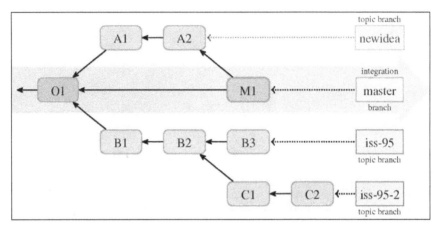

Fig 3. The topic branches workflow with one integration branch (`master`) and three topic or feature branches. Among the topic branches, there is one (namely, `newidea`) already merged in the integration branch and one (`iss-95-2`) dependent on the feature developed in the other feature branch (`iss-95` here).

In the **topic branches workflow** (also called the **feature branches workflow**), you have are at least two different types of branches. First, there needs to be at least one permanent (or just long-lived) *integration branch*. This type of branches is used purely for merging. Integration branches are public.

Second, there are separate short-lived temporary *feature branches*, each intended for the development of a topic or the creation of a bug fix. They are used to carry all the steps, and only the steps required in the development of a feature or a fix; a unit of work for a developer. These branches can be deleted after the feature or the bug fix is merged. Topic branches are usually private and are often not present in public repositories.

When a feature is ready for review, its topic branch is often rebased to make integration easier, and optionally to make history more clear. It is then sent for review as a whole. The topic branch can be used in a pull request, or can be sent as a series of patches (for example, using `git format-patch` and `git send-email`). It is often saved as a separate topic branch in a maintainer's working repository (for example, `git am --3way` if it was sent as patches) to help in examining and managing it.

Then, the integration manager (the maintainer in the blessed repository workflow, or simply another developer in the central repository workflow) reviews each topic branch and decides whether it is ready for inclusion in selected integration branch. If it is, then it will get merged in (perhaps, with the `--no-ff` option).

Graduation branches in a topic branch workflow

The simplest variant of the topic branches workflow uses only one integration branch. Usually, however, one would combine the graduation branches workflow with topic branches.

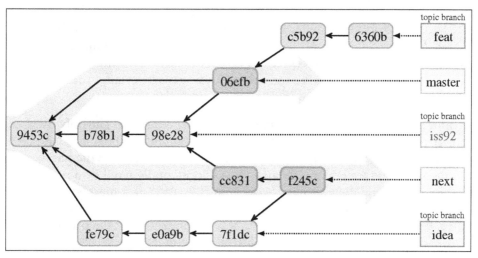

Fig 4. The topic branches workflow with two graduation branches. Among topic branches, there is one (`iss92`) that is considered stable enough to be merged into both the `next` (unstable) and `master` (stable) graduation branches. One (`idea`) that got merged into `next` for testing and one (`feat`) just created from master.

In this often used variant, the feature branch is started from the tip of a given stable branch (usually) or from the last major release, unless the branch requires some other feature. In the last case, the branch needs to be forked from (created from) the topic branch it depends on, such as the `feat` branch in *Fig 4*. Bugfix topic branches are created on top of the maintenance branch.

When the topic is considered done, it is first merged into the development-work integration branch (for example, `next`) to be tested. For example, in *Fig 4*, topic branches `idea` and `iss92` are both merged into `next`, while `feat` is not considered ready yet. Adventurous users can use builds from given unstable branch to exercise the feature, though they better take into the account the possibility of crashes and data loss.

After this examination, when the feature is considered to be ready to be included in the next release, it is merged into the stable-work integration branch (for example, master). *Fig 4* includes one such branch: iss92. At this point, after merging it into the stable integration branch, the topic branch can be deleted.

Using a feature branch allows topical revision to be kept together and not mixed with other commits. The topic branch workflow allows for the easy undoing of topic as a whole, and for removing of all bad commits together (removing a series of commits as a whole unit), instead of using a series of reverts.

If the feature turns out to be not ready, it is simply not merged into the stable branch, and it remains present only in the development-work branch. If we, however, realize too late that it was not ready, after the topic was merged into the stable branch, we would need to revert the merge. This is a slightly more advanced operation than reverting a single commit, but it is less troublesome than reverting commits one, by one while ensuring that all the commits get correctly reverted. Problems with reverting merges will be covered in *Chapter 8, Keeping History Clean*.

The workflow for topic branches containing bugfixes is similar. The only difference is that one needs to consider into which of integration branches the bugfix branch is to be merged into. This, of course, depends on the situation. Perhaps the bugfix applies only to the maintenance branch, because it was accidentally fixed by a new feature in the stable-work and development-work branches; then, it is merged only to this branch. Perhaps, the bug applies only to the stable-work and development-work branches, because it is about the feature that was not present in the previous version, thus the maintenance branch is excluded from being merged into.

Using a separate topic branch for bug fixing, instead of committing bugfix directly, has an additional advantage. It allows us to easily correct the misstep, if it turns out after the fact that the fix applies to more branches than we thought.

For example, if it turns out that the fix needs to be applied also to the maintained version and not only to the current work, with the topic branch you can simply merge the fix into additional branches. This is not the case if we were to commit the fix directly on the stable branch. In the latter situation, you cannot use merging, as it would destabilize the maintenance branch. You would need to copy the revision with the fix, by cherry-picking it from the branch it was committed on into the maintenance branch (see *Chapter 7, Merging Changes Together* for detailed description of this operation). But it means that duplicated commits; additionally cherry-picked commits can sometimes interact wrongly with the act of merging.

The topic branches workflow also allows us to check whether the features conflict with each other, and then fix them as necessary. You can simply create a throw-away integration branch and merge into it topic branches containing these features, to test the interaction between them. You can even publish such branches meant for integration testing (named `proposed-updates` or just `pu` for example) to allow for other developers to examine the works in progress. You should however state explicitly in the developer documentation that said branch should not be used as a basis to work on, as it is recreated each time from scratch.

Branch management for a release in a topic branch workflow

Let's assume that we are using three graduation (integration) branches: `maint` for maintenance work on the last release, `master` for stable work, `next` for development.

The first thing that the maintainer (the release manager) needs to do before creating a new release is to verify that `master` is a superset of `maint`, that is, all the bugs are fixed also in the version considered for the next release. You can do this by checking whether the following command gives an empty output (see *Chapter 2, Exploring Project History*):

```
$ git log master..maint
```

If the preceding command show some unmerged commits, the maintainer needs to decide what to do with them. If these bug fixes don't break anything, he/she can simply merge `maint` into `master` (as it is merging the more stable branch into the less stable one).

Now that the maintainer knows that `master` is a superset of `maint`, he/she can create the new release from remote `master` by tagging it, and then pushing just created tag to the distribution point (to the public repository), for example with the following:

```
$ git tag -s -m "Foo version 1.4" v1.4 master
$ git push origin v1.4 master
```

The preceding command assumed that the public repository of the `Foo` project is the one described by the `origin`, and that we use the double-digit version for major releases (following the semantic versioning specification: `http://semver.org/`).

> If the maintainer wants to support more than one older version, he or she would need to copy an old maintenance branch, as the next step would be to prepare it for maintaining just released revision:
>
> ```
> $ git branch maint-1.3.x maint
> ```

Then, the maintainer updates `maint` to the new release, advancing the branch (note that step one ensured that `maint` was a subset of `master`):

```
$ git checkout maint
$ git merge --ff-only master
```

If the second command fails, it means that there are some commits on the branch `maint` that are not present in `master`, or to be more exact that `master` is not a strict descendant of `maint`.

Because we usually consider features for inclusion in `master` one by one, there might be some topic branches that are merged into `next`, but they were abandoned before they were merged into `master` (or they are not merged because they were not ready.) This means that though the `next` branch contains a superset of topic branches that compose the `master` branch, `master` is not necessarily the ancestor of `next`.

That's why advancing the `next` branch after a release can be more complicated than advancing the `maint` branch. One solution is to rewind and rebuild the `next` branch:

```
$ git checkout next
$ git reset --hard master
$ git merge ai/topic_in_next_only_1...
```

You can find unmerged topics to be merged to rebuild `next` with:

```
$ git branch --no-merged next
```

After creating the release following rebuilding of `next`, other developers would have to force fetch the `next` branch (see the next section), as it would not fast-forward if it is not already configured to force fetch:

```
$ git pull
From git://git.example.com/pub/scm/project
   62b553c..c2e8e4b  maint        -> origin/maint
   a9583af..c5b9256  master       -> origin/master
 + 990ffec...cc831f2 next         -> origin/next  (forced update)
```

Notice the forced update for the `next` branch here.

Git-flow – a successful Git branching model

One can see that the more advanced version of the topic branching workflow builds on top of the graduation branch's one. In some cases, even more involved branching model might be necessary, utilizing more types of branches: graduation branches, release branches, hotfix branches, and topic branches. Such model is sometimes called `gitflow` or `git-flow`.

This development model uses two main long-running graduation branches to separate the production-ready stable state from the work involved with integration of the latest delivered ongoing development. Let's call these branches for example `master` (stable work) and `develop` (gathers changes for the next release). The latter can be used for nightly builds. These two integration branches have an infinite lifetime.

These branches are accompanied in this workflow by supporting branches, namely, feature branches, release branches, and hotfix branches.

Each new feature is developed on a topic branch (such branches are sometimes called feature branch), named after a feature. Such branches are forked off the tip of either the `devel` or `master` branch, depending on the details of the workflow and the requirements of the feature in question. When work on a feature is finished, its topic branch is merged, with the `--no-ff` option (so that there is always a merge commit where a feature can be described), into `devel` for integration testing. When they are ready for the next release, they are merged into the `master` branch. A topic branch exists only as long as a feature is in development, and are deleted when merged (or when abandoned).

The purpose of a release branch is twofold. When created, the goal is to prepare a new production release. This means doing last minute clean-up, applying minor bug fixes, and preparing metadata for a release (for example, version numbers, release names, and so on). All but the last should be done using topic branches; preparing metadata can be done directly on the release branch. This use of the release branch allows us to separate the quality assurance for the upcoming release from the work developing features for the next big release.

Such release branches are forked off when the stable state reflects, or is close to, the desired state planned for the new release. Each such branch is named after a release, usually something such as `release-1.4` or `release-v1.4.x`. One would usually create a few release candidates from this branch (tagging them `v1.4-rc1` and so on) before tagging the final state of the new release (for example, `v1.4`).

The release branch might exist only until the time the project release it was created for is rolled out, or it might be left to gather maintenance work: bug fixes for the given release (though, usually, maintenance is done only for a few latest versions or the most popular versions). In the latter situation, it replaces the `maint` branch of other workflows.

Hotfix branches are like release branches, but for an unplanned release usually connected with fixing serious security bugs. They are usually named `hotfix-1.4.1` or something similar. A hotfix branch is created out of an old release tag if the respective release (maintenance) branch does not exist. The purpose of this type of branches is to resolve critical bugs found in a production version. After putting a fix on such branches, the minor release is cut (for each such branch).

Fixing a security issue

Let's examine another situation now. How can we use branches to manage fixing a bug, for example, a security issue. This requires a slightly different technique than an ordinary development.

As explained in *Topic branches workflow*, while it is possible to create a bugfix commit directly on the most stable of the integration branches that is affected by the bug, it is usually better to create a separate topic branch for the bugfix in question.

You start by creating a bugfix branch forking from the oldest (most stable) integration branch the fix needs to be applied to, perhaps even at the branching point of all the branches it would apply to. You put the fix (perhaps, consisting of multiple commits) on the branch that you have just created. After testing it, you simply merge the bugfix branch into the integration branches that need the fix.

This model can be also used to resolve conflicts (dependencies) between branches at an early stage. Let's assume that you are working on some new feature (on a topic branch), which is not ready yet. While writing it, you have noticed some bugs in the development version and you know how to fix them. You want to work on top of the fixed state, but you realize that other developers would also want the bugfix. Committing the fix on top of the feature branch takes the bugfix hostage. Fixing the bug directly on an integration branch has a risk of forgetting to merge the bugfix into the feature in progress.

The solution is to create a fix on a separate topic branch and to merge it into both the topic branch for the feature being developed, and into the test integration branch (and possibly the graduation branches).

 You can use similar techniques to create and manage some features that are requested by a subset of customers. You need to simply create a separate topic branch for each such feature and merge it into the individual, per customer branches.

The matter complicates a bit if there is security involved. In the case of a severe security bug, you would want to fix it not only in the current version, but also in all the widely used versions.

To do this, you need to create a hotfix branch for various maintenance tracks (forking it from the specified version):

```
$ git checkout -b hotfix-1.9.x v1.9.4
```

Then, you need to merge the topic branch with the fix in question into the just created hotfix branch, to finally create the bugfix release:

```
$ git merge CVE-2014-1234
$ git tag -s -m "Project 1.9.5" v1.9.5
```

Interacting with branches in remote repositories

We see that having many branches in a single repository is very useful. Easy branching and merging allows for powerful development models, which are utilizing advanced branching techniques, such as topic branches. This means that remote repositories will also contain many branches. Therefore, we have to go beyond just the repository to the repository interaction, which was described in *Chapter 5, Collaborative Development with Git*. We have to consider how to interact with multiple branches in the remote repositories.

We also need to think about how many local branches in our repository relate to the branches in the remote repositories (or, in general, other refs). The other important knowledge is how the tags in the local repository relate to the tags in other repositories.

Understanding the interaction between repositories, the branches in these repositories, and how merge changes (in *Chapter 7, Merging Changes Together*) is required to truly master collaboration with Git.

Upstream and downstream

In software development, the **upstream** refers to a direction toward the original authors or the maintainers of the project. We can say that the repository is upstream from us if it is closer (in the repository-to-repository steps) to the blessed repository — the canonical source of the software. If a change (a patch or a commit) is accepted upstream, it will be included either immediately or in a future release of an application, and all the people **downstream** would receive it.

Similarly, we can say that a given branch in a remote repository (the maintainer repository) is an **upstream branch** for given local branch, if changes in that local branch are to be ultimately merged and included in the remote branch.

> A quick reminder: the upstream repository and the upstream branch in the said remote repository for a given branch are defined, respectively, by the branch.<branchname>.remote and branch.<branchname>.merge configuration variables. The upstream branch can be referred to with the @{upstream} or @{u} shortcut.
>
> The upstream is set while creating a branch out of the remote-tracking branch, and it can be modified using either git branch --set-upstream-to or git push --set-upstream.

The upstream branch does not need to be a branch in the remote repository. It can be a local branch, though we usually say then that it is a **tracked branch** rather than saying that it is an upstream one. This feature can be useful when one local branch is based on another local branch, for example, when a topic branch is forked from other topic branch (because it contains the feature that is a prerequisite for the latter work).

Remote-tracking branches and refspec

While collaborating on a project, you would be interacting with many repositories (see the *Collaborative Development With Git* section of this chapter). Each of these remote (public) repositories you are interacting with will have their own notion of the position of the branches. For example, the master branch in the remote repository origin needs not to be at the same place as your own local master branch in your clone of the repository. In other words, they need not point to the same commit in the DAG of revisions.

Remote-tracking branches

To be able to check the integration status, for example, what changes are there in the origin remote repository that are not yet in yours, or what changes did you make in your working repository that you have not yet published, you need to know where the branches in the remote repositories are (well, where they were the last time you contacted these repositories). This is the task of remote-tracking branches— the references that track where the branch was in the remote repository.

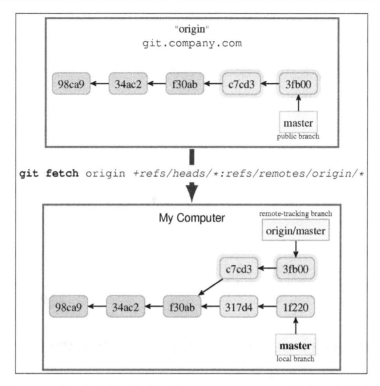

Fig 5: Remote-tracking branches. The branch `master` in remote `origin` is fetched into the
remote-tracking branch `origin/master` (full name `refs/remotes/origin/master`).
Grayed out text in the fetch command denotes the default implicit parameters.

To track what happens in the remote repository, remote-tracking branches are
updated automatically; this means that you cannot create new local commits on
top of them (as you would lose these commits during update). You need to create
the local branch for it. This can be done, for example, with simply `git checkout`
`<branchname>`, assuming that the local branch with the given name does not
already exist. This command creates a new local branch out of the remote branch
`<branchname>` and sets the upstream information for it.

Refspec – remote to local branch mapping specification

As described in *Chapter 2*, *Exploring Project History*, local branches are in the
`refs/heads/` namespace, while remote-tracking branches for a given remote are
in the `refs/remotes/<remote name>/` namespace. But that's just the default. The
`fetch` (and `push`) lines in the `remote.<remote name>` configuration describe the
mapping between branches (or refs in general) in the remote repository and the
remote-tracking branches (or other refs) in the local repository.

This mapping is called **refspec**; it can be either explicit, mapping branches one by one, or globbing, describing a mapping pattern.

For example, the default mapping for the `origin` repository is:

```
[remote "origin"]
    fetch = +refs/heads/*:refs/remotes/origin/*
```

This says that, for example, the contents of the `master` branch (whose full name is `refs/heads/master`) in the remote repository `origin` is to be stored in the local clone of repository in the remote-tracking branch `origin/master` (whose full name is `refs/remotes/origin/master`). The plus + sign at the beginning of the pattern tells Git to accept the updates to the remote-tracking branch that are not fast-forward, that is, are not descendants of the previous value.

The mapping can be given using the fetch lines in the configuration for the remote, as above, or can be also passed as arguments to a command (it is often enough to specify just the short name of the reference instead of the full refspec). The configuration is taken into account only if there are no refspecs on the command line.

Fetching and pulling versus pushing

Sending changes (publishing) to the remote repository is done with `git push`, while getting changes from it is done with `git fetch`. These commands send changes in the opposite direction. You should remember, however, that your local repository has the very important difference—it has you sitting at the keyboard available to run other Git commands.

That is why there is no equivalent in the local-to-remote direction to `git pull`, which combines getting and integrating changes (see the next section). There is simply nobody there to resolve possible conflicts (problems doing automated integration).

In particular, there is a difference between how branches and tags are fetched, and how are they are pushed. This will be explained in detail later on.

Pull – fetch and update current branch

Many times, you want to incorporate changes from a specific branch of a remote repository into the current branch. The pull command downloads changes (running `git fetch` with parameters given); then, it automatically integrates the retrieved branch head into the current branch. By default, it calls `git merge` to integrate changes, but you can make it to run `git rebase` instead The latter can be done either with the `--rebase` option, or the `pull.rebase` configuration option to `git pull`, or with `branch.<branch name>.rebase` to configure this for the individual branch.

Note that if there is no configuration for the remote (you are doing the pull by URL), Git uses the FETCH_HEAD ref to store tips of the fetched branches.

There is also the `git request-pull` command to create information about published or pending changes for the pull-based workflows, for example, for a variant of the blessed repository workflow. It creates a plain text equivalent of the GitHub merge requests, one which is particularly suitable to send by e-mail.

Pushing to the current branch in a nonbare remote repository

Usually, the repositories you push to are created for synchronization and are bare, that is, without a working area. A bare repository doesn't even have the concept of the current branch (HEAD)–there is no work tree, therefore, there is no checked out branch.

Sometimes, however, you might want to push to the nonbare repository. This may happen, for example, as a way of synchronizing two repositories, or as a mechanism for deployment (for example, of a web page or a web application). By default, Git on the server (in the nonbare repository you are pushing into) will deny the ref update to the currently checked out branch. This is because it brings HEAD out of sync with the working tree and the staging area, which is very confusing if you don't expect it. You can, however, enable such a push by setting `receive.denyCurrentBranch` to `warn` or `ignore` (changing it from the default value of `refuse`).

You can even make Git update the working directory (which must be clean, that is, without any uncommitted changes) by setting the said configuration variable to `updateInstead`.

An alternative and a more flexible solution to using `git push` for deployment is to configure appropriate hooks on the receiving side — see *Chapter 10, Customizing and Extending Git,* for information on hooks in general, and *Chapter 11, Git Administration,* for details on their use on the server.

The default fetch refspec and push modes

We usually fetch from public repositories with all the branches made public. We most often want to get a full update of all the branches. That's why `git clone` sets up the default fetch refspec in a way shown in the *Refspec – remote to local branch mapping specification* section of this chapter. The common exception to "fetch all" rule is following a pull request. But in this case, we have the repository and the branch (or the signed tag) stated explicitly in the request, and we will run the pull command with provided parameters: `git pull <URL> <branch>`.

On the other side, in the private working repository, there are usually many branches that we don't want to publish or, at least, we don't want to publish them yet. In most cases, we would want to publish a single branch: the one we were working on and the one we know is ready. However, if you are the integration manager, you would want to publish a carefully selected subset of the branches instead of just one single branch.

This is yet another difference between fetching and pushing. That's why Git doesn't set up push refspec by default (you can configure it manually nonetheless), but instead relies on the so-called *push modes* (configured using `push.default`) to decide what should be pushed where. This configuration variable, of course, applies only while running the `git push` command without branches to push stated explicitly on the command line.

Using git push to sync out of a host that one cannot pull from

When you work on two machines, `machineA` and `machineB`, each with its own work tree, a typical way to synchronize between them is to run `git pull` from each other. However, in certain situations, you may be able to make the connection only in one direction, but not in the other (for example, because of a firewall or intermittent connectivity). Let's assume that you can fetch and push from `machineB`, but you cannot fetch from `machineA`.

You want to perform push from `machineB` to `machineA` in such way, that the result of the operation is practically indistinguishable from doing fetch while being on `machineA`. For this you need to specify, via refspec, that you want to push local branch into its remote-tracking branch.

```
machineB$ git push machineA:repo.git \
    refs/heads/master:refs/remotes/machineB/master
```

The first parameter is the URL in the scp-like syntax, the second parameter is refspec. Note that you can set these all up in the `config` file in case you need to do something like this more often.

Fetching and pushing branches and tags

The next section will describe which push modes are available and when to use them (for which collaboration workflows). But first, we need to know how Git behaves with respect to tags and branches while interacting with remote repositories.

Because, pushing is not the exact opposite of fetching, and because branches and tags have different objectives (branches point to the lines of development and tags name specific revisions), their behavior is subtly different.

Fetching branches

Fetching branches is quite simple. With the default configuration, the `git fetch` command downloads changes and updates remote-tracking branches (if possible). The latter is done according to the fetch refspec for the remote.

There are, of course, exceptions to this rule. One such exception is mirroring the repository. In this case all the refs from the remote repository are stored under the same name in the local repository. The `git clone --mirror` would generate the following configuration for `origin`:

```
[remote "origin"]
  url = https://git.example.com/project
  fetch = +refs/*:refs/*
  mirror = true
```

The names of refs that are fetched, together with the object names they point at, are written to the `.git/FETCH_HEAD` file. This information is used, for example, by `git pull`; this is necessary if we are fetching via URL and not via a remote name. It is done because, when we fetch by the URL, there are simply no remote-tracking branches to store the information on the fetched branch to be integrated.

You can delete remote-tracking branches on case by case basis with `git branch -r -d`; you can remove on case by case basis remote-tracking branches for which the corresponding branch in the remote repository no longer exists with `git remote prune` (or in modern Git with `git fetch --prune`).

Fetching tags and automatic tag following

The situation with tags is a bit different. While we would want to make it possible for different developers to work independently on the same branch (for example, an integration branch such as `master`), though in different repositories, we would need all developers to have one specific tag to always refer to the same specific revision. That's why the position of branches in remote repositories is stored using a separate per-remote namespace `refs/remotes/<remote name>/*` in remote-tracking branches, but tags are mirrored — each tag is stored with the same name, in `refs/tags/*` namespace.

Though where the positions of tags in the remote repository are stored can, of course, be configured with the appropriate fetch refspec; Git is that flexible. One example where it might be necessary is the fetching of a subproject, where we want to store its tags in a separate namespace (more information on this issue in *Chapter 9, Managing Subprojects - Building a Living Framework*).

This is also why, by default, while downloading changes, Git would also fetch and store locally all the tags that point to the downloaded objects. You can disable this automatic tag following with the `--no-tags` option. This option can be set on the command line as a parameter, or it can be configured with the `remote.<remote name>.tagopt` setting.

You can also make Git download all the tags with the `--tags` option, or by adding the appropriate fetch refspec value for tags:

```
fetch = +refs/tags/*:refs/tags/*
```

Pushing branches and tags

Pushing is different. Pushing branches are (usually) governed by the selected push mode. You push a local branch (usually just a single current branch) to update a specific branch in the remote repository, from `refs/heads/` locally to `refs/heads/` in remote. It is usually a branch with the same name, but it might be a differently named branch configured as upstream—details will be provided later. You don't need to specify the full refspec: using the ref name (for example, name of a branch) means pushing to the ref with the same name in the remote repository, creating it if it does not exist. Pushing HEAD means pushing the current branch into the branch with the same name (not to the HEAD in remote—it usually does not exist).

Usually, you push tags explicitly with `git push <remote repository> <tag>` (or `tag <tag>` if by accident there is both a tag and branch with the same name—both mean the `+refs/tags/<tag>:refs/tags/<tag>` refspec). You can push all the tags with `--tags` (and with appropriate refspec), and turn on the automatic tag following with `--follow-tags` (it is not turned on by default as it is for fetch).

As a special case of refspec, pushing an "empty" source into some ref in remote deletes it. The `--delete` option to `git push` is just a shortcut for using this type of refspec. For example, to delete a ref matching `experimental` in the remote repository, you can run:

```
$ git push origin :experimental
```

Note that the remote server might forbid the deletion of refs with `receive.denyDeletes` or hooks.

Push modes and their use

The behavior of `git push`, in the absence of the parameters specifying what to push, and in the absence of the configured push refspec, is specified by the push mode. Different modes are available, each suitable for different collaborative workflows from *Chapter 5, Collaborative Development with Git.*

The simple push mode – the default

The default push mode in Git 2.0 and later is the so-called `simple` mode. It was designed with the idea of *minimum surprise*: the idea that it is better to prevent publishing a branch, than to make some private changes accidentally public.

With this mode, you always push the current local branch into the same named branch in the remote repository. If you push into the same repository you fetch from (the centralized workflow), it requires the upstream to be set for the current branch. The upstream is named the same as the branch.

This means that, in the centralized workflow (push into the same repository you fetch from), it works like `upstream` with the additional safety that the upstream must have the same name as the current (pushed) branch. With triangular workflow, while pushing to a remote that is different from the remote you normally pull from, it works like `current`.

This is the safest option; it is well-suited for beginners, which is why it is the default mode. You can turn it on explicitly with `git config push.default simple`.

The matching push mode for maintainers

Before version 2.0 of Git, the default push mode was `matching`. This mode is most useful for the maintainer (also known as the integration manager) in a blessed repository workflow. But most of the Git users are not maintainers; that's why the default push mode was changed to `simple`.

The maintainer would get contributions from other developers, be it via pull request or patches sent in an e-mail, and put them into topic branches. He or she could also create topic branches for their own contributions. Then, the topic branches considered to be suitable are merged into the appropriate integration branches (for example, `maint`, `master`, and `next`) – merging will be covered in *Chapter 7, Merging Changes Together*. All this is done in the maintainer's private repository.

The public blessed repository (one that everyone fetches from, as described in *Chapter 5, Collaborative Development with Git*) should contain only long-running branches (otherwise, other developers could start basing their work on a branch that suddenly vanishes). Git cannot know by itself which branches are long-lived and which are short-lived.

With the matching mode, Git will push all the local branches that have their equivalent with the same name in the remote repository. This means that only the branches that are already published will be pushed to the remote repository. To make a new branch public you need to push it explicitly the first time, for example:

```
$ git push origin maint-1.4
```

 Note that with this mode, unlike with other modes, using `git push` command without providing list of branches to push can publish multiple branches at once, and may not publish the current branch.

To turn on the matching mode globally, you can run:

```
$ git config push.default matching
```

If you want to turn it on for a specific repository, you need to use a special refspec composed of a sole colon. Assuming that the said repository is named `origin` and that we want a not forced push, it can be done with:

```
$ git config remote.origin push :
```

You can, of course, push matching branches using this refspec on the command line:

```
$ git push origin :
```

The upstream push mode for the centralized workflow

In the centralized workflow, there is the single shared central repository every developer with commit access pushes to. This shared repository will have only long-lived integration branches, usually only `maint` and `master`, and sometimes only `master`.

One should rather never work directly on `master` (perhaps with the exception of simple single-commit topics), but rather fork a topic branch for each separate feature out of the remote-tracking branch:

```
$ git checkout -b feature-foo origin/master
```

In the centralized workflow, the integration is distributed: each developer is responsible for merging changes (in their topic branches), and publishing the result to the master branch in the central repository. You would need to update the local master branch, merge the topic branch to it, and push it:

```
$ git checkout master
$ git pull
$ git merge feature-foo
$ git push origin master
```

An alternate solution is to rebase the topic branch on the top of the remote-tracking branch, rather than merging it. After rebasing, the topic branch should be an ancestor of master in the remote repository, so we can simply push it into master:

```
$ git checkout feature-foo
$ git pull --rebase
$ git push origin feature-foo:master
```

In both the cases, you are pushing the local branch (master in the merge-based workflow, the feature branch in the rebase-based workflow) into the branch it tracks in the remote repository; in this case, origin's master.

That is what the upstream push mode was created for:

```
$ git config push.default upstream
```

This mode makes Git push the current branch to the specific branch in the remote repository — the branch whose changes are usually integrated into the current branch. This branch in the remote repository is the upstream branch (and can be referenced as @{upstream}). Turning this mode on makes it possible to simplify the last command in both examples to the following:

```
$ git push
```

The information about the upstream is created either automatically (while forking off the remote-tracking branch), or explicitly with the --track option. It is stored in the configuration file and it can be edited with ordinary configuration tools. Alternatively, it can be changed later with the following:

```
$ git branch --set-upstream-to=<branchname>
```

The current push mode for the blessed repository workflow

In the blessed repository workflow, each developer has his or her own private and public repository. In this model, one fetches from the blessed repository and pushes to his or her own public repository.

In this workflow, you start working on a feature by creating a new topic branch for it:

```
$ git checkout -b fix-tty-bug origin/master
```

When the features are ready, you push it into your public repository, perhaps rebasing it first to make it easier for the maintainer to merge it:

```
$ git push origin fix-tty-bug
```

Here, it is assumed that you used `pushurl` to configure the triangular workflow, and the push remote is `origin`. You would need to replace `origin` here with the appropriate name of the publishing remote if you are using a separate remote for your own public repository (using a separate repository makes it possible to use it not only for publishing, but also for synchronization between different machines).

To configure Git so when on `fix-tty-bug` branch it is enough to just run `git push`, you need to set up Git to use the `current` push mode, which can be done with the following:

```
$ git config push.default current
```

This mode will push the current branch to the branch with the same name at the receiving end.

Note that, if you are using a separate remote for the publishing repository, you would need to set up the `remote.pushDefault` configuration option to be able to use just `git push` for publishing.

Summary

This chapter has shown how to effectively use branches for development and for collaboration.

We got to know a wide set of the various uses of branches, from integration, through release management and the parallel development of features, to fixing bugs. You have learned different branching workflows, including the very useful and widely used topic branch workflow. The knowledge should help you make the best use of branching, customizing the model of work to fit the project and your own preferences.

You have also learned how to deal with multiple branches per repository while downloading or publishing changes. Git provides flexibility in how the information on branches and other refs in the remote repository are managed using the so-called refspecs to define mapping to local refs: remote-tracking branches, local branches, and tags. Usually, fetching is governed by fetch refspec, but pushing is managed by the configured push mode. Various collaborative workflows require a different handling of branch publishing; this chapter describes which push mode to use with which workflow and explains why.

You also got to know a few useful tricks. One of them is how to store the project's web page or the generated HTML documentation in a single repository with the "orphan" branch trick (which is used, for example, by GitHub Project Pages). You found out how to synchronize the working directory of the remote repository (for example, for the deployment of a web application) with `git push`; one of the possible solutions. You have learned how to do fetch equivalent with push, if the connection is possible only in the opposite direction.

The next chapter, *Chapter 7, Merging Changes Together*, will explain how to integrate changes from other branches and other developers. You will learn about merging and rebasing, and how to deal with situations where Git could not do it automatically (how to handle various types of merge conflicts). You will also learn about cherry-picking and reverting commits.

Merging Changes Together

The previous chapter, *Advanced Branching Techniques*, described how to use branches effectively for collaboration and development.

This chapter will teach you how to integrate changes from different parallel lines of development (that is, branches) together by creating a merge commit, or by reapplying changes with the rebase operation. Here, the concepts of merge and rebase are explained, including the differences between them and how they both can be used. This chapter will also explain the different types of merge conflicts, and teach how to examine them, and how to resolve them.

In this chapter, we will cover the following topics:

- Merging, merge strategies, and merge drivers
- Cherry-picking and reverting a commit
- Applying a patch and a patch series
- Rebasing a branch and replaying its commits
- Merge algorithm on file and contents level
- Three stages in the index
- Merge conflicts, how to examine them, and how to resolve them
- Reusing recorded [conflict] resolutions with `git rerere`
- External tool: `git-imerge`

Methods of combining changes

Now that you have changes from other people in the remote-tracking branches (or in the series of e-mails), you need to combine them, perhaps also with your changes. Or perhaps, your work on a new feature, created and performed on a separate topic branch, is now ready to be included in the long-lived development branch, and made available to other people. Maybe you have created a bugfix and want to include it in all the long-lived graduation branches. In short, you want to join two divergent lines of development, to combine them together.

Git provides a few different methods of combining changes and variations of these methods. One of these methods is a *merge* operation, joining two lines of development with a two-parent commit. Another way to copy introduced work from one branch to another is via cherry-picking, which is creating a new commit with the same changeset on another line of development (this is sometimes necessary to use). Or, you can reapply changes, transplanting one branch on top of another with *rebase*. We will now examine all these methods and their variants, see how they work, and when they can be used.

In many cases, Git will be able to combine changes automatically; the next section will talk about what you can do if it fails and if there are merge conflicts.

Merging branches

The merge operation joins two (or more) separate branches together, including *all* the changes since the point of divergence into the current branch. You do this with the `git merge` command:

```
$ git checkout master
$ git merge bugfix123
```

Here, we first switched to a branch we want to merge into (`master` in this example), and then provided the branch to be merged (here, `bugfix123`).

No divergence – fast-forward and up-to-date cases

Say that you need to create a fix for a bug somebody found. Let's assume that you have followed the recommendations of the topic branch workflow from *Chapter 6, Advanced Branching Techniques*, and created a separate bugfix branch, named `bugfix123`, off the maintenance branch `maint`. You have run your tests (that were perhaps just created), making sure that the fix is correct and is what you want. Now you are ready to merge it, at least, into `maint` to make this fix available for other people, and perhaps, also into `master` (into the stable branch). The latter can be configured to deploy the fix to production environment.

In such cases, there is often no real divergence, which means that there were no commits on the maintenance branch (the branch we are merging into), since a bugfix branch was created. Because of this, Git would, by default, simply move the branch pointer of the current branch forward:

```
$ git checkout maint
$ git merge i18n
Updating f41c546..3a0b90c
Fast-forward
 src/random.c | 2 ++
 1 file changed, 2 insertions(+)
```

You have probably seen this Fast-forward phrase among output messages during git pull, when there are no changes on the branch you are pulling into. The fast-forward merge situation is shown on Fig. 1:

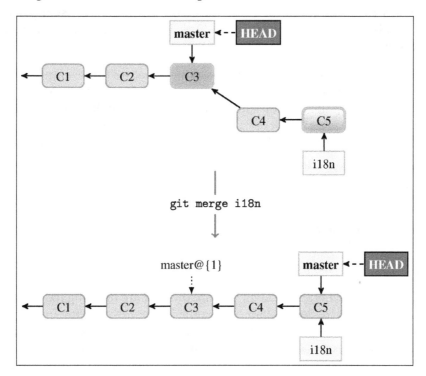

Fig 1: The master branch is fast-forwarded to i18n during merge

This case is important for the centralized and the peer-to-peer workflows (described in *Chapter 5, Collaborative Development with Git*), as it is the fast-forward merge that allows you to ultimately push your changes forward.

In some cases, it is not what you want. See that, for example, after the fast-forward merge in *Fig 1*, we have lost the information that the **C4** and **C5** commits were done on the i18n topic branch, and are a part of internationalization efforts. We can force creating a merge commit (described in the next section) even in such cases with the git merge --no-ff command. The default is --ff; to fail instead of creating a merge commit you can use --ff-only (ensuring fast-forward only).

There is another situation where the head (tip) of one branch is the ancestor of the other, namely, the up-to-date case where the branch we are trying to merge is already included (merged) in the current branch. Git doesn't need to do anything in this case; it just informs the user about it.

Creating a merge commit

When you are merging fully fledged feature branches, rather than merging bugfix branches as in the previous section, the situation is usually different from the previously described Fast-forward case. Then, the development usually had diverged. You began work on a feature of a topic branch to separate and isolate it from other developments.

Suppose that you have decided that your work on a feature (for example, work on adding support for internationalization on the i18n topic branch) is complete and ready to be included in the master stable branch. In order to do so with a merge operation, you need to first check out the branch you want to merge into, and then run the git merge command with the branch being merged as a parameter:

```
$ git checkout master
Switched to branch 'master'
$ git merge i18n
Merge made by the 'recursive' strategy.
Src/random.c |    2 ++
1 file changed, 2 insertions(+)
```

Because the top commit on the branch you are on (and are merging into) is not a direct ancestor or a direct descendant of the branch you are merging in, Git has to do more work than just moving the branch pointer. In this case, Git does a merge of changes since the divergence, and stores it as a merge commit on the current branch. This commit has two parents denoting that it was created based on more than one commit (more than one branch): the first parent is the previous tip of the current branch and the second parent is the tip of branch you are merging in.

Note that Git does commit the result of merge if it can be done automatically (there are no conflicts). But the fact that the merge succeeded at the text level doesn't necessarily mean that the merge result is correct. You can either ask Git to not autocommit a merge with `git merge --no-commit` to examine it first, or you can examine the merge commit and then use the `git commit --amend` command if it is incorrect.

In contrast, most other version control systems do not automatically commit the result of a merge.

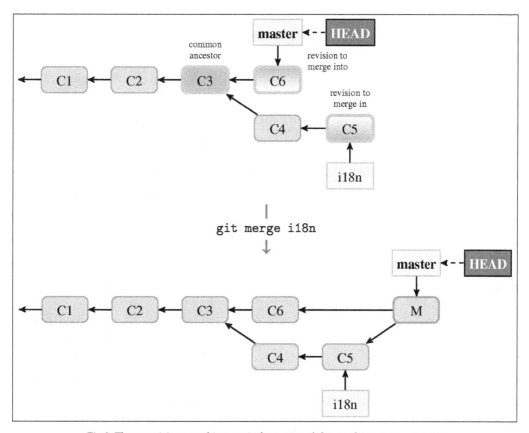

Fig 2: Three revisions used in a typical merge and the resulting merge commit

Git creates contents of a merge commit (**M** in Fig 2) using by default (and in most cases) the three way merge, which in turn uses the snapshots pointed to the tips of the branches being merged (`master`: **C6** and `i18n`: **C5**) and the common ancestor of the two (**C3** here, which you can find with the `git merge-base` command).

It's worth pointing out that Git can determine the common ancestor automatically thanks to storing revisions in the DAG and remembering merges. This was not the case in the older revision control systems.

A very important issue is that Git creates the merge commit contents based usually only on the three revisions: merged into (ours), merged in (theirs), and the common ancestor (merge base). It does not examine what had happened on the divergent parts of the branches; this is what makes merging fast. But because of this, Git also does not know about the cherry-picked or reverted changes on the branches being merged, which might lead to surprising results (see, for example, the section about reverting merges in *Chapter 8, Keeping History Clean*).

Merge strategies and their options

In the merge message, we have seen that it was made by the *recursive* strategy. The *merge* strategy is an algorithm that Git uses to compose the result of joining two or more lines of development, which is basing this result on the DAG of revisions.

There are a few merge strategies that you can select to use with the `--strategy/ -s` option. By default, Git uses the recursive merge strategy while joining two branches and a very simple *octopus* merge strategy while joining more than two branches. You can also choose the *resolve* merge strategy if the default one fails; it is fast and safe, though less capable in merging.

The two remaining merge strategies are special purpose algorithms. The *ours* merge strategy can be used when we want to abandon changes in the merged in branch, but keep them in the history of the merged into branch, for example, for documentation purposes. This strategy simply repeats the current snapshot (ours version) as a merge commit. Note that ours merge strategy, invoked with `--strategy=ours` or `-s ours`, should be not confused with the "ours" option to the default recursive merge strategy, `--strategy=recursive --strategy-option=ours` or just `-Xours`, which means something different.

The *subtree* merge strategy can be used for subsequent merges from an independent project into a subdirectory (subtree) in a main project. It automatically figures out where the subproject was put. This issue, and the idea of subtrees, will be described in more detail in *Chapter 9, Managing Subprojects – Building a Living Framework*.

The default *recursive* merge strategy is named after how it deals with multiple merge bases and criss-cross merges. In case of more than one merge base (more than one common ancestor that can be used for a three-way merge), it creates a merge tree (conflicts and all) from the ancestors as a merge base, that is, it merges recursively. Of course, these common ancestors being merged can have more than one merge base again.

Some strategies are customizable and take their own options. You can pass an option to a merge algorithm with `-X<option>` (or `--strategy-option=<option>`) on the command line, or set it with the appropriate configuration variables. You will find more about merge options in a later section, when we will be talking about solving merge conflicts.

Reminder – merge drivers

Chapter 4, Managing Your Worktree, introduced `gitattributes`, among others merge drivers. These *drivers* are user-defined and deal with merging file contents if there is a conflict, replacing the default three-way file-level merge. Merge strategies in contrast deal with the DAG level merging (and tree-level, that is, merging directories) and you can only choose from the built-in options.

Reminder – signing merges and merging tags

In *Chapter 5, Collaborative Development with Git*, you have learned about signing your work. While using merge to join two lines of development, you can either merge a signed tag or sign a merge commit (or both). Signing a merge commit is done with the `-S` / `--gpg-sign` option to use the `git merge` or the `git commit` command; the latter is used if there were conflicts or the `--no-commit` option was used while merging.

Copying and applying a changeset

The merging operation is about joining two lines of development (two branches), including all the changes since their divergence. This means, as described in *Chapter 6, Advanced Branching Techniques*, that if there is one commit on the less stable branch (for example, `master`) that you want to have also in a more stable branch (for example, `maint`), you cannot use the merge operation. You need to create a copy of such commit. Entering such situation should be avoided (using topic branches), but it can happen, and handling it is sometimes necessary.

Sometimes, the changes to be applied come not from the repository (as a revision in the DAG to be copied), but in the form of a patch, that is, a unified diff or an e-mail generated with `git format-patch` (with patch, plus a commit message). Git includes the `git am` tool to handle mass applying of commit-containing patches.

Both of these are useful on their own, but understanding these methods of getting changes is necessary to understand how rebasing works.

Cherry-pick – creating a copy of a changeset

You can create a copy of a commit (or a series of commits) with the `cherry-pick` command. Given a series of commits (usually, just a single commit), it applies the changes each one introduces, recording a new commit for each.

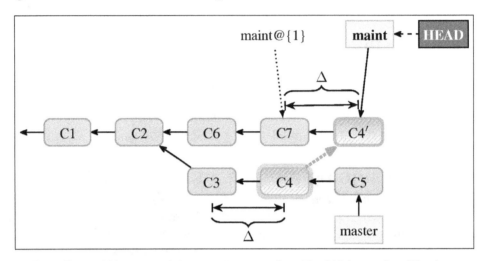

Fig 3: Cherry-picking a commit from `master` to `maint`. The thick brown dotted line from C4 to C4' denotes copy; it is not a reference.

This does not mean that the snapshot (that is, the state of a project) is the same in the original and in the copy; the latter will include other changes. Also, while the changes will usually be the same (as in *Fig 3*), they can also in some cases be different, for example if part of the changes was already present in the earlier commits.

Note that, by default, Git does not save information about where the cherry-picked commit came from. You can append this information to an original commit message, as a (`cherry-picked from the commit <sha-1>`) line with `git cherry-pick -x <commit>`. This is only done for cherry-picks without conflicts. Remember that this information is only useful if you have an access to the copied commit. Do not use it if you are copying commits from the private branch, as other developers won't be able to make use of that information.

Revert – undoing an effect of a commit

Sometimes it turns out that, even with code review, there will be some bad commits that you need to back out (perhaps it turned out to be a not so good idea, or it contains bugs). If the commit is already made public, you cannot simply remove it. You need to undo its effects; this issue will be explained in detail in *Chapter 8, Keeping History Clean*.

This "undoing of a commit" can be done by creating a commit with a reversal of changes, something like cherry-pick but applying the reverse of changes. This is done with the `revert` command.

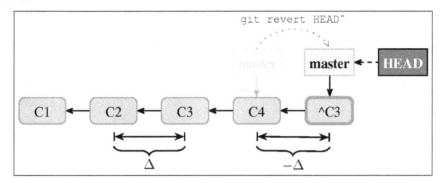

Fig 4: The effect of using `git revert` C3 on a `master` branch, creating a new commit named `^C3`

The name of this operation might be misleading. If you want to revert all the changes made to the whole working area, you can use `git reset` (in particular, the `--hard` option). If you want to revert changes made to a single file, use `git checkout` `<file>`. Both of these are explained in detail in *Chapter 4, Managing Your Worktree*. The `git revert` command records a new commit to reverse the effect of the earlier commit (often, a faulty one).

Applying a series of commits from patches

Some collaborative workflows include exchanging the changes as patches via an e-mail (or another communication medium). This workflow is often encountered in open-source projects; it is often easier for a new or a sporadic contributor to create a specially crafted e-mail (for example, with `git format-patch`) and send it to a maintainer or a mailing list, than to set up a public repository and send a pull request.

You can apply a series of patches from a mailbox (in the mbox or maildir format; the latter is just a series of files) with the `git am` command. If these emails (or files) were created from the `git format-patch` output, you can use `git am --3way` to use the three-way file merge in the case of conflicts. Resolving conflicts will be discussed in later section of this chapter.

You can find both tools to help use the patch submission process by sending a series of patches, for example from the `pull` request on GitHub (for example, the `submitGit` web app for Git project), and tools that track web page patches sent to a mailing list (for example, the `patchwork` tool).

Cherry-picking and reverting a merge

This is all good, but what happens if you want to cherry-pick or revert a merge commit? Such commits have more than one parent, thus they have more than one change associated with them.

In this case, you have to tell Git which change you want to pick up (in the case of cherry-pick), or back out (in the case of revert) with the -m <parent number> option.

Note that reverting a merge undoes the changes, but it does not remove the merge from the history of the project. See the section on reverting merges in *Chapter 8, Keeping History Clean*.

Rebasing a branch

Besides merging, Git supports additional way to integrate changes from one branch into another: namely the rebase operation.

Like a merge, it deals with the changes since the point of divergence (at least, by default). But while a merge creates a new commit by joining two branches, rebase takes the new commits from one branch (takes the commits since the divergence) and reapplies them on top of the other branch.

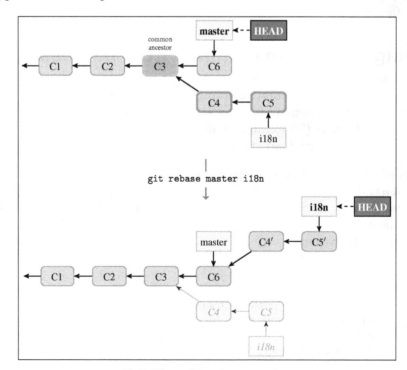

Fig 5: Effects of the rebase operation

With merge, you first switched to the branch to be merged and then used the merge command to select a branch to merge in. With rebase, it is a bit different. First you select a branch to rebase (changes to reapply) and then use the `rebase` command to select where to put it. In both the cases, you first check out the branch to be modified, where a new commit or commits would be (a merge commit in the case of merging, and a replay of commits in the case of rebasing):

```
$ git checkout i18n
$ git rebase master
First, rewinding head to replay your work on top of it...
Applying: Mark messages for translation
```

Or, you can use `git rebase master i18n` as a shortcut. In this form, you can easily see that the rebase operation takes the `master..i18n` range of revisions (this notation is explained in *Chapter 2*, *Exploring Project History*), replays it on top of `master`, and finally points `i18n` to the replayed commits.

Note that old versions of commits doesn't vanish, at least not immediately. They would be accessible via reflog (and `ORIG_HEAD`) for a grace period. This means that it is not that hard to check how replaying changed the snapshots of a project, and with a bit more effort how changesets themselves have changed.

Merge versus rebase

We have these two ways of integrating changes: merge and rebase. How do they differ and what are their advantages and disadvantages? You can compare *Fig 2* in the *Creating a merge commit* section with *Fig 5* in the *Rebasing a branch* section.

First, merge doesn't change history (see *Chapter 8*, *Keeping History Clean*). It creates and adds a new commit (unless it was a fast-forward merge; then it just advances the branch head), but the commits that were reachable from the branch remain reachable. This is not the case with rebase. Commits get rewritten, old versions are forgotten, and the DAG of revisions changes. What was once reachable might no longer be reachable. This means that you should not rebase published branches.

Secondly, merge is a one-step operation with one place to resolve merge conflicts. The rebase operation is multi-step; the steps are smaller (to keep changes small, see *Chapter 12*, *Git Best Practices*), but there are more of them.

Linked to this is a fact that the merge result is based (usually) on three commits only, and that it does not take into the account what happened on either of the branches being integrated step by step; only the endpoints matter. On the other hand, rebase reapplies each commit individually, so the road to the final result matters here.

Thirdly, the history looks different: you get a simple linear history with rebase, while using the merge operation leads to complex history with the lines of development forking and joining. The history is simpler for rebase, but you lose information that the changes were developed on a separate branch and that they were grouped together, which you get with merge (at least with `--no-ff`). There is even the `git-resurrect` script in the Git `contrib` tools, that uses the information stored in the commit messages of the merge commits to resurrect the old, long deleted feature branches.

The last difference is that, because of the underlying mechanism, rebase does not, by default, preserve merge commits while reapplying them. You need to explicitly use the `--preserve-merges` option. The merge operation does not change the history, so merge commits are left as it is.

Types of rebase

The previous section described two mechanisms to copy or apply changes: the `git cherry-pick` command, and the pipeline from `git format-patch` to `git am --3way`. Either of them can be used by `git rebase` to reapply commits.

The default is to use the patch-based workflow, as it is faster. With this type of rebase, you can use some additional options with rebase, which are actually passed down to the `git apply` command that does the actual replaying of changesets. These options will be described later while talking about conflicts.

Alternatively, you can use the `--merge` option to utilize merge strategies to do the rebase (kind of cherry-picking each commit). The default recursive merge strategy allows rebase to be aware of the renames on the upstream side (where we put the replayed commits). With this option, you can also select a specific merge strategy and pass options to it.

There is also an interactive rebase with its own set of options. This is one of the main tools in *Chapter 8, Keeping History Clean*. It can be used to execute tests after each replayed commit to check that the replay is correct.

Advanced rebasing techniques

You can also have your rebase operation replay on something other than the target branch of the rebase with `--onto <newbase>`, separating selected range of revisions to replay from the new base to replay onto.

Let's assume that you had based your `featureA` topic branch on the unstable development branch named `next`, because it is dependent on some feature that was not yet ready and not yet present in the stable branch (`master`). If the functionality on which `featureA` depends was deemed stable and was merged into `master`, you would want to move this branch from being forked from the `next` to being forked from `master`. Or perhaps, you started the `server` branch from the related `client` branch, but you want to make it more obvious that they are independent.

You can do this with `git rebase --onto master next featureA` in the first case, and `git rebase --onto master server client` in the second one.

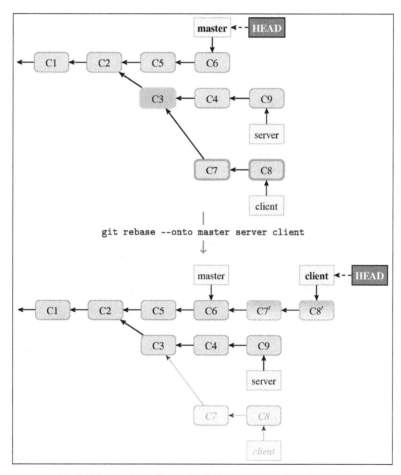

Fig 6: Rebasing branch, moving it from one branch to the other

Or perhaps, you want to rebase only a part of the branch. You can do this with `git rebase --interactive`, but you can also use `git rebase --onto <new base> <starting point> <branch>`.

You can even choose to rebase the whole branch (usually, an orphan branch) with the --root option. In this case, you would replay the whole branch and not just a selected subset of it.

Resolving merge conflicts

Merging in Git is typically fairly easy. Since Git stores and has access to the full graph of revisions, it can automatically find where the branches diverged, and merge only those divergent parts. This works even in the case of repeated merges, so you can keep a very long-lived branch up to date by repeatedly merging into it or by rebasing it on top of new changes.

However, it is not always possible to automatically combine changes. There are problems that Git cannot solve, for example because there were different changes to the same area of a file on different branches: these problems are called **merge conflicts**. Similarly, there can be problems while reapplying changes, though you would still get merge conflicts in case of problems.

The three-way merge

Unlike some other version control systems, Git does not try to be overly clever about merge conflict resolutions, and does not try to solve them all automatically. Git's philosophy is to be smart about determining the cases when a merge can be easily done automatically (for example, taking renames into account), and if automatic resolution is not possible, to not be overly clever about trying to resolve it. It is better to bail out and ask users to resolve merge, perhaps unnecessary with a smart algorithm, than to automatically create an incorrect one.

Git uses the three-way merge algorithm to come up with the result of the merge, comparing the common ancestors (*base*), side merged in (*theirs*), and side merged into (*ours*). This algorithm is very simple, at least at the tree level, that is, the granularity level of files. The following table explains the rules of the algorithm:

ancestor (base)	HEAD (ours)	branch (theirs)	result
A	A	A	A
A	A	B	B
A	B	A	B
A	B	B	B
A	B	C	merge

The rules for the trivial tree-level three-way merges are (see the preceding table):

- If only one side changes a file, take the changed version
- If both the sides have the same changes, take the changed version
- If one side has a different change from the other, there is **merge conflict** at the contents level

It is a bit more complicated if there are more than one ancestor or if a file is not present in all the versions. But usually it is enough to know and understand these rules.

If one side changed the file differently from the other (where the type of the change counts, for example, renaming a file on one branch doesn't conflict with the changing contents of the file on the other branch), Git tries to merge the files at the contents level, using the provided merge driver if it is defined, and the contents level three-way merge otherwise (for text files).

The three-way file merge examines whether the changes touch different parts of the file (different lines are changed, and these changes are well separated by more than diff context sizes away from each other). If these changes are present in different parts of the file, Git resolves the merge automatically (and tells us which files are automerged).

However, if you changed the same part of the same file differently in the two branches you're merging together, Git won't be able to merge them cleanly:

```
$ git merge i18n
Auto-merging src/rand.c
CONFLICT (content): Merge conflict in src/rand.c
Automatic merge failed; fix conflicts and then commit the result.
```

Examining failed merges

In the case Git is unable to automatically resolve a merge (or if you have passed the `--no-commit` option to the `git merge` command), it would not create a merge commit. It will pause the process, waiting for you to resolve the conflict.

You can then always abort the process of merging with `git merge --abort`, in modern Git. With the older version, you would need to use `git reset` and delete `.git/MERGE_HEAD`.

Conflict markers in the worktree

If you want to see which files are yet unmerged at any point after a merge conflict, you can run git status:

```
$ git status
On branch master
You have unmerged paths.
  (fix conflicts and run "git commit")


Unmerged paths:
  (use "git add <file>..." to mark resolution)


    both modified:      src/rand.c


no changes added to commit (use "git add" and/or "git commit -a")
```

Anything that has not been resolved is listed as unmerged. In the case of content conflicts, Git uses standard conflict markers, putting them around the place of conflict with the *ours* and *theirs* version of the conflicted area in question. Your file will contain a section that would look somewhat like the following:

```
<<<<<<< HEAD:src/rand.c
fprintf(stderr, "Usage: %s <number> [<count>]\n", argv[0]);
=======
fprintf(stderr, _("Usage: %s <number> [<count>\n"), argv[0]);
>>>>>>> i18n:src/rand.c
```

This means that the ours version on the current branch (HEAD) in the src/rand.c file is there at the top of this block between the <<<<<<< and ======= markers, while the theirs version on the i18n branch being merged (also from src/rand.c) is there at the bottom part between the ======= and >>>>>>> markers.

You need to replace this whole block by the resolution of the merge, either by choosing one side (and deleting the rest) or combining both changes, for example:

```
fprintf(stderr, _("Usage: %s <number> [<count>]\n"), argv[0]);
```

To help you avoid committing unresolved changes by mistake, Git by default checks whether committed changes include something that looks like conflict markers, refusing to create a merge commit without --no-verify if it finds them.

If you need to examine a common ancestor version to be able to resolve a conflict, you can switch to `diff3` like conflict markers, which have an additional block:

```
<<<<<<< HEAD:src/rand.c
fprintf(stderr, "Usage: %s <number> [<count>]\n", argv[0]);
|||||||
fprintf(stderr, "Usage: %s <number> [<count>\n", argv[0]);
=======
fprintf(stderr, _("Usage: %s <number> [<count>\n"), argv[0]);
>>>>>>> i18n:src/rand.c
```

You can replace merge conflict markers individually on a file-per-file basis by rechecking the file again with the following command:

```
$ git checkout --conflict=diff3 src/rand.c
```

If you prefer to use this format all the time, you can set it as the default for future merge conflicts, by setting `merge.conflictStyle` to `diff3` (from the default of `merge`).

Three stages in the index

But how does Git keep track of which files are merged and which are not? Conflict markers in the working directory files would not be enough. Sometimes, there are legitimate contents that look like commit markers (for example, test files for merge, or files in the AsciiDoc format), and there are more conflict types than `CONFLICT(content)`. How does Git, for example, represent the case where both sides renamed the file but in a different way, or where one side changed the file and the other side removed it?

It turns out that it is another use for the staging area of the commit (a merge commit in this case), which is also known as the index. In the case of conflicts, Git stores all of conflicted files versions in the index under `stages`; each stage has a number associated with it. Stage 1 is the common ancestor (`base`), stage 2 is the merged into version from `HEAD`, that is, the current branch (`ours`), and stage 3 is from `MERGE_HEAD`, the version you're merging in (`theirs`).

You can see these stages for the unmerged files with the low level (plumbing) command `git ls-files --unmerged` (or for all the files with `git ls-files --stage`):

```
$ git ls-files --unmerged
100755 ac51efdc3df4f4fd318d1a02ad05331d8e2c9111 1  src/rand.c
100755 36c06c8752c78d2aaf89571132f3bf7841a7b5c3 2  src/rand.c
100755 e85207e04dfdd50b0a1e9febbc67fd837c44a1cd 3  src/rand.c
```

You can refer to each version with the `:<stage number>:<pathname>` specifier. For example, if you want to view a common ancestor version of `src/rand.c`, you can use the following:

```
$ git show :1:src/rand.c
```

If there is no conflict, the file is in stage 0 of the index.

Examining differences – the combined diff format

You can use the `status` command to find which files are unmerged, and conflict markers do a good job of showing conflicts. How to see only conflicts before we work on them, and how to see how they were resolved? The answer is `git diff`.

One thing to remember is that for merges, even the merges in progress, Git will show the so-called **combined diff** format. It will look as follows (for a conflicted file during a merge):

```
$ git diff
diff --cc src/rand.c
index 293c8fc,4b87d29..0000000
--- a/src/rand.c
+++ b/src/rand.c
@@@ -14,16 -14,13 +14,26 @@@ int main(int argc, char *argv[]
       return EXIT_FAILURE;
    }


++<<<<<<< HEAD
 +  int max = atoi(argv[1]);
 +  if (max > RAND_MAX) {
 +    fprintf(stderr, "Cannot handle <number> larger than %d (%d)\n",
 +            RAND_MAX, max);
 +    return EXIT_FAILURE;
 +  } else if (max < 2) {
 +    fprintf(stderr, "<number> cannot be smaller than %d (%d)\n",
 +            2, max);
 +    return EXIT_FAILURE;
 +  }
```

```
++=======
+    char *endptr = NULL;
+    long int val = strtol(argv[1], &endptr, 10);
+    if (*endptr) {
+        fprintf(stderr, "Invalid argument(s)\n");
+        return EXIT_FAILURE;
+    }
+    int max = (int) val;
++>>>>>>> 8c4ceca59d7402fb24a672c624b7ad816cf04e08

     srand(time(NULL));
     int result = random_int(max)
```

You can see a few differences from the ordinary unified `diff` format described in *Chapter 3, Developing with Git*. First, it uses `diff --cc` in the header to denote that it uses the compact combined format (it uses `diff --combined` instead if you used the `git diff -c` command). The extended header lines, such as `index 293c8fc,4b87d29..0000000`, take into account that there is more than one source version. The chunk header, `@@@ -14,16 -14,13 +14,26 @@@`, is modified (different from the one for the ordinary patch) to prevent people from trying to apply a combined diff as unified diff, for example, with the `patch -p1` command.

Each line of the `diff` command is prefixed by two or more characters (two in the most common cases of merging two branches): the first character tells about the state of the line in the first preimage (*ours*) as compared to the result, the second character tells about the other preimage (*theirs*), and so on. For example, `++` means that the line was not present in either of versions being merged (here, in this example, you can find it on the line with the conflict marker).

Examining differences is even more useful for checking the resolution of a merge conflict.

To compare the result (current state of the working directory) with the version from the current branch (merged into), that is, *ours* version, you can use `git diff --ours`; similarly, for the version being merged (*theirs*), and the common ancestor version (*base*).

How do we get there: git log --merge

Sometimes, we need more context to decide which version to choose or to otherwise resolve a conflict. One such technique is reviewing a little bit of history, to remember why the two lines of development being merged were touching the same area of code.

To get the full list of divergent commits that were included in either branch, we can use the triple-dot syntax that you learned in *Chapter 2, Exploring Project History*, adding the `--left-right` option to make Git show which side the given commit belongs to:

```
$ git log --oneline --left-right HEAD...MERGE_HEAD
```

We can further simplify this and limit the output to only those commits that touched at least one of the conflicted files, with a `--merge` option to `git log`, for example:

```
$ git log --oneline --left-right --merge
```

This can be really helpful in quickly giving you the context you need to help understand why something conflicts and how to more intelligently resolve it.

Avoiding merge conflicts

While Git prefers to fail to automerge in a clear way, rather than to try elaborate merge algorithms, there are a few tools and options that one can use to help Git avoid merge conflicts.

Useful merge options

One of the problems while merging branches might be that they use different end of line normalization or clean/smudge filters (see *Chapter 4, Managing Your Worktree*). This might happen when one branch added such configuration (changing gitattributes file), while the other did not. In the case of end of line character configuration changes, you would get a lot of spurious changes, where lines differ only in the EOL characters. In both cases, while resolving a three-way merge, you can make Git run a virtual check out and check in of all the three stages of a file. This is done by passing the `renormalize` option to the recursive merge strategy (`git merge -Xrenormalize`). This would, as the name suggests, normalize end of line characters, and make them the same for all stages.

Changing end of line can lead to what can be considered a part of *whitespace-related conflicts*. It's pretty easy to tell that it is the case while looking at the conflict, because every line is removed on one side and added again on the other, and `git diff --ignore-whitespace` shows a more manageable conflict (or even a conflict that is resolved). If you see that you have a lot of whitespace issues in a merge, you can abort and redo it, but this time, with `-Xignore-all-space` or `-Xignore-space-change`. Note that whitespace changes mixed with other changes to a line are not ignored.

Sometimes, mismerges occur due to unimportant matching lines (for example, braces from distinct functions). You can make Git spend more time minimizing differences by selecting *patience diff algorithm* with `-Xpatience` or `-Xdiff-algorithm=patience`.

If the problem is misdetected renames, you can adjust the rename threshold with `-Xrename-threshold=<n>`.

Rerere – reuse recorded resolutions

The **rerere** (reuse recorded resolutions) functionality is a bit of a hidden feature. As the name of the feature implies, it makes Git remember how each conflict was resolved chunk by chunk, so that the next time Git sees the same conflict it would be able to resolve it automatically. Note, however, that Git will stop at resolving conflicts and that it does not autocommit the said rerere-based resolution, even if it resolves it cleanly (if it is superficially correct).

Such a functionality is useful in many scenarios. One example is the situation when you want a long-lived (long development) branch to merge cleanly at the end, but you do not want to create intermediate merge commits. In this situation, you can do trial merges (merge, then delete merge), saving information about how merge conflicts were resolved to the `rerere` cache. With this technique, the final merge should be easy, because most of it would be cleanly resolved from the resolutions recorded earlier.

Another situation you can make use of the `rerere` cache, is when you merge a bunch of topic branches into a testable permanent branch. If the integration test for a branch fails, you would want to be able to rewind the failed branch, but you would rather not lose the work spent on resolving a merge.

Or perhaps, you have decided that you rather use rebase than merge. The rerere mechanism allows us to translate the merge resolution to the rebase resolution.

To enable this functionality, simply set `rerere.enabled` to true, or create the `.git/rr-cache` file.

Dealing with merge conflicts

Let's assume that Git was not able to automerge cleanly, and that there are merge conflicts that you need to resolve to be able to create a new merge commit. What are your options?

Aborting a merge

First, let's cover how to get out of this situation. If you weren't perhaps prepared for conflicts or if you do not know enough about how to resolve them, you can simply back out from the merge you started with `git merge --abort`.

This command tries to reset to the state before you started a merge. It might be not able to do this if you have not started from a clean state. Therefore it is better to stash away changes, if there are any, before performing a merge operation.

Selecting ours or theirs version

Sometimes, it is enough to choose one version in the case of conflicts. If you want to have all the conflicts resolved this way, forcing all the chunks to resolve in favor of the *ours* or *theirs* version, you can use the `-Xours` (or `-Xtheirs`) option or the recursive merge strategy. Note that `-Xours` (merge option) is different from `-s ours` (merge strategy); the latter creates a fake merge, where the merge contents are the same as the *ours* version, instead of taking ours version only for conflicted files.

If you want to do this only for selected files, you can recheckout the file with the ours or theirs version with `git checkout --ours / --theirs`.

You can examine the base, ours, or theirs version with `git show :1:file`, `:2:file`, `:3:file`, respectively.

Scriptable fixes – manual file remerging

There are types of changes that Git can't handle automatically, but they are scriptable fixes. The merge can be done automatically, or at least is much easier, if we could transform the "ours", "theirs" and "base" version first. Renormalization after changing how the file is checked out and stored in the repository (eol and clean/smudge filters) and handling the whitespace change are built-in options. Another non built-in example could be changing the encoding of a file, or other scriptable set of changes such as renaming variables.

To perform a scripted merge, first you need to extract a copy of each of these versions of the conflicted file, which can be done, with the `git show` command and a `:<stage>:<file>` syntax:

```
$ git show :1:src/rand.c >src/rand.common.c
$ git show :2:src/rand.c >src/rand.ours.c
$ git show :3:src/rand.c >src/rand.theirs.c
```

Now that you have in the working area the contents of all the three stages of the files, you can fix each version individually, for example with `dos2unix` or with `iconv`, and so on. You can then remerge the contents of the file with the following:

```
$ git merge-file -p \
      rand.ours.c rand.common.c rand.theirs.c >rand.c
```

Using graphical merge tools

If you want to use a graphical tool to help you resolve merge conflicts, you can run `git mergetool`, which fires up a visual merge tool and guides invoked tool through all the merge conflicts.

It has a wide set of preconfigured support for various graphical merge helpers. You can configure which tool you want to use with `merge.tool`. If you don't do this, Git would try all the possible tools in the sequence which depends on the operating system and the desktop environment.

You can also configure a set up for your own tool.

Marking files as resolved and finalizing merges

As described earlier, if there is a merge conflict for a file, it will have three stages in the index. To mark a file as resolved, you need to put the contents of a file in stage 0. This can be done by simply running `git add <file>`.

When all the conflicts get resolved, you need to simply run `git commit` to finalize the merge commit (or you can skip marking each file individually as resolved and just run `git commit -a`). The default commit message for merge summarizes what we are merging, including a list of the conflicts if any, and adds a shortlog of the merged-in branches by default. The last is controlled by the `--log` option and the `merge.log` configuration variable.

Resolving rebase conflicts

When there is a problem with applying a patch or a patch series, cherry-picking or reverting a commit, or rebasing a branch, Git will fall back to using the three-way merge algorithm. How to resolve such conflicts is described in earlier sections.

However, for some of these methods, such as rebase, applying mailbox, or cherry-picking a series of commits, that are done stage by stage (a sequencer operation), there are other issues, namely, what to do if there is a conflict during such an individual stage.

You have three options. You can resolve the conflict, and continue the operation with the --continue parameter (or in case of git am, also --resolved). You can abort the operation and reset HEAD to the original branch with --abort. Finally, you can use --skip to drop a revision, perhaps because it is already present in the upstream and we can drop it during replaying.

git-imerge – incremental merge and rebase for git

Both rebase and merge have their disadvantages. With merge, you need to resolve one big conflict (though using test merges and rerere to keep up-to-date proposed resolutions could help with this) in an all-or-nothing fashion. There is almost no way to save partially a done merge or to test it; git stash can help, but it might be an inadequate solution.

Rebase, on the other hand, is done in step-by-step fashion. But it is unfriendly to collaboration; you should not rebase published parts of the history. You can interrupt a rebase, but it leaves you in a strange state (on an anonymous branch).

That's why the git imerge third-party tool was created. It presents conflicts pair wise in small steps. It records all the intermediate merges in such a way that they can be shared, so one person can start merging and the other can finish it. The final resolution can be stored as an ordinary merge, as an ordinary rebase, and as a rebase with history.

Summary

This chapter has shown us how to effectively join two lines of development together, combining commits they gathered since their divergence.

First, we got to know various methods of combining changes: merge, cherry-pick, and rebase. This part focused on explaining how these functionalities work at higher levels: at the level of the DAG of revisions. You learned how merge and rebase works, and what is the difference between them. Some of the more interesting uses of rebase, such as transplanting a topic branch from one long-lived branch to another, were also shown.

Then, you learned what to do in case Git is not able to automatically combine changes, that is, what can be done in the presence of a merge conflict. The important part of this process is to understand how the three-way merge algorithm works, and how the index and the working area are affected in case of conflicts. You now know how to examine failed merges and how to examine proposed resolutions, how to try avoiding conflicts, and finally how to resolve them and mark them as resolved.

The next chapter, *Keeping History Clean*, will explain why we might want to rewrite history to keep it clean (and what does it mean). One of the tools to rewrite history is an interactive rebase, a close cousin of an ordinary rebase operation described there. You will learn various methods of rewriting commits: how to reorder them, how to split them if they are too large, how to squash fix with the commit it is correcting, and how to remove a file from the history. You will find what you can do if you cannot rewrite history (understanding why rewriting published history is bad), but you still need to correct it: with the mechanisms of replacing and of notes. While at it, we will talk about other applications of these mechanisms.

8
Keeping History Clean

The previous chapter, *Merging Changes Together*, described how to join changes developed by different people (as described in *Chapter 5, Collaborative Development with Git*), or just developed in a separate feature branch (as shown in *Chapter 6, Advanced Branching Techniques*). One of the techniques was rebase, which can help bring a branch to be merged to a better state. But if we are rewriting history, perhaps it would be possible to also modify the commits being rebased to be easier for review, making the development steps of a feature clearer? If rewriting is forbidden, can one make history cleaner without it? How do we fix mistakes if we cannot rewrite history?

This chapter will answer all those questions. It will explain why one might want to keep clean history, when it can and should be done, and how it can be done. Here you will find step-by-step instructions on how to reorder, squash, and split commits. This chapter will also describe how to do large-scale history rewriting (for example clean up after imports from other VCS) and what to do if one cannot rewrite history (how to use reverts, replacements, and notes).

To really understand some of the topics presented here and to truly master their use, you need some basics of Git internals that are presented at beginning of this chapter.

In this chapter, we will cover the following topics:

- The basics of the object model of Git repositories
- Why you shouldn't rewrite published history and how to recover from it
- The interactive rebase: reordering, squashing, splitting, and testing commits
- Large-scale scripted history rewriting
- Reverting revision, reverting a merge, and remerging after reverted merge
- Amending history without rewriting with grafts and replacements
- Appending additional information to the objects with notes

An introduction to Git internals

To really understand and make good use of at least some of the methods described in this chapter, you would need to understand at least the very basics of Git internals. Among others, you would need to know how Git stores the information about revisions.

One would also require to know how to manipulate such data and how to do it from a script. Git provides a set of low-level commands to use in scripts, as a supplement to the user-facing high-level commands. These commands are very flexible and powerful, though perhaps not very user-friendly. Knowledge about this scripted interface will help us also administer the Git repositories via hooks in *Chapter 11, Git Administration*.

Git objects

In *Chapter 2, Exploring Project History*, you have learned that Git represents history as the Directed Acyclic Graph (DAG) of revisions, where each revision is a graph node represented as a **commit object**. Each commit is identified by a SHA-1 identifier. We can use this identifier (in full, or in an ambiguous shortened form) to refer to any given version.

The commit object consists of revision metadata, links to zero or more parent commits, and the snapshot of the project's files at the revision it represents. The revision metadata includes authorship (who and when made the changes), committership (who and when created the commit object), and of course the commit message.

It is interesting to see how Git represents the snapshot of project's files at the given revision. Git uses **tree objects** to represent directories, and **blob objects** (Binary Large OBject (**BLOB**)) to represent contents of a file. Besides the commit, tree, and blob objects, there might also be **tag objects** representing annotated and signed tags.

Each object is identified by the SHA-1 hash function over its contents or, to be more exact, over the type and the size of the object, plus its contents. Such a content-based identifier does not require a central naming service. Thanks to this fact, each and every distributed repository of the same project will use the same identifiers and we do not have to worry about name collisions:

```
# calculate SHA-1 identifier of blob object with Git
$ printf "foo" | git hash-object -t blob —stdin
# calculate SHA-1 identifier of blob object by hand
$ printf "blob 3\0foo" | sha1sum
```

We can say that the Git repository is the content-addressed object database. That's, of course, not all there is; there are also references (branches and tags) and various configurations, and other things.

Let's describe Git objects in more detail, starting bottom-up. We can examine objects with the low-level `git cat-file` command:

- **Blob**: These objects store the contents of the file at the given revision. Such an object can be created using the low-level `git hash-object -w` command. Note that, if different revisions have the same contents of a file, it is stored only once thanks to content-based addressing:

  ```
  $ git cat-file blob HEAD:COPYRIGHT

  Copyright (c) 2014 Company

  All Rights Reserved
  ```

- **Tree**: These objects represent directories. Each tree object is a list of entries sorted by the filename. Each entry is composed of combined permissions and type, name of the file or directory, and a link (that is SHA-1 identifier) of an object connected with the given path, either the tree object (representing the subdirectory), the blob object (representing the file contents), or rarely the commit object (representing the submodule). Note that, if different revisions have the same contents of a subdirectory, it will be stored only once thanks to content-based addressing:

  ```
  $ git cat-file -p HEAD^{tree}

  100644 blob 862aafd...   COPYRIGHT

  100644 blob 25c3d1b...   Makefile

  100644 blob bdf2c76...   README

  040000 tree 7e44d2e...   src
  ```

  Note that the real output includes full 40-character SHA-1 identifiers, not a shortened one, as shown in the preceding example. You can create tree objects out of the index (that you can create using the `git update-index` command) with `git write-tree`.

- **Commit**: These objects represent revisions. Each commit is composed of a set of headers (key-value data) that includes zero or more parent lines, and exactly one tree line with the link to the `tree` object representing a snapshot of the repository contents: the top directory of a project. You can create a commit with a given tree object as a revision snapshot by using the low-level `git commit-tree` command or by simply using `git commit`:

  ```
  $ git cat-file -p HEAD

  tree 752f12f08996b3c0352a189c5eed7cd7b32f42c7
  ```

```
parent cbb91914f7799cc8aed00baf2983449f2d806686

parent bb71a804f9686c4bada861b3fcd3cfb5600d2a47

author Joe Hacker <joe@example.com> 1401584917 +0200

committer Bob Developer <bob@example.com> 1401584917 +0200


Merge remote branch 'origin/multiple'
```

- **Tag**: These objects represent annotated tags, of which signed tags are a special case. Tag objects also consist of a series of headers (among others link to the tagged object) and a tag message. You can create a tag object with a low-level `git mktag` command, or simply with `git tag`:

```
$ git cat-file tag v0.2

object 5d2584867fe4e94ab7d211a206bc0bc3804d37a9

type commit

tag v0.2

tagger John Tagger <john@example.com> 1401585007 +0200


random v0.2
```

> The Git internal format for the author, committer, and tagger dates is `<unix timestamp> <timezone offset>`. The Unix timestamp (POSIX time) is the number of seconds since the Unix epoch, which is 00:00:00 Coordinated Universal Time (UTC), Thursday, 1 January 1970 (1970-01-01T00:00:00Z), not counting leap seconds. This denotes when the event took place. You can print the Unix timestamp with `date "%s"` and convert it into other formats with `date --date="@<timestamp>"`.
>
> The timezone offset is a positive or negative offset from UTC in the HHMM (hours, minutes) format. For example, CET (that is 2 hours ahead UTC) is +0200. This can be used to find local time for an event.

Some Git commands work on any type of objects. For example, you can tag any type of objects, not only commits. You can, among others, tag a blob object to keep some unrelated piece of data in the repository and have it available in each clone. Public keys can be such data.

Notes and replacements, which will be described later in this chapter, also work on any type of objects.

The plumbing and porcelain Git commands

Git was developed in the bottom-up fashion. This means that its development started from basic blocks and built upward. Many user-facing commands were once built as shell scripts utilizing these basic low-level blocks to do their work. Because of this, we can distinguish between the two types of Git commands.

The better known types are the so-called **porcelain** commands, which are high-level, user-facing commands ("porcelain" is a play of words on calling *engine* level commands *plumbing*). The output of these commands is intended for the end user. This means that its output can be changed to be more user-friendly , and therefore its output can be different in different Git versions. with the Git version. The user (you) is smart enough to understand what happened, if presented, for example, with an additional information, or with a changed wording, or with a changed formatting.

This is not the case for the scripts that you may write (here, in this chapter, for example as a part of the scripted rewrite with `git filter-branch`). Here, you need unchanging output; well, at least, for the scripts that are used more than once (as hooks, as the `gitattribute` drivers, and as helpers). You can often find a switch, usually named `--porcelain`, that ensures the command output is immutable. For other commands, the solution is to specify the format fully. Alternatively, you can use low-level commands intended for scripting: the so-called **plumbing** commands. These commands usually do not have user-friendly defaults, not to mention do-what-I-mean-ness. Their output does not depend on the Git configuration; not that many of them can be configured via Git configuration file.

The `git(1)` manpage includes a list of all the Git commands separated into porcelain and plumbing. The distinction between plumbing and porcelain commands was mentioned as a tip in *Chapter 4*, *Managing Your Worktree*, when we encountered the first low-level plumbing command without a user-facing and user-friendly porcelain equivalent.

Environment variables used by Git

Git uses a number of shell environment variables to determine how it behaves. For user-facing porcelain commands that are shell scripts, they are used to pass data to the low-level plumbing commands doing the work, in addition to using standard input (pipelines) and command parameters.

Occasionally, it comes in handy to know what these environment variables are and how they can be used to make Git behave the way you want it to. This will be very visible in the section about scripted history rewriting with `git filter-branch` (especially, `--env-filter`) later in this chapter.

Environment variables fall between the Git configuration and command parameters in priority: environment variables overriding configuration and command parameters overriding environment variables. Well, except for fallback non-Git-specific environment variables, such as PAGER and EDITOR, that take lowest precedence and can be overridden by configuration variables, such as core.pager and core.editor.

What follows is not meant to be an exhaustive list of all the environment variables that Git uses, but only a selected set of the ones especially useful and connected to the topic of this chapter.

Environment variables affecting global behavior

Some of Git's general behavior as a whole (the paths it searches and the external programs its uses) depends on environment variables.

GIT_EXEC_PATH determines where the core git programs are installed. You can check and set the current setting with git --exec-path. The default value is set at installation.

Where Git looks for configuration files is also affected by environment variables. The user-specific configuration file (also called the *global* configuration file) can be found either at $XDG_CONFIG_HOME/git/config (or $HOME/.config/git/config if XDG_CONFIG_HOME is not set or empty) or at $HOME/.gitconfig, values in the latter file taking precedence. You can override the values of either of these variables, namely HOME and XDG_CONFIG_HOME (which many other things depend on) in a shell profile for a truly portable Git installation.

The location of the system-wide configuration file is set at installation (usually, /etc/gitconfig), but you can skip reading from this file by setting the GIT_CONFIG_NOSYSTEM environment variable. This can be useful if your system configuration is interfering with your commands. Or, you can set the single configuration file to be used by Git with GIT_CONFIG environment variable (for git config this is equivalent to using the --file option).

The GIT_PAGER environment variable controls the program used to display a multipage output on the command line if the standard output is a terminal. If this is unset, then the core.pager configuration variable, the PAGER environment variable, and the built-in value — that is, the less program — will be used as a fallback, whichever is set, in this order.

A similar situation exists with GIT_EDITOR which is used to configure the editor to launch in the interactive mode when the user needs to edit some text (a commit message, for example). Note that the editor can be a script that is generating required output, instead of a real editor. The fallback environment variable is EDITOR or VISUAL, depending on the environment (after core.editor).

Environment variables affecting repository locations

Git uses several environment variables to determine how it interfaces with the current repository. These environment variables apply to all the core Git commands.

The GIT_DIR and GIT_WORK_TREE environment variables specify, if set, the location of the .git directory (the administrative area containing the repository) and its work tree (working area), respectively. The --git-dir command-line option can also be used to set the location of the repository. The location of the work tree can be controlled by the --work-tree option and the core.worktree configuration variable; well, if the repository is not bare and there exists a working area. By default, the repository that ends in /.git is considered to be not bare; you can also set the core.bare configuration variable explicitly.

If the location of the repository is not set explicitly, Git will starting from the current directory walk up the directory tree, looking for a .git directory at each step. If it finds it, the directory it was in when it found .git becomes the work tree (the top directory of the project), and the found .git directory is the location of the repository. You can specify a set of directories as a colon-separated list of absolute paths where Git should stop this walk with GIT_CEILING_DIRECTORIES (for example, to exclude slow-loading network directories); by default, Git would stop only at filesystem boundaries (unless GIT_DISCOVERY_ACROSS_FILESYSTEM is set to true).

You can use the GIT_INDEX_FILE environment variable to specify the location of an alternate index file. The default is to use $GIT_DIR/index. Note that the index is not present in bare repositories. This variable can be used to create or modify a state of commit without touching the working area, that is, without touching the filesystem.

The GIT_OBJECT_DIRECTORY variable can be used to specify the location of the object storage directory; the default is to use $GIT_DIR/objects.

Also, due to the immutable nature of git objects and the fact that they are content-addressed, old objects can be archived into shared, read-only directories and, which can be outside GIT_OBJECT_DIRECTORY. Of course you need to tell Git where to find them. Or, in other words, Git repositories can share the object database (with some caveats). See git clone --reference <repository> <URL>, for example. This issue is covered in detail in *Chapter 9, Managing Subprojects - Building a Living Framework*.

You can use the GIT_ALTERNATE_OBJECT_DIRECTORIES environment variable to specify additional directories that can be used to search for the git objects. This variable specifies a ":" separated list of paths the object would be read from, in addition to what is in the $GIT_DIR/objects/info/alternates file and the repository's own object database. New objects will not be written to these alternates.

How to compare two local repositories?

Let's assume that you want to compare two local repositories, but for some reason, you cannot just add one as a remote of the other, and then fetch from that remote. One example of such restriction would be using a read-only storage.

Being in one of repositories, you can do the following:

```
GIT_ALTERNATE_OBJECT_DIRECTORIES=../repo/.git/objects \
git diff \
    $(GIT_DIR=../repo/.git git rev-parse --verify HEAD) \
    HEAD
```

For the other repository, you need to get the universal identifier for an object, that is, its SHA-1. You can do so with the git rev-parse command. To turn a reference, such as HEAD or HEAD:README, it needs to be run in the other repository, which can be done with either the GIT_DIR environment variable (as in the example) or the --git-dir command-line option.

Environment variables affecting committing

The final creation of a Git commit object is usually done internally by the git commit-tree plumbing command. While parent information is provided as command parameters on the command line and git commit-tree gets a commit message on standard input, author and committer information is taken from the following environment variables.

The GIT_AUTHOR_NAME and GIT_COMMITTER_NAME commands are the human-readable name in the author and committer fields, respectively. The e-mail address can be set with GIT_AUTHOR_EMAIL for the author field and GIT_COMMITTER_EMAIL for the committer field, with generic EMAIL environment variable used as a fallback if the configuration variable core.email is not set. GIT_AUTHOR_DATE is the timestamp used for the author field with a date in the RFC 2822 e-mail format (Fri, 08 May 2015 01:35:42 +0200), the ISO 8601 standard date format (2015-05-08T01:36:48+0200), the Git internal format that is Unix time plus +hhmm numeric time zone (1431041884 +0200), or the any other datetime format supported by Git; similar for GIT_COMMITTER_DATE.

In case, (some of) these environment variables are not set, the information is taken from the configuration or Git tries to guess it. If the required information is not provided, and Git cannot guess it, then commit will fail.

Rewriting history

Many times, while working on a project, you may want to revise your commit history. One reason for this could be to make it easier to review before submitting changes upstream. Another reason would be to take reviewer comments into account in the next improved version of changes. Or perhaps you'd like to have a clear history while finding regressions using bisection, as described in *Chapter 2, Exploring Project History*.

One of the great things about Git is that it makes revising and rewriting history possible, while providing a wide set of tools to revise history and make it clean.

 There are two conflicting views among users of the version control system: one states that history is sacred and you should better show the true history of the development, warts and all, and another that states that you should clean up the new history for better readability before publishing it.

An important issue to note is that, even though we talk about rewriting history, objects in Git (including commits) are *immutable*. This means that rewriting is really creating a modified copy of commits, a new path in the DAG of revisions. Then appropriate branch reference is switched to point to the just created new path. The original, pre-rewrite commits are there in the repository, referenced and available from the reflog (and also, ORIG_HEAD). Well, at least, until they get pruned (that is, deleted) as unreferenced and unreachable objects during garbage-collecting. Though, this happens only after the reflog expires.

Amending the last commit

The simplest case of history rewriting is correcting the latest commit on a branch (the current commit).

Sometimes, you notice a typo (an error) in a commit message, or that you have committed incomplete change in the last revision. If you have not pushed (published) your changes, you can amend the last commit. This is done with the --amend option to git commit.

The result of amending a commit is shown in *Fig 6* in *Chapter 3, Developing with Git*. Note that there is no functional difference between amending the last commit and changing the commits deeper in history. In both the cases you are creating a new commit, leaving the old version referenced by the reflog.

Here, the index (that is, the explicit staging area for commits) shows its usefulness again. For example, if you want to simply fix only the commit message, and you do not want to make any changes, you can use `git commit --amend` (note the lack of `-a / --all` option). This works even if you started work on a new commit; at least, assuming that you didn't add any changes to the index. If you did, you can put them away temporarily with `git stash`, fix the commit message of the last commit, and then pop stashed changes and restore the index with `git stash pop --index`.

If, on the other hand, you realize that you have forgotten some changes, you can just edit the files and use `git commit --amend --all`. And if the changes are interleaved, you can use `git add`, or its interactive version (utilizing knowledge from *Chapter 5, Managing Your Worktree*), to create the contents you want to have, finalizing it with `git commit --amend`.

An interactive rebase

Sometimes, you might want to edit commit deeper in history, or reorganize commits into a logical sequence of steps. One of the built-in tools that you can use in Git for this purpose is `git rebase --interactive`.

Here, we will assume that you are working on a feature using a separate topic branch and a topic branch workflow described and recommended in *Chapter 6, Advanced Branching Techniques*. We will also assume that you are doing the work in the series of logical steps, rather than in one large commit.

While implementing a new feature, you usually don't do it perfectly from the very beginning. You would want to introduce it in a series of self-contained small steps (see *Chapter 12, Git Best Practices*) to make code review (or code audit) and bisection (finding the cause of regressions) easier. Often only after finishing work you see how to split it better. It is also unreasonable to expect that you would not make mistakes while implementing a new feature.

Before submitting the changes (either pushing to a central repository, pushing to your own public repository and sending pull requests, or using some other workflows described in *Chapter 5, Collaborative Development with Git*), you would often want to update your branch to the current up-to-date state of a project . By rebasing your changes on top of current state, and having them up to date, you would make it easier for the maintainer (the integration manager) to ultimately merge your changes in, when they are accepted for the inclusion in the mainline. Interactive rebase allows you to clean up history, as described earlier, while doing it.

Besides tidying up before publishing changes, there is also additional use for tools such as an interactive rebase. While working on a more involved feature, the very first submission is not always accepted into an upstream and added to the project. Often, patch review finds problem with the code or with the explanation of the changes. Perhaps, something is missing (for example, the feature lacks documentations or tests), some commit needs to be fixed, or the submitted series of patches (or a branch submitted in a pull request) should be split into smaller commits for easy review. In this case, you would also use an interactive rebase (or an equivalent tool) to prepare a new version to submit, taking into account the results of code inspection.

Reordering, removing, and fixing commits

Rebase, as described in *Chapter 7, Merging Changes Together*, consists of taking a series of changes of the commits being rebased and reapplying them on top of a new base (a new commit). In other words, rebase moves changesets, not snapshots. Git starts the interactive rebase by opening the instructions sheet corresponding to those series operations of reapplying changes in an editor.

You can configure the text editor used for editing the rebase instruction file separately from the default editor (used, for example, to edit commit message) with the sequence.editor configuration variable, which in turn can be overridden by the GIT_SEQUENCE_EDITOR environment variable.

Like in the case of the template for editing commits, the instruction sheet is accompanied by the comments explaining what you can do with it (note that if you use older Git version, some interactive rebase commands might be missing):

```
pick 89579c9 first commit in a branch
pick d996b71 second commit in a branch
pick 6c89dee third commit in a branch

# Rebase 89579c9..6c89dee onto b8fffe1
```

```
#
# Commands:
#  p, pick = use commit
#  r, reword = use commit, but edit the commit message
#  e, edit = use commit, but stop for amending
#  s, squash = use commit, but meld into previous commit
#  f, fixup = like "squash", but discard this commit's log message
#  x, exec = run command (the rest of the line) using shell
#  d, drop = remove commit
#
# These lines can be re-ordered; they are executed from top to bottom.
#
# If you remove a line here THAT COMMIT WILL BE LOST.
#
# However, if you remove everything, the rebase will be aborted.
#
# Note that empty commits are commented out
```

As explained in the comments, the instructions are in the order of execution, starting from the instruction on the top to create the first commit with the new base as its parent, and ending with the instruction copying commit at the tip of the branch being rebased at the bottom. This means that revisions are listed in an increasing chronological order, older commits first. This is the reverse order as compared to the git log output with the most recent commit first (unless using git log --reverse). This is quite understandable; the rebase reapplies changesets in the order they were added to the branch, while the log operation shows commits in the order of reachability from the tips.

Each line of the instruction sheet consists of three elements separated by spaces. First, there is a one-word command; by default, the interactive rebase starts with pick. Each command has a one-letter shortcut that you can use instead of the long form, as shown in the comments (for example you can use "`p`" in place of "`pick`").

Next, there is a uniquely shortened SHA-1 identifier of a commit to be used with the command. Strictly speaking, it is the identifier of a commit being rebased, which it had before the rebase started. This shortened SHA-1 identifier is used to pick the appropriate commit (for example while reordering lines, which means reordering commits).

Last, there is the description (the subject) of a commit. It is taken from the first line of the commit message (specifically, it is the first paragraph of the commit message with the line breaks removed, where a paragraph is defined as the set of subsequent lines of text separated from other paragraphs by at least one empty line — that is, two or more end-of-line characters). This is one of the reasons why the first line of the commit message should be a short description of changes (see *Chapter 12, Git Best Practices*). This description is for you to help decide what to do with the commit; Git uses its SHA-1 identifier and ignores the rest of the line.

Reordering commits with the interactive rebase is as simple as reordering lines in the instruction sheet. Note, however, that if the changes were not independent, you might need to resolve conflicts, even if they would be no merge conflicts without doing reordering. In such cases, as instructed by Git, you would need to fix conflicts, mark conflicts as resolved, (for example, with `git add`), and then run `git rebase --continue`. Git will remember that you are in the middle of an *interactive* rebase, so you don't need to repeat the `--interactive` option.

The other possibility of dealing with a conflict, namely, skipping a commit, rather than resolving a conflict, by running `git rebase --skip`, is here as well. By default, rebase removes changes that are already present in upstream; you might want to use this command in case the rebase doesn't detect correctly that the commit in question is already there in the branch we are transplanting revisions onto. In other words, do skip a commit if you know that the correct resolution of a conflict is an empty changeset.

 You can also make Git present you again with the instruction sheet at any time when rebase stops for some reason (including an error in the instruction sheet, like using the `squash` command with the first commit) with `git rebase --edit-todo`. After editing it, you can continue the rebase.

To **remove changes**, you simply need to remove the relevant line from the instruction sheet, or to comment it out, or -- with the newest Git -- use the `drop` command. You can use it to drop failed experiments, or to make it easier on the rebase by deleting changesets that you know are already present in the rebase onto the upstream, though perhaps in a different form. Note, though, that removing the instruction sheet altogether aborts the rebase.

To **fix a commit**, change the `pick` command preceding the relevant commit in the instruction sheet to `edit` (or just `e`). This would make rebase stop at this commit, that is, at the step of reapplying changes, similar to the case with a conflict. To be precise, the interactive rebase applies the commit in question, so it is the `HEAD` commit and stops the process giving control to the user. You can then fix this commit, as if it were a current one with `git commit --amend`, as described in *Amending the last commit*. After changing it to your liking, run `git rebase --continue`, as explained in the instruction that Git prints.

A proper `git-aware` command-line prompt, such as the one from the Git `contrib` command, would tell you if you are in the middle of the rebase (see *Chapter 10, Customizing and Extending Git*). If you are not using such a prompt, you can always check what's happening with `git status`:

```
$ git status
rebase in progress; onto b3cebef
You are currently rebasing branch 'subsys' on 'b3cebef'.
  (fix conflicts and then run "git rebase --continue")
  (use "git rebase --skip" to skip this patch)
  (use "git rebase --abort" to check out the original
branch)
```

As you can see, you can always go to the state before starting the rebase with `git rebase --abort`.

If you only want to change the commit message (for example, to fix spellings or include additional information), you can skip the need to run `git commit --amend` and then `git rebase --continue` by using `reword` (or `r`) instead of `edit`. Git would then automatically open the editor with the commit message. Saving changes and exiting the editor will commit the changes, amend the commit, and continue the rebase.

Squashing commits

Sometimes, you might need to make one commit out of two or more, squashing them together. Maybe, you decided that it didn't make sense to split the changes and they are better together.

With the interactive rebase, you can reorder these commits, as needed, so they are next to each other. Then, leave the `pick` command for the first of the commits to be concatenated together (or change it to `edit`). For the rest of the commits, use the `squash` or `fixup` command. Git will then accumulate the changes and create the commit with all of them together. The suggested commit message for the folded commit is the commit message of the first commit with the messages of the commits with the `squash` command appended; commit messages with the `fixup` command are omitted. This means that the `squash` command is useful while squashing changes, while `fixup` is useful for adding fixes. If the commits had different authors, the folded commit will be attributed to the author of the first commit. The committer will be you, the person performing the rebase.

Let's assume that you noticed that you forgot to add some part of the changes to the commit. Perhaps, it is missing tests (or just negative tests) or the documentation. The commit is in the past, so you cannot just add to it by amending. You could use an interactive rebase or the patch management interface to fix it, but often it is more effective to create the commit with forgotten changes and squash it later.

Similarly, when you notice that the commit you created a while ago has a bug, instead of trying to edit it immediately, you can create a `fixup` commit with a bugfix to be squashed later.

If you are using this technique, some time might pass between noticing the need to append new changes or fix a bug and creating an appropriate commit, and the time taken to rebase. How to mark the said commit to squash or fixup? If you use the commit message beginning with the magic string `squash!` ... or `fixup!` ..., respectively, preceding the description (the first line of the commit message that is sometimes called **subject**) of a commit to be squashed into, you can ask Git to autosquash them, thus automatically modifying the to-do list of `rebase -i`. You can request this on an individual basis with the `--autosquash` option or you can enable this behavior by default with the `rebase.autoSquash` configuration variable. To create the appropriate magic commit message, you can use `git commit --squash/--fixup.` (with commit to be squashed into / commit to be fixes as a parameter to this option)

Splitting commits

Sometimes, you might want to make two commits or more out of one commit, splitting it in two or more parts. You may have noticed that the commit is too large, perhaps it tries to do too much, and should be split in two. Or perhaps, you have decided that some part of a changeset should be moved from one commit to another, and extracting it into a separate commit is a first step towards that.

Git does not provide a one-step built-in command for this operation. Nevertheless, splitting commits is possible with the clever use of the interactive rebase.

To split a given commit, first mark it with the `edit` action. As described earlier, Git will stop at the specified commit and give the control back to the user. In the case of splitting a commit, when you return the control to Git with `git rebase --continue`, you would want to have two commits in place of one.

The problem of splitting a commit is comparable to the problem of having different changes tangled together from *Chapter 3, Developing with Git* (the section about interactive commit). The difference is that the commit is already created and copied from the branch being rebased. It is simple to fix it with `git reset HEAD^`; as described in *Chapter 4, Managing Your Worktree*, this command will keep the working area at the (entangled) state of the commit to be split while moving the HEAD pointer and the staging area for the commit to the state before this revision. Then you can interactively add to the index the changes that you want to have in the first commit, composing the intermediate step in the staging area. Next, check whether you have what you want in the index, then create a commit from it using `git commit` without the `-a` / `--all` option. Repeat these last two steps as often as necessary.

Alternatively, instead of adding changes interactively, you can interactively remove changes to create the intermediate state for split commit. This can be done with interactive reset, mentioned in *Chapter 4, Managing Your Worktree*.

For the last commit in the series (the second one if you are splitting the commit in two), you can either add everything to the index making a working copy clean and create a commit from the index, or you can create a commit from the state of the working area (`git commit --all`). If you want to keep, or start from, the commit message of the original commit to be split, you can provide it with the `--reuse-message=<commit>` or `--reedit-message=<commit>` option while creating a commit. I think, the simplest way of naming a commit that was split (or that is being split) is to use reflog — it will be the HEAD@{n} entry just before `reset: moving to HEAD^` in the `git reflog` output.

Instead of crafting the commit in the staging area (in the index) starting from the parent of the commit to be split, and adding changes, perhaps interactively, you could start from the final state (that is, the commit to be split) and remove the changes that are to be in second step, for example, with `git reset --patch HEAD^` (interactive removal). Frankly, you can use any combination of techniques from *Chapter 4, Managing Your Worktree*. I find, for example, graphical commit tools such as `git gui` quite useful (you can find what are the graphical commit tools, and their examples in *Chapter 11, Customizing and Extending Git*).

If you are not absolutely sure that the intermediate revisions you are creating in the index are consistent (they compile, pass the test suite, and so on), you should use `git stash save --keep-index` to stash away the not-yet-committed changes, bringing the working area to the state composed in the index. You can the test the changes (for example by using the testsuite), and if fixes are necessary amend the staging area. Alternatively, you can create the commit from the index and use plain `git stash` to save the state of the working area after each commit. You can then test and amend the created intermediate commit if the fixes are necessary. In both the cases, you need to restore changes with `git stash pop` before you work on a new commit in the split.

Testing each rebased commit

A good software development practice is to test each change before committing it. But it does not always happen. Let's assume that you forgot to test some commits or skipped it because the change seemed trivial and you were pressed for time. The interactive rebase allows you to execute tests (to be precise, any command) during the rebase process by adding the `exec` (x) action with an appropriate command after the commit you want to test.

The `exec` command launches the command (the rest of the line) in a shell: the one specified in `SHELL` environment variable, or the default shell if `SHELL` is not set. This means that you can use shell features (for POSIX shell, it would be using `cd` to change directories, ">" to command output redirection, and ";" and "&&" to sequence multiple commands, and so on). It's important to remember that the command to be executed is run from the root of the working tree, not from the current directory (the subdirectory you were in while starting the interactive rebase).

If you are strict about not publishing untested changes, you might have worried about the fact that rewritten commits, rebased on the top of the new changes, might not pass the tests, even if the originals have. You can, however, make the interactive rebase test each commit with the `--exec` option, for example:

```
$ git rebase --interactive --exec "make test"
```

This would modify the staring instruction sheet, inserting `exec make test` after each entry:

```
pick 89579c9 first commit in a branch
exec make test
pick d996b71 second commit in a branch
exec make test
pick 6c89dee third commit in a branch
exec make test
```

External tools – patch management interfaces

You might prefer fixing the old commit immediately at the time you have noticed the bug, and not postponing it till the branch is rebased. The latter is usually done just before the branch is sent for review (to publish it). This might be quite some time after realizing the need to edit the past commit.

Git itself doesn't make it easy to fix the found bug straight away, not with built-in tools. You can, however, find third-party external tools that implement the patch management interface on the top of Git. Examples of such tools include **Stacked Git (StGit)** and **Git Quilt (Guilt)**.

These tools provide similar functionality to Quilt (that is, pushing/popping patches to/from a stack). With them, you have a set of work-in-progress *floating* patches in the Quilt-like stack. You have also accepted changes in the form of proper Git commits. You can convert between patch and commit and vice versa, move and edit patches around, move and edit commits (that is done by turning the commit and its children into patches and back again), squash patches, and so on.

This is, however, an additional tool to install, additional set of operations to learn (even if they make your work easier), and additional set of complications coming from the boundary between the Git and the tool in question. An interactive rebase is powerful enough nowadays and, with autosquash, the need for another layer on top of Git is lessened.

Scripted rewrite with the git filter-branch

In some cases, you might need to use more powerful tools than the interactive rebase to rewrite and clean up the history. You might want something that would rewrite the full history, and would do the rewrite noninteractively, given some specified algorithm to do the rewrite. Such situations are the task for `git filter-branch`.

The calling convention of this command is rather different than for the interactive rebase. First, you need to give it a branch or a set of branches to rewrite, for example, `--all` to rewrite all the branches. Strictly speaking, you give it the `rev-list` options as arguments, that is, a series of positive and negative references (see *Chapter 2, Exploring Project History* for definition). The command will only rewrite the positive refs mentioned in the command line. This means that positive references, which are the upper limits of revision ranges, need to be able to be rewritten—to be branch names. Negative revisions are used to limit what is ran through the rewriting process; you can, of course, also specify a pathspec on a command line to limit the changes.

This command rewrites the Git revision history by applying custom filters (scripts) on each revision to be rewritten. That's another difference: rebase works by reapplying changesets, while filter-branch works with snapshots. One of the consequences of this is that, for the filter-branch, a merge is just a kind of a commit object, while the rebase skips merges, unless you use the --preserve-merges option that does not work well combined with the interactive mode.

And, of course, with the filter-branch, you use scripts for rewrite (that are called **filters**), instead of rewriting interactively: editing instruction sheets and running commands by hand to edit, reword, squash, split, or test commits during the rebase process. This means that the speed of the filter-branch operation is not limited by the speed of the user interaction, but by I/O. It is recommended to use an off-disk temporary directory for rewriting (if the filter requires it) with the -d <directory> option.

> Because git filter-branch is usually used for massive rewrites, it saves the original refs, pointing to the pre-rewritten history in the refs/original/ namespace (you can override it with the --original <namespace> option).
>
> The command would also refuse to start, unless forced, if there are already existing refs starting with refs/original/, or if there is anything in a temporary directory.

Running the filter-branch without filters

If you specify no filters, the commits will be recommitted without any changes. Such usage would normally have no effect, but it is permitted to allow in the future to compensate for (to fix) some Git bugs.

It is important to note that this command respects both *grafts* (it honors .git/info/grafts file) and *replacements* (refs in the refs/replace/ namespace), thought you can ask Git with a command line option to not follow the latter. Grafts and replacements are techniques to affect the history (or a rather a view of it) without rewriting any revisions. Both will be explained later in the *Replacements mechanism* section.

This means that running git filter-branch without any filter can be used to make permanent the effects of grafts or replacements by rewriting the selected commits. This way, you can use the following technique: use git replace on the specified commits to alter the view of a history, ensure that it looks correct (like you wanted it to look like), and then make the modification permanent with a filter-branch.

Additionally, while rewriting commits, `git filter-branch` respects the current value of a few relevant configuration variables. The values of those variables might have changed since the original creation of the commits being rewritten. This feature might be used, for example, to fix history if you have used nonstandard encoding for the commit messages (not UTF-8), but forgot to set `i18n.commitEncoding`. Rewriting history with no filters, with 'i18n.commitEncoding' set correctly at that tome, will nevertheless add the `encoding` header to the commit objects.

Available filter types for filter-branch and their use

There is a large set of different types of possible filters to specify how to rewrite history. You can specify more than one type of filter; they are applied in the listed order. Note that different filters have different performance considerations.

The command argument is always evaluated in the shell context and is called once per commit undergoing the rewrite. Information about a pre-rewrite SHA-1 identifier of a current commit (that is, the commit being rewritten) is passed to the filter using the `GIT_COMMIT` environment variable. In addition, there is a `map` shell function available that takes the original SHA-1 of a commit as an argument, and outputs either the rewritten or original SHA-1 depending on whether the commit was rewritten or not at the time this shell function was invoked.

Also, `GIT_AUTHOR_NAME`, `GIT_AUTHOR_EMAIL`, `GIT_AUTHOR_DATE`, `GIT_COMMITTER_NAME`, `GIT_COMMITTER_EMAIL`, and `GIT_COMMITTER_DATE` are taken from the current commit and exported to the environment to make it easier to write the contents of the filter, and to affect the author and committer identities of the replacement commit. The filter-branch command uses `git commit-tree` to create a replacement commit if the filter function succeeds; if the command returns a nonzero exit status, then the whole rewrite will get aborted.

When writing filter scripts, just like for normal scripts, it is usually better to use low-level plumbing commands, rather than high-level porcelain commands designed for interactive use. In particular, the filter-branch command uses plumbing itself... without all the do what I mean (DWIM) niceties(like following gitignore files). If you prefer, though, you can use programs for filters, instead of shell scripts.

The `git filter-branch` command supports the following types of filters:

- `--env-filter`: This may be used to modify environments in which a commit is performed. You might use it to change author or committer information, namely their name, e-mail, or time of operation. Note that variables need to be re-exported.

- `--tree-filter`: This may be used to rewrite the contents of the commit, that is, the tree object the commit refers to. The command is evaluated in the shell, with the working directory set to the root of the project and current commit checked out. After the command finishes, the contents of the working area are used *as-is*, new files are auto-added, and disappeared files are auto-removed without considering any ignore rules (for example, from `.gitignore`).

- `--index-filter`: This may be used to rewrite the index and the staging area from which the rewritten commit will be created. It is similar to the tree filter, but is much faster, because it doesn't need to check out files into the working area (into the filesystem).

- `--parent-filter`: This may be used to rewrite the commit's parent list. It receives a parent string in the form of the parent's command-line parameters to the `git commit-tree` command (`-p <parent full SHA-1>`) on a standard input, and shall output a new parent string on a standard output.

- `--msg-filter`: This may be used to rewrite the commit messages. It receives the original commit message on a standard input, and shall output a new commit message on a standard output.

- `--commit-filter`: This may be used to specify the command to be called instead of `git commit-tree`. This means getting `<tree> [(-p <parent>)...]` as arguments to the filter command, and getting the log message on the standard input.

  You can use in this filter a few convenience functions: `skip_commit "$@"` to leave out the current commit (but not its changes!), and `git_commit_non_empty_tree "$@"` to automatically skip no-change commits.

> `"$@"` expands to the positional parameters of the command starting from one. When the expansion occurs within double quotes, each parameter expands to a separate word. This is a standard POSIX shell feature, and can be used to pass all the parameters down unchanged.

- `--tag-name-filter`: This may be used to rewrite tag names. The original tag name is passed on a standard input, and the command shall write a new name to a standard output. The original tags are not deleted, but can be overwritten; use `--tag-name-filter cat` to simply update tags (stripping signatures).

  Note that the signature gets stripped, because by definition, it is impossible to preserve them. Tags with rewritten names are properly rewritten to point to the changed object. Currently, there is no support to change the tagger, timestamp, tag message, or re-signing tags.

- `--subdirectory-filter <directory>`: This may be used to leave only the history of the given directory, and make this directory a project root. Can be used to change a subdirectory of a project into a subproject; see also *Chapter 9: Managing Subprojects - Building a Living Framework*.

Note that if you use the `git log` / `git rev-list` options to limit the set of revisions to rewrite (for example, `--all` to rewrite all the branches), you must separate them with "`--`" from the specification of filters and other `git filter-branch` options.

Examples of using the git filter-branch

Let's assume that you committed a wrong file to a repository by mistake and you want to **remove the file from the history**. Perhaps this was a site-specific configuration file with passwords or their equivalent. Perchance, during "`git add .`", you have included a generated file that was not properly ignored (maybe it was a large binary file). Or mayhap, it turned out that you don't have the distribution rights to a file and you need to have it removed to avoid copyright violation.

Now you need to remove it from the project. Using `git rm --cached` would remove it only from future commits. You can also quite easily remove the file from the latest version by amending the commit (as described earlier in this chapter).

To excise the file from the entire history, (let's assume it is called `passwords.txt`), you can use `git filter-branch` with the `--tree-filter` option:

```
$ git filter-branch --tree-filter 'rm -f passwords.txt' HEAD
Rewrite fdfb73095fc0d594ff8d7f507f5fc3ab36859e3d (32/32)
Ref 'refs/heads/master' was rewritten
```

There is, however, a faster alternative—instead of using a tree filter, which involves writing out files, you can use delete files from the index using `git rm --cached` with the index filter. You need to ensure that the filter runs successfully and does not exit even if there are no files to delete; there is also no need for output:

```
$ git filter-branch --index-filter \
    'git rm -f --cached -q --ignore-unmatch passwords.txt' HEAD
```

Or, you can use the BFG Repo-Cleaner third-party tool described in a later section.

You can use a filter branch to **remove all the specific types of commits** from the history, for example, commits by a specific author (one that, for example, didn't fulfill the copyright obligations, such as the contributor agreement). Note, however, that there is a very important difference between removing commits with filter-branch and removing them using a interactive rebase. A filter-branch removes nodes in the DAG of revisions, but does not remove the changes—there is simply no longer an intermediate step between two snapshots, and changes move to the child commit. On the other hand, an interactive rebase removes both commit and changes. This means that all the child commits are modified so that their snapshot does not include removed changes.

To remove a commit, you can use the `skip_commit` shell function in a commit filter:

```
$ git filter-branch --commit-filter '
if [ "$GIT_AUTHOR_NAME" = "Bad Contributor" ];
then
  skip_commit "$@"
else
  git commit-tree "$@"
fi' HEAD
```

You can use a filter-branch to permanently **join two repositories**, connect histories, and split the history in two. You can do this directly with a parent filter. For example to join repositories, making the commit `<root-id>` from the history of one of repositories being joined have `<graft-id>` commit (from the other repository) as a parent, you can use:

```
$ git filter-branch --parent-filter \
'test "$GIT_COMMIT" = <root-id> && echo "-p <graft-id>" || cat' HEAD
```

You can **split history** at a given commit in two in a similar way, by setting parents to an empty set with `echo ""`.

If you know that you have only one root commit (only one commit with no parents), you can simplify the method to join the history to the following command:

```
$ git filter-branch --parent-filter 'sed "s/^\$/-p <graft id>/"' HEAD
```

In my opinion, however, it is simpler to use grafts or replacements, check whether the joined/split history renders correctly, and then make replacements permanent by running filter-branch without filters with the revision range starting, at least, from the rewritten joint/root commit. Still, the `--parent-filter` approach has an advantage if you can tell programmatically which revision or revisions to split (or join); a simple version of this technique is presented in the single-root join as shown in the preceding example.

Another common case is to **fix erroneous names or e-mail addresses in commits**. Perhaps, you forgot to run `git config` to set your name and e-mail address before you started working and Git guessed it incorrectly (if it couldn't guess it, it would ask for it before allowing the commit), and `.mailmap` is not enough. Maybe, you want to open the sources of the formerly proprietary closed-source program and need to change the internal corporate e-mail to a personal address.

In any case, you can change the e-mail addresses in the whole history with a filter-branch. You need to ensure that you are changing your commits. You can use `--env-filter` for this (though `--commit-filter` would work too, with just `git commit-tree "$@"` and no export lines):

```
$ git filter-branch --env-filter '
if test "$GIT_AUTHOR_EMAIL" = "joe@localhost"; then
   GIT_AUTHOR_NAME="Joe Hacker"
   GIT_AUTHOR_EMAIL=joe@company.com
   export GIT_AUTHOR_NAME GIT_AUTHOR_EMAIL
fi' HEAD
```

This example presents a simplified solution, you would want to change the committer data too, and the code is nearly identical.

If you are open-sourcing a project, you could also want to add the `Signed-off-by:` lines for the Digital Certificate of Origin (see *Chapter 12, Git Best Practices*):

```
$ git filter-branch --msg-filter \
'cat && echo && echo "Signed-off-by: Joe Hacker <joe@company.com>"' \
HEAD
```

Suppose that you have noticed **a typo in the name of a subdirectory**, for example, `inlude/` instead of `include/`. If there is no problem rewriting it, you could fix it by using `--tree-filter` with `mv -f inlude include`; but with some ingenuity, we can use `--index-filter` faster:

```
$ git filter-branch --index-filter '
  git ls-files --stage |
  sed -e "s!\(\t\"*\)inlude/!\1include/!" |
  GIT_INDEX_FILE=$GIT_INDEX_FILE.new \
    git update-index --index-info &&
  mv "$GIT_INDEX_FILE.new" "$GIT_INDEX_FILE"
' HEAD
```

The explanation is as follows: we use the fact that the output of `git ls-files --stage` matches the format of input for `git update-index --index-info` (the latter command is a plumbing command underlying the `git add` porcelain). To replace text and fix a typo in a path name, the `sed` (streaming editor) utility is used. Here, we needed to write the regular expression to take care that some file names may require quoting. A temporary index file is used to make an atomic operation.

Often, some part of a larger project takes life on its own and it begins to make sense to use it separate from the project it started in. We would want to extract the history of this part to make its **subdirectory the new root**. To rewrite history in this way and discard all the other history, you can run:

```
$ git filter-branch --subdirectory-filter lib/foo -- --all
```

Though, perhaps, a better solution would be to use a specialized third-party tool, namely, `git subtree`. This tool (and its alternatives) will be discussed in *Chapter 9, Managing Subprojects – Building a Living Framework*.

External tools for large-scale history rewriting

The `git filter-branch` command is not the only solution for the large-scale rewriting of the project's history. There are other tools that might be easier to use, either because they include lots of predefined clean-up operations, or because they provide some level of interactivity with the ability for scripted rewrite (with read-evaluate-print loop (REPL), similar to interactive shells in some interpreted programming languages).

Removing files from the history with BFG Repo Cleaner

The BFG Repo Cleaner is a simpler, faster, and specialized alternative to using the `git filter-branch` command for cleansing bad data out of your Git repository history: removing files and directories and replacing text in files (for example, passwords with placeholders). It is faster than filter-branch for its area of application, because it can assume that we don't care where in the directory hierarchy the bad file is, only that we want it to be gone. Also, it can use multiple cores with parallel processing, and it doesn't need to fork and the `exec` shell to run filter script for each commit—BFG is written in Scala and uses JGit as a Git implementation.

BFG is simpler to use in typical use cases, because it provides a set of command-line parameters specialized for removing files and fixing them, such as `--delete-files` or `--replace-text`, a query language of sorts It lacks the flexibility (often unnecessary one) of filter-branch, though.

One issue you need to remember is that BFG assumes that you have fixed the contents of your current commit.

Editing the repository history with reposurgeon

The reposurgeon was originally created to help clean up artefacts created by the repository conversion (migrating from one version control system to another). It relies on being able to parse, modify, and emit the command stream in the `git fast-import` format, which is nowadays a common export and import format among source control systems thanks to it being version control agnostic.

It can be used for history rewriting, including editing past commits and metadata, excising commits, squashing (coalescing) and splitting commits, removing files and directories from history, and splitting and joining history.

The major advantage `reposurgeon` has over using `git filter-branch` is that it can be run in two modes: either as an interactive interpreter, a kind of debugger/editor for history with command history and tab completion, and a batch mode to execute commands given as arguments. This allows to interactively inspect history and test changes, and then batch run them for all the revisions.

The disadvantage is having to install and then learn to use a separate tool.

The perils of rewriting published history

There is, however, a very important principle. Namely, that you should never (or, at least, not without a very, very good reason) rewrite published history, especially when it comes to commits that got pushed to the public repository, or were otherwise made public. What you can do is to change those parts of the graph of the revisions that are private.

The reason behind this rule is that rewriting published history could cause trouble for downstream developers, if they based their changes on revisions that got rewritten.

This means that it is safe to rewrite and rebuild those public branches that are explicitly stated and documented to be in flux, for example, as a way of showing work in progress (such as pu: proposed updates type of branch). Another possibility for the safe rewriting of a public branch is to do it at specific stages of the project's life, namely, after creating a new release; again, this needs to be documented.

The consequences of upstream rewrite

Now, you will see on a simple example the perils of rewriting published history (for example, rebasing) and how it causes trouble. Let's assume that there are two public branches that are of interest: master and subsys. The latter branch is based on (forked from) the former. Let's also assume that a downstream developer (who might be you) created a new topic branch based on subsys for his/her own work, but did not published it yet; it is present only in his/her local repository. This situation is shown in *Fig 1* (the darker blue color denotes the revisions present only in the local repository of the downstream developer):

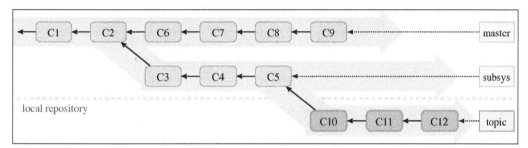

Fig 1: The state of the local repository of a downstream developer before the rewrite of the published history with the new local work that was put on a topic branch

Then, upstream rewrites the subsys branch to start from the current (topmost) revision in the master branch. This operation is called **rebase**, and was described in the previous chapter, *Chapter 7, Merging Changes Together*. During rewrite, one of the commits was dropped; perhaps the same change was already present in master and was skipped, or perhaps it was dropped for some reason or squashed into the previous commit with an interactive rebase (this operation will be described later in the *Interactive rebase* section). The public repository now looks as follows:

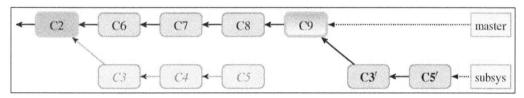

Fig 2: The state of a public upstream repository after rewrite. You can see the emphasized old base of the rebased branch, new base, and rewritten commits (after rebase)

Note that, in the default configuration, Git would refuse to push rewritten history (would deny a nonfast-forward push). You would need to force the push.

The problem is with merging changes based on the pre-rewrite versions of the revisions, such as the `topic` branch in this example:

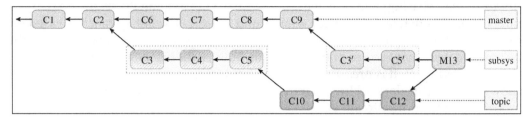

Fig 3: The situation after merging the changes that were based on pre-rewrite revisions into post-rewrite branches. Notice that the merge brings the pre-rewrite version of the revisions, including the commits dropped during rebase

If neither the downstream developer, nor the upstream one, notices that the published history has been rewritten, and merges the changes from the `topic` branch into, for example, the `subsys` branch it was based on, the merge would bring duplicated commits. As we can see in the example in *Fig 3*, after such a merge (denoted by `M13` here), we have both the `C3`, `C4`, and `C5` pre-rewrite commits brought by the topic branch, and the `C3'` and `C5'` post-rewrite commits. Note that the commit `C4` that was removed in the rewrite is back; it might have been a security bug!

Recovering from an upstream history rewrite

But what can we do if the upstream has rewritten the published history (for example, rebased it)? Can we avoid bringing the abandoned commits back, and merging a duplicate or near-duplicate of the rewritten revisions? After all, if the rewrite is published, changing it would be yet another rewrite.

The solution is to rebase your work to fit with the new version from the upstream, moving it from the pre-rewrite upstream revisions to the post-rewrite ones.

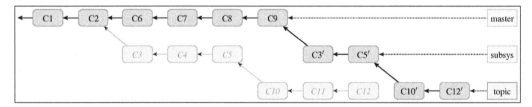

Fig 4: After a downstream rebase of a topic branch, done to recover from upstream rewrite

In the case of our example, it would mean rebasing the `topic` branch onto a new (post-rewrite) version of `subsys`, as shown in *Fig 4*.

You might not have a local copy of the subsys branch; in this case, substitute subsys with the respective remote-tracking branch, for example, origin/subsys.

Depending on whether the topic branch is public or not, it might mean that now you are breaking the promise of unaltered public history for your downstream. Recovering from an upstream rewrite might then result in a ripple of rebases following the rewrite down the river of downstreams (of dependent repositories).

An easy case is when subsys is simply rebased, and the changes remain the same (which means that C4 vanished because one of C6-C9 included it). Then, you can simply rebase topic on top of its upstream, that is, subsys, with:

```
$ git rebase subsys topic
```

The topic part is not necessary if you are currently on it (if topic is the current branch). This rebases everything: the old version of subsys and your commits in topic. This solution, however, relies on the fact that git rebase would skip repeated commits (removing C3, C4, and C5, and leaving only C10' and C12'). It might be better and less error-prone to assume the more difficult case.

The hard case is when rewriting subsys involved some changes and was not only a pure rebase, or when an interactive rebase was used. In this case, it is better to explicitly move just your changes, namely subsys@{1}..topic (assuming that the subsys@{1} entry in subsys reflog is before rewrite), stating that they are moved on top of new subsys. This can be done with the --onto option:

```
$ git rebase --onto subsys subsys@{1} topic
```

You can make Git use reflog to find a better common ancestor with the --fork-point option to Git rebase, for example:

```
$ git rebase --fork-point subsys topic
```

The rebase would then move the changes to topic, starting with the result of the git merge-base --fork-point subsys topic command; though if the reflog of the subsys branch does not contain necessary information, Git would fall back to upstream; here subsys.

 Note that you can use an interactive rebase instead of an ordinary rebase like in the narration mentioned earlier, for a better control at the cost of more work (for example, to drop commits that are already present, but are not detected by the rebase machinery as such).

Amending history without rewriting

What to do if what you need to fix is in the published part of the history? As described in *Perils of rewriting published history section*, changing the parts of the history that were made public (which is actually creating a changed copy and replacing references) can cause problems for downstream developers. You better not to touch this part of the graph of revisions.

There are a few solutions to this problem. The most commonly used is to put a new fixup commit with appropriate changes (for example, a typo fix in a documentation). If you need to remove changes, deciding that they turned out to be bad to have, you can create a commit to revert the changes.

If you fix a commit or revert one, it would be nice to annotate that commit with the information that it was buggy, and which commit fixed (or reverted) it. Even though you cannot (should not) edit the fixed commit to add this information if the commit is public, Git provides a notes mechanism to append extra information to existing commits, which is a bit like publishing an addendum, errata, or amendment. You need however to remember that notes are not published by default, nonetheless it is easy to publish them too (you just need to remember to do it).

Reverting a commit

If you need to back-out an existing commit, undoing the changes it brought, you can use `git revert`. As described in *Chapter 7, Merging Changes Together* (see, for example, *Fig 4*), the *revert* operation creates a commit with reverse of changes. For example, where original commit adds a line, reversion removes it, where original commit removes a line, reversion adds it.

> Note that different version control systems use the name *revert* for different operations. In particular, it is often used to mean resetting the changes to a file back to latest committed version, throwing away uncommitted changes. It is something that `git reset -- <file>` does in Git.

It is best shown on an example. Let's take for example of the last commit on branch `multiple`, and check the summary of its changes:

```
$ git show --stat multiple
commit bb71a804f9686c4bada861b3fcd3cfb5600d2a47
Author: Alice Developer <alice@company.com>
Date:   Sun Jun 1 03:02:09 2014 +0200
```

```
    Support optional <count> parameter
```

```
  src/rand.c | 26 ++++++++++++++++++++++-----
  1 file changed, 21 insertions(+), 5 deletions(-)
```

Reverting this commit (which requires a clean working directory) would create a new revision. This revision undoes the changes that the reverted commit brought:

```
$ git revert bb71a80
[master 76d9e25] Revert "Support optional <count> parameter"
  1 file changed, 5 insertions(+), 21 deletions(-)
```

Git would ask for a commit message, which should explain why you reverted a revision, how it was faulty, and why it needed to be reverted rather than fixed. The default is to give the SHA-1 of the reverted commit:

```
$ git show --stat
commit 76d9e259db23d67982c50ec3e6f371db3ec9efc2
Author: Alice Developer <alice@example.com>
Date:   Tue Jun 16 02:33:54 2015 +0200
Revert "Support optional <count> parameter"

This reverts commit bb71a804f9686c4bada861b3fcd3cfb5600d2a47.

  src/rand.c | 26 ++++++--------------------
  1 file changed, 5 insertions(+), 21 deletions(-)
```

An often found practice is to leave alone the subject (which allows to easily find reverts), but replace the content with a description of the reasoning behind the revert.

Reverting a faulty merge

Sometimes, you might need to undo an effect of a merge. Suppose that you have merged changes, but it turned out that they were merged prematurely, and that the merge brings regressions.

Let's say that the branch that got merged is a `topic` branch and that you were merging it into the `master` branch. This situation is shown in *Fig 5*:

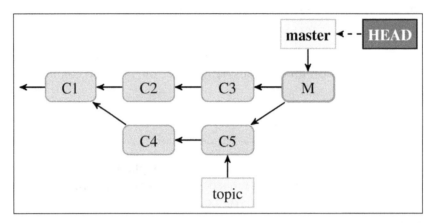

Fig 5: An accidental or premature merge commit, a starting point to reverting merges and redoing reverted merges

If you didn't publish this merge commit before you noticed the mistake and the unwanted merge exists only in your local repository, the easiest solution is to drop this commit with `git reset --hard HEAD^` (see *Chapter 4, Managing Your Worktree* for an explanation of the hard mode of `git reset`).

What do you do if you realize only later that the merge was incorrect, for example, after one more commit was created on the `master` branch and published? One possibility is to revert the merge.

However, a merge commit has more than one parent, which means more than one delta (more than one changeset). To run revert on a merge commit, you need to specify which patch you are reverting or, in other words, which parent is the mainline. In this particular scenario, assuming that there was one more commit after the merge (and that the merge was two commits back), the command would look as follows:

```
$ git revert -m 1 HEAD^^
[master b2d820c] Revert "Merge branch 'topic'"
```

The situation after reverting a merge is shown in *Fig 6*:

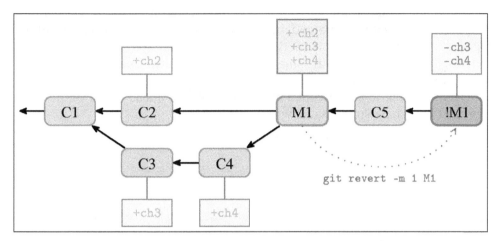

Fig 6: The history from the previous figure after `git revert -m 1 <merge commit>`. The square boxes attached to the selected commits symbolize their changesets in a diff-like format (combined diff format for the merged commit)

Starting with the new !M1 commit (the symbol !M1 was used to symbolize negation or reversal of commit M1), it's as if the merge never happened, at least, with respect to the changes.

Recovering from reverted merges

Let's assume that you continued work on a branch whose merge was reverted. Perhaps it was prematurely merged, but it doesn't mean that the development on it stopped. If you continue to work on the same branch, perhaps by creating commits with fixes, they will get ready in some time and then you will need to be able to merge them correctly into the mainline, again. Or perhaps, the mainline would mature enough to be able to accept a merge. Trouble lies ahead if you simply try to merge your branch again, the same way as the last time.

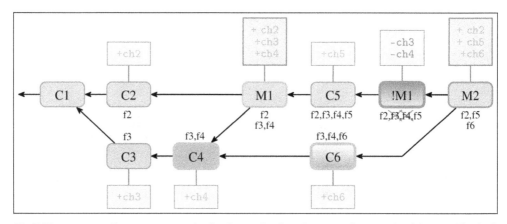

Fig 7: The unexpectedly erroneous result of trying to simply redo reverted merges in a history with a bad merge. The text beside the commits represents a list of features present in or absent from a commit. The three commits with a thick outline are merged commits ("ours" and "theirs" version) and the merge base: the common ancestor ("base")

The unexpected result is that Git has brought only the changes since the reverted merge. The changes brought by the commits on a side branch whose merge got reverted are not here. In other words, you would get a strange result: the new merge would not include the changes that were created on your branch (on side branch) before the merge that got reverted.

This is caused by the fact that revert undoes changes (the data), but does not undo the history (the DAG of revisions). This means that a new merge sees C4, the commit on the side branch just before the reverted merge, as a common ancestor. Because the default three-way merge strategy looks only at the state of the ours, theirs, and base snapshot, it doesn't search through the history to find that there was a revert there. It sees that both the common ancestor C4 and the merged branch (that is, *theirs*) C6 do include features brought by the commits C3 and C4, namely f3 and f4, while the branch that we merged into (that is, *ours*) doesn't have them because of the revert.

For the merge strategy, it looks exactly like the case where one branch deleted something, which means that this change (this removal) is the result of the merge (looks like the case when there was change only in one side). Particularly, it looks like the base has a feature, the side branch has a feature, but the current branch doesn't (because of the revert), so the result doesn't have it. You can find the explanation of the merging mechanism in *Chapter 7, Merging Changes Together*.

There is more than one option to fix this issue and make Git re-merge the `topic` branch correctly, which means including features `f3` and `f4` in the result. Which option you should choose depends on the exact circumstances, for example, whether the branch being merged is published or not. You don't usually publish topic branches, and if you do, perhaps in the form of the `proposed-updates` branch with all the topic branches merged in, it is with the understanding that they can and probably will be rewritten.

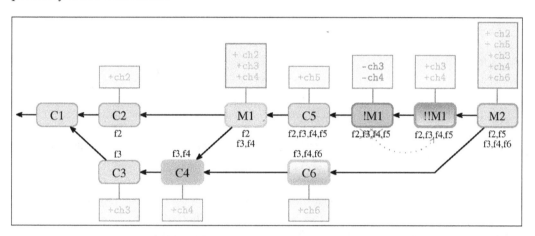

Fig 8: The history after remerging (as M2) a reverted merge M1 by reverting the revert !!M1. Notation used like in Fig 7

One option is to bring back deleted changes by reverting the revert. The result is shown in *Fig 8*. In this case, you have brought changes to match the recorded history.

Another option would be to change the view of the history (perhaps temporarily), for example amending it with `git replace`, by changing the merge !M1 to a nonmerge commit. Both these options are suitable in the situation where at least the parts of the branch being merged, namely `topic`, were published.

If the problem was some bugs in the commits being merged (on the branch `topic`) and the branch being merged was not published, you can fix these commits with the interactive rebase, as described earlier. Rebasing changes the history anyway, so if you additionally ensure that the new history you are creating with the rebase does not have any revision in common with the old history that includes the said failed and reverted merge, re-merging the topic branch would pose no challenges.

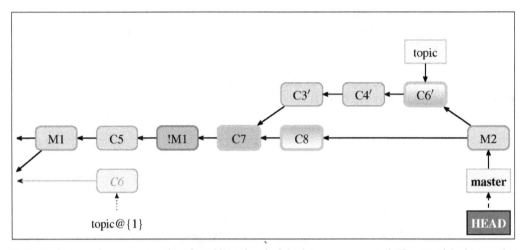

Fig 9: The history after remerging the rebased branch, which had its merge reverted. The rest of the history that is not visible here is like in Fig 6. The three commits with a thick outline are merged commits (the "ours" and "theirs" version) and the new merge base is the common ancestor ("base")

Usually, you would rebase a topic branch, `topic` here, on top of the current state of the branch it was forked from, which here is the `master` branch. This way, your changes are kept up to date with the current work, which makes a later merge easier. Now that the `topic` branch has new history, merging it again into `master`, like in *Fig 9*, is easy and it doesn't give any surprises or troubles.

A more difficult case would be if the `topic` branch is for some reason (like being able to merge it into the `maint` branch too) required to keep its base. Not more difficult in the sense that there would be problems with re-merging the `topic` branch after rebase, but that we need to ensure that the branch after rebase doesn't share history with the reverted merge arc. The goal is to have history in a shape as shown in *Fig 10*. By default, rebase tries to fast-forward revisions if they didn't change (for example, leaving C3 in place if the rebase didn't modify it), so we need to use `-f` / `--force-rebase` to force rebasing also of unchanged skippable commits. (or `--no-ff`, which is equivalent).

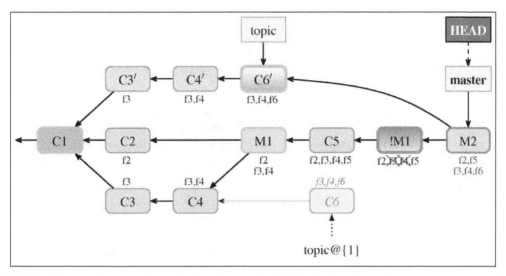

Fig 10: The history after remerging an "in place" rebased topic branch, where a pre-rebase merge was reverted. The notations used to mark the commits are the same as in Fig 7

So, you should not be blindly reverting the revert of a merge. What to do with the problem of re-merging after reverted merge depends on how you want to handle the branch being merged. If the branch is being rewritten (for example, using interactive rebase), then reverting the revert would be actively a wrong thing to do, because you could bring back errors fixed in the rewrite.

Storing additional information with notes

The notes mechanism is a way to store additional information for an object, usually a commit, without touching the objects themselves. You can think of it as an attachment, or an appendix, "*stapled*" to an object. Each note belongs to some category of notes, so that notes used for different purposes can be kept separate.

Adding notes to a commit

Sometimes, you want to add extra information to a commit— an information that is available only after its creation. It might be, for example, a note that there was a bug found in the said commit, and perhaps, even that it got fixed in some specified future commit (in case of regression). Perhaps, we realized, after the commit got published, that we forgot to add some important information to the commit message, for example, explain why it was done. Or maybe, we realized that there is another way of doing it and we want to note it to not forget about it, and for other developers to share the idea.

Because in Git history is immutable; you cannot do this without rewriting the history (creating a modified copy and forgetting the old version of the history). Immutability of history is important: it allows people to sign revisions and trust that, once inspected, history cannot change. What you can do instead is to add the extra message as a note.

Let's assume that codevelopers have switched from `atoi()` to `strtol()`, because the former is deprecated. The change was since then made public. But the commit message didn't include an explanation of why it was deprecated and why it is worth it to switch, even if the code after the change is longer. Let's add the information as a note:

```
$ git notes add \
  -m 'atoi() invokes undefined behaviour upon error' v0.2~3
```

We have added the note directly from the command line without invoking the editor by using the `-m` flag (the same as for `git commit`) to simplify the explanation of this example. The note will be visible while running `git log` or `git show`:

```
$ git show --no-patch v0.2~3
commit 8c4ceca59d7402fb24a672c624b7ad816cf04e08
Author: Bob Hacker <bob@company.com>
Date:   Sun Jun 1 01:46:19 2014 +0200

    Use strtol(), atoi() is deprecated


Notes:
    atoi() invokes undefined behaviour upon error
```

As you can see from the preceding output, our note is shown after the commit message in the `Notes:` section. Displaying notes can be disabled with the `--no-notes` option and (re)enabled with `--show-notes`.

How notes are stored

In Git, notes are stored using extra references in the `refs/notes/` namespace. By default, commit notes are stored using the `refs/notes/commits` ref; this can be changed using the `core.notesRef` configuration variable, which in turn can be overridden with the `GIT_NOTES_REF` environment variable.

The value of either variable must be fully qualified (that is, it must include the `refs/notes/`prefix, though this requirement got relaxed in newest Git). If the given ref does not exist, it is not an error, but it means that no notes should be printed. These variables decide both which type of notes are displayed with the commit after the `Notes:` line, and where to write the note created with `git notes add`.

You can see that the new type of reference has appeared in the repository:

```
$ git show-ref --abbrev
2b953b4 refs/heads/bar
5d25848 refs/heads/master
bb71a80 refs/heads/multiple
fcac4a6 refs/notes/commits
5d25848 refs/remotes/origin/HEAD
5d25848 refs/remotes/origin/master
b35871a refs/stash
995a30b refs/tags/v0.1
ee2d7a2 refs/tags/v0.2
```

If you examine the new reference, you will see that each note is stored in a file named after the SHA-1 identifier of the annotated object. This means that you can have only one note of the given type for one object. You can always edit the note, append to it (with `git notes append`), or replace its content (with `git notes add --force`). In the interactive mode, Git opens the editor with the contents of the note, so edit/append/replace is the same here. As opposed to commits, notes are mutable:

```
$ git show refs/notes/commits
commit fcac4a649d2458ba8417a6bbb845da4000bbfa10
Author: Alice Developer <alice@example.com>
Date:   Tue Jun 16 19:48:37 2015 +0200

    Notes added by 'git notes add'


diff --git a/8c4ceca59d7402fb24a672c624b7ad816cf04e08 b/8c4ceca59d7402fb2
4a672c624b7ad816cf04e08
new file mode 100644
index 0000000..a033550
```

```
--- /dev/null
+++ b/8c4ceca59d7402fb24a672c624b7ad816cf04e08
@@ -0,0 +1 @@
+atoi() invokes undefined behaviour upon error
```

```
$ git log -1 --oneline 8c4ceca59d7402fb24a672c624b7ad816cf04e08
8c4ceca Use strtol(), atoi() is deprecated
```

Notes for commits are stored in a separate line of (meta-)history, but this need not be the case for the other categories of notes: the notes reference can point directly to the *tree* object instead of to the *commit* object such as for `refs/notes/commits`.

One important issue that is often overlooked in books and articles is that it is the full path to file with notes contents, not the base name of the file, that identifies the object the note is attached to. If there are many notes, Git can and would use a fan-out directory hierarchy, for example storing the preceding note at the `8c/4c/eca59d7402fb24a672c624b7ad816cf04e08` path (notice the slashes).

Other categories and uses of notes

Notes are usually added to commits. But even for those notes that are attached to commits it makes sense, at least in some cases, to store different pieces of information using different categories of notes. This makes it possible to decide on an individual basis which parts of information to display, and which parts to push to the public repository, and it allows to query for specific parts of information individually.

To create a note in a namespace (category) different from the default one (where the default means `notes/commits`, or `core.notesRef` if set), you need to specify the category of notes while adding it:

```
$ git notes --ref=issues add -m '#2' v0.2~3
```

Now, by default, Git would display only the `core.notesRef` category of notes after the commit message. To include other types of notes, you must either select the category to display with `git log --notes=<category>` (where `<category>` is either the unqualified or qualified reference name, or a glob; you can use `--notes=*` to show all the categories), or configure which notes to display in addition to the default with the `display.notesRef` configuration variable (or the `GIT_NOTES_DISPLAY_REF` environment variable). You can either specify the the configuration variable value multiple times, just like for `remote.<remote-name>.push` (or specify a colon-separated list of pathnames in the case of using an environment variable), or you can specify a globing pattern:

```
$ git config notes.displayRef 'refs/notes/*'
$ git log -1 v0.2~3
commit 8c4ceca59d7402fb24a672c624b7ad816cf04e08
Author: Bob Hacker <bob@company.com>
Date:    Sun Jun 1 01:46:19 2014 +0200

    Use strtol(), atoi() is deprecated

Notes:
    atoi() invokes undefined behaviour upon error

Notes (issues):
    #2
```

There are many possible uses of notes. You can, for example, use notes to reliably mark which patches (which commits) were *upstreamed* (forward-ported to the development branch) or *downstreamed* (back-ported to the more stable branch or to the stable repository), even if the upstreamed/downstreamed version is not identical, and mark a patch as being *deferred* if it is not ready for either upstream or downstream.

This is a bit more reliable, if requiring manual input, than relying on the mechanism of `git patch-id` to detect when changeset is already present (which you can use by rebasing, using `git cherry`, or with the `--cherry` / `--cherry-pick` / `--cherry-mark` option to `git log`). This is, of course, in case we are not using topic branches from the start, but rather we are cherry-picking commits.

Notes can be used to store results of the post-commit (but pre-merge) code audit, and to notify other developers why this version of the patch was used.

Notes can also be used to handle **marking bugs and bug fixes**, and **verifying fixes**. You often find bugs in commits long after they got published, that's why you need notes for this; if you find a bug before publishing, you would rewrite the commit instead.

In this case, first, when the bug gets reported, and if it was regression, you find which revision introduced the bug (for example with `git bisect`, as described in *Chapter 2, Exploring Project History*). Then you would want to mark this commit, putting the identifier of a bug entry in an issue tracker for the project (usually, a number or number preceded by some specific prefix such as `Bug:1385`) in the `bugs`, or `defects`, or `issues` category of notes; perhaps you would want to also include the description of a bug. If the bug affects security, it might be assigned a vulnerability identifier, for example, a Common Vulnerabilities and Exposures (CVE) number; this information could be put into the note in the `CVE-IDs` category.

Then, after some time, hopefully, the bug will get fixed. Just like we marked the commit that it contains the bug, we can annotate it additionally with the information on which commit fixes it, for example, in note under `refs/notes/fixes`. Unfortunately, it might happen that the first attempt at fixing it didn't handle the bug entirely correct, and you have to amend a fix, or perhaps even create a fix for a fix. If you are using bugfix or hotfix branches (topic branches for bugfixes), as described in *Chapter 6, Advanced Branching Techniques*, it will be easy to find them together and to apply them together–by merging said bugfix branch. If you are not well, then it would be a good idea to use notes to annotate fixes that should be cherry-picked together with a supplementary commit, for example by adding note in `alsoCherryPick`, or `seeAlso`, or whatever you want to name this category of notes. Perhaps also an original submitter, or a Q&A group, would get to the fix and test that it works correctly; it would be better if the commit was tested before publishing, but it is not always possible, so `refs/notes/tests` it is.

Third-party tools use (or could use) notes to store additional **per-commit tool-specific information**. For example, Gerrit, which is a free, web-based team code collaboration tool, stores information about code reviews in `refs/notes/reviews`: including the name and e-mail address of the Gerrit user that submitted the change, the time the commit was submitted, the URL to the change review in the Gerrit instance, review labels and scores (including the identity of the reviewer), the name of project and branch, and so on:

```
Notes (review):
    Code-Review+2: John Reviewer <john@company.com>
    Verified+1: Jenkins
    Submitted-by: Bob Developer <bob@company.com>
    Submitted-at: Thu, 20 Oct 2014 20:11:16 +0100
    Reviewed-on: http://localhost:9080/7
    Project: common/random
    Branch: refs/heads/master
```

Similarly, `git svn`, a tool for bidirectional operation between the Subversion repository and Git working as a fat client for Subversion (`svn`), could have stored the original Subversion identifiers in notes, rather than appending this information to a commit message (or dropping it altogether).

Going to a more exotic example, you can use the notes mechanism to store the result of a build (either the archive, the installation package, or just the executable), attaching it to a commit or a tag. Theoretically, you could store a build result in a tag, but you usually expect for a tag to contain **Pretty Good Privacy** (**PGP**) signature and perhaps also the release highlights. Also, you would in almost all the cases want to fetch all the tags, while not everyone wants to pay the cost of disk space for the convenience of pre-build executables. You can select from case to case whether you want or not to fetch the given category of notes (for example, to skip pre-built binaries), while you autofollow tags. That's why notes are better than tags for this purpose.

Here the trouble is to correctly generate a binary note. You can binary-safely create a note with the following trick:

```
# store binary note as a blob object in the repository
$ blob=$(git hash-object -w ./a.out)
# take the given blob object as the note message
$ git notes --ref=built add --allow-empty -C "$blob" HEAD
```

You cannot simply use `-F ./a.out`, as this is not binary safe — comments (or rather what was misdetected as comment, that is lines starting with #) would be stripped.

The notes mechanism is also used as a mechanism to enable storing cache for the `textconv` filter (see the section on gitattributes in *Chapter 4, Managing Your Worktree*). All you need to do is configure the filter, setting its `cachetextconv` to `true`:

```
[diff "jpeg"]
   textconv = exif
   cachetextconv = true
```

Here, notes in the `refs/notes/texconv/jpeg` category (named after the filter) are used to attach the text of the conversion to a blob object.

Rewriting history and notes

Notes are attached to the objects they annotate, usually commits, by their SHA-1 identifier. What happens then with notes when we are rewriting history? In the new, rewritten history, SHA-1 identifiers of objects in most cases are different.

It turns out that you can configure this quite extensively. First, you can select which categories of notes should be copied along with the annotated object during rewrite with the `notes.rewriteRef` multi-value configuration variable. This setting can be overridden with the `GIT_NOTES_REWRITE_REF` (see the naming convention) environment variable with a colon-separated list (like for the well-known `PATH` environment variable) of fully qualified note references, and globs denoting reference patterns to match. There is no default value for this setting; you must configure this variable to enable rewriting.

Second, you can also configure whether to copy a note during rewriting depending on the exact type of the command doing the rewriting (currently supported are `rebase` and `amend` as the value of the command) . This can be done with the Boolean-valued configuration variable `notes.rewrite.<command>`.

In addition, you can decide what to do if the target commit already has a note while copying notes during a rewrite, for example while squashing commits using an interactive rebase. You have to decide between `overwrite` (take the note from the appended commit), `concatenate` (which is the default value), and `ignore` (use the note from the original commit being appended to) for the `notes.rewriteMode` configuration variable, or the `GIT_NOTES_REWRITE_MODE` environment variable.

Publishing and retrieving notes

So, we have notes in our own local repository. What to do if we want to share these notes? How do we make them public? How can we and other developers get notes from other public repositories?

We can employ our knowledge of Git here. Section *How notes are stored* explained that notes are stored in an object database of the repository using special references in the `refs/notes/` namespace. The contents of note are stored as a blob object, referenced through this special ref. Commit notes (notes in `refs/notes/commits`) store the history of notes, though Git allows you to store notes without history as well. So, what you need to do is to get notes references, and the contents of notes will follow. This is the usual mechanism of repository synchronization (of object transfer).

This means that to **publish your notes**, you need to configure appropriate `push` lines in the appropriate remote repository configuration (see *Chapter 5, Collaborative Development with Git*). Assuming that you are using a separate `public` remote (if you are the maintainer, you will probably use simply `origin`), which is perhaps set as `remote.pushDefault`, and that you would like to publish notes in any category, you can run:

```
$ git config --add remote.public.push '+refs/notes/*:refs/notes/*'
```

In the case when `push.default` is set to `matching` (or Git is old enough to have this as the default behavior), or the "push" lines use special refspec ":" or "+:", then it is enough to push notes refs the first time, and they would be pushed automatically each time after:

```
$ git push origin 'refs/notes/*'
```

Fetching notes is only slightly more involved. If you don't produce specified types of notes yourself, you can fetch notes in the mirror-like mode to the ref with the same name:

```
$ git config --add remote.origin.fetch '+refs/notes/*:refs/notes/*'
```

However, if there is a possibility of conflict, you would need to fetch notes from the remote into the remote-tracking notes reference, and then use `git notes merge` to join them into your notes; see the documentation for details.

> If you wanted to make it easy to merge `git` notes, perhaps even automatically, then following the convention of the `Key: Value` entries on separate lines for the content of notes with the duplicates removed would help.

There is no standard naming convention for remote-tracking notes references, but you can use either `refs/notes/origin/*` (so that the shortened notes category `commits` from the remote `origin` is `origin/commits` and so on), or go whole works and fetch `refs/*` from the remote origin into `refs/remotes/origin/refs/*` (so the `commits` category would land in `refs/remotes/origin/refs/notes/commits`).

Using the replacements mechanism

The original idea for the replace-like/replacement-like mechanism was to make it possible to join the history of two different repositories.

The original impulse was to be able to switch from the other version control system to Git by creating two repositories: one for the current work, starting with the most recent version in the empty repository, and the second one for the historical data, storing the conversion from the original system. That way, it would be possible to take time doing the faithful conversion of historical data, and even fix it if the conversion were incorrect, without affecting the current work.

What was needed is some mechanism to connect histories of those two repositories, to have full history for inspection going back to the creation of a project (for example, for `git blame`, that is, the line-history annotation).

The replacements mechanism

The modern incarnation of such tools is a replace (or replacements) mechanism. With it, you can replace any object, with any object or rather create a virtual history (virtual object database of a repository) by creating an overlay so that most Git commands return a replacement in place of the original object.

But the original object is still there, and Git's behavior with respect to the replacement mechanism was done in such a way as to eliminate the possibility of losing data. You can get the original view with the `--no-replace-objects` option to the `git` wrapper before the command, or the `GIT_NO_REPLACE_OBJECTS` environment variable. For example, to view the original history, you can use `git --no-replace-objects log`.

The information about replacement is saved in the repository by storing the ref named after SHA-1 of the replaced object in the `refs/replace/` namespace, with the SHA-1 of replacement as its sole content. However, there is no need to edit it by hand or with the low-level plumbing commands; you can use the `git replace` command.

Almost all the commands use replacements, unless told not too, as explained previously. The exception are the reachability analysis commands; this means that Git would not remove the replaced objects because there are no longer reachable if we take replacement into account. Of course, replacement objects are reachable from the replaced refs.

You can replace any object with any object, though changing the type of an object requires telling Git that you know what you are doing with `git replace -f <object> <replacement>`. This is because such a change might lead to troubles with Git, because it was expecting one type of object and getting another.

With `git replace --edit <object>`, you can edit its contents interactively. What really happens is that Git opens the editor with the object contents and, after editing, Git creates a new object and a replacement ref. The object format (in particular, the commit object format, as one would almost always edit commits) was described at beginning of this chapter. You can change the commit message, commit parents, authorship, and so on.

Example – joining histories with git replace

Let's assume that you want to split the repository into two, perhaps for performance reasons. But you want to be able to treat joined history as if it were one. Or perhaps, there was a history split after the SCM change, with the fresh repository with the current work (started after switching from the current state of a project with an empty history) and the converted historical repository kept separate.

How to split history was described in the examples of using `git filter-branch` here in this chapte. One of solutions shown here was to run `git replace --graft <to be root>` on a commit where you want to split and then use `git filter-branch -- --all` without filters to make the split permanent.

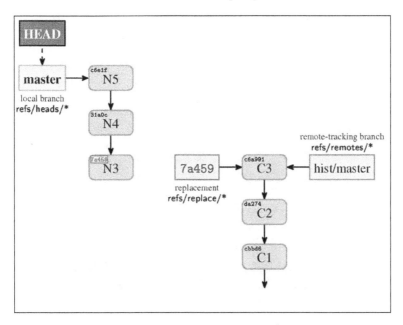

Fig 11: The view of a split history with the replacements turned off (`git --no-replace-objects`). The SHA-1 in the left upper corner of a commit denotes its identifier. Note that SHA-1 identifiers were all shortened to 5 hex-digits in this figure

In many cases, you might want to create a kind of informational commit on top of the historical repository, for example, adding to the README file the notification where one can find the current work repository. Such commits for simplicity are not shown in *Fig 11*.

How to join history depends a bit on whether the history was originally split or was originally joined. If it was originally joined, then split; just tell Git to replace post-split with the pre-split version with `git replace <post-split> <pre-split>`. If the repository was split from beginning, use the `--edit` or `--graft` option to `git replace`.

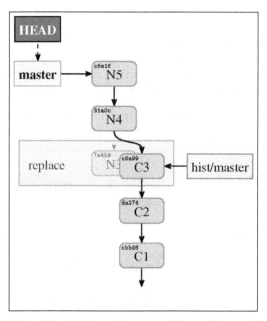

Fig 12: The view of a split history joined using replacements. The notations are the same as in the previous figure, but with the replace ref shown in a different way—as the result of the replacement

The split history is there, just hidden from the view. For all the Git commands, the history looks like *Fig 12*. You can, as described earlier, turn off using replacements; in this case, you would see the history as in *Fig 11*.

Historical note – grafts

The first attempt to create a mechanism to make it possible to join lines of history was `grafts`. It is a simple `.git/info/grafts` file with the SHA-1 of the affected commit and its replacement parents in line separated by spaces.

This mechanism was only for commits and allowed only to change the parentage. There was no support for transport, that is, for propagating this information from inside of Git. You could not turn grafts mechanism off temporarily, at least not easily. Moreover, it was inherently unsafe, because there were no exceptions for the reachability-checking commands, making it possible for Git to remove needed objects by accident during pruning (garbage collecting).

However, you can find its use in examples. Nowadays, it is obsolete, especially with the existence of the `git replace --graft` option. If you use grafts, consider replacing them with the replacements objects; there is the `contrib/convert-grafts-to-replace-refs.sh` script that can help with this in the Git sources.

 The **shallow clone** (the result of `git clone --depth=<N>`, a clone with the shortened history) is managed with a graft-like `.git/shallow` file. This file is managed by Git, however, not by the user.

Publishing and retrieving replacements

How to publish replacements and how to get them from the remote repository? Because replacements use references, this is quite simple.

Each replacement is a separate reference in the `refs/replaces/` namespace. Therefore, you can get all the replacements with the globing `fetch` or `push` line:

```
+refs/replace/*:refs/replace/*
```

There can be only one replacement for an object, so there are no problems with merging replacements. You can only choose between one replacement or the other.

Theoretically, you could also request individual replacements by fetching (and pushing) individual replacement references instead of using glob.

Summary

This chapter, along with *Chapter 6, Advanced Branching Techniques*, provided all the tools required to manage a clean, readable, and easy-to-review history of a project.

You have learned how to make history more clean by rewriting it, and what does rewriting history mean in Git, when and why to avoid it, and how to recover from an untimely upstream rewrite. You have learned to use an interactive rebase to delete, reorder, squash, and split commits, and how to test each commit during rebase. You know how to do large-scale scripted rewrite with filter-branch: how to edit commits and commit metadata and how to permanently change history, for example, splitting it in two. You also got to know some third-party external tools, which can help with these tasks.

You learned what to do if you cannot rewrite history: how to fix mistakes by creating commits with appropriate changes (for example with `git revert`), how to add extra information to the existing commits with notes, and how to change the virtual view of the history with replacements. You learned to handle reverting a faulty merge and re-merging after reverted merge. You know how to fetch and publish both notes and replacements.

To really understand advanced history rewriting and the mechanism behind notes and replacements, this chapter explained the basics of Git internals and low-level commands usable for scripting (including scripted rewrite).

The following chapter, *Chapter 9, Managing Subprojects - Building a Living Framework*, will explain and show different ways to connect different subprojects in one repository, from submodules to subtrees.

You will also learn techniques to manage or mitigate managing large-size assets inside a repository. Splitting a large project into submodules is one, but not the only way to handle this issue.

9
Managing Subprojects – Building a Living Framework

In *Chapter 5*, *Collaborative Development with Git*, you have learned how to manage multiple repositories, while *Chapter 6*, *Advanced Branching Techniques*, taught us various development techniques utilizing multiple branches and multiple lines of development in these repositories. Up till now, these multiple repositories were all repositories of a single project. Different projects were all being developed independent of each other. Repositories of the different projects were autonomous.

This chapter will explain and show different ways to connect different subprojects in the one single repository of the framework project, from the strong inclusion by embedding the code of one project in the other (subtrees), to the light connection between projects by nesting repositories (submodules). You will learn how to add a subproject to a master project, how to update the superproject state, and how to update a subproject. We will find out how to send our changes upstream, backporting them into the appropriate project , and pushing to appropriate repository. Different techniques of managing subprojects have different advantages and drawbacks here.

Submodules are sometimes used to manage large size assets. This chapter would also present alternate solutions to the problem of handling large binary files, and other large assets in Git.

In this chapter, we will cover the following topics:

- Managing library and framework dependencies
- Dependency management tools — managing dependencies outside Git
- Importing code into a superproject as a subtree
- Using subtree merges; the `git-subtree` and `git-stree` tools
- Nested repositories: a subproject inside a superproject
- Internals of submodules: `gitlinks`, `.gitmodules`, the `.git` file
- Use cases for subtrees and submodules, comparison of approaches
- Alternative third-party solutions and tools/helpers
- Git and large files

Managing library and framework dependencies

There are various reasons to join an external project to your own project. Because there are different reasons to include a project (let's call it a *subproject*, or a *module*) inside another project (let's call it *superproject*, or a *master project*, or a *container*), there are different types of inclusions geared towards different circumstances. They all have their advantages and disadvantages, and it is important to understand these to be able choose the correct solution for your problem.

Let's assume that you work on a web application, and that your webapp uses JavaScript (for example, for AJAX, as single-page app perhaps). To make it easier to develop, you probably use some JavaScript library or a web framework, such as jQuery.

Such a library is a separate project. You would want to be able to pin it to a known working version (to avoid problems where future changes to the library would make it stop working for your project), while also being able to review changes and automatically update it to the new version. Perhaps, you would want to make your own changes to the library, and send the proposed changes to the upstream (of course, you would want for users of your project to be able to use the library with your out-of-tree fixes, even if they are not yet accepted by original developers). Conceivably, you might have customizations and changes that you don't want to publish (send to the upstream), but you might still make them available.

This is all possible in Git. There are two main solutions for including subprojects: importing code into your project with the *subtree* merge strategy and linking subprojects with *submodules*.

Both submodules and subtrees aim to reuse the code from another project, which usually has its own repository, putting it somewhere inside your own repository's working directory tree. The goal is usually to benefit from the central maintenance of the reused code across a number of container repositories, without having to resort to clumsy, unreliable manual maintenance (usually by copy-pasting).

Sometimes, it is more complicated. The typical situation in many companies is that they use many in-house produced applications, which depend on the common utility library or on a set of libraries. You would usually want to develop each of such applications separately, use it together with others, branch and merge, and apply your own changes and customizations, all in a separate Git repository. Though there are cases for having a single monolithic repository, such as simplified organizations, dependencies, cross-project changes, and tooling if you can get away with it.

But this division, one Git repository for one application, is not without problems. What to do with the common library? Each application uses some specific version of the library and you need to supervise which one. If the library gets improved, you need to test whether this new version correctly works with your code and doesn't crash your application. But the common library is not usually developed as a standalone; its development is driven by the needs of projects that use it. Developers improve it to enhance it with new features needed for their applications. At some point of time, they would want to send their changes to the library itself to share their changes with other developers, if only to share the burden of maintaining these features (the out-of-tree patches bring maintenance costs to keep them current).

What to do then? This chapter describes a few strategies used to manage subprojects. For each technique, we will detail how to add such subprojects to superprojects, how to keep them up to date, how to create your own changes, and how to publish selected changes upstream.

 Note that all the solutions require that all the files of a subproject are contained in a single subdirectory of a superproject. No currently available solution allows you to mix the subproject files, with other files or have them occupy more than one directory.

However you manage subprojects, be it subtrees, submodules, third-party tools or dependency management outside Git, you should strive for the module code to remain independent of the particularities of the superproject (or at least, handle such particularities using an external, possibly nonversioned configuration). Using superproject-specific modifications goes against modularization and encapsulation principles, unnecessarily coupling the two projects.

Managing dependencies outside Git

In many cases, the technological context (the development stack used) allows to use for packaging and formal dependency management. If it is possible, it is usually preferable to go this route. It lets you split your codebase better and avoid a number of side effects, complications, and pitfalls that litter the submodule and subtree solution space (with different complications for different techniques). It removes the version control systems from the managing modules. It also lets you benefit from versioning schemes, such as **semantic versioning** (http://semver.org/), for your dependencies.

As a reminder, here's a partial list (in the alphabetical order) of the main languages and development stacks, and their dependency management/packaging systems and registries (see the full comparison at http://www.modulecounts.com/):

- Clojure has Clojars
- Go has GoDoc
- Haskell has Hackage (registry) and cabal (application)
- Java has Maven Central (Maven and Gradle)
- JavaScript has npm (for Node.js) and Bower
- .NET has NuGet
- Objective-C has CocoaPods
- Perl has CPAN (Comprehensive Perl Archive Network) and carton
- PHP has Composer, Packagist, and good old PEAR and PECL
- Python has PyPI (Python Package Index) and pip
- Ruby has Bundler and RubyGems
- Rust has Crates

Sometimes, these are not enough. You might need to apply some out-of-tree patches (changes) to customize the module (subproject) for your needs. But for some reason, you are unable to publish these changes upstream, to have them accepted. Perhaps, the changes are relevant only to your specific project, or the upstream is slow to respond to the proposed changes, or perhaps there are license considerations Maybe the subproject in question is a in-house module that cannot be made public and which you are required to use for your company projects.

In all these cases, you need for the custom package registry (the package repository) to be used in addition to the default one , or you need to make subprojects be managed as private packages, which these systems often allow. If there is no support for private packages, a tool to manage the private registry, such as Pinto or CPAN::Mini for Perl, would be also needed.

Manually importing the code into your project

Let's take a look at one of the possibilities: why don't we simply import the library into some subdirectory in our project? If you need to bring it up to date, you would just copy the new version as a new set of files. In this approach, the subproject code is embedded inside the code of the superproject.

The simplest solution would be to just overwrite the contents of the subproject's directory each time we want to update the superproject to use the new version. If the project you want to import doesn't use Git, or if it doesn't use a version control system at all, or if the repository it uses is not public, this will indeed be the only possible solution.

Using repositories from a foreign VCS as a remote

If the project you want to import (to embed) uses a version control system other than Git, but there is a good conversion mechanism (for example, with a fast-import stream), you can use **remote helpers** to set up a foreign VCS repository as a remote repository (via automatic conversion). You can check *Chapter 5, Collaborative Development with Git*, and *Chapter 10, Customizing and Extending Git* for more information.

This can be done, for example, with the Mercurial and Bazaar repositories, thanks to the git-remote-hg and git-remote-bzr helpers.

Moving to the new version of the imported library is quite simple (and the mechanism easy to understand). Remove all the files from the directory, add files from the new version of the library, for example by extracting them from the archive, then use git add command to the directory:

```
$ rm -rf mylib/
$ git rm mylib
$ tar -xzf /tmp/mylib-0.5.tar.gz
$ mv mylib-0.5 mylib
$ git add mylib
$ git commit
```

This method works quite well in simple cases with the following caveats:

- In Git, in the history of your project, you have only the versions of the library at the time of imports. On the one hand, this makes your project history clean and easy to understand, on the other hand, you don't have access to the fine-grained history of a subproject. For example, when using git bisect, you would be able only find that it was introduced by upgrading the library, but not the exact commit in the history of the library that introduced the bug in question.

- If you want to customize the code of the library, fitting it to your project by adding the changes dependent on your application, you would need to reapply those customization in some way after you import a new version. You could extract your changes with `git diff` (comparing it to the unchanged version at the time of import) and then use `git apply` after upgrading the library. Or, you could use a rebase, an interactive rebase, or some patch management interface; see *Chapter 8, Keeping History Clean*. Git won't do this automatically.

- Each importing of the new version of the library requires running a specific sequence of commands to update superproject: removing the old version of files, adding new ones, and committing the change. It is not as easy as running `git pull`, though you can use scripts or aliases to help.

A Git subtree for embedding the subproject code

In a slightly more advanced solution, you use the **subtree merge** to join the history of a subproject to the history of a superproject. This is only somewhat more complicated than an ordinary pull (at least, after the subproject is imported), but provides a way to automatically merge changes together.

Depending on your requirements, this method might fit well with your needs. It has the following advantages:

- You would always have the correct version of the library, never using the wrong library version by an accident

- The method is simple to explain and understand, using only the standard (and well-known) Git features. As you will see, the most important and most commonly used operations are easy to do and easy to understand, and it is hard to go wrong.

- The repository of your application is always self-contained; therefore, cloning it (with plain old `git clone`) will always include everything that's needed. This means that this method is a good fit for the *required dependencies*.

- It is easy to apply patches (for example, customizations) to the library inside your repository, even if you don't have the commit rights to the upstream repository.

- Creating a new branch in your application also creates a new branch for the library; it is the same for switching branches. That's the behavior you expect. This is contrasted with the submodule's behavior (the other technique for managing subprojects).

- If you are using the `subtree` merge strategy (described shortly in *Chapter 7, Merging Changes Together*), for example with `git pull -s subtree`, then getting a new library version will be as easy as updating all the other parts of your project.

Unfortunately however, this technique is not without its disadvantages. For many people and for many projects, these disadvantages do not matter. The simplicity of the subtree-based method usually prevails over its faults.

Here are the problems with the subtree approach:

- Each application using the library doubles its files. There is no easy and safe way to share its objects among different projects and different repositories. Though see the following about the possibility of sharing Git object database.

- Each application using the library has its files checked out in the working area, though you can change it with the help of the **sparse checkout** (described later in the chapter).

- If your application introduces changes to its copy of the library, it is not that easy to publish these changes and send them upstream. Third-party tools such as `git subtree` or `git stree` can help here. They have specialized subcommands to extract the subproject's changes.

- Because of the lack of separation between the subproject files and the superproject files, it is quite easy to mix the changes to the library and the changes to the application in one commit. In such cases, you might need to rewrite the history (or the copy of a history), as described in *Chapter 8, Keeping History Clean*.

The first two issues mean that subtrees are not a good fit to manage the subprojects that are *optional dependencies* (needed only for some extra features) or *optional components* (such as themes, extensions, or plugins), especially those that are installed by a mere presence in the appropriate place in the filesystem hierarchy.

Sharing objects between forks (copies) with alternates

You can mitigate the duplication of objects in the repository with alternates or, in other words, with `git clone --reference`. However, then you would need to take greater care about garbage collection. The problematic parts are those parts of the history that are referenced in the borrower repository (that is, one with alternates set up), but are not referenced in the lender reference's repository. The description and explanation of the alternative mechanisms will be presented in *Chapter 11, Git Administration*.

There are different technical ways to handle and manage the subtree-imported subprojects. You can use classic Git commands, just using the appropriate options while affecting the subproject, such as `--strategy=subtree` (or the `subtree` option to the default `recursive` merge strategy, `--strategy-option=subtree=<path>`) for `merge`, `cherry-pick`, and related operations. This manual approach works everywhere, is actually quite simple in most cases, and offers the best degree of control over operations. It requires, however, a good understanding of the underlying concepts.

In modern Git (since version 1.7.11), there is the `git subtree` command available among installed binaries. It comes from the `contrib/` area and is not fully integrated (for example, with respect to its documentation). This script is well tested and robust, but some of its notions are rather peculiar or confusing , and this command does not support the whole range of possible subtree operations. Additionally, this tool supports only the *import with history* workflow (which will be defined later), which some say clutters the history graph.

There are also other third-party scripts that help with subtrees; among them is `git-stree`.

Creating a remote for a subproject

Usually, while importing a subproject, you would want to be able to update the embedded files easily. You would want to continue interacting with the subproject. For this, you would add that subproject (for example, the common library) as a remote reference in your own (super) project and fetch it:

```
$ git remote add mylib_repo https://git.example.com/mylib.git
$ git fetch mylib_repo
warning: no common commits
remote: Counting objects: 12, done.
remote: Total 12 (delta 0), reused 0 (delta 0)
Unpacking objects: 100% (12/12), done.
From https://git.example.com/mylib.git
* [new branch]      master      -> mylib_repo/master
```

You can then examine the `mylib_repo/master` remote-tracking branch, which can be done either by checking it out into the detached HEAD with `git checkout mylib_repo/master`, or by creating a local branch out of it and checking this local branch out with `git checkout -b mylib_branch mylib_repo/master`. Alternatively, you can just list its files with `git ls-tree -r --abbrev mylib_repo/master`. You will see then that the subproject has a different project root from your superproject. Additionally, as seen from the `warning: no common commits` message, this remote-tracking branch contains a completely different history coming from a separate project.

Adding a subproject as a subtree

If you are not using specialized tools like `git subtree` but a manual approach, the next step will be a bit complicated and will require you to use some advanced Git concepts and techniques. Fortunately, it needs to be done only once.

First, if you want to import the subproject history, you would need to create a merge commit that will import the subproject in question. You need to have the files of the subproject in the given directory in a superproject. Unfortunately, at least, with the current version of Git as of writing this chapter, using the `-Xsubtree=mylib/` merge strategy option would not work as expected. We would have to do it in two steps: prepare the parents and then prepare the contents.

The first step would then be to prepare a merge commit using the `ours` merge strategy, but without creating it (writing it to the repository). This strategy joins histories, but takes the current version of the files from the current branch:

```
$ git merge --no-commit --strategy=ours mylib_repo/master
Automatic merge went well; stopped before committing as requested
```

If you want to have *simple history*, similar to the one we get from just copying files, you can skip this step.

We now need to update our index (the staging area for the commits) with the contents of the `master` branch from the library repository, and update our working directory with it. All this needs to happen in the proper subfolder too. This can be done with the low-level (plumbing) `git read-tree` command:

```
$ git read-tree --prefix=mylib/ -u mylib_repo/master
$ git status
On branch master
All conflicts fixed but you are still merging.
  (use "git commit" to conclude merge)


Changes to be committed:

        new file:    mylib/README
        [...]
```

We have used the `-u` option, so the working directory is updated along with the index.

It is important to not forget the trailing slash in the argument of the `--prefix` option. Checked out files are *literally* prefixed with it.

This set of steps is described in the HOWTO section of the Git documentation, namely in the *How to use the subtree merge strategy* moved earlier `https://www.kernel.org/pub/software/scm/git/docs/howto/using-merge-subtree.html`.

It is much easier to use tools such as `git subtree`:

```
$ git subtree add --prefix=mylib mylib_repo master
git fetch mylib_repo master
Added dir 'mylib'
```

The `git subtree` command would fetch the subtree's remote when necessary; there's no need for the manual fetch that you had to perform in the manual solution.

If you examine the history, for example, with `git log --oneline --graph --decorate`, you will see that this command merged the library's history with the history of the application (of the superproject). If you don't want this, tough luck. The `--squash` option that `git subtree` offers on its `add`, `pull`, and `merge` subcommands won't help here. One of the peculiarities of this tool is that this option doesn't create a **squash merge**, but simply merges the squashed subproject's history (as if it were squashed with an interactive rebase). See, *Fig 2* later in the chapter.

If you want a subtree without its history attached to the superproject history, consider using `git-stree`. It has the additional advantage that it remembers the subtree settings and that it would create a remote if necessary:

```
$ git stree add mylib_repo -P mylib \
  https://git.example.com/mylib.git master
warning: no common commits
[master 5e28a71] [STree] Added stree 'mylib_repo' in mylib
 5 files changed, 32 insertions(+)
 create mode 100644 mylib/README
[...]

  STree 'mylib_repo' configured, 1st injection committed.
```

The information about the subtree's prefix (subdirectory), the branch, and so on is stored in the local configuration in the `stree.<name>` group This stays in contrast to the behavior of `git subtree`, where you need to provide the prefix argument on each command.

Cloning and updating superprojects with subtrees

All right! Now that we have our project with a library embedded as a subtree, what do we need to do to get it? Because the concept behind subtrees is to have just one repository: the container, you can simply clone this repository.

To get an up-to-date repository you just need a regular pull; this would bring both superproject (the container) and subproject (the library) up to date. This works regardless of the approach taken, the tool used, and the manner in which the subtree was added. It is a great advantage of the subtrees approach.

Getting updates from subprojects with a subtree merge

Let's see what happens if there are some new changes in the subproject since we imported it. It is easy to bring the version embedded in the superproject up to date:

```
$ git pull --strategy subtree mylib_repo master
From https://git.example.com/mylib.git
 * branch            master      -> FETCH_HEAD
Merge made by the 'subtree' strategy.
```

You could have fetched and then merged instead, which allows for greater control. Or, you could have rebased instead of merging, if you prefer; that works too.

> Don't forget to select the merge strategy with `-s subtree` while pulling a subproject. Merging could work even without it, because Git does rename detection and would usually be able to discover that the files were moved from the root directory (in the subproject) to a subdirectory (in the superproject we are merging into). The problematic case is when there are conflicting files inside and outside of the subproject. Potential candidates are `Makefiles` and other standard filenames.
>
> If there are some problems with Git detecting the correct directory to merge into, or if you need advanced features of an ordinary `recursive` merge strategy (which is the default), you can instead use `-Xsubtree=<path/to/subproject>`, the `subtree` option of the `recursive` merge strategy.

You may need to adjust other parts of the application code to work properly with the updated code of the library.

Note that, with this solution, you have a subproject history attached to your application history, as you can see in *Fig 1*:

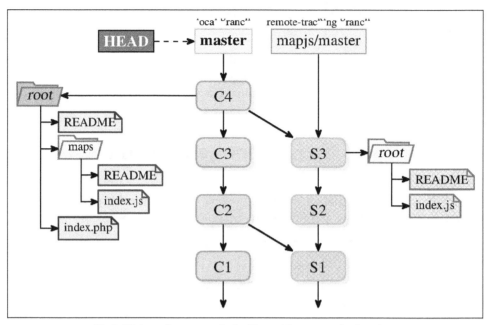

Fig 1: History of a superproject with a subtree-merged subproject

If you don't want to have the history of a subproject entangled in the history of a master project, and prefer a simple-looking history (as shown on *Fig. 2*), you can use the `--squash` option of `git merge` (or `git pull`) command to squash it.

```
$ git merge -s subtree --squash mylib_repo/master
Squash commit -- not updating HEAD
Automatic merge went well; stopped before committing as requested
$ git commit -m "Updated the library"
```

In this case, you would have in the history only the fact that the version of the subproject had changed, which has its advantages and disadvantages. You get simpler history, but also simplified history.

With the `git subtree` or `git stree` tools, it is enough to use their `pull` subcommand; they supply the `subtree` merge strategy themselves. However, currently `git subtree pull` requires you to respecify `--prefix` and the entire subtree settings.

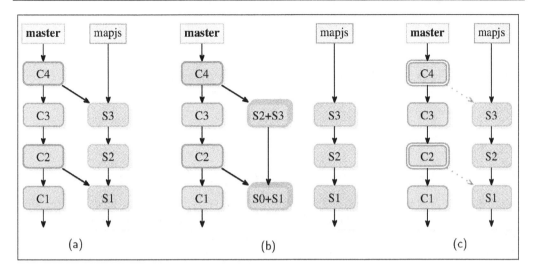

Fig 2: Different types of subtree merges: (a) subtree merge: `git pull -s subtree` and `git subtree pull`, (b) subtree merge of squashed commits: `git subtree pull --squash`, (c) squashed subtree merge: `git pull -s subtree --squash` and `git stree`. Note that dotted line in (c) denotes how commits C2 and C4 were made, and not that it is parent commit.

Note that the `git subtree` command always merges, even with the `--squash` option; it simply squashes the subproject commits before merging (such as the `squash` instruction in the interactive rebase). In turn, `git stree pull` always squashes the merge (such as `git merge --squash`), which keeps the superproject history and subproject history separated without polluting the graph of the history. All this can be seen in *Fig 2*.

Showing changes between a subtree and its upstream

To find out the differences between the subproject and the current version in the working director, you need nontypical selector syntax for `git diff`. This is because all the files in the subproject (for example, in the `mylib_repo/master` remote-tracking branch) are in the root directory, while they are in the `mylib/` directory in the superproject (for example, in `master`). We need to select the subdirectory to be compared with `master`, putting it after the revision identifier and the colon (skipping it would mean that it would be compared with the root directory of the superproject).

The command looks as follows:

```
$ git diff master:mylib mylib_repo/master
```

Similarly, to check after the subtree merge whether the commit we just created (HEAD) has the same contents in the `mylib/` directory as the merged in commit, that is, HEAD^2, we can use:

```
$ git diff HEAD:mylib HEAD^2
```

Sending changes to the upstream of a subtree

In some cases, the subtree code of a subproject can only be used or tested inside the container code; most themes and plugins have such constraints. In this situation, you'll be forced to evolve your subtree code straight inside the master project code base, before you finally backport it to the subproject upstream.

These changes often require adjustments in the rest of the superproject code; though it is recommended to make two separate commits (one for the subtree code change and one for the rest), it is not strictly necessary. You can tell Git to extract only the subproject changes. The problem is with the commit messages of the split changes, as Git is not able to automatically extract relevant parts of the changeset description.

Another common occurrence, which is best avoided but is sometimes necessary, is the need to customize the subproject's code in a container-specific way (configure it specifically for a master project), usually without pushing these changes back upstream. You should carefully distinguish between both the situations, keeping each use case's changes (backportable and nonbackportable) in their own commits.

There are different ways to deal with this issue. You can avoid the problem of extracting changes to be sent upstream by requiring that all the subtree changes have to be done in a separate module-only repository. If it is possible, we can even require that all the subproject changes have to be sent upstream first, and we can get the changes into the container only through upstream acceptance.

If you need to be able to extract the subtree changes, then one possible solution is to utilize `git filter-branch --directory-filter` (or `--index-filter` with the appropriate script). Another simple solution is to just use `git subtree push`. Both the methods, however, backport every commit that touches the subtree in question.

If you want to send upstream only a selection of the changes to the subproject of those that made it into the master project repository, then the solution is a bit more complicated. One possibility is to create a local branch meant specifically for backporting out of the subproject remote-tracking branch. Forking it from said subtree-tracking branch means that it has the subtree as the root and it would include only the submodule files.

This branch intended for backporting changes to the subproject would need to have the appropriate branch in the remote of the subproject upstream repository as its upstream branch. With such setup, we would then be able to `git cherry-pick --strategy=subtree` the commits we're interested in sending to the subproject's upstream onto it. Then, we can simply `git push` this branch into the subproject's repository.

> It is prudent to specify `--strategy=subtree` even if cherry-pick would work without it, to make sure that the files outside the subproject's directory (outside subtree) will get quietly ignored. This can be used to extract the subtree changes from the mixed commit; without this option, Git will refuse to complete the cherry-pick.

This requires much more steps than ordinary `git push`. Fortunately, you need to face this problem only while sending the changes made in the superproject repository back to the subproject. As you have seen, fetching changes from the subproject into the superproject is much, much simpler.

Well, it using `git-stree` would make this trivial: you just need to list the commits to be pushed to backport:

```
$ git stree push mylib_repo master~3 master~1
  5e28a71 [To backport] Support for creating debug symbols
  5b0aa4b [To backport] Timestamping (requires application tweaks)
  STree 'mylib_repo' successfully backported local changes to its remote
```

In fact, this tool uses internally the same technique, creating and using a backport-specific local branch for the subproject.

The Git submodules solution: repository inside repository

The subtrees method of importing the code (and possibly also history) of a subproject into the superproject has its disadvantages. In many cases, the subproject and the container are two different projects: your application depends on the library, but it is obvious that they are separate entities. Joining the histories of the two doesn't look like the best solution.

Additionally, the embedded code and imported history of a subproject is always here. Therefore, the subtrees technique is not a good fit for optional dependencies and components (such as plugins or themes). It also doesn't allow you to have different access control for the subproject's history, with the possible exception of restricting write access to the subproject (actually to the subdirectory of a subproject), by using Git repository management solutions such as gitolite (you can find more in *Chapter 11, Git Administration*).

The submodule solution is to keep the subproject code and history in its own repository and to embed this repository inside the working area of a superproject, but not to add its files as superproject files.

Gitlinks, .git files, and the git submodule command

Git includes the command named git submodule, which is intended to work with submodules. Unfortunately, using this tool is not easy. To utilize it correctly, you need to understand at least some of the details of its operation. It is a combination of two distinct features: the so-called **gitlinks** and the git submodule tool itself.

Both in the subtree solution and the submodule solution, subprojects need to be contained in their own folder inside the working directory of the superproject. But while with subtrees the code of the subproject belongs to superproject repository, it is not the case for submodules. With submodules, each subproject has instead its own repository somewhere inside the working directory of its container repository. The code of the submodule belongs to its repository, and the superproject itself simply stores meta-information required to get appropriate revision of the subproject files.

In practice, in modern Git, submodules use a simple .git file with a single gitdir: line containing a relative path to the actual repository folder. The submodule repository is actually located inside superproject's .git/modules folder (and has core.worktree set up appropriately). This is done mostly to handle the case when the superproject has branches that don't have submodule at all. It allows to avoid having to scrap the submodule's repository while switching to the superproject revision without it.

You can think of the .git file with gitdir: line as a symbolic reference equivalent for the .git directories, an OS-independent symbolic link replacement. The path to the repository doesn't need to be a relative path.

```
$ ls -aloF plugins/demo/
total 10
```

```
drwxr-xr-x 1 user   0 Jul 13 01:26 ./
drwxr-xr-x 1 user   0 Jul 13 01:26 ../
-rw-r--r-- 1 user 32 Jul 13 01:26 .git
-rw-r--r-- 1 user  9 Jul 13 01:26 README
[...]
$ cat plugins/demo/.git
gitdir: ../../.git/modules/plugins/demo
```

Be that as it may, the contained superproject and the subproject module truly act as and, in fact, are independent repositories: they have their own history, their own staging area, and their own current branch. You should, therefore, take care while typing commands, minding if you're inside the submodule or outside it, because the context and impact of your commands differ drastically!

The main idea behind submodules is that the superproject commit remembers the exact revision of the subproject; this reference uses the SHA1 identifier of subproject commit. Instead of using a manifest-like file like in some dependency management tools, submodules solution stores this information in a tree object using the so-called gitlinks. Gitlink is a reference from a tree object (in the superproject repository) to a commit object (usually, in the submodule repository); see *Fig 3*.

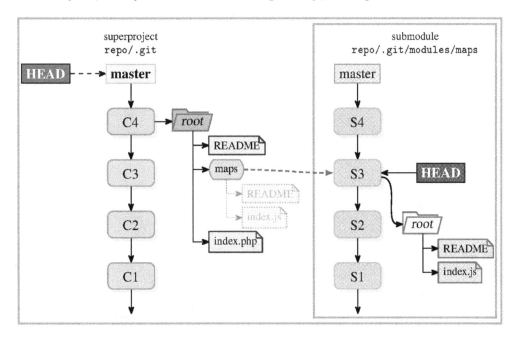

Fig 3: The history of a superproject with a subproject linked as a submodule . The faint shade of submodule files on left hand side denotes that there are present as files in the working directory of the superproject, but are not in the superproject repository themselves.

Recall that, following the description of the types of objects in the repository database from *Chapter 8*, *Keeping History Clean*, each commit object (representing a revision of a project) points exactly to one tree object with the snapshot of the repository contents. Each tree object references blobs and trees, representing file contents and directory contents, respectively. The tree object referenced by the commit object uniquely identifies the set of files contents, file names, and file permissions contained in a revision associated with the commit object.

Let's remember that the commit objects themselves are connected with each other, creating the Directed Acyclic Graph (DAG) of revisions. Each commit object references zero or more parent commits, which together describe the history of a project.

Each type of the references mentioned earlier took part in the reachability check. If the object pointed to was missing, it means that the repository is corrupt.

It is not so for gitlinks. Entries in the tree object pointing to the commits refer to the objects in the other separate repository, namely in the subproject (submodule) repository. The fact that the submodule commit being unreachable is not an error is what allows us to optionally include submodules; no submodule repository, no commit referenced in gitlink.

The results of running `git ls-tree --abbrev HEAD` on a project with all the types of objects is as follows:

```
040000 tree 573f464    docs
100755 blob f27adc2    executable.sh
100644 blob 1083735    README.txt
040000 tree ef9bcb4    subdirectory
160000 commit 5b0aa4b   submodule
120000 blob 3295d66    symlink
```

Compare it with the contents of the working area (with `ls -l -o -F`):

```
drwxr-xr-x    5 user    12288 06-28 17:18 docs/
-rwxr-xr-x    1 user    36983 02-20 20:11 executable.sh*
-rw-r--r--    1 user     2628 2015-01-03  README.txt
drwxr-xr-x    3 user     4096 06-28 17:19 subdirectory/
drwxr-xr-x   48 user    36864 06-28 17:19 submodule/
lrwxrwxrwx    1 user       32 06-28 17:18 symlink -> docs/toc.html
```

Adding a subproject as a submodule

With subtrees, the first step was usually to add a subproject repository as a remote, which meant that objects from the subproject repository were fetched into the superproject object database.

With submodules, the subproject repository is kept separate. You could manage cloning the subproject repository manually from inside the superproject worktree and then add the gitlink also by hand with `git add <submodule directory>` (without a trailing slash).

Important note!

Normally, commands `git add subdir` and `git add subdir/` (the latter with a forward slash, which following the POSIX standard denotes a subdirectory) are equivalent. This is not true if you want to create gitlink! If `subdir` is a top directory of an embedded Git repository of a subproject, the former would create a gitlink reference, while the latter in the form of `git add subdir/` would add all the files in the `subdir` individually, which is not probably what you expect.

A simpler and better solution is to use the `git submodule` command, which was created to help manage the filesystem contents, the metadata, and the configuration of your submodules, as well as inspect their status and update them. To add the given repository as a submodule at a specific directory in the superproject, use the add subcommand of the `git submodule`:

```
$ git submodule add https://git.example.com/demo-plugin.git \
  plugins/demo
Cloning into 'plugins/demo'...
done.
```

Note:

While using paths instead of URLs for remotes, you need to remember that the relative paths for remotes are interpreted relative to our main remote, not to the root directory of our repository.

This command stores the information about the submodule, for example the URL of the repository, in the `.gitmodules` file. It creates this file if it does not exist:

```
[submodule "plugins/demo"]
        path = plugins/demo
        url = https://git.example.com/demo-plugin.git
```

Note that a submodule gets a name equal to its path. You can set the name explicitly with the --name option (or by editing the configuration); git mv on a submodule directory will change the submodule path but keep the same name.

Reuse of authentication while fetching submodules

While storing the URL of a remote repository, it is often acceptable and useful to store the username with the subproject information (for example, storing the username in a URL, like user@git.company. com:mylib.git).

However, remembering the username as a part of URL is undesirable in .gitmodules, because this file must be visible by other developers (which often use different usernames for authentication). Fortunately, the commands that descend into submodules can reuse the authentication from cloning (or fetching) a superproject.

The add subcommand also runs an equivalent of git submodule init for you, assuming that if you have added a submodule, you are interested in it. This adds some submodule-specific settings to the local configuration of the master project:

```
[submodule "plugins/demo"]
        url = https://git.example.com/demo-plugin.git
```

Why the duplication? Why store the same information in .gitmodules and in .git/config? Well, because while the .gitmodules file is meant for all developers, we can fit our local configuration to specific local circumstances. The other reason for using two different files is that while the presence of the submodule information in .gitmodules means only that the subproject is available, having it also in .git/config implies that we are interested in a given submodule (and that we want it to be present).

You can create and edit the .gitmodules file by hand or with git config -f .gitmodules. This is useful if, for example, you have added a submodule by hand by cloning it, but want to use git submodule from now on.

This file is usually committed to the superproject repository (similar to .gitignore and .gitattributes files), where it serves as the list of possible subprojects.

All the other subcommands require this file to be present; for example, if we would run git submodule update before adding it, we would get:

```
$ git submodule update
No submodule mapping found in .gitmodules for path
'plugins/demo'
```

That's why `git submodule add` stages both the `.gitmodules` file and the submodule itself:

```
$ git status
On branch master
Changes to be committed:
  (use "git reset HEAD <file>..." to unstage)


        new file:    .gitmodules
        new file:    plugins/demo
```

Note that the whole submodule, which is a directory, `looks to the git status like the new file`. By default, most Git commands are limited to the active container repository only, and do not descend to the nested repositories of the submodules. As we will see, this is configurable.

Cloning superprojects with submodules

One important issue is that, by default, if you clone the superproject repository, you would not get any submodules. All the submodules will be missing from the working duplicated directory; only their base directories are here. This behavior is the basis of the optionality of submodules.

We need then to tell Git that we are interested in a given submodule. This is done by calling the `git submodule init` command. What this command does is it copies the submodule settings from the `.gitmodules` file into the superproject's repository configuration, namely, `.git/config`, registering the submodule:

```
$ git submodule init plugins/demo
Submodule 'plugins/demo' (https://git.example.com/demo-plugin.git)
registered for path 'plugins/demo'
```

The `init` subcommand adds the following two lines to the `.git/config` file:

```
[submodule "plugins/demo"]
        url = https://git.example.com/demo-plugin.git
```

This separate local configuration for the submodules you are interested in allows you also to configure your local submodules to point to a different location URL (perhaps, a per-company reference clone of a subproject's repository) than the one that is present in `.gitmodules` file.

This mechanism also makes it possible to provide the new URL if the repository of a subproject moved. That's why the local configuration overrides the one that is recorded in `.gitmodules`; otherwise you would not be able to fetch from current URL when switched to the version before the URL change. On the other hand, if the repository moved , and the `.gitmodules` file was updated accordingly, we can re-extract new URL from `.gitmodules` into local configuration with `git submodule sync`.

We have told Git that we are interested in the given submodule. However, we have still not fetched the submodule commits from its remote and neither have we checked it out and have its files present in the working directory of the superproject. We can do this with `git submodule update`.

 In practice, while dealing with submodule using repositories, we usually group the two commands (`init` and `update`) into one with `git submodule update --init`.

well, at least if we don't need to customize the URL.

If you are interested in all the submodules, you can use `git clone --recursive` to automatically initialize and update each submodule right after cloning.

To temporarily remove a submodule, retaining the possibility of restoring it later, you can mark it as not interesting with `git remote deinit`. This just affects `.git/config`. To permanently remove a submodule, you need to first deinit it and then remove it from `.gitmodules` and from the working area (with `git rm`).

Updating submodules after superproject changes

To update the submodule so that the working directory contents reflect the state of a submodule in the current version of superproject, you need to perform `git submodule update`. This command updates the files of the subproject or, if necessary, clones the initial submodule repository:

```
$ rm -rf plugins/demo    # clean start for this example
$ git submodule update
Submodule path 'plugins/demo': checked out '5e28a713d8e87…'
```

The `git submodule update` command goes to the repository referenced by `.git/config`, fetches the ID of the commit found in the index (`git ls-tree HEAD -- plugins/demo`), and checks out this version into the directory given by `.git/config`. You can, of course, specify the submodule you want to update, giving the path to the submodule as a parameter.

Because we are here checking out the revision given by gitlink, and not by a branch, `git submodule update` detaches the subprojects' HEAD (see *Fig 3*). This command rewinds the subproject straight to the version recorded in the supermodule.

There are a few more things that you need to know:

- If you are changing the current revision of a superproject in any way, either by changing a branch, by importing a branch with `git pull`, or by rewinding the history with `git reset`, you need to run `git submodule update` to get the matching content to submodules. This is not done automatically, because it could lead to potentially losing your work in a submodule.

- Conversely, if you switch to another branch, or otherwise change the current revision in a superproject, and do not run `git submodule update`, Git would consider that you changed your submodule directory deliberately to point to a new commit (while it is really an old commit, that you used before, but you forgot to update). If, in this situation, you would run `git commit -a`, then by accident, you will change gitlink, leading to having an incorrect version of a submodule stored in the superproject history.

- You can upgrade the gitlink reference simply by fetching (or switching to) the version of a submodule you want to have by using ordinary Git commands inside the subproject, and then committing this version in the supermodule. You don't need to use the `git submodule` command here.

You can have Git to automatically fetch the initialized submodules while pulling the updates from the master project's remote repository. This behavior can be configured using `fetch.recurseSubmodules` (or `submodule.<name>.fetchRecurseSubmodules`). The default value for this configuration is `on-demand` (to fetch if gitlink changes, and the submodule commit it points to is missing). You can set it to `yes` or `no` to turn recursively fetching submodules on or off unconditionally. The corresponding command-line option is `--recurse-submodules`.

It is however critical to remember that even though Git can automatically fetch submodules, it *does not auto-update*. Your local clone of the submodule repository is up to date with the submodule's remote, but the submodule's working directory is stuck to its former contents. If you don't explicitly update the submodule's working directory, the next commit in the container repository will regress the submodule. Currently, there are no configuration settings or command-line options that can autoupdate all the auto-fetched submodules on pull. Well, there were no such options at the time of this writing, but hopefully the management of submodules in Git will improve.

Note that instead of checking out the gitlinked revision on detached HEAD, we can merge the commit recorded in the superproject into the current branch in the submodule with --merge, or rebase the current branch on top of the gitlink with --rebase, just like with `git pull`. The submodule repository branch used defaults to master, but the branch name may be overridden by setting the submodule.<name>.branch option in either .gitmodules or .git/config, the latter taking precedence.

As you can see, using gitlinks and the `git submodule` command is quite complicated. Fundamentally, the concept of gitlink might fit well to the relationship between subprojects and your superproject, but using this information correctly is harder than you think. On the other hand, it gives great flexibility and power.

Examining changes in a submodule

By default, the status, logs, and diff output is based solely on the state of the active repository, and does not descend into submodules. This is often problematic; you would need to remember to run `git submodule summary`. It is easy to miss a regression if you are limited to this view: you can see that the submodule has changed, but you can't see how.

You can, however, set up Git to make it use a *submodule-aware status* with the status.submoduleSummary configuration variable. If it is set to a nonzero number, this number will provide the --summary-limit restriction; a value of true or -1 will mean an unlimited number.

After setting this configuration, you would get something like the following redundant:

```
$ git status
On branch master
Changes to be committed:
  (use "git reset HEAD <file>..." to unstage)


        new file:    .gitmodules
        new file:    plugins/demo


Submodule changes to be committed:

* plugins/demo 0000000...5e28a71 (3):
  > Fix repository name in a README file
```

The status extends the always present information that the submodule changed (`new file: plugins/demo`), adding the information that the submodule present at `plugins/demo` got three new commits, and showing the summary for the last one (`Fix repository name in a README file`). The right pointing angle bracket `>` preceding the summary line means that the commit was added, that is, present in the working area but not (yet) in the superproject commit.

 Actually, this added part is just the `git submodule summary` output.

For the submodule in question, a series of commits in the submodule between the submodule version in the given superproject's commit and the submodule version in the index or the working tree (the former shown by using `--cached`) are listed. There is also `git submodule status` for short information about each module.

The `git diff` command's default output also doesn't tell much about the change in the submodule, just that it is different:

```
$ git diff HEAD -- plugins/demo
diff --git a/plugins/demo b/plugins/demo
new file mode 160000
index 0000000..5e28a71
--- /dev/null
+++ b/plugins/demo
@@ -0,0 +1 @@
+Subproject commit 5e28a713d8e875f2cf1060c2580886dec3e5b04c
```

Fortunately, there is the `--submodule=log` command-line option (that you can enable by default with the `diff.submodule` configuration setting) that lets us see something more useful:

```
$ git diff HEAD --submodule=log -- plugins/demo
Submodule subrepo 0000000...5e28a71 (new submodule)
```

Instead of using `log`, we can use the `short` format that shows just the names of the commits, which is the default if the format is not given (that is, with just `git diff --submodule`).

Getting updates from the upstream of the submodule

To remind you, the submodule commits are referenced in gitlinks using the SHA1 identifier, which always resolves to the same revision; it is not a volatile (inconstant) reference such as a branch name. Because of this, a submodule in a superproject does not automatically upgrade (which could possibly be breaking the application). But sometimes you may want to update it.

Let's assume that the subproject repository got new revisions published and we want, for our superproject, to update to the new version of a submodule.

To achieve this, we need to update the local repository of a submodule, move the version we want to the working directory of the superproject, and finally commit the submodule change in the superproject.

We can do this manually, starting by first changing current directory to be inside the working directory of the submodule. Then, inside the submodule, we perform `git fetch` to get the data to the local clone of the repository (in `.git/modules/` in the superproject). After verifying what we have with `git log`, we can then update the working directory. If there are no local changes, you can simply checkout the desired revision. Finally, you need to create a commit in a superproject.

In addition to the finer-grained control, this approach has the added benefit of working regardless of your current state (whether you are on an active branch or on a detached HEAD).

Another way to go about this would be, working from the container repository, to explicitly upgrade the submodule to its tracked remote branch with `git submodule update --remote`. Similarly to the ordinary `update` command, you can choose to merge or rebase instead of checking out a branch; you can configure the default way of updating with the `submodule.<name>.update` configuration variable, and the default upstream branch with `submodule.<name>.branch`.

> In short, `submodule update --remote --merge` will merge upstream's subproject changes into the submodule, while `submodule update --merge` will merge the superproject gitlink changes into the submodule.

The `git submodule update --remote` command would fetch new changes from the submodule remote site automatically, unless told not to with `--no-fetch`.

Sending submodule changes upstream

One of the major dangers in making changes live directly in a submodule (and not via its standalone repository) is forgetting to push the submodule. A good practice for submodules is to commit changes to the submodule first, push the module changes, and only then get back to the container project, commit it, and push the container changes.

If you only push to the supermodule repository, forgetting about the submodule push, then other developers would get an error while trying to get the updates. Though Git does not complain while fetching the superproject, you would see the problem in the `git submodule summary` output (and in the `git status` output, if properly configured) and while trying to update the working area:

```
$ git submodule summary
* plugins/demo 12e3a52...0e90143:

  Warn: plugins/demo doesn't contain commit 12e3a529698c519b2fab790…

$ git submodule update
fatal: reference is not a tree: 12e3a529698c519b2fab790…

Unable to checkout '12e3a529698c519b2fab790…' in submodule path 'plugins/demo'
```

You can plainly see how important it is to remember to push the submodule. You can ask Git to automatically push the submodules while pushing the superproject, if it is necessary, with `git push --recurse-submodules=on-demand` (the other option is just to check). With Git 2.7.0 or later you can also use the `push.recurseSubmodules` configuration option.

Transforming a subfolder into a subtree or submodule

The first issue that comes to mind while thinking of the use cases of subprojects in Git is about having source code of the base project be ready for such division. Submodules and subtrees are always expressed as subdirectories of the superproject (the master project). You can't mix files from different subsystems in one directory.

Experience shows that most systems use such a directory hierarchy, even in monolithic repositories, which is a good beginning for modularization efforts. Therefore, transforming a subfolder into a real submodule/subtree is fairly easy and can be done in the following sequence of steps:

1. Move the subdirectory in question outside the working area of a superproject to have it beside the top directory of superproject. If it is important to keep the history of a subproject, consider using `git filter-branch --subdirectory-filter` or its equivalent, perhaps together with tools such as `reposurgeon` to clean up the history. See *Chapter 8, Keeping History Clean* for more details.

2. Rename the directory with the subproject repository to better express the essence of the extracted component. For example, a subdirectory originally named `refresh` could be renamed to `refresh-client-app-plugin`.

3. Create the public repository (upstream) for the subproject, as a first class project (for example, create a new project on GitHub to keep extracted code, either under the same organization as a superproject, or under a specialized organization for application plugins).

4. Initialize now a self-sufficient and standalone plugin as a Git repository with `git init`. If in step 1 you have extracted the history of the subdirectory into some branch, then push this branch into the just created repository. Set up the public repository created in step 3 as a default remote repository and push the initial commit (or the whole history) to the just created URL to store the subproject code.

5. In the superproject, read the subproject you have just extracted; this time, as a proper submodule or subtree, whichever solution is a better fit and whichever method you prefer to use. Use the URL of the just created public repository for the subproject.

6. Commit the changes in the superproject and push them to its public repository, in the case of submodules including the newly created (or the just modified) `.gitmodules` file.

The recommended practice for the transformation of a subdirectory into a standalone submodule is to use a read-only URL for cloning (adding back) a submodule. This means that you can use either the `git://` protocol (warning: in this case the server is unauthenticated) or `https://` without a username. The goal of this recommendation is to enforce separation by moving the work on a submodule code to a standalone separate subproject repository. In order to ensure that the submodule commits are available to all other developers, every change should go through the public repository for a subproject.

If this recommendation (best practice) is met with a categorical refusal, in practice you could work on the subproject source code directly inside the superproject, though it is more error prone. You would need to remember to commit and push in the submodule first, doing it from inside of the nested submodule subdirectory; otherwise other developers would be not able to get the changes. This combined approach might be simpler to use, but it loses the true separation between implementing and consuming changes, which should be better assumed while using submodules.

Subtrees versus submodules

In general, subtrees are easier to use and less tricky. Many people go with submodules, because of the better built-in tooling (they have their own Git command, namely `git submodule`), detailed documentation, and similarity to the Subversion externals, making them feel falsely familiar. Adding a submodule is very simple (just run `git submodule add`), especially compared to adding a subtree without the help of third-party tools such as `git subtree` or `git stree`.

The major difference between subtrees and submodules is that, with subtrees, there's only one repository, which means just one lifecycle. Submodules and similar solutions use nested repositories, each with its own lifeline.

Though submodules are easy to set up and fairly flexible, they are also fraught with peril, and you need to practice vigilance while working with them. The fact that the submodules are opt-in also means that the changes touching the submodules demand a manual update by every collaborator. Subtrees are always there, so getting the superproject's changes mean getting the subproject's too.

Commands such as `status`, `diff`, and `log` display precious little information about submodules, unless properly configured to cross the repository boundary; it is easy to miss a change. With subtrees, `status` works normally, while `diff` and `log` need some care, because the subproject commits have a different root directory. The latter assumes that you did not decide to not include the subproject history (by squashing subtree merges). Then, the problem is only with the remote-tracking branches in subproject's repository, if any.

Because the lifecycles of different repositories are separate, updating a submodule inside its containing project requires two commits and two pushes. Updating a subtree-merged subproject is very simple: only one commit and one push. On the other hand, publishing the subproject changes upstream is much easier with submodules, while it requires changeset extraction with subtrees (here tools such as `git subtree` help a lot).

The next major issue, and a source of problems, is that the submodule has two sources of the current revision: the gitlink in the superproject and the branches in the submodule's clone of the repository. This means that `git remote update` works a bit like a sideways push into a nonbare repository (see *Chapter 6, Advanced Branching Techniques*). Submodule heads are therefore generally detached, so any local update requires various preparatory actions to avoid creating a lost commit. There is no such issue with subtrees. All the revision changing commands work as usual with subtrees, bringing the subproject directory to the correct version without the requirement of any additional action. Getting changes from the subproject repository is just a subtree merge away. The only difference between ordinary pull is the `-s subtree` option.

Still, sometimes submodules are the right choice. Compared to subtrees, they allow for a subproject (a module) to be not fetched, which is helpful when your code base is massive. Submodules are also useful when the heavy modularization is not natively handled, or not well natively handled, by the development stack's ecosystem.

Submodules might also themselves be superprojects for other submodules, creating a hierarchy of subprojects. Using nested submodules is made easier thanks to `git submodule status`, `update`, `foreach`, and `sync` subcommands all supporting the `--recursive` switch.

Use cases for subtrees

With subtrees, there is only one repository, no nested repositories, just like a regular codebase. This means that there is just one lifecycle. One of the key benefits of subtrees is being able to mix container-specific customizations with general purpose fixes and enhancements.

Projects can be organized and grouped together in whatever way you find to be most logically consistent. Using a single repository also reduces the overhead from managing dependencies.

The basic example of using subtrees is managing the customized version of a library, a required dependency. It is easy to get a development environment set up to run builds and tests. Monorepo makes it also viable to have one universal version number for all the projects. Atomic cross-submodule commits are possible; therefore, a repository can always be in a consistent state.

You can also use subtrees for embedding related projects, such as a GUI or a web interface, inside a superproject. In fact, many use cases for submodules can also apply to the subtrees solution, with an exception of the cases where there is a need for a subproject to be optional, or to have different access permissions than a master project. In those cases you need to use submodules.

Use cases for submodules

The strongest argument for the use of submodules is the issue of modularization. Here, the main area of use for submodules is handling plugins and extensions. Some programming ecosystems, such as ANSI C and C++, and also Objectve-C, lack good and standard support for managing version-locked multimodule projects. In this case, a plugin-like code can be included in the application (superproject) using submodules, without sacrificing the ability to easily update to the latest version of a plugin from its repository. The traditional solution of putting instructions about how to copy plugins in the README, disconnects it from the historical metadata.

This schema can be extended also to the noncompiled code, such as the Emacs List settings, configuration in dotfiles, (including frameworks such as oh-my-zsh), and themes (also for web applications). In these situations, what is usually needed to use a component is the physical presence of a module code at conventional locations inside the master project tree, which are mandated by the technology or framework being used. For instance, themes and plugins for Wordpress, Magento, and so on are often de facto installed this way. In many cases, you need to be in a superproject to test these optional components.

Yet another particular úse case for submodules is the division based on access control and visibility restriction of a complex application. For example, the project might use a cryptographic code with license restrictions, limiting access to it to the small subset of developers. With this code in a submodule with restricted access to its repository, other developers would simply be unable to clone this submodule. In this solution, the common build system needs to be able to skip cryptographic component if it is not available. On the other hand, the dedicated build server can be configured in such a way that the client gets the application build with crypto enabled.

A similar visibility restriction purpose, but in reverse, is making the source code of examples available long before it was to be published. This allows for better code thanks to the social input. The main repository for a book itself can be closed (private), but having an examples/ directory contain a submodule intended for a sample source code allows you to make this subrepository public. While generating the book in the PDF and EPUB (and perhaps also MOBI) formats, the build process can then embed these examples (or fragments of them), as if they were ordinary subdirectory.

Third-party subproject management solutions

If you don't find a good fit in either `git subtree` or `git submodule`, you can try to use one of the many third-party projects to manage dependencies, subprojects, or collections of repositories. One such tool is the `externals` (or `ext`) project by Miles Georgie. You can find it at `http://nopugs.com/ext-tutorial`. This project is VCS-agnostic, and can be used to manage any combination of version control systems used by subprojects and superprojects.

Another is the `repo` tool (`https://android.googlesource.com/tools/repo/`) used by the Android Open Source project to unify the many Git repositories for across-network operations. You can find many other such tools.

 When choosing between native support and one of the many tools to manage many repositories together, you should check whether the tool in question uses a subtree-like or submodule-like approach to find if it would be a good fit for your project.

Managing large Git repositories

Because of its distributed nature, Git includes the full change history in each copy of the repository. Every clone gets not only all the files, but every revision of every file ever committed. This allows for efficient development (local operations not involving a network are usually fast enough so that they are not a bottleneck) and efficient collaboration with others (distributed nature allows for many collaborative workflows).

But what happens when the repository you want to work on is really huge? Can we avoid taking a large amount of disk space for version control storage? Is it possible to reduce the amount of data that end users need to retrieve while cloning the repository?

If you think about it, there are broadly two main reasons for repositories to grow massive: they can accumulate a very long history (the every revision direction), or they can include huge binary assets that need to be managed together with code (the every file direction), or both. For those two scenarios, the techniques and workarounds are different, and can be applied independently.

Handling repositories with a very long history

Even though Git can effectively handle repositories with a long history, very old projects spanning huge number of revisions can become a pain to clone. In many cases, you are not interested in ancient history and do not want to pay the time to get all the revisions of a project and the disk space to store them.

For example, if you want to propose a new feature or a bugfix (the latter might require running `git bisect` on your machine, where the regression bug is easily reproducible; see *Chapter 2, Exploring Project History* for how to use bisection), you don't want to wait for the full clone to finish, which may take quite a while.

> Some Git repository hosting services, such as GitHub, offer a web-based interface to manage repositories, including in-browser file management and editing. They may even automatically create a fork of the repository for you to enable writing and proposing changes.
>
> But a web-based interface doesn't cover everything, and you might be using self-hosted repositories or a service that doesn't provide this feature anyway.

Using shallow clones to get truncated history

The simple solution to a fast clone and to saving disk space is to perform shallow clone using Git. This operation allows you to get a local copy of the repository with the history truncated to a particular specified depth, that is, the number of latest revisions.

How do you do it? Just use the `--depth` option:

```
$ git clone --depth=1 https://git.company.com/project
```

The preceding command clones only the most recent revision of the primary branch. This trick can save quite a bit of time and relieve a great deal of load from the servers. Often, shallow clone finishes in seconds rather than in minutes; a significant improvement.

Since version 1.9, Git supports pull and push operations even with shallow clones, though some care is still required. You can change the depth of a shallow clone by providing the `--depth=<n>` option to `git fetch` (note however that tags for the deepened commits are not fetched). To turn a shallow repository into a complete one, use `--unshallow`.

Note, also `git clone --depth=1` may still get all the branches and all the tags. This can happen if the remote repository doesn't have `HEAD`, thus it doesn't have a primary branch selected; otherwise only the tip of the said single branch is fetched. Long-lived projects usually had many releases during their long history. To really save time, you would need then to combine shallow clone with the next solution: branch limiting.

Cloning only a single branch

Git, by default, clones all the branches and tags (if you want to fetch notes or replacements, you need to specify them explicitly). You can limit the amount of the history you clone by specifying that you want to clone only a single branch:

```
$ git clone --branch master --single-branch \
  https://git.company.com/project
```

Because most of the project history (most of the DAG of revisions) is shared among branches, with very few exceptions, you probably won't see a huge difference using this.

This feature might be quite useful if you don't want detached orphan branches or the opposite: you want only an orphan branch (for example, with a web page for a project). It also works well used together with a shallow clone.

Handling repositories with large binary files

In some specific circumstances, you might need to track *huge binary assets* in the code base. Gaming teams have to handle huge 3D models, web development teams might need to track raw image assets or Photoshop documents, and both might require having video files under version control. Sometimes, you might want the convenience of including large binary deliverables that are difficult or expensive to generate, for example, storing a snapshot of a virtual machine image.

There are some tweaks to improve the handling of binary assets by Git. For binary files that change significantly from version to version (and not just change some metadata headers), you might want to turn off the delta compression by adding `-delta` explicitly for specific types of files in a `.gitattributes` file (see *Chapter 4, Managing Your Worktree*, and *Chapter 10, Customizing and Extending Git*). Git would automatically turn off delta compression for any file above the `core.bigFileThreshold` size, 512 MiB by default. You might also want to turn the compression off (for example if a file is in the compressed format already); though because `core.compression` and `core.looseCompression` are global for the whole repository, it makes more sense if binary assets are in a separate repository (submodule).

Splitting the binary asset folder into a separate submodule

One possible way of handling large binary asset folders is, as mentioned earlier, to split them into a separate repository and pull the assets into your main project as submodule. The use of submodules gives a way to control when assets are updated. Moreover, if a developer does not need those binary assets to work, he or she can simply exclude the submodule with assets from fetching.

The limitation is that you need to have a separate folder with these huge binary assets that you want to handle this way.

Sparse checkout

Git includes the technique that allows you to explicitly detail which files and folders you want to populate on checkout. This mode is turned on by setting the `core.sparseCheckout` configuration variable to `true`, and uses the `.git/info/sparse-checkout` file with the `gitignore` syntax to specify what is to appear in the working directory. The index is populated in full, with `skip-worktree` set for files missing from the checkout.

While it can be helpful if you have a huge tree of folders, it doesn't affect the overall size of the local repository itself.

Storing large binary files outside the repository

Another solution is to use one of the many third-party tools that try to solve the problem of handling large binary files in Git repositories. Many of them are using a similar paradigm, namely, storing the contents of huge binary files outside the repository, while providing some kind of pointers to the contents in the checkout.

There are three parts of each such implementation: how they store the information about the contents of the managed files inside the repository, how they manage sharing the large binary files between a team, and how they integrate with Git (and what is their performance penalty). While choosing a solution, you would need to take this data into account, together with the operating system support, ease of use, and the size of the community.

What is stored in the repository and what is checked in might be a *symlink* to the file or to the key, or it might be a *pointer file* (often plain text), which acts as a reference to the actual file contents (by name or by the cryptographic hash of file contents). The tracked files need to be stored in some kind of backend for a collaboration (cloud service, rsync, shared directory, and so on). Backends might be accessed directly by the client, or there might be a separate server with a defined API into which the blobs are written to, which would in turn offload the storage elsewhere.

The tool might either require the use of separate commands for checking out and committing large files and for fetching from and pushing to the backend, or it might be integrated into Git. The integrated solution uses the `clean`/`smudge` filters to handle check-out and check-in transparently, and the `pre-push` hook to send large file contents transparently together. You only need to state which files to track and, of course, initialize the repository for the tool use.

The advantage of a filter-based approach is the ease of use; however, there is a performance penalty, because of how it works. Using separate commands to handle large binary assets makes the learning curve a bit steeper, but provides for better performance. Some tools provide both interfaces.

Among different solutions, there are **git annex** with a large community and support for various backends, and Git LFS (Large File Storage) created by GitHub, which provides good MS Windows support, client-server approach, and transparency (with support for filter-based approach). There are many other such tools, for example, **git-fat**, **git-media**, **git-bigstore**, and **git-sym**.

Summary

This chapter provided all the tools you need to manage multicomponent projects with Git, from libraries and graphical interfaces, through plugins and themes, to frameworks.

You learned the concept behind the subtrees technique and how to use it to manage subprojects. You know how to create, update, examine, and manage subprojects using subtrees.

You got to know the submodule approach of nested repositories for optional dependencies. You learned the ideas behind gitlinks, `.gitmodules`, and the `.git` files. You encountered the pitfalls and traps for the unwary that you need to be vigilant about while using submodules. You know the reason for these problems and understand the notions behind them. You know how to create, update, examine, and manage subprojects using submodules.

You learned when to use subtrees and submodules, and their advantages and disadvantages. You know a few use cases for each technique.

Now that you know how to use Git effectively in a variety of circumstances, and learned the high-level ideas behind Git behavior that helps you understand it, it's time to tackle how to make Git easier to use in *Chapter 10, Customizing and Extending Git*.

10
Customizing and Extending Git

Earlier chapters were designed to help you understand and master Git as a version control system, from examining history, through managing your contributions, to collaborating with other developers, ending with handling the composite projects in the last chapter: *Chapter 9, Managing Subprojects – Building a Living Framework*.

The following two chapters would help set up and configure Git, so that you can use it more effectively for yourself (this chapter) and help other developers use it (the next chapter).

This chapter will cover configuring and extending Git to fit one's needs. First, it will show how to set up a Git command line to make it easier to use. For some tasks though it is easier to use visual tools; the short introduction to graphical interfaces in this chapter should help you in choosing one. Next, there will be an explanation on how to change and configure Git behavior, from configuration files (with the selected configuration options described), to a per-file configuration with the `gitattributes` file.

Then this chapter will cover how to automate Git with hooks, describing for example how to make Git check whether the commit being created passes coding guidelines for a project. This part will focus on the client-side hook, and will only touch upon the server-side hooks— those are left for the, *Chapter 11, Git Administration*. The last part of the chapter will describe how to extend Git, from the Git command aliases, through integrating new user-visible commands, to helpers and drivers (new back-end abilities).

Many issues, such as `gitattributes`, remote and credential helpers, and the basics of the Git configuration should be known from the previous chapters. This chapter will gather this information in a single place and expand it a bit.

In this chapter, we will cover the following topics:

- Setting up shell prompt and TAB completion for a command line
- Types and examples of graphical user interfaces
- Configuration files and basic configuration options
- Installing and using various types of hooks
- Simple and complex aliases
- Extending Git with new commands and helpers

Git on the command line

There are a lot of different ways to use the Git version control system. There are many graphical user interfaces (GUIs) of varying use cases and capabilities, and there exists tools and plugins that allow integration with an integrated development environment (IDE) or a file manager.

However, the command line is the only place you can run all of the Git commands and which provides support for all their options. New features, which you might want to use, are developed for the command line first. Also, most of the GUIs implement only some subsets of the Git functionality. Mastering the command line always guarantees a deep understanding of tools, mechanisms, and their abilities. Just knowing how to use a GUI is probably not enough to get a founded knowledge.

Whether you use Git on a command line from choice, as a preferred environment, or you need it because it is the only way to access the required functionality, there are a few shell features that Git can tap into to make your experience a lot friendlier.

Git-aware command prompt

It's useful to customize your **shell prompt** to show information about the state of the Git repository we are in.

 Shell prompt is a short text message that is written to the terminal or the console output to notify the user of the interactive shell that some typed input is expected (usually a shell command).

This information can be as simple or as complex as you want. Git's prompt might be similar to the ordinary command-line prompt (to reduce dissonance), or visibly different (to be able to easily distinguish that we are inside the Git repository).

There is an example implementation for bash and zsh shells in the contrib/ area. If you install Git from the sources, just copy the contrib/completion/git-prompt. sh file to your home directory; if you have installed Git on Linux via a package manager, you will probably have it at /etc/bash_completion.d/git-prompt.sh. This file provides the __git_ps1 shell function to generate a Git-aware prompt in the Git repositories, but first you need to source this file in your .bashrc or .zshrc:

```
if [ -f /etc/bash_completion.d/git-prompt.sh ]; then
    source /etc/bash_completion.d/git-prompt.sh
fi
```

The shell prompt is configured using environment variables. To set up prompt, you must change directly or indirectly the PS1 (*prompt string one*, the default interaction prompt) environment variable. Thus, one solution to create a Git-aware command prompt is to include a call to the __git_ps1 shell function in the PS1 environment variable, by using command substitution:

```
export PS1='\u@\h:\w$(__git_ps1 " (%s)")\$ '
```

Note that, for zsh, you would also need to turn on the command substitution in the shell prompt with setopt PROMPT_SUBST command.

Alternatively, for a slightly faster prompt and with a possibility of color, you can use __git_ps1 to set PS1. This is done with the PROMPT_COMMAND environment variable in bash and with the precmd() function in zsh. You can find more information about this option in comments in the git-prompt.sh file; for bash, it could be:

```
PROMPT_COMMAND='__git_ps1 "\u@\h:\w""\\\$ "" (%s)"'
```

With this configuration (either solution), the prompt will look as follows:

```
bob@host.company.org:~/random/src (master)$
```

The bash and zsh shell prompts can be customized with the use of special characters, which get expanded by a shell. In the example used here, \u means the current user (bob), \h is the current hostname (host.company.org), \w means the current working directory (~/random/src), while \$ prints the $ part of the prompt (# if you are logged in as the root user). $(...) in the PS1 setup is used to call external commands and shell functions .__git_ps1 " (%s)" here calls the __git_ps1 shell function provided by git-prompt.sh with a formatting argument: the %s token is the place-holder for the presented Git status. Note that you need to either use single quotes while setting the PS1 variable from the command line, as in the example shown here, or escape shell substitution, so it is expanded while showing the prompt and not while defining the variable.

If you are using the __git_ps1 function, Git will also display information about the current ongoing multistep operation: merging, rebasing, bisecting, and so on. For example, during an interactive rebase (-i) on the branch master, the relevant part of the prompt would be master|REBASE-i. It is very useful to have this information right here in the command prompt, especially if you get interrupted in the middle of operation.

It is also possible to indicate in the command prompt the state of the working tree, the index, and so on. We can enable these features by exporting the selected subset of these environment variables (for some features you can additionally turn it off on per-repository basis with provided boolean-valued configuration variables):

Variable/Configuration	Values	Effect
GIT_PS1_SHOWDIRTYSTATE bash.showDirtyState	Nonempty	This shows * for the unstaged changes and + for the staged changes.
GIT_PS1_SHOWSTASHSTATE	Nonempty	This shows $ if something is stashed.
GIT_PS1_SHOWUNTRACKEDFILES bash.showUntrackedFiles	Nonempty	This shows % if there are untracked files in workdir.
GIT_PS1_SHOWUPSTREAM bash.showUpstream	Space-separated list of values: • verbose • name • legacy • git • svn	This autoshows whether you are behind <, up to date "=", or ahead > of the upstream. name shows the upstream name and verbose shows the number of commits ahead/behind (with a sign). git compares HEAD to @{upstream} and svn to SVN upstream.
GIT_PS1_DESCRIBE_STYLE	One of values: • contains • branch • describe • default	This provides extra information when on detached HEAD. contains uses newer annotated tags, branch newer tag or branch, describe uses older annotated tags, default shows if there is exactly matching tag.

Variable/Configuration	Values	Effect
GIT_PS1_SHOWCOLORHINTS (prompt command / precmd only)	Nonempty	Colored hint about the current dirty state and so on.
GIT_PS1_HIDE_IF_PWD_IGNORED bash.hideIfPwdIgnored	Nonempty	Does not show a Git-aware prompt if the current directory is set to be ignored by Git.

If you are using the zsh shell, you can take a look at the zsh-git set of scripts, the zshkit configuration scripts, or the oh-my-zsh framework available for zsh, instead of using bash—first completion and prompt setup from the Git contrib/. Alternatively you can use the vcs_info subsystem built-in into zsh.

Well, there are alternate prompt solutions also for bash, for example git-radar.

> You can, of course, generate your own Git-aware prompt. For example, you might want to split the current directory into the repository path part and the project subdirectory path part with the help of the git rev-parse command.

Command-line completion for Git

Another shell feature that makes it easier to work with command-line Git is the programmable command-line completion. This feature can dramatically speed up typing Git commands. Command-line completion allows you to type the first few characters of a command, or a filename, and press the completion key (usually *Tab*) to fill the rest of the item. With the Git-aware completion, you can also fill in subcommands, command-line parameters, remotes, branches, and tags (ref names), each only where appropriate (for example, remote names are completed only if the command expects the remote name at a given position).

Git comes with built-in (but not always installed) support for the auto-completion of Git commands for the bash and zsh shells.

For bash, if the completion is not installed with Git (at /etc/bash_completion.d/ git.sh in Linux by default), you need to get a copy of the contrib/completion/ git-completion.bash file out of the Git source code. Copy it somewhere accessible, like your home directory, and source it from your .bashrc or .bash_profile:

```
. ~/git-completion.bash
```

Once the completion for Git is enabled, to test it you can type for example:

```
$ git check<TAB>
```

With Git completion enabled `bash` (or `zsh`) would autocomplete this to `git checkout`.

Similarly, in an ambiguous case, double *Tab* shows all the possible completions (though it is not true for all the shells):

```
$ git che<TAB><TAB>
checkout        cherry        cherry-pick
```

The completion feature also works with options; this is quite useful if you don't remember the exact option but only the prefix:

```
$ git config --<TAB><TAB>
--add            --get-regexp      --remove-section    --unset
--file=          --global          --rename-section    --unset-all
--get            --list            --replace-all
--get-all        --local           --system
```

Instead of the list of possible completions, some shells use (or can be configured to use) rotating completion, where with multiple possible completions, each *Tab* shows a different completion for the same prefix (cycling through them).

Note that the command-line completion (also called **tab completion**) generally works only in the interactive mode, and is based on the unambiguous prefix, not on the unambiguous abbreviation.

Autocorrection for Git commands

An unrelated, but similar to **tab completion**, built-in Git tool is **autocorrection**. By default, if you type something that looks like a mistyped command, Git helpfully tries to figure out what you meant. It still refuses to do it, even if there is only one candidate:

```
$ git chekout
git: 'chekout' is not a git command. See 'git --help'.

Did you mean this?
        checkout
```

However, with the `help.autoCorrect` configuration variable set to a positive number, Git will automatically correct and execute the mistyped commands after waiting for the given number of deciseconds (0.1 of second). You can use a negative value of this option for immediate execution, or zero to go back to default:

```
$ git chekout
WARNING: You called a Git command named 'chekout', which does not exist.
Continuing under the assumption that you meant 'checkout'
in 0.1 seconds automatically...
Your branch is up-to-date with 'origin/master'.
```

If there is more than one command that can be deduced from the entered text, nothing will be executed. This mechanism works only for Git commands; you cannot autocorrect subcommands, parameters, and options (as opposed to tab completion).

Making the command line prettier

Git fully supports a colored terminal output, which greatly aids in visually parsing the command output. A number of options can help you set the coloring to your preference.

First, you can specify when to use colors and for output of which commands. There is a `color.ui` master switch to control output coloring to turn off all the Git's colored terminal outputs and set them to `false`. The default setting for this configuration variable is `auto`, which makes Git color the output when it's going straight to a terminal, but omit the color-control codes when the output is redirected to a file or a pipe.

You can also set `color.ui` to `always`, though you'd rarely want this: if you want color codes in your redirected output, simply pass a `--color` flag to the Git command; conversely, the `--no-color` option would turn off colored output.

If you want to be more specific about which commands are colored and which parts of the output are colored, Git provides appropriate coloring settings: `color.branch`, `color.diff`, `color.interactive`, `color.status`, and so on. Like with the master switch `color.ui`, each of these can be set to `true`, `false`, `auto`, and `always`.

In addition, each of these settings has subsettings that you can use to set specific colors for specific parts of the output. The color value of such configuration variables, for example, `color.diff.meta` (to configure the coloring of meta information in your `diff` output), consists of space-separated names of the foreground color, the background color (if set), and the text attribute.

You can set the color to any of the following values: `normal`, `black`, `red`, `green`, `yellow`, `blue`, `magenta`, `cyan`, or `white`. As for the attributes, you can choose from `bold`, `dim`, `ul` (underline), `blink`, and `reverse` (swap the foreground color with the background one).

The pretty formats for `git log` also include an option to set colors; see the git log documentation.

Alternative command line

To understand some of the rough edges of the Git user's interface, you need to remember that Git was developed to a large extent in the bottom-up fashion. Historically, Git began as a tool to write version control systems (you can see how early Git was used in the *A Git core tutorial for developers* documentation available at `https://www.kernel.org/pub/software/scm/git/docs/gitcore-tutorial.html` or `https://git-scm.com/docs/gitcore-tutorial`).

The first alternative "porcelain" for Git (alternative user interface) was Cogito. Nowadays, Cogito is no more; all of its features are long incorporated into Git (or replaced by better solutions). There were some attempts to write wrapper scripts (alternative UIs) designed to make it easy to learn and use, for example, **Easy Git** (**eg**).

There are also external Git porcelains that do not intend to replace the whole user interface, but either provide access to some extra feature, or wrap Git to provide some restricted feature set. Patch management interfaces, such as **StGit**, **TopGit**, or **Guilt** (formerly **Git Queues** (**gq**)), are created to make it easy to rewrite, manipulate, and clean up selected parts of the unpublished history; these were mentioned as an alternative to an interactive rebase in *Chapter 8, Keeping History Clean*. Then, there are single-file version control systems, such as Zit and SRC, which use Git as a backend.

Besides alternative user interfaces, there are also different implementations of Git (defined as reading and writing Git repositories). They are at different stages of completeness. Besides core C implementation, there is JGit in Java, and also the `libgit2` project—the modern basis of Git bindings for various programming languages.

Graphical interfaces

You have learned how to use Git on the command line. The previous section told you how to customize and configure it to make it even more effective. But the terminal is not the end. There are other kinds of environments you can use to manage Git repositories. Sometimes, a visual representation is what you need.

Now, we'll take a short look at the various kinds of user-centered graphical tools for Git; the tour of Git administrative tools is left for the next chapter, *Chapter 11, Git Administration*.

Types of graphical tools

Different tools and interfaces are tailored for different workflows. Some tools expose only a selected subset of the Git functionality, or encourage a specific way of working with version control.

To be able to make an informed choice selecting a graphical tool for Git, you need to know what types of operations the different types of tools do support. Note that one tool can support more than one type of uses.

First there is a **graphical history viewer**. You can think of it as a powerful GUI over `git log`. This is the tool to be used when you are trying to find something that happened in the past, or you are visualizing and browsing your project's history and the layout of branches. Such tools usually accept revision selection command-line options, such a s`--all`. Command-line Git has `git log --graph` and less used `git show-branch` that use ASCII-art to show the history.

A similar tool is **graphical blame**, showing the line-wise history of a file. For each line, it can show when that line was created and when it was moved or copied to the current place. You can examine the details of each of the commits shown, and usually browse through the history of the lines in a file. Other tools with similar applications, namely examining the evolution of the line range (`git log -L`) and the so called pickaxe search (`git log -S`) does not have many GUIs.

Next, there are **commit tools** meant primarily to craft (and amend) commits, though usually they also include some kind of worktree management (for example ignoring files and switching branches) and **management of remotes**. Such tools would usually show unstaged and staged changes, allowing you to move files between these states . Some of those tools even allow to stage and unstage individual chunks of changes, like interactive versions of `git add`, `git reset`, and so on. A graphical version of an interactive add is described in *Chapter 4, Managing Your Worktree*, and mentioned in *Chapter 3, Developing with Git*.

Then, we have **file manager integration** (or **graphical shell integration**). These plugins usually show the status of the file in Git (tracked/untracked/ignored) using icon overlays. They can offer a context menu for a repository, directory, and file, often with accompanying keyboard shortcuts. They may also bring drag and drop support.

Programmer editors and integrated development environments (IDEs) often offer support for **IDE integration** with Git (or version control in general). These offer repository management (as a part of team project management), make it possible to perform Git operations directly from the IDE, show the status of the current file and the repository, and perhaps even annotate the view of the file with version control information. They often include the commit tool, remote management, the history viewer, and the diff viewer.

Git repository's hosting sites often offer workflow-oriented **desktop clients**. These mostly focus on a curated set of commonly used features that work well together in the flow. They automate common Git tasks. They are often designed to highlight their service, offering extra features and integration, but they will work with any repository hosted anywhere.

Graphical diff and merge tools

Graphical diff tools and graphical merge tools are somewhat special case. In these categories, Git includes the commands for integration with third-party graphical tools, namely, git difftool and git mergetool. These tools would then be called from the Git repository. Note that this is different from the external diff or diff merge drivers, which replace ordinary git diff or augment it.

Although Git has an internal implementation of diff and a mechanism for merge conflict resolutions (see *Chapter 7, Merging Changes Together*), you can use an external graphical diff tool instead. These are often used to show the differences better (usually, as a side-by-side diff, possibly with refinements), and help resolve a merge (often with a three-pane interface).

Configuring the graphical diff tool, or the graphical merge tool, takes a number of custom settings. To tell which tool to use for diff and merge, respectively, you can set up diff.tool and merge.tool, respectively . Without setting for example "merge.tool" the "git mergetool" command would print the information on how to configure it, and will attempt to run one of predefined tools:

```
$ git mergetool

This message is displayed because 'merge.tool' is not configured.
See 'git mergetool --tool-help' or 'git help config' for more details.
'git mergetool' will now attempt to use one of the following tools:
tortoisemerge emerge vimdiff
No files need merging
```

Running `git mergetool --tool-help` will show all the available tools, including those that are not installed. In case the tool you use is not in `$PATH`, or it has a wrong version of the tool, you can use `mergetool.<tool>.path` to set or override the path for the given tool:

```
$ git mergetool --tool-help
'git mergetool --tool=<tool>' may be set to one of the following:
                vimdiff
                [...]


The following tools are valid, but not currently available:
                araxis
                [...]


Some of the tools listed above only work in a windowed
environment. If run in a terminal-only session, they will fail.
```

If there is no built-in support for your tool, you can still use it; you just need to configure it. The `mergetool.<tool>.cmd` configuration variable specifies how to run the command, while `mergetool.<tool>.trustExitCode` tells Git whether the exit code of that program indicates a successful merge resolution or not. The relevant fragment of the configuration file (for a graphical merge tool named `extMerge`) could look as follows:

```
[merge]
    tool = extMerge
[mergetool "extMerge"]
    cmd = extMerge "$BASE" "$LOCAL" "$REMOTE" "$MERGED"
```

Graphical interface examples

In this section, you will be presented with a selection of tools around Git that you could use, or that might prompt you to research further. A nice way to start such a research is to list some selected GUI clients.

There are two visual tools that are a part of Git and are usually installed with it, namely `gitk` and `git-gui`. They are written in Tcl/Tk. `Gitk` is a graphical history viewer, while `git gui` is a commit tool; there is also `git gui blame`, a visually interactive line-history browser. These tools are interconnected, for example, browsing history from `git gui` opens `gitk`.

Visual tools do not need to use the graphical environment. There is `tig` (Text Interface for Git), a nurses-based text-mode interface, which functions as a repository browser and a commit tool, and can act as a Git pager.

There is `git cola` developed in Python and available for all the operating systems, which includes commit tools and remotes management, and also a diff viewer. Then, there is the simple and colorful `Gitg` tool for GNOME; you will get a graphical history viewer, diff viewer, and file browser.

One of the more popular open-source GUI tools for MacOS is `GitX`. There are a lot of forks of this tool; one of the more interesting ones is `Gitbox`. It features both the history viewer and commit tools.

For MS Windows, there is `TortoiseGit` and `git-cheetah`, both of which offer integration into the Windows context menu, so you can perform Git commands inside Windows Explorer (the file manager integration and shell interface).

Both GitHub Inc. and Atlassian released a desktop GUI tool that you can easily use with your GitHub or Bitbucket repository, respectively, but it is not limited to it. Both `GitHub Client` and `SourceTree` feature repository management in addition to other common facilities.

Configuring Git

So far, while describing how Git works and how to use it, we have introduced a number of ways to change its behavior. Here, it will be explained in the systematic fashion how to configure Git operations on a temporary and permanent basis. We will also see how you can make Git behave in a customized fashion by introducing and reintroducing several important configuration settings. With these tools, it's easy to get Git to work the way you want it to.

Command-line options and environment variables

Git processes the switches that change its behavior in a hierarchical fashion, from the least specific to the most specific one, with the most specific one (and shortest term) moved earlier taking precedence.

The most specific one, overriding all the others, is the command-line options. They affect, obviously, only the current Git command.

One issue to note is that some command-line options, for example `--no-pager` or `--no-replace-objects` go to the `git` wrapper, not to the Git command itself. Examine, for example, the following line to see the distinction:

```
$ git --no-replace-objects log -5 --oneline --graph
--decorate
```

You can find the conventions used through the Git command-line interface on `https://www.kernel.org/pub/software/scm/git/docs/gitcli.html` manpage manpage.

The second way to change how the Git command works is to use environment variables. They are specific to the current shell, and you need to use `export` to propagate the variables to the subprocesses if replacement is used. There are some environment variables that apply to all core Git commands, and some that are specific to a given (sub)command.

Git also makes use of some nonspecific environment variables. These are meant as a last resort; they are overridden by their Git specific equivalents. Examples include variables such as `PAGER` and `EDITOR`.

Git configuration files

The final way to customize how Git works is with the configuration files. In many cases, there is a command-line option to configure an action, an environment variable for it, and finally a configuration variable, in the descending order of preference.

Git uses a series of configuration files to determine nondefault behavior that you might want to have. There are three layers of those that Git looks for configuration values. Git reads all these files in order from the least specific to the most specific one. The settings in the later ones override those set in the earlier ones. You can access the Git configuration with the `git config` command: by default, it operates on the union of all the files, but you can specify which one you want to access with the command-line options. You can also access any given file following the configuration file syntax (such as the `.gitmodules` file mentioned in *Chapter 9*, *Managing Subprojects - Building a Living Framework*) by using the `--file=<pathname>` option (or the `GIT_CONFIG` environment variable).

You can also read the values from any blob with configuration-like contents; for example, you may use `git config --blob=master:.gitmodules` to read from the `.gitmodules` file in the `master` branch.

The first place Git looks for configuration is the system-wide configuration file. If Git is installed with the default settings, it can be found in /etc/gitconfig. Well, at least, on Linux it is there, as the Filesystem Hierarchy Standard (FHS) states that /etc is the directory for storing the host-specific system-wide configuration files; Git for Windows puts this file in the subdirectory of its Program Files folder. This file contains the values for every user on the system and all their repositories. To make git config read and write from and to this file specifically (and to open it with --edit), pass the --system option to the git config command.

You can skip the reading settings from this file with the GIT_CONFIG_NOSYSTEM environment variable. This can be used to set up a predictable environment or to avoid using a buggy configuration you can't fix.

The next place Git looks is ~/.gitconfig, falling back to ~/.config/git/config if it exists (with the default configuration). This file is specific to each user and it affects all the user's repositories. If you pass the option --global to git config, it would read and write from this file specifically. Reminder: here, as in the other places, ~ (the tilde character) denotes the home directory of the current user ($HOME).

Finally, Git looks for the configuration values in the per-repository configuration file in the Git repository you are currently using, which is (by default and for nonbare repositories) .git/config. Values set there are specific to that local single repository. You can make Git read and write to this file by passing the --local option.

Each of these levels (system, global, and local) overrides values in the previous level, so for example, values in .git/config trump those in ~/.gitconfig; well, unless the configuration variable is multivalued.

 You can use this to have your default identity in the per-user file and to override it if necessary on a per-repository basis with a per-repository configuration file.

The syntax of Git configuration files

Git's configuration files are plain text, so you can also customize Git's behavior by manually editing the chosen file. The syntax is fairly flexible and permissive; whitespaces are mostly ignored (contrary to .gitattributes). The hash # and semicolon ; characters begin comments, which last until the end of the line. Blank lines are ignored.

The file consists of sections and variables, and its syntax is similar to the syntax of INI files. Both the section names and variable names are case-insensitive. A section begins with the name of the section in square brackets `[section]` and continues until the next section. Each variable must begin at some section, which means that there must be a section header before the first setting of a variable. Sections can repeat and can be empty.

Sections can be further divided into subsections. Subsection names are case-sensitive and can contain any character except newline (double quotes " and backslash \ must be escaped as \" and \\, respectively). The beginning of the subsection will look as follows:

```
[section "subsection"]
```

All the other lines (and the remainder of the line after the section header) are recognized as a setting variable in the `name = value` form. As a special case, just `name` is a shorthand for `name = true` (boolean variables). Such lines can be continued to the next line by ending it with "\" (the backslash character), that is by escaping the end-of-line character. Leading and trailing whitespaces are discarded; internal whitespaces within the value are retained verbatim. You can use double quotes to preserve leading or trailing whitespaces in values.

You can include one `config` file from another by setting the special variable `include.path` to the path of the file to be included. The included file will be expanded immediately, similar to the mechanism of `#include` in C and C++. The path is relative to the configuration file with the include directive. You can turn this feature off with `--no-includes`.

Types of configuration variables and type specifiers

While requesting (or writing) a `config` variable, you may give a *type specifier*. It can be `--bool`, which ensures that the returned value is `true` or `false`; `--int`, which expands the optional value suffix of k (1024 elements), m (1024k), or g (1024m); `--path`, which expands ~ for the value of $HOME; and ~user for the home directory of the given user. There is also `--bool-or-int` and a few options related to storing colors and retrieving color escape codes; see the `git config` documentation.

Accessing the Git configuration

You can use the `git config` command to access the Git configuration, starting from listing the configuration entries in a canonical form, through examining individual variables, to editing and adding entries.

You can query the existing configuration with `git config --list`, adding an appropriate parameter if you want to limit to a single configuration layer. On a Linux box with the default installation, in the fresh empty Git repository just after `git init`, the local (per-repository) setting would look approximately like the following:

```
$ git config --list --local
core.repositoryformatversion=0
core.filemode=false
core.bare=false
core.logallrefupdates=true
```

You can also query a single key with `git config`, limiting or not the scope to the specified file, by giving the name of configuration variable as a parameter (optionally preceded by `--get`), with the section, optional subsection, and variable name (key) separated by dot:

```
$ git config user.email
alice@example.com
```

This would return the last value, that is, the one with the most precedence. You can get all the values with `--get-all`, or specific keys with `--get-regexp=<match>`. This is quite useful while accessing a multivalued option like refspecs for a remote.

With `--get`, `--get-all`, and `--get-regexp`, you can also limit the listing (and the settings for multiple-valued variables) to only those variables matching the value regexp (which is passed as an optional last parameter). For example:

```
$ git config --get core.gitproxy 'for kernel\.org$'
```

You can also use the `git config` command to set the configuration variable value. For example, to set the e-mail address of the user, which is to be common to most of his or her repositories, you can run the following:

```
$ git config --global user.name "Alice Developer"
```

To change multivar, you can use:

```
$ git config core.gitproxy '"ssh" for kernel.org'  'for kernel\.org$'
```

The local layer (per-repository file) is the default for writing, if nothing else is specified. For multivalue configuration options, you can add multiple lines to it by using the `--add` option.

It is also very easy to delete configuration entries with `git config --unset`.

Instead of setting all the configuration values on the command line, as shown in the preceding example, it is possible to set or change them just by editing the relevant configuration file directly. Simply open the configuration file in your favorite editor, or run the `git config --edit` command.

The local repository configuration file just after a fresh init on Linux looks as follows:

```
[core]
        repositoryformatversion = 0
        filemode = true
        bare = false
        logallrefupdates = true
```

Basic client-side configuration

You can divide the configuration options recognized by Git into two categories: client-side and server-side. The majority of the options are about configuring your personal working preferences; they are client-side. The server-side configuration will be touched upon in more detail in *Chapter 11, Git Administration*; here you will find only basics.

There are many supported configuration options, but only a small fraction of them needs to be set; a large fraction of them has sensible defaults , and explicitly setting them is only useful in certain edge cases. There are a lot of options available; you can see a list of all the options with `git config --help`. Here we'll be covering only the most common and most useful options.

Two variables that really need to be set up are `user.email` and `user.name`. Those configuration variables define the author's identity. Also, if you are signing annotated tags or commits (as discussed in *Chapter 5, Collaborative Development with Git*), you might want to set up your GPG signing key ID. This is done with the `user.signingKey` configuration setting.

By default, Git uses whatever you've set on the system as your default text editor (defined with the `VISUAL` or `EDITOR` environment variables; the first only for the graphical desktop environment) to create and edit your commit and tag messages. It also uses whatever you have set as the pager (`PAGER`) for paginating and browsing the output of the Git commands. To change this default to something else, you can use the `core.editor` setting. The same goes for `core.pager`. Git would ultimately fall back on the `vi` editor and on the `less` pager.

With Git, the pager is invoked automatically. The default less pager supports not only pagination, but also incremental search for example. Also, with the default configuration (the LESS environment variable is not set) less invoked by Git works as if it was invoked with LESS=FRX. This means that it would skip pagination of there is less than one page of output, it would pass through ANSI color codes, and it would not clear screen on exit.

Creating commit messages is also affected by commit.template. If you set this configuration variable, Git will use that file as the default message when you commit. The template is not distributed with the repository in general. Note that Git would add the status information to the commit message template, unless it is forbidden to do it by setting commit.status to false.

Such a template is quite convenient if you have a commit-message policy, as it greatly increases the chances of this policy being followed. It can, for example, include the commented-out instructions for filling the commit message. You can augment this solution with an appropriate hook that checks whether the commit message matches the policy (see the *Commit process hooks* section in this chapter).

The status of the files in the working area is affected by the ignore patterns and the file attributes (see *Chapter 4, Managing Your Worktree*). You can put ignore patterns in your project's in-tree .gitignore file (usually tracked '.gitignore' is about which files are tracked, and is tracked itself by Git (not by itself). itself), or in the .git/info/excludes file for local and private patterns, to define which files are not interesting. These are project-specific; sometimes, you would want to write a kind of global (per-user) .gitignore file. You can use core.excludesFile to customize the path to the said file; in modern Git, there is a default value for this path, namely,~/.config/git/ignore. There is also a corresponding core.attributesFile for this kind of global .gitattributes files, which defaults to ~/.config/git/attributes.

 Actually, it is $XDG_CONFIG_HOME/git/ignore; if the $XDG_CONFIG_HOME environment variable is not set or is empty, $HOME/.config/git/ignore is used.

Although Git has an internal implementation of diff, you can set up an external tool to be used instead with the help of diff.external. You would usually want to create a wrapper script that massages the parameters that Git passes to it, and pass the ones needed in the order external diff requires. By default, Git passes the following arguments to the diff program:

```
path old-file old-hex old-mode new-file new-hex new-mode
```

See also the *Graphical diff and merge tools* section for the configuration of git difftool and git mergetool.

The rebase and merge setup, configuring pull

By default, when performing `git pull` (or equivalent), Git would use the `merge` operation to join the local history and the history fetched from the remote. This would create a merge commit if the history of the local branch has diverged from the remote one. Some argue that it is better to avoid all these merge commits and create mostly a linear history by using `rebase` instead (for example, with `git pull --rebase`) to join histories. You can find more information on this topic in *Chapter 7, Merging Changes Together*.

There are several configuration settings that can be used to make the `git pull` default to rebase, to set up tracking, and so on. There is the `pull.rebase` configuration option and a branch-specific `branch.<name>.rebase` option that, when set to `true`, tells Git to perform rebase instead of merge during pull (for the `<name>` branch only in a later case). Both can also be set to `preserve` to run rebase with the `--preserve-merges` option, to have local merge commits not be flattened in the rebase.

You can make Git automatically set up the per-branch "pull to rebase" configuration while creating specific kinds of new branches with `branch.autoSetupRebase`. You can set it to `never`, `local` (for locally tracked branches only), `remote` (for remote tracked branches only), or `always` (for local plus remote).

Preserving undo information – the expiry of objects

By default, Git will automatically remove unreferenced objects, clean `reflogs` of stale entries, and pack loose objects, all to keep the size of the repository down. You can also run the garbage collection manually with the `git gc` command. You should know about repository's object-oriented structure from *Chapter 8, Keeping History Clean*.

Git will, for safety reasons, use a grace period of two weeks while removing unreferenced objects for; this can be changed with the `gc.pruneExpire` configuration: the setting is usually a relative date (for example, `1.month.ago`; you can use dots as a word separator). To disable the grace period (which is usually done from the command line), the value `now` can be used.

The branch tip history is kept for 90 days by default (or `gc.reflogExpire`, if set) for reachable revisions, and for 30 days (or `gc.reflogExpireUnreachable`) for reflog entries that are not a part of the current history. Both settings can be configured on a per-refname basis, by supplying a pattern of the ref name to be matched as a subsection name, that is, `gc.<pattern>.reflogExpire`, and similar for the other setting. This can be used to change the expire settings for HEAD or for `refs/stash` (see *Chapter 4, Managing Your Worktree*), or for remote-tracking branches `refs/remotes/*` separately. The setting is a length of time (for example, `6.months`); to completely turn of reflog expiring use the value of `never`. You can use the latter for example to switch off expiring of `stash` entries.

Formatting and whitespace

Code formatting and whitespace issues are some of the more frustrating and subtle problems you may encounter while collaborating, especially with cross-platform development. It's very easy for patches and merges to introduce subtle whitespace changes, because of editors silently introducing such changes (often not visible) and a different notion of line endings on different operating systems: MS Windows, Linux, and MacOS X. Git has a few configuration options to help with these issues.

One important issue for cross-platform work is the notion of **line-ending**. This is because MS Windows uses a combination of a carriage return (CR) character and a linefeed (LF) character for new lines in text files, whereas MacOS and Linux use only a linefeed character. Many editors on MS Windows will silently replace existing LF-style line endings with CRLF or use CRLF for new lines, which leads to subtle but annoying troubles.

Git can handle this issue by auto-converting line endings into LF when you add a file to the index. If your editor uses CRLF line endings, Git can also convert line-endings to the native form when it checks out code in your filesystem. There are two configuration settings that affect this matter: `core.eol` and `core.autocrlf`. The first setting, `core.eol`, sets the line ending to be used while checking out files into the working directory for files that have the `text` property set (see the next section, *Per-file configuration with gitattributes*, which summarizes and recalls information about the file attributes from *Chapter 4, Managing Your Worktree*).

The second and older setting, `core.autocrlf`, can be used to turn on the automatic conversion of line endings to CRLF. Setting it to `true` converts the LF line endings in the repository into CRLF when you check out files, and vice versa when you stage them; this is the setting you would probably want on a Windows machine. (This is almost the same as setting the `text` attribute to `auto` on all the files and `core.eol` to `crlf`.) You can tell Git to convert CRLF to LF on a commit but not the other way around by setting `core.autocrlf` to `input` instead; this is the setting to use if you are on a Linux or Mac system. To turn off this functionality, recording the line-endings in the repository as they are set this configuration value to `false`.

This handles one part of the whitespace issues: line-ending variance, and one vector of introducing them: editing files. Git also comes with the way to detect and fix some of other whitespace issues. It can look for a set of common whitespace problems to notice. The `core.whitespace` configuration setting can be used to activate them (for those disabled by default), or turn them off (for those enabled by default). The three that are turned on by default are:

- `blank-at-eol`: This looks for trailing spaces at the end of a line

- `blank-at-eof`: This notices blank lines at the end of a file
- `space-before-tab`: This looks for spaces immediately before the tabs at the initial (beginning) indent part of the line

The `trailing-space` value in `core.whitespace` is a shorthand to cover both `blank-at-eol` and `blank-at-eof`. The three that are disabled by default but can be turned on are:

- `indent-with-non-tab`: This treats the line that is indented with space characters instead of the equivalent tabs as an error (where equivalence is controlled by the `tabwidth` option); this option enforces indenting with *Tab* characters.
- `tab-in-indent`: This watches for tabs in the initial indentation portion of the line (here, `tabwidth` is used to fix such whitespace errors); this option enforces indenting with space characters.
- `cr-at-eol`: This tells Git that carriage returns at the end of the lines are OK (allowing CRLF endings in the repository).

You can tell Git which of these you want enabled or disabled by setting `core.whitespace` to the comma separated list of values. To disable an option, prepend it with the "-" prefix in front of the value. For example, if you want all but `cr-at-eol` and `tab-in-indent` to be set, and also while setting the tab space value to 4, you can use:

```
$ git config --local core.whitespace \
    trailing-space,space-before-tab,indent-with-non-tab,tabwidth=4
```

You can also set these options on a per-file basis with the `whitespace` attribute. For example, you can use it to turn off checking for whitespace problems in test cases to handle whitespace issues, or ensure that the Python 2 code indents with spaces:

```
*.py whitespace=tab-in-indent
```

Git will detect these issues when you run a `git diff` command and inform about them using the `color.diff.whitespace` color, so you can notice them and possibly fix them before you create a new commit. While applying patches with `git apply`, you can ask Git to either warn about the whitespace issues with `git apply --whitespace=warn`, error out with `--whitespace=error`, or you can have Git try to automatically fix the issue with `--whitespace=fix`. The same applies to the `git rebase` command as well.

Server-side configuration

There are a few configuration options available for the server-side of Git. They would be described in more detail in *Chapter 11, Git Administration*; here you will find a short summary of some of the more interesting parameters.

You can make the Git server check for object consistency, namely, that every object received during a push matches its SHA-1 identifier and that points to a valid object with a `receive.fsckObjects` Boolean-valued configuration variable. It is turned off by default because `git fsck` is a fairly expensive operation, and it might slow down operation, especially on large pushes (which are common in large repositories). This is a check against faulty or malicious clients.

If you rewrite commits that you have already pushed to a server (which is bad practice, as explained in *Chapter 8, Keeping History Clean*) and try to push again, you'll be denied. The client might, however, force-update the remote branch with the `--force` flag to the `git push` command. However, the server can be told to refuse force-pushes by setting `receive.denyNonFastForward` to `true`.

The `receive.denyDeletes` setting blocks one of the workarounds to the `denyNonFastForward` policy, namely, deleting and recreating a branch. This forbids the deletion of branches and tags; you must remove refs from the server manually.

All of these features could also be implemented via the server-side receive-like hooks; this will be covered in the *Installing a Git hook* section, and also to some extent in *Chapter 11, Git Administration*.

Per-file configuration with gitattributes

Some of the customizations can also be specified for a path (perhaps via glob) so that Git applies these settings only for a subset of files or for a subdirectory. These path-specific settings are called gitattributes.

The order of precedence of applying this type of settings starts with the per-repository local (per-user) per-path settings in the `$GIT_DIR/info/attributes` file. Then, the `.gitattributes` files are consulted, starting with the one in the same directory as the path in question, going up through the `.gitattributes` files in the parent directories, up to the top level of the worktree (the root directory of a project). Finally, the global per-user attributes file (specified by `core.attributesFile`, or at `~/.config/git/attributes` if this is not set) and the system-wide file (in `/etc/gitattributes` in the default installation) are considered.

Available Git attributes are described in detail in *Chapter 4*, *Managing Your Worktree*. Using attributes, you can, among others, do things such as specify the separate merge strategies via merge drivers for the specific kind of files (for example, ChangeLog), tell Git how to diff non-text files, or have Git filter content during checkout (on writing to the working area, that is, to the filesystem) and checkin (on staging contents and committing changes to the repository, that is, creating objects in the repository database).

Syntax of the Git attributes file

A gitattributes file is a simple text file that sets up the local configuration on a per-path basis. Blank lines, or lines starting with the hash character (#) are ignored; thus, a line starting with # serves as a comment, while blank lines can serve as separators for readability. To specify a set of attributes for a path, put a pattern followed by an attributes list, separated by a horizontal whitespace:

```
pattern   attribute1 attribute2
```

When more than one pattern matches the path, a later line overrides an earlier line, just like for the .gitignore files (you can also think that the Git attributes files are read from the least specific system-wide file to the most specific local repository file).

Git uses a backslash (\) as an escape character for patterns. Thus, for patterns that begin with a hash, you need to put a backslash in front of the first hash (that is written as \#). Because the attributes information is separated by whitespaces, trailing spaces in the pattern are ignored and inner spaces are treated as end of pattern, unless they are quoted with a backslash (that is, written as "\ ").

If the pattern does not contain a slash (/), which is a directory separator, Git will treat the pattern as a shell glob pattern and will check for a match against the pathname relative to the location of the .gitattributes file (or top level for other attribute files). Thus, for example, the *.c patterns match the C files anywhere down from the place the .gitattributes file resides. A leading slash matches the beginning of the pathname. For example, /*.c matches bisect.c but not builtin/bisect--helper.c., while *.c pattern would match both.

If the pattern includes at least one slash, Git will treat it as a shell glob suitable for consumption by the `fnmatch(3)` function call with the `FNM_PATHNAME` flag. This means that the wildcards in the pattern will not match the directory separator, that is, the slash (/) in the pathname; the match is anchored to beginning of the path. For example, the `include/*.h` pattern matches `include/version.h` but not `include/linux/asm.h` or `libxdiff/includes/xdiff.h`. Shell glob wildcards are: `*` matching any string (including empty), `?` matching any single character, and the [...] expression matching the character class (inside brackets, asterisks and question marks lose their special meaning); note that unlike in regular expressions, the complementation/negation of character class is done with ! and not ^. For example to match anything but a number one can use `[!0-9]` shell pattern, which is equivalent to `[^0-9]` regexp.

Two consecutive asterisks (`**`) in patterns may have a special meaning, but only between two slashes (`/**/`), or between a slash and at the beginning or the end of pattern. Such a wildcard matches zero or more path components. Thus, a leading `**` followed by a slash means match in all directories, while trailing `/**` matches every file or directory inside the specified directory.

Each attribute can be in one of the four states for a given path. First, it can be *set* (the attribute has special value of `true`); this is specified by simply listing the name of the attribute in the attribute list, for example, `text`. Second, it can be *unset* (the attribute has a special value of `false`); this is specified by listing the name of the attribute prefixed with minus, for example,`-text`. Third, it can be set to a specific value; this is specified by listing the name of the attribute followed by an equal sign and its value, for example, `-text=auto` (note that there cannot be any whitespace around the equal sign as opposed to the configuration file syntax). If no pattern matches the path, and nothing says if the path has or does not have attributes, the attribute is said to be unspecified (you can override a setting for the attribute, forcing it to be explicitly unspecified with `!text`).

If you find yourself using the same set of attributes over and over for many different patterns, you should consider defining a macro attribute. It can be defined in the local, or global, or system-wide attributes file, but only in the top level `.gitattributes` file. The macro is defined using `[attr]<macro>` in place of the file pattern; the attributes list defines the expansion of the macro. For example, the built-in `binary` macro attribute is defined as if using:

```
[attr]binary -diff -merge -text
```

Automating Git with hooks

There are usually certain prerequisites to the code that is produced, either self-induced or enforced externally. The code should be always able to compile and pass at least a fast subset of the tests. With some development workflows, each commit message may need to reference an issue ID (or fit message template), or include a digital certificate of origin in the form of the Signed-off-by line. In many cases, these parts of the development process can be automated by Git.

Like many programming tools, Git includes a way to fire custom functionality contained in the user-provided code (custom scripts), when certain important pre-defined actions occur, that is, when certain events trigger. Such a functionality invoked as a event handler is called a **hook**. It allows to take an additional action and, at least for some hooks, also to stop the triggered functionality.

Hooks in Git can be divided into the client-side and the server-side hooks. **Client-side hooks** are triggered by local operations (on client) such as committing, applying a patch series, rebasing, and merging. **Server-side hooks** on the other hand run on the server when the network operations such as receiving pushed commits occur.

You can also divide hooks into pre hooks and post-hooks. **Pre hooks** are called before an operation is finished, usually before the next step while performing an operation. If they exit with a nonzero value, they will cancel the current Git operation. **Post hooks** are invoked after an operation finishes and can be used for notification and logs; they cannot cancel an operation.

Installing a Git hook

The hooks in Git are executable programs (usually scripts), which are stored in the hooks/ subdirectory of the Git repository administrative area, that is in .git/hooks/ for non-bare repositories. Hook programs are named each after an event that triggers it; this means that if you want for one event to trigger more than one script, you will need to implement multiplexing yourself.

When you initialize a new repository with git init (this is done also while using git clone to create a copy of the other repository; clone calls init internally), Git populates the hooks directory with a bunch of inactive example scripts. Many of these are useful by themselves, but they also document the hook's API. All the examples are written as shell or Perl scripts, but any properly named executable would work just fine. If you want to use bundled example hook scripts, you'll need to rename them, stripping the .sample extension and ensuring that they have the executable permission bit.

A template for repositories

Sometimes you would want to have the same set of hooks for all your repositories. You can have a global (per-user and system-wide) configuration file, a global attributes file, and a global ignore list. It turns out that it is possible to select hooks to be populated during the creation of the repository. The default sample hooks that get copied to the .git/hooks repository are populated from /usr/share/git-core/ templates.

Also, the alternative directory with the repository creation templates can be given as a parameter to the --template command-line option (to git clone and git init), as the GIT_TEMPLATE_DIR environment variable, or as the init.templateDir configuration option (which can be set in a per-user configuration file). This directory must follow the directory structure of .git (of $GIT_DIR), which means that the hooks need to be in the hooks/ subdirectory there.

Note, however, that this mechanism has some limitations. As the files from the template directory are only copied to the Git repositories on their initialization, updates to the template directory do not affect the existing repositories. Though you can re-run git init in the existing repository to reinitialize it, just remember to save any modifications made to the hooks.

Maintaining hooks for a team of developers can be tricky. One possible solution is to store your hooks in the actual project directory (inside project working area), or in a separate hooks repository, and create a symbolic link in .git/hooks, as needed.

There are even tools and frameworks for Git hook management; you can find examples of such tools listed on http://githooks.com/.

Client-side hooks

There are quite a few client-side hooks. They can be divided into the commit-workflow hooks (a set of hooks invoked by the different stages of creating a new commit), apply-email workflow hooks, and everything else (not organized into a multihook workflow).

It is important to note that hooks are *not* copied when you clone a repository. This is done partially for security reasons, as hooks run unattended and mostly invisible. You need to copy (and rename) files themselves, though you can control which hooks get installed while creating or reinitializing a repository (see the previous subsection). This means that you cannot rely on the client-side hooks to enforce a policy; if you need to introduce some hard requirements, you'll need to do it on the server-side.

Commit process hooks

There are four client-side hooks invoked (by default) while committing changes. They are as follows:

1. The `pre-commit` hook is run first, even before you invoke the editor to type in the commit message. It is used to inspect the snapshot to be committed, to see whether you haven't forgotten anything. A nonzero exit from this hook aborts the commit. You can bypass invoking this hook altogether with `git commit --no-verifies`. This hook takes no parameters.

    This hook can, among others, be used to check for the correct code style, run the static code analyzer (linter) to check for problematic constructs, make sure that the code compiles and that it passes all the tests (and that the new code is covered by the tests), or check for the appropriate documentation on a new functionality. The default hook checks for whitespace errors (trailing whitespace by default) with `git diff --check` (or rather its plumbing equivalent), and optionally for non-ASCII filenames in the changed files. You can, for example, make a hook that asks for a confirmation while committing with a dirty work-arena (for the changes in the worktree that would not be a part of the commit being created); though it is an advanced technique. Or, you can try to have it check whether there are documentations and unit tests on the new methods.

2. The `prepare-commit-msg` hook is run after the default commit message is created (including the static text of the file given by `commit.template`, if any), and before the commit message is opened in the editor. It lets you edit the default commit message or create a template programmatically, before the commit author sees it. If the hook fails with a nonzero status, the commit will be aborted. This hook takes as parameters the path to the file that holds the commit message (later passed to the editor) and the information about source of the commit message (the latter is not present for ordinary `git commit`): `message` if the `-m` or `-F` option was given, `template` if the `-t` option was given or `commit.template` was set, `merge` if the commit is merged or the `.git/MERGE_MSG` file exists, `squash` if the `.git/SQUASH_MSG` file exists, or `commit` if the message comes from the other commit: the `-c`, `-C`, or `--amend` option was given. In the last case, the hook gets additional parameters, namely, a SHA-1 of the commit that is the source of the message.

    The purpose of this hook is to edit or create the commit message, and this hook is not suppressed by the `--no-verify` option. This hook is most useful when it is used to affect commits where the default message is autogenerated, such as the templated commit message, merged commits, squashed commits, and amended commits. The sample hook that Git provides comments out the `Conflict:` part of the merge commit message.

Another example of what this hook can do is to use the description of the current branch given by `branch.<branch-name>.description`, if it exists, as a base for a branch-dependent dynamic commit template. Or perhaps, check whether we are on the topic branch, and then list all the issues assigned to you on a project issue tracker, to make it easy to add the proper artefact ID to the commit message.

3. The `commit-msg` hook is run after the developer writes the commit message, but before the commit is actually written to the repository. It takes one parameter, a path to the temporary file with the commit message provided by user (by default `.git/COMMIT_EDITMSG`).

   If this script exits with a nonzero status, Git aborts the commit process, so you can use it to validate that, for example, the commit message matches the project state, or that the commit message conforms to the required pattern. The sample hook provided by Git can check, sort, and remove duplicated `Signed-off-by:` lines (which might be not what you want to use, if signoffs are to be a chain of provenance). You could conceivably check in this hook whether the references to the issue numbers are correct (and perhaps expand them, adding the current summary of each mentioned issue).

   Gerrit Code Review provides a `commit-msg` hook (which needs to be installed in the local Git repository) to automatically create, insert, and maintain a unique `Change-Id:` line above the signoffs during `git commit`. This line is used to track the iterations of coming up with a commit; if the commit message in the revision pushed to Gerrit lacks such information, the server will provide instructions on how to get and install that hook script.

4. The `post-commit` hook runs after the entire process is completed. It doesn't take any parameters, but at this point of the commit operation the revision that got created during commit is available as HEAD. The exit status of this hook is ignored.

   Generally, this script (like most of the `post-*` scripts) is most often used for notifications and logging, and it obviously cannot affect the outcome of `git commit`. You can use it, for example, to trigger a local build in a continuous integration tool such as Jenkins. In most cases, however, you would want to do this with the `post-receive` hook on the dedicated continuous integration server.

   Another use case is to list information about all the TODO and FIXME comments in the code and documentation (for example, the author, version, file path, line number, and message), printing them to standard output of the hook, so that that they are not forgotten and remain up to date and useful.

Hooks for applying patches from e-mails

You can set up three client-side hooks for the e-mail based workflow (where commits are sent in an e-mail). They are all invoked by the `git am` command (which name comes from the apply mailbox), which can be used to take saved e-mails with patches (created, for example, with `git format-patch` for example and sent, for example, with `git sent-email`) and turn them into a series of commits. Those hooks are as follows:

1. The first hook to run is `applypatch-msg`. It is run after extracting the commit message from the patch and before applying the patch itself. As usual, for a hook which is not a `post-*` hook, Git aborts applying the patch if this hook exists with a nonzero status. It takes a single argument: the name of the temporary file with the extracted commit message.

    You can use this hook to make sure that the commit message is properly formatted, or to normalize the commit message by having the script alter the file. The example `applypatch-msg` hook provided by Git simply runs the `commit-msg` hook if it exists as a hook (the file exists and is executable).

2. The next hook to run is `pre-applypatch`. It is run after the patch is applied to the working area, but before the commit is created. You can use it to inspect the state of the project before making a commit, for example, running tests. Exiting with a nonzero status aborts the `git am` script without committing the patch.

    The sample hook provided by Git simply runs the `pre-commit` hook, if present.

3. The last hook to run is `post-applypatch`, which runs after the commit is made. It can be used for notifying or logging, for example, notifying all the developers or just the author of the patch that you have applied it.

Other client-side hooks

There are a few other client-side hooks that do not fit into a series of steps in a single process.

The `pre-rebase` hook runs before you rebase anything. Like all the `pre-*` hooks, it can abort the rebase process with a nonzero exit code. You can use this hook to disallow rebasing (and thus rewriting) any commits that were already published. The hook is called with the name of the base branch (the upstream the series was forked from) and the name of the branch being rebased. The second parameter is passed to the hook only if the branch being rebased is not the current branch. The sample `pre-rebase` hook provided by Git tries to do this, though it makes some assumptions specific to Git's project development that may not match your workflow (take note that amending commits also rewrites them, and that rebasing may create a copy of a branch instead of rewriting it).

The pre-push hook runs during the git push operation, after it has checked the remote status (and exchange finding which revisions are absent on server), but before anything has been pushed. The hook is called with the reference to the remote (the URL or the remote name) and the actual push URL (the location of remote) as script parameters. Information about the commits to be pushed is provided on the standard input, one line per ref to be updated. You can use this hook to validate a set of ref updates before a push occurs; a nonzero exit code aborts the push. The example installed simply checks whether there are commits beginning with WIP in a set of revisions to be pushed or marked with the nopush keyword in the commit message, and when either of those is true, it aborts the push. You can even make a hook prompt the user if he or she is sure. This hook compliments the server-side checks, avoiding data transfer that would fail validation anyway.

The post-rewrite hook is run by commands that rewrite history (that replace commits), such as git commit --amend and git rebase. Note, however, that it is not run by large scale history rewriting, such as git filter-branch. The type of command that triggered the rewrite (amend or rebase) is passed as a single argument, while the list of rewrites is sent to the standard input. This hook has many of the same uses as the post-checkout and post-merge hooks, and it runs after automatic copying of notes, which is controlled by the notes.rewriteRef configuration variable (you can find more about notes mechanism in *Chapter 8, Keeping History Clean*).

The post-checkout hook is run after successful git checkout (or git checkout <file>) after having updated the worktree. The hook is given three parameters: the SHA-1s of the previous and current HEAD (which may or may not be different) and a flag indicating whether it was a whole project checkout (you were changing branches, the flag parameter is 1) or a file checkout (retrieving files from the index or named commit, the flag parameter is 0). As a special case, during initial checkout after git clone, this hook passes the all-zero SHA-1 as the first parameter (as a source revision). You can use this hook to set up your working directory properly for your use case. This may mean handling large binary files outside the repository (as an alternative to per-file the filter Git attribute) that you don't want to have in the repository, or setting the working directory metadata properties such as full permissions, owner, group, times, extended attributes, or ACLs. It can also be used to perform repository validity checks, or enhance the git checkout output by auto-displaying the differences (or just the diff statistics) from the previous checked out revision (if they were different).

The post-merge hook runs after a successful merge operation. You can use it in a way similar to post-checkout to restore data and metadata in the working tree that Git doesn't track, such as full permissions data (or just make it invoke post-checkout directly). This hook can likewise validate the presence of files external to Git control that you might want copied in when the working tree changes.

For Git, objects in the repository (for example, commit objects representing revisions) are immutable; rewriting history (even amending a commit) is in fact creating a modified copy and switching to it, leaving the pre-rewrite history abandoned. Deleting a branch also leaves abandoned history. To prevent the repository from growing too much, Git occasionally performs garbage collection by removing old unreferenced objects. In all but ancient Git, this is done as a part of normal Git operations by them invoking `git gc --auto`. The `pre-auto-gc` hook is invoked just before garbage collection takes place and can be used to abort the operation, for example, if you are on battery power. It can also be used to notify you that garbage collection is happening.

Server-side hooks

In addition to the client-side hooks, which are run in your own repository, there are a couple of important server-side hooks that a system administrator can use to enforce nearly any kind of policy for your project.

These hooks are run before and after you do a push to the server. The pre hooks (as mentioned earlier) can exit nonzero to reject a push or part of it; messages printed by the pre hooks will be sent back to the client (sender). You can use these hooks to set up complex push policies. Git repository management tools, such as `gitolite` and Git hosting solutions, use these to implement more involved access control for repositories. The post hooks can be used for notification, starting a build process (or just to rebuild and redeploy the documentation) or running a full test suite, for example as a part of a continuous integration solution.

While writing server-side hooks, you need to take into account where in the sequence of operations does the hook take place and what information is available there, both as parameters or on the standard input, and in the repository.

That's what happens on the server when it receives a push:

1. Simplifying it a bit, the first step is that all the objects that were present in the client and missing on the server are sent to the server and stored (but are not yet referenced). If the receiving end fails to do this correctly (for example, because of the lack of disk space), the whole push operation will fail.

2. The `pre-receive` hook is run. It takes a list describing the references that are being pushed on its standard input. If it exits with a nonzero status, it aborts the whole operation and none of the references that were pushed are accepted.

3. For each ref being updated, the following happens:

    1. The built-in sanity checks may reject the push to the ref, including the check for an update of a checked out branch, or a non-fast-forward push (unless forced), and so on

    2. The `update` hook is run, passing ref to be pushed in arguments; if this script exits nonzero, only this ref will be rejected the sample hook blocks unannotated tags from entering the repository.

    3. The ref is updated (unless, in modern Git, the push is requested to be atomic)

4. If the push is atomic, all the refs are updated (if none were rejected).

5. The `post-receive` hook is run, taking the same data as the `pre-receive` one. This one can be used to update other services (for example, notify continuous integration servers) or notify users (via an e-mail or a mailing list, IRC, or a ticket-tracking system).

6. For each ref that was updated, the `post-update` hook is run. This can also be used for logging. The sample hook runs `git update-server-info` to prepare a repository, saving extra information to be used over *dumb* transports, though it would work better if run once as `post-receive`.

7. If push tries to update the currently checked out branch and the `receive.denyCurrentBranch` configuration variable is set to `updateInstead`, then `push-to-checkout` is run.

You need to remember that in pre hooks, you don't have refs updated yet, and that post hooks cannot affect the result of an operation. You can use pre hooks for access control (permission checking), and post hooks for notification and updating side data and logs.

You will see example hooks (server-side and client-side) for the Git-enforced policy in *Chapter 11, Git Administration*. You will also learn how other tools use those hooks, for example, for use in access control and triggering actions on push.

Extending Git

Git provides a few mechanisms to extend it. You can add shortcuts and create new commands, and add support for new transports; all without requiring to modify Git sources.

Command aliases for Git

There is one little tip that can make your Git command-line experience simpler, easier, and more familiar, namely, Git aliases. It is very easy in theory to create an alias. You simply need to create an `alias.<command-name>` configuration variable; its value is the expansion of alias.

One of the uses for aliases is defining short abbreviations for commonly used commands and their arguments. Another is creating new commands. Here are a couple of examples you might want to set up:

```
$ git config --global alias.co checkout
$ git config --global alias.ci commit
$ git config --global alias.lg log --graph --oneline --decorate
$ git config --global alias.aliases 'config --get-regexp ^alias\.'
```

The preceding setup means that typing, for example, `git ci` would be the same as typing `git commit`. Aliases take arguments just as the regular Git commands do. Git does not provide any default aliases that are defining shortcuts for the common operations, unless you use a friendly fork of Git by Felipe Contreras: `git-fc`.

Arguments are split by space, the usual shell quoting and escaping is supported; in particular, you can use a quote pair (`"a b"`) or a backslash (`a\ b`) to include space in a single argument.

> Note, however, that you cannot have the alias with the same name as a Git command; in other words, you cannot use aliases to change the behavior of commands. The reasoning behind this restriction is that it could make existing scripts and hooks fail unexpectedly. Aliases that hide existing Git commands (with the same name as Git commands) are simply ignored.

You might, however, want to run external command rather than a Git command in an alias. Or, you might want to join together the result of a few separate commands. In this case, you can start the alias definition with the `!` character (with the exclamation mark):

```
$ git config --global alias.unmerged \
'!git ls-files --unmerged | cut -f2 | sort -u'
```

Because here the first command of the expansion of an alias can be an external tool, you need to specify the `git` wrapper explicitly, as shown in the preceding example.

> Note that in many shells, for example, in `bash`, `!` is the history expansion character and it needs to be escaped as `\!`, or be within single quotes.

Note that such shell command will be executed from the top-level directory of a repository (after `cd` to a top level), which may not necessarily be the current directory. Git sets the `GIT_PREFIX` environment variable to the current directory path relative to the top directory of a repository, that is, `git rev-parse --show-prefix`. As usual, `git rev-parse` (and some `git` wrapper options) may be of use here.

The fact mentioned earlier can be used while creating aliases. The `git serve` alias, running `git daemon` to read-only serve the current repository at `git://127.0.0.1/`, makes use of the fact that the shell commands in aliases are executed from the top-level directory of a repo:

```
[alias]
serve = !git daemon --reuseaddr --verbose  --base-path=.  --export-all
./.git
```

Sometimes, you need to reorder arguments, use an argument twice, or pass an argument to the command early in the pipeline. You would want to refer to subsequent arguments as `$1`, `$2`, and so on, or to all arguments as `$@`, just like in shell scripts. One trick that you can find in older examples is to run a shell with a `-c` argument, like in the first of the examples mentioned next; the final dash is so that the arguments start with `$1`, not with `$0`. A more modern idiom is to define and immediately execute a shell function, like in the second example (it is a preferred solution because it has one of the fewer level of quoting, and lets you use standard shell argument processing):

```
[alias]
record-1 = !sh -c 'git add -p -- $@ && git commit' -
record-2 = !f() {  git add -p -- $@ && git commit }; f
```

Aliases are integrated with command-line completion. While determining which completion to use for an alias, Git searches for a `git` command, skipping an opening brace or a single quote (thus, supporting both of the idioms mentioned earlier). With modern Git (version 2.1 or newer), you can use the null command `":"` to declare the desired completion style. For example, alias expanding to `!f() { : git commit ; ... } f` would use a command completion for `git commit`, regardless of the rest of the alias.

Git aliases are also integrated with the help system; if you use the `--help` option on an alias, Git would tell you its expansion (so you can check the relevant man page):

```
$ git co --help
'git co' is aliased to `checkout'
```

Adding new Git commands

Aliases are best at taking small one-liners and converting them into small useful Git commands. You can write complex aliases, but when it comes to larger scripts, you would probably like to incorporate them into Git directly.

Git subcommands can be standalone executables that live in the Git execution path (which you can find by running `git --exec-path`); on Linux, this normally is `/usr/libexec/git-core`. The `git` executable itself is a thin wrapper that knows where the subcommands live. If `git foo` is not a built-in command, the wrapper searches for the `git-foo` command first in the Git `exec` path, then in the rest of your `$PATH`. The latter makes it possible to write local Git extensions (local Git commands) without requiring access to the system's space.

This feature is what it makes possible to have user interface more or less integrated with the rest of Git in projects such as `git imerge` (see *Chapter 7, Merging Changes Together*) or `git annex` (see *Chapter 9, Managing Subprojects - Building a Living Framework*). It is also how projects such as Git Extras, providing extra Git commands, were made.

Note, however, that if you don't install the documentation for your command in typical places, or configure documentation system to find its help,, `git foo --help` won't work correctly.

Credential helpers and remote helpers

There is another place where simply dropping appropriately named executable enhances and extends Git. **Remote helper** programs are invoked by Git when it needs to interact with remote repositories and remote transport protocols Git does not support natively. You can find more about them in *Chapter 5, Collaborative Development with Git*.

When Git encounters a URL of the form `<transport>://<address>`, where `<transport>` is a (pseudo)protocol that is not natively supported, it automatically invokes the `git remote-<transport>` command with a remote and full remote URL as arguments. A URL of the form `<transport>::<address>` also invokes this remote helper, but with just `<address>` as a second argument in the place of a URL. Additionally, with `remote.<remote-name>.vcs` set to `<transport>`, Git would explicitly invoke `git remote-<transport>` to access that remote.

The **helpers mechanism** in Git is about interacting with external scripts using a well-specified format.

Each remote helper is expected to support a subset of commands. You can find more information about the issue of creating new helpers in the `gitremote-helpers(1)` man page.

There is another type of helpers in Git, namely, **credentials helpers**. They can be used by Git to get the credentials from the user required, for example, to access the remote repository over HTTP. They are specified by the configuration though, just like the merge and diff drivers, and like the clean and smudge filters.

Summary

This chapter provided all the tools you need to use Git effectively. You got to know how to make the command-line interface easier to use and more effective with the Git-aware dynamic command prompt, command-line completion, autocorrection for Git commands, and using colors. You learned of the existence of alternative interfaces, from alternative porcelains to the various types of graphical clients.

You were reminded of the various ways to change the behavior of Git commands. You discovered how Git accesses its configuration, and learned about a selected subset of configuration variables. You have learned how to automate Git with hooks and how to make use of them. Finally, you have learned how to extend Git with new commands and support new URLs schemes.

This chapter was mainly about making Git more effective for you; the next chapter, *Chapter 11, Git Administration*, would explain how to make Git more effective for other developers. You will find there more about server-side hooks and see their usage. You will also learn about repository maintenance.

11
Git Administration

The previous chapter, *Customizing and Extending Git*, explained among others how to use Git hooks for automation moved earlier in the chapter. The client-side hooks were described in detail, while the server-side hooks were only sketched. Here, in this chapter, we will present the server-side hooks comprehensively, and mention the client-side hooks' usage as helpers.

The earlier chapters helped master your work with Git as a developer, as a person collaborating with others, and as a maintainer. When the book was talking about setting up repositories and branch structure, it was from the point of view of a Git user.

This chapter is intended to help readers who are in a situation of having to take up the administrative side of Git. This includes setting up remote Git repositories and configuring their access. It covers the work required to make Git go smoothly (that is, Git maintenance), and finding and recovering from the repository errors. This chapter will also describe transfer protocols and how to use server-side hooks for implementing and enforcing development policy. Additionally, you will find here a short description of the various types of tools that can be used to manage remote repositories, to help you choose among them.

In this chapter, we will cover the following topics:

- Server-side hooks—implementing a policy and notifications
- Transport protocols, authentication and authorization
- How to set up Git on the server
- Third-party tools for management of remote repositories
- Signed pushes to assert updating refs and enable audits
- Reducing the size of hosted repositories with alternates and namespaces
- Improving server performance and helping the initial clone

- Checking for repository corruption and fixing the repository
- Recovering from errors with the help of reflogs and `git fsck`
- Git repository maintenance and repacking
- Augmenting development workflows with Git

Repository maintenance

Occasionally, you may need to do some clean up of a repository, usually to make it more compact. Such clean ups are a very important step after migrating a repository from another version control system.

Modern Git (or rather all but ancient Git) from time to time runs the `git gc --auto` command in each repository. This command checks whether there are too many loose objects (objects stored as separate files, one file per object, rather than stored together in a packfile; objects are almost always created as loose), and if these conditions are met, then it would launch the garbage collection operation. The garbage collection means to gather up all the loose objects and place them in packfiles, and to consolidate many small packfiles into one large packfile. Additionally, it packs references into the `packed-refs` file. Objects that are unreachable even via reflog, and are safely old, do not get picked in the repack. Git would then delete loose objects and packfiles that got repacked (with some safety margin with respect to the age of the loose object's files), thus pruning old unreachable objects. There are various configuration knobs in the `gc.*` namespace to control garbage collection operations.

You can run `auto gc` manually with `git gc --auto`, or force garbage collection with `git gc`. The `git count-objects` command (perhaps with the help of the `-v` parameter) can be used to check whether there are signs that repack is needed. You can even run individual steps of the garbage collection individually with `git repack`, `git pack-refs`, `git prune`, and `git prune-packed`.

By default, Git would try to reuse the results of the earlier packing to reduce CPU time spent on the repacking, while still providing good disk space utilization. In some cases, you would want to more aggressively optimize the size of repository at the cost of it taking more time: this is possible with `git gc --aggressive` (or with repacking the repository by hand with `git repack`, run with appropriate parameters). It is recommended to do this after import from other version control systems; the mechanism that Git uses for importing (fast-import stream) is optimized for the speed of the operation, not for the final repository size.

There are issues of maintenance not covered by `git gc`, because of their nature. One of them is pruning (deleting) remote-tracking branches that got deleted in the remote repository. This can be done with `git fetch --prune` or `git remote prune`, or on a per-branch basis with `git branch --delete --remotes <remote-tracking branch>`. This action is left to the user, and not run by `git gc`, because Git simply cannot know whether you have based your own work on the remote-tracking branch that is to be pruned.

Data recovery and troubleshooting

It is almost impossible to never make any mistakes. This applies also to using Git. The knowledge presented in this book, and your experience with using Git, should help in reducing the number of mistakes. Note that, Git tries quite hard not to make you lose your work; many mistakes are recoverable.

Recovering a lost commit

It may happen that you accidentally lost a commit. Perhaps, you force-deleted an incorrect branch that you were to be working on, or you rewound the branch to an incorrect place, or you were on an incorrect branch while starting an operation. Assuming something like this happened, is there any way to get your commits back and to undo the mistake?

Because Git does not delete objects immediately, but keeps them for a while, and only deletes them if they are unreachable during the garbage collection phase, the commit you lost will be there; you just need to find it. The garbage collection operation has, as mentioned, its own safeties; though if you find that you need troubleshooting, it would be better to turn off automatic garbage collection temporarily with git config gc.auto never.

Often, the simplest way to find and recover lost commits is to use the `git reflog` tool. For each branch, and separately for HEAD, Git silently records (logs) where the tip of the branch was in your local repository, at what time it was there, and how it got there. This record is called the reflog. Each time you commit or rewind a branch, the reflog for the branch and for the HEAD is updated. Each time you change the branches, the HEAD reflog is updated, and so on.

You can see where the tip of branch has been at any time by running `git reflog` or `git reflog <branch>`. You can run `git log -g` instead, where `-g` is a short way of saying `--walk-reflog`; this gives you a normal configurable log output. There is also `--grep-reflog=<pattern>` to search the reflog:

```
$ git reflog
6c89dee HEAD@{0}: commit: Ping asynchronously
```

```
d996b71 HEAD@{1}: rebase -i (finish): returning to refs/heads/ajax
d996b71 HEAD@{2}: rebase -i (continue): Ping asynchronously WIP
89579c9 HEAD@{3}: rebase -i (pick): Use Ajax mode
7c6d322 HEAD@{4}: commit (amend): Simplify index()
e1e6f65 HEAD@{5}: cherry-pick: fast-forward
eea7a7c HEAD@{6}: checkout: moving from ssh-check to ajax
c3e77bf HEAD@{7}: reset: moving to ajax@{1}
```

You should remember the `<ref>@{<n>}` syntax from *Chapter 2*, *Exploring Project History*. With the information from reflogs, you can rewind the branch in question to the version from before the set of operations, or you can start a new branch starting with any commit in the list.

Let's assume that your loss was caused by deleting a wrong branch. Because of the way reflogs are implemented (because logs for a branch named `foo`, that is, for the `refs/heads/foo` ref, are kept in the `.git/logs/refs/heads/foo` file), reflog for a given branch is deleted together with the branch. You might still have the necessary information in the `HEAD` reflog, unless you have manipulated the branch tip without involving the working area, but it might not be easy to find it.

In the case when the information is not present in reflogs, one way to find the necessary information to recover lost objects is to use the `git fsck` utility, which checks your repository for integrity. With the `--full` option, you can use this command to show all unreferenced objects:

```
$ git fsck --full
Checking object directories: 100% (256/256), done.
Checking objects: 100% (58/58), done.
dangling commit 50b836cb93af955ca99f2ccd4a1cc4014dc01a58
dangling blob 59fc7435baf79180a3835dddc52752f6044bab99
dangling blob fd64375c1f2b17b735f3145446d267822ae3ddd5
[...]
```

You can see the SHA1 identifiers of the unreferenced (lost) commits in the lines with the `dangling commit` string prefix. To examine all these dangling commits, you can filter the `git fsck` output for the commits with `grep "commit"`, extract their SHA1 with `cut -d' ' -f3`, and then feed these revisions into `git log --stdin --no-walk`.

```
$ git fsck --full | grep "commit" | cut -d' ' -f3 | git log --stdin --no-walk
```

Troubleshooting Git

The main purpose of `git fsck` is to check for repository corruption. Besides having an option to find dangling objects, it runs sanity checks for each object and tracks the reachability fully. It can find corrupted and missing objects; if the corruption was limited to your clone and the correct version can be found in other repositories (in backups and other archives), you can try to recover those objects from an uncorrupted source.

Sometimes, however, the error might be deeper. You can try to find a Git expert outside your team, but often the data in the repository is proprietary. Creating a minimal reproduction of the problem is not always possible. With modern Git, if the problem is structural, you can try to use `git fast-export --anonymize` to strip the repository from the data while reproducing the issue.

If the repository is fine, but the problem is with the Git operations, you can try to use various tracking and debugging mechanisms built into Git, or you can try to increase the verbosity of the commands. You can turn on tracing with the appropriate environment variables, shown later. The trace output can be written to standard error stream by setting the value of the appropriate environment variable to `1`, `2`, or `true`. Other integer values between 2 and 10 will be interpreted as open file descriptors to be used for trace output. You can also set such environment variables to the absolute path of the file to write trace messages to.

These tracking-related variables include the following (see the manpage of the `git` wrapper for the complete list):

- `GIT_TRACE`: This enables general trace messages, which do not fit into any specific category. This includes the expansion of the Git aliases (see *Chapter 10, Customizing and Extending Git*), built-in command execution, and external command execution (such as pager, editor, or helper).

- `GIT_TRACE_PACKET`: This enables packet-level tracking of the network operations for the "smart" transport protocols. This can help with debugging protocol issues or the troubles with the remote server that you set up. For debugging and fetching from shallow repositories, there is `GIT_TRACE_SHALLOW`.

- `GIT_TRACE_SETUP`: This enables trace messages, printing information about the location of the administrative area of the repository, the working area, and the current working directory and the prefix (the last one is the subdirectory inside the repository directory structure).

- `GIT_TRACE_PERFORMANCE`: This shows the total execution time of each Git command.

There is also GIT_CURL_VERBOSE to emit all the messages generated by the curl library for the network operations over HTTP, and GIT_MERGE_VERBOSITY to control the amount of output shown by the recursive merge strategy.

Git on the server

The previous chapters should give you enough knowledge to master most of the day-to-day version control tasks. The *Chapter 5, Collaborative Development with Git*, explained how one can lay out repositories for the collaboration. Here, we will explain how to actually set up remote Git repositories to serve.

The topic of administration of the Git repositories covers a large area. There are books written about specific repository management solutions, such as Gitolite, Gerrit, GitHub, or GitLab. Here, you will hopefully find enough information to help you with choosing a solution, or with crafting your own.

Let's start with the tools and mechanisms to manage remote repositories themselves, and then move on to the ways of serving Git repositories (putting Git on the server).

Server-side hooks

Hooks that are invoked on the server can be used for server administration; among others, these hooks can control the access to the remote repository by performing the authorization step, and can ensure that the commits entering the repository meet certain minimal criteria. The latter is best done with the additional help of client-side hooks, which were described in *Chapter 10, Customizing and Extending Git*. That way users are not left with being notified that their commits do not pass muster only at the time they want to publish them. On the other hand, client-side hooks implementing validation are easy to skip with the --no-verify option (so server-side validation is necessary), and you need to remember to install them.

Note, however, that server-side hooks are invoked only during push; you need other solutions for access control to fetch (and clone).

Hooks are also obviously not run while using *dumb* protocols—there is no Git on the server invoked then.

While writing hooks to implement some Git-enforced policy, you need to remember at what stage the hook in question is run and what information is available then. It is also important to know how the relevant information is passed to the hook—but you can find the last quite easily in the Git documentation in the githooks manpage. The previous chapter included a simple summary of server-side hooks. Here, we will expand a bit on this matter.

All the server-side hooks are invoked by `git receive-pack`, which is responsible for receiving published commits (which are received in the form of the packfile, hence the name of the command). For each hook, except for the `post-*` ones, if the hook exits with the nonzero status, then the operation is interrupted and no further stages are run. The post hooks are run after the operation finishes, so there is nothing to interrupt.

Both the standard output and the standard error output are forwarded to `git send-pack` at the client end, so the hooks can simply pass messages for the user by printing them (for example with `echo`, if the hook was written as a shell script). Note that the client doesn't disconnect until all the hooks complete their operation, so be careful if you try to do anything that may take a long time, such as automated tests. It is better to have a hook just start such long operations asynchronously and exit, allowing the client to finish.

You need to remember that, in pre hooks, you don't have refs updated yet, and that post hooks cannot affect the result of an operation. You can use pre hooks for access control (permission checking), and post hooks for notification, updating the side data, and logging. Hooks are listed in the order of operation.

The pre-receive hook

The first hook to run is `pre-receive`. It is invoked just before you start updating refs (branches, tags, notes, and so on) in the remote repository, but after all the objects are received. It is invoked once for the receive operation. If the server fails to receive published objects, for example, because of the lack of the disk space or incorrect permissions, the whole `git push` operation will fail before Git invokes this hook.

This hook receives no arguments; all the information is received on the standard input of the script. For each ref to be updated, it receives a line in the following format:

```
<old-SHA1-value> <new-SHA1-value> <full-ref-name>
```

Refs to be created would have the old SHA1 value of 40 zeros, while refs to be deleted will have a new SHA1 value equal to the same. The same convention is used in all the other places, where the hooks receive the old and the new state of the updated ref.

This hook can be used to quickly bail out if the update is not to be accepted, for example, if the received commits do not follow the specified policy or if the signed push (more on this is mentioned later) is invalid. Note that to use it for access control, (for authorization) you need to get the authentication token somehow, be it with the `getpwuid` command or with an environment variable such as `USER`. This depends on the server setup and on the server configuration.

Push-to-update hook for pushing to nonbare repositories

When pushing to the nonbare repositories, if push tries to update the currently checked out branch then push-to-checkout will be run. This is done if the configuration variable receive.denyCurrentBranch is set to the updateInstead value (instead of one of the values: true or refuse, warn or false, or ignore) This hook receives the SHA1 identifier of the commit that is to be the tip of the current branch that is going to be updated.

This mechanism is intended to synchronize working directories when one side is not easily accessible interactively (for example, accessible via interactive ssh), or as a simple deploy scheme. It can be used to deploy to a live website, or to run code tests on different operating systems.

If this hook is not present, Git will refuse the update of the ref if either the working tree or the index (the staging area) differs from HEAD, that is, if the status is "not clean". This hook is to be used to override this default behavior.

You can craft this hook to have it make changes to the working tree and to the index that are necessary to bring them to the desired state. For example, it can simply run git read-tree -u -m HEAD "$1" in order to switch to the new branch tip (the -u option updates the files in the worktree), while keeping the local changes (the -m option makes it perform a fast-forward merge with two commits/trees). If this hook exits with a nonzero status, then it will refuse pushing to the currently checked out branch.

The update hook

The next to run is the update hook, which is invoked *separately* for each ref being updated. This hook is invoked after the non-fast-forward check (unless the push is forced), and the per-ref built-in sanity checks that can be configured with receive.denyDeletes, receive.denyDeleteCurrent, receive.denyCurrentBranch, and receive.denyNonFastForwards.

Note that exiting with nonzero refuses the ref to be updated; if the push is atomic, then refusing any ref to be updated will abandon the whole push. With an ordinary push, only the update of a single ref will be refused; the push of other refs will proceed normally.

This hook receives the information about the ref to be updated as its parameters, in order: the full name of the ref being updated, the old SHA1 object name stored in the ref before the push, and the new SHA1 object name to be stored in the ref after the push.

The example `update.sample` hook can be used to block unannotated tags from entering the repository, and to allow or deny deleting and modifying tags, and deleting and creating branches. All the configurable of this sample hook is done with the appropriate `hooks.*` configuration variables, rather than being hard-coded. There is also the `update-paranoid` Perl script in `contrib/hooks/`, which can be used as an example on how to use this hook for the access control. This hook is configured with an external configuration file, where, among others, you can set up access so that only commits and tags from specified authorsare allowed, and authors additionally have correct access permissions.

Many repository management tools, for example Gitolite, set up and use this hook for their work. You need to read the tool documentation if you want for some reason to run your own `update` hook moved earlier together with the one provided by such a tool.

The post-receive hook

Then, after all the refs are updated, the `post-receive` hook is run. It takes the same data as the `pre-receive` one. Only now, all the refs point to the new SHA1s. It can happen that another user has modified the ref after it was updated, but before this hook was able to evaluate it. This hook can be used to update other services (for example, notify the continuous integration server), notify users (via an e-mail or a mailing list, an IRC channel, or a ticket-tracking system), or log the information about the push for audit (for example, about signed pushes). It supersedes and should be used in the place of the `post-update` hook.

There is no default `post-receive` hook, but you can find the simple `post-receive-email` script, and its replacement `git-multimail`, in the `contrib/hooks/` area. These two example hooks are actually developed separately from Git itself, but for convenience they are provided with the Git source. `git-multimail` sends one e-mail summarizing each changed ref, one e-mail for each new commit with the changes — threaded (as a reply) to the corresponding ref change e-mail, and one *announce* e-mail for each new annotated tag; each of these is separately configurable with respect to the e-mail address used and, to some extent, also with respect to the information included in the e-mails.

To provide an example of third-party tools, `irker` includes the script to be used as the Git's `post-receive` hook to send notifications about the new changes to the appropriate IRC channel using the `irker` daemon (set up separately).

The post-update hook (legacy mechanism)

Then the post-update hook is run. Each ref that was actually successfully updated passes its name as one of parameters; this hook takes a variable number of parameters. This is only a partial information; you don't know what the original (old) and updated (new) values of the updated refs were, and the current position of the ref is prone to race conditions (as explained before). Therefore, if you actually need the position of the refs, post-receive hook is a better solution.

The sample hook runs git update-server-info to prepare a repository for use over the dumb transports, by creating and saving some extra information. If the repository is to be published, or copied and published to be accessible via plain HTTP or other walker-based transport, you may consider enabling it. However, in modern Git, it is enough to simply set receive.updateServerInfo to true, so that hook is no longer necessary.

Using hooks to implement the Git-enforced policy

The only way to truly enforce policy is to implement it using server-side hooks, either pre-receive or update; if you want a per-ref decision, you need to use the latter. Client-side hooks can be used to help developers pay attention to the policy, but these can be disabled, or skipped, or not enabled.

Enforcing the policy with server-side hooks

One part of the development policy could be requiring that each commit message adheres to the specified template. For example, one may require for each nonmerge commit message to include the Digital Certificate of Origin in the form of the Signed-off-by: line, or that each commit refers to the issue tracker ticket by including a string that looks like ref: 2387. The possibilities are endless.

To implement such a hook, you first need to turn the old and new values for a ref (that you got by either reading them line by line from the standard input in pre-receive, or as the update hook parameters) into a list of all the commits that are being pushed. You need to take care of the corner cases: deleting a ref (no commits pushed), creating a new ref, and a possibility of non-fast-forward pushes (where you need to use the merge base as the lower limit of the revision range, for example, with the git merge-base command), pushes to tags, pushes to notes, and other nonbranch pushes. The operation of turning a revision range into a list of commits can be done with the git rev-list command, which is a low-level equivalent (plumbing) of the user-facing git log command (porcelain); by default, this command prints out only the SHA1 values of the commits in the specified revision range, one per line, and no other information.

Then, for each revision, you need to grab the commit message and check whether it matches the template specified in the policy. You can use another plumbing command, called `git cat-file`, and then extract the commit message from this command output by skipping everything before the first blank line. This blank line separates commit metadata in the raw form from the commit body:

```
$ git cat-file commit a7b1a955
tree 171626fc3b628182703c3b3c5da6a8c65b187b52
parent 5d2584867fe4e94ab7d211a206bc0bc3804d37a9
author Alice Developer <alice@example.com> 1440011825 +0200
committer Alice Developer <alice@example.com> 1440011825 +0200

Added COPYRIGHT file
```

Alternatively, you can use `git show -s` or `git log -1`, which are both porcelain commands, instead of `git cat-file`. However, you would then need to specify the exact output format, for example, `git show -s --format=%B <SHA1>`.

When you have these commit messages, you can then use the regular expression match or another tool on each of the commit messages caught to check whether it matches the policy.

Another part of the policy may be the restrictions on how the branches are managed. For example, you may want to prevent the deletion of long-lived development stage branches (see *Chapter 6, Advanced Branching Techniques*), while allowing the deletion of topic branches. To distinguish between them, that is to find out whether the branch being deleted is a topic branch or not, you can either include a configurable list of branches to manage strictly , or you can assume that topic branches always use the `<user>/<topic>` naming convention. The latter solution can be enforced by requiring the newly created branches, which should be topic branches only, to match this naming convention.

Conceivably, you could make a policy that topic branches can be fast-forwarded only if they are not merged in, though implementing checks for this policy would be nontrivial.

Usually, you have only specific people with the permission to push to the official repository of the project (having holding so-called commit bit). With the server-side hooks, you can configure the repository so that it allows anyone to push, but only to the special `mob` branch; all the other push access is restricted.

You can also use server-side hooks to require that only annotated tags are allowed in the repository, that tags are signed with a public key that is present in the specified key server (and thus, can be verified by other developers), and that tags cannot be deleted or updated. If needed, you can restrict signed tags to those coming from the selected (and configured) set of users, for example enforcing a policy that only one of the maintainers can mark a project for a release (by creating an appropriately named tag, for example, `v0.9`).

Early notices about policy violations with client-side hooks

It would be not a good solution to have a strict enforcement of development policies, and not provide users with a way to help watch and fulfill the said policies. Having one's work rejected during push can be frustrating; to fix the issue preventing one from publishing the commit, one would have to edit their history. See *Chapter 8, Keeping History Clean* for details on how to do it.

The answer to that problem is to provide some client-side hooks that users can install, to have Git notify them immediately when they are violating the policy, which would make their changes rejected by the server. The intent is to help correct any problem as fast as possible, usually before committing the changes. These client-side hooks must be distributed somehow, as hooks are not copied when cloning a repository. Various ways to distribute these hooks are described in *Chapter 10, Customizing and Extending Git*.

If there are any limitations on the contents of the changes, perhaps that some file might be changed only by specified developers, the warning can be done with `pre-commit`. The `prepare-commit-msg` hook (and the `commit.template` configuration variable) can provide the developer with the customized template to be filled while working on a commit message. You can also make Git check the commit message, just before the commit would be recorded, with the `commit-msg` hook. This hook would find out and inform you whether you have correctly formatted the commit, message and if this message includes all the information required by the policy. This hook can also be used instead of or in addition to `pre-commit` to check whether you are not modifying the files you are not allowed to.

The `pre-rebase` hook can be used to verify that you don't try to rewrite history in a manner that would lead to non-fast-forward push (with `receive.deny NonFastForwards` on the server, forcing push won't work anyway).

As a last resort, there is a `pre-push` hook, which can check for correctness before trying to connect to the remote repository.

Signed pushes

Chapter 5, Collaborative Development with Git, includes a description of various mechanisms that a developer can use to ensure integrity and authenticity of their work: signed tags, signed commits, and signed merges (merging signed tags). All these mechanisms assert that the objects (and the changes they contain) came from the signer.

But signed tags and commits do not assert that the developer wanted to have a particular revision at the tip of a particular branch. Authentication done by the hosting site cannot be easily audited later, and it requires you to trust the hosting site and its authentication mechanism. Modern Git (version 2.2 or newer) allows you to sign pushes for this purpose.

Signed pushes require the server to set up `receive.certNonceSeed` and the client to use `git push --signed`. Handling of signed pushes is done with the server-side hooks.

The signed push certificate sent by client is stored in the repository as a blob object and is verified using GPG. The `pre-receive` hook can then examine various `GIT_PUSH_CERT_*` environment variables (see the `git-receive-pack` manpage for the details) to decide whether to accept or deny given signed push.

Logging signed pushes for audit can be done with the `post-receive` hook. You can have it send an e-mail notification about the signed push or have it append information about the push to a log file. The push, certificate that is signed includes an identifier for the client's GPG key, the URL of the repository, and the information about the operations performed on the branches or tags in the same format as the `pre-receive` and `post-receive` input.

Serving Git repositories

In *Chapter 5, Collaborative Development with Git*, we have examined four major protocols used by Git to connect with remote repositories: local, HTTP, SSH (Secure Shell), and Git (the native protocol). This was done from the point of view of a client connecting to the repository, discussing what these protocols are and which one to use if the remote repository offers more than one.

This chapter will offer the administrator's side of view, explaining how to set up moved later, rephrased Git repositories to be served with these different transport protocols. Here we will also examine, for each protocol, how the authentication and authorization look like.

Local protocol

This is the most basic protocol, where a client uses the path to the repository or the `file://` URL to access remotes. You just need to have a shared filesystem, such as an NFS or CIFS mount, which contains Git repositories to serve. This is a nice option if you already have access to a networked filesystem, as you don't need to set up any server.

Access to repositories using a file-based transport protocol is controlled by the existing file permissions and network access permissions. You need read permissions to fetch and clone, and write permissions to push.

In a later case, if you want to enable push, you'd better set up a repository in such way that pushing does not screw up the permissions. This can be helped by creating a repository with the `--shared` option to `git init` (or to `git clone`). This option allows users belonging to the same group to push into the repository by using the *sticky group ID* to ensure that the repositories stay available to all the group members.

The disadvantage of this method is that shared access to a networked filesystem is generally more difficult to set up and reach safely from multiple remote locations, than a basic network access and setting up appropriate server. Mounting the remote disk over the Internet can be difficult and slow.

This protocol does not protect the repository against accidental damage. Every user has full access to the repository's internal files and there is nothing preventing from accidentally corrupting the repository.

SSH protocol

SSH (Secure Shell) is a common transport protocol (common especially for Linux users) for self-hosting Git repositories. SSH access to servers is often already set up in many cases as a way to safely log in to the remote machine; if not, it is generally quite easy to set up and use. SSH is an authenticated and encrypted network protocol.

On the other hand, you can't serve anonymous access to Git repositories over SSH. People must have at least limited access to your machine over SSH; this protocol does not allow anonymous read-only access to published repositories.

Generally, there are two ways to give access to Git repositories over SSH. The first is to have a separate account on the server for each client trying to access the repository (though such an account can be limited and does not need full shell access, you can in this case use `git-shell` as a login shell for Git-specific accounts). This can be used both with ordinary SSH access, where you provide the password, or with a public-key login. In a one-account-per-user case, the situation with respect to the access control is similar to the local protocol, namely, the access is controlled with the filesystem permissions.

A second method is to create a single shell account, which is often the `git` user, specifically to access Git repositories and to use public-key login to authenticate users. Each user who is to have an access to the repositories would then need to send his or her SSH public key to the administrator, who would then add this key to the list of authorized keys. The actual user is identified by the key he or she uses to connect to the server.

Another alternative is to have the SSH server authenticated from an LDAP server, or some other centralized authentication scheme (often, to implement single sign-ons). As long as the client can get (limited) shell access, any SSH authentication mechanism can be used.

Anonymous Git protocol

Next is the Git protocol. It is served by a special really simple TCP daemon, which listens on a dedicated port (by default, port 9418). This is (or was) a common choice for fast anonymous unauthenticated read-only access to Git repositories.

The Git protocol server, `git daemon`, is relatively easy to set up. Basically, you need to run this command, usually in a daemonized manner. How to run the daemon (the server) depends on the operating system you use. It can be an `upstart` script, a `systemd` unit file, or a `sysvinit` script. A common solution is to use `inetd` or `xinetd`.

You can remap all the repository requests as relative to the given path (a project root for the Git repositories) with `--base-path=<directory>`. There is also support for virtual hosting; see the `git-daemon` documentation for the detail. By default, `git daemon` would export only the repositories that have the `git-daemon-export-ok` file inside `gitdir`, unless the `--export-all` option is used. Usually, you would also want to turn on `--reuseaddr`, to allow the server to restart without waiting for the connection to time out.

The downside of the Git protocol is the lack of authentication and the obscure port it runs on (that may require you to punch a hole in the firewall). The lack of authentication is because by default it is used only for read access, that is for fetching and cloning repositories. Generally, it is paired with either SSH (always authenticated, never anonymous) or HTTPS for pushing.

You can configure it to allow for push (by enabling the `receive-pack` service with the `--enable=<service>` command-line option or, on a per repository basis, by setting the `daemon.receivePack` configuration to `true`), but it is generally not recommended. The only information available to hooks for implementing access control is the client address, unless you require all the pushes to be signed. You can run external commands in an access hook, but this would not provide much more data about the client.

 One service you might consider enabling is `upload-archive`, which serves `git archive --remote`.

The lack of authentication means not only that the Git server does not know who accesses the repositories, but also that the client must trust the network to not spoof the address while accessing the server. This transport is not encrypted; everything goes in the plain.

Smart HTTP(S) protocol

Setting up the so-called "smart" HTTP(S) protocol consists basically of enabling a server script that would invoke `git receive-pack` and `git upload-pack` on the server. Git provides a CGI script named `git-http-backend` for this task. This CGI script can detect if the client understands smart HTTP protocol; if not, it will fall back on the "dumb" behavior (a backward compatibility feature).

To use this protocol, you need some CGI server, for example, Apache (with this server you would also need the `mod_cgi` module or its equivalent, and the `mod_env` and `mod_alias` modules). The parameters are passed using environment variables (hence, the need for `mod_env` in case of using Apache): `GIT_PROJECT_ROOT` to specify where repositories are and an optional `GIT_HTTP_EXPORT_ALL` if you want to have all the repositories exported, not only those with the `git-daemon-export-ok` file in them.

The authentication is done by the web server. In particular, you can set it up to allow unauthenticated anonymous read-only access, while requiring authentication for push. Utilizing HTTPS gives encryption and server authentication, like for the SSH protocol. The URL for fetching and pushing is the same when using HTTP(S); you can also configure it so that the web interface for browsing Git repositories uses the same URL as for fetching.

The documentation of `git-http-backend` includes a set up for Apache for different situations, including unauthenticated read and authenticated write. It is a bit involved, because initial ref advertisements use the query string, while the `receive-pack` service invocation uses path info.

On the other hand, requiring authentication with any valid account for reads and writes and leaving the restriction of writes to the server-side hook is simpler and often acceptable solution.

If you try to push to the repository that requires authentication, the server can prompt for credentials. Because the HTTP protocol is stateless and involves more than one connection sometimes, it is useful to utilize credential helpers (see *Chapter 10, Customizing and Extending Git*) to avoid either having to give the password more than once for a single operation, or having to save the password somewhere on the disk (perhaps, in the remote URL).

Dumb protocols

If you cannot run Git on the server, you can still use the dumb protocol, which does not require it. The dumb HTTP(S) protocol expects the Git repository to be served as normal static files from the web server. However, to be able to use this kind of protocol, Git requires the extra `objects/info/packs` and `info/refs` files to be present on the server, and kept up to date with `git update-server-info`. This command is usually run on push via one of the earlier mentioned smart protocols (the default `post-update` hook does that, and so does `git-receive-pack` if `receive.updateServerInfo` is set to `true`).

It is possible to push with the dumb protocol, but this requires a set up that allows updating files using a specified transport; for the dumb HTTP(S) transport protocol, this means configuring WebDAV.

Authentication in this case is done by the web server for static files. Obviously, for this kind of transport, Git's server-side hooks are not invoked, and thus they cannot be used to further restrict access.

Note that for modern Git, the dumb transport is implemented using the `curl` family of remote helpers, which may be not installed by default.

This transport works (for fetch) by downloading requested refs (as plain files), examining where to find files containing the referenced commit objects (hence, the need for server information files, at least for objects in packfiles), getting them, and then walking down the chain of revisions, examining each object needed, and downloading new files if the object is not present yet in the local repository. This walker method can be horrendously inefficient if the repository is not packed well with respect to the requested revision range. It requires a large number of connections and always downloads the whole pack, even if only one object from it is needed.

With smart protocols, Git on the client-side and Git on the server negotiate between themselves which objects are needed to be sent (want/have negotiation). Git then creates a customized packfile, utilizing the knowledge of what objects are already present on the other side, and usually including only deltas, that is, the difference from what the other side has (a thin packfile). The other side rewrites the received packfile to be self-contained.

Remote helpers

Git allows us to create support for new transport protocols by writing remote helper programs. This mechanism can be also used to support foreign repositories. Git interacts with a repository requiring a remote helper by spawning the helper as an independent child process, and communicating with the said process through its standard input and output with a set of commands.

You can find third-party remote helpers to add support to the new ways of accessing repositories, for example, there is `git-remote-dropbox` to use Dropbox to store the remote Git repository. Note, however, that remote helpers are (possibly yet) limited in features as compared to the built-in transport support.

Tools to manage Git repositories

Nowadays, there is no need to write the Git repositories management solution yourself. There is a wide range of various third-party solutions that you can use. It is impossible to list them all, and even giving recommendations is risky. The Git ecosystem is actively developed; which tool is the best can change since the time of writing this.

I'd like to focus here just on the types of tools for administrators, just like it was done for GUIs in *Chapter 10, Customizing and Extending Git*.

First, there are **Git repository management** solutions (we have seen one example of such in the form of the update-paranoid script in the contrib/ area). These tools focus on access control, usually the authorization part, making it easy to add repositories and manage their permissions. An example of such a tool is Gitolite. They often support some mechanism to add your own additional access constraints.

Then, there are **web interfaces**, allowing us to view Git repositories using a web browser. Some make it even possible to create new revisions using a web interface. They differ in capabilities, but usually offer at least a list of available Git repositories, a summary view for each repository, an equivalent of the git log and git show commands, and a view with a list of files in the repository. An example of such tools is gitweb script in Perl that is distributed with Git; another is cgit used by https://www.kernel.org/ for the Linux kernel repositories (and others).

Often useful are the **code review (code collaboration)** tools. These make it possible for developers in a team to review each other's proposed changes using a web interface. These tools often allow the creation of new projects and the handling of access management. An example of such a tool is Gerrit Code Review.

Finally, there are **Git hosting** solutions, usually with a web interface for the administrative side of managing repositories, allowing us to add users, create repositories, manage their access, and often work from the web browser on the Git repositories. An example of such a tool is GitLab. There are also similar **source code management** systems, which provide (among other web-based interfaces) repository hosting services together with the features to collaborate and manage development. Here, Phabricator and Kallithea can be used as examples.

Of course, you don't need to self-host your code. There is a plethora of third-party hosted options: GitHub, Bitbucket, and so on. There are even hosted solutions using open source hosting management tools, such as GitLab.

Tips and tricks for hosting repositories

If you want to self-host Git repositories, there are a few things that may help you with server performance and user satisfaction.

Reducing the size taken by repositories

If you are hosting many forks (clones) of the same repository, you might want to reduce disk usage by somehow sharing common objects. One solution is to use alternates (for example, with git clone --reference) while creating a fork. In this case, the derived repository would look to its parent object storage if the object is not found on its own.

There are, however, two problems with this approach. First is that you need to ensure that the object the borrowing repository relies on does not vanish from the repository set as the alternate object storage (the repository you borrow from). This can be done, for example, by linking the borrowing repository refs in the repository lending the objects, for example, in the `refs/borrowed/` namespace. Second is that the objects entering the borrowing repository are not automatically de-duplicated: you need to run `git repack -a -d -l`, which internally passes the `--local` option to `git pack-objects`.

An alternate solution would be to keep every fork together in a single repository, and use `gitnamespaces` to manage separate views into the DAG of revisions, one for each fork. With plain Git, this solution means that the repository is addressed by the URL of the common object storage and the namespace to select a particular fork. Usually, this is managed by a server configuration or by a repository management tool; such mechanism translates the address of the repository into a common repository and the namespace. The `git-http-backend` manpage includes an example configuration to serve multiple repositories from different namespaces in a single repository. Gitolite also has some support for namespaces in the form of logical and backing repositories and `option namespace.pattern`, though not every feature works for logical repositories.

Storing multiple repositories as the namespace of a single repository avoids storing duplicated copies of the same objects. It automatically prevents duplication between new objects without the need for ongoing maintenance, as opposed to the alternates solution. On the other hand, the security is weaker; you need to treat anyone with access to the single namespace, which is within the repository as if he or she had an access to all the other namespaces, though this might not be a problem for your case.

Speeding up smart protocols with pack bitmaps

Another issue that you can stumble upon while self-hosting repositories is the performance of smart protocols. For the clients of your server, it is important that the operations finish quickly; as an administrator, you would not want to generate high CPU load on the server due to serving Git repositories.

One feature, ported from JGit, should significantly improve the performance of the counting objects phase, while serving objects from a repository that uses this trick. This feature is a bitmap-index file, available since Git 2.0.

This file is stored alongside the packfile and its index. It can be generated manually by running `git repack -A -d --write-bitmap-index`, or be generated automatically together with the packfile by setting the `repack.writeBitmaps` configuration variable to `true`. The disadvantage of this solution is that bitmaps take additional disk space, and the initial repack requires extra time to create bitmap-index.

Solving the large nonresumable initial clone problem

Repositories with a large codebase and a long history can get quite large. The problem is that the initial clone, where you need to get all of a possibly large repository, is an all-or-nothing operation, at least for modern (safe and effective) smart transfer protocols: SSH, `git://`, and smart HTTP(S). This might be a problem if a network connection is not very reliable. There is no support for a resumable clone, and it unfortunately looks like it is fundamentally hard problem to solve for Git developers. This does not mean, however, that you, as a hosting administrator, can do nothing to help users get this initial clone.

One solution is to create, with the `git bundle` command, a static file that can be used for the initial clone, or as reference repository for the initial clone (the latter can be done with the `git clone --reference=<bundle> --dissociate` command if you have Git 2.3 or a newer looks unnecessary). This bundle file can be distributed using any transport; in particular, one that can be resumed if interrupted, be it HTTP, FTP, rsync, or BitTorrent. The conventions people use, besides explaining how to get such a bundle in the developer documentation, is to use the same URL as for the repository, but with the `.bundle` extension (instead of an empty extension or a `.git` suffix).

There are also more esoteric approaches like a step by step deepening of a shallow clone (or perhaps, just using a shallow clone with `git clone --depth` is all that's needed), or using approaches such as GitTorrent.

Augmenting development workflows

Handling version control is only a part of the development workflow. There is also work management, code review and audit, running automated tests, and generating builds.

Many of these steps can be helped using specialized tools. Many of them offer Git integration. For example, code review can be managed using Gerrit, requiring that each change passes a review before being made public. Another example is setting up development environments so that pushing changes to the public repository can automatically close tickets in the issue tracker based on the patterns in the commit messages. This can be done with the server-side hooks or with the hosting service's webhooks.

A repository can serve as a gateway, running automated tests (for example, with the help of Jenkins/Hudson continuous integration service), and deploying changes to ensure quality environments only after passing all of these tests. Another repository can be configured to trigger builds for various supported systems. Many tools and services support push to deploy mechanisms (for example, Heroku or Google's App Engine).

Git can automatically notify users and developers about the published changes. It can be done via e-mail, using the mailing list or the IRC channel, or a web-based dashboard application. The possibilities are many; you only need to find them.

Summary

This chapter covered various issues related to the administrative side of working with Git. You have learned the basics of maintenance, data recovery, and repository troubleshooting. You have also learned how to set up Git on the server, how to use server-side hooks, and how to manage remote repositories. The chapter covered tips and tricks for a better remote performance. The information in this chapter should help you choose the Git repository management solution, or even write your own.

The next chapter will include a set of recommendations and best practices, both specific to Git and those that are version control agnostic. A policy based on these suggestions can be enforced and encouraged with the help of the tools described here in this chapter.

12
Git Best Practices

The last chapter of *Mastering Git* presents a collection of generic and Git-specific version control recommendations and best practices. You have encountered many of these recommendations already in the earlier chapters; they are here as a summary and as a reminder. For details and the reasoning behind each best practice, you would be referred to specific chapters.

This chapter will cover issues of managing the working directory, creating commits and series of commits (pull requests), submitting changes for inclusion, and the peer review of changes.

In this chapter, we will cover the following topics:

- How to separate projects into repositories
- What types of data to store in a repository and which files should Git ignore
- What to check before creating a new commit
- How to create a good commit and a good commit series (or, in other words, how to create a good pull request)
- How to choose an effective branching strategy, and how to name branches and tags
- How to review changes and how to respond to the review

Starting a project

When starting a project, you should choose and clearly define a project governance model (who manages work, who integrates changes, and who is responsible for what). You should decide about the license and the copyright of the code: whether it is work for hire, whether contributions would require a copyright assignment, a contributor agreement, or a contributor license agreement, or simply a digital certificate of origin.

Dividing work into repositories

In centralized version control systems, often everything under the sun is put under the same project tree. With distributed version control systems such as Git, it is better to split separate projects into separate repositories.

There should be one conceptual group per repository; divide it beforehand correctly. If some part of the code is needed by multiple separate projects, consider extracting it into its own project and then incorporating it as a submodule or subtree, grouping concepts into a superproject. See *Chapter 9, Managing Subprojects - Building a Living Framework* for the details.

Selecting the collaboration workflow

You need to decide about the collaboration structure, whether your project would use a dispersed contributor model, a "blessed" repository model, or a central repository, and so on (as found in *Chapter 5, Collaborative Development with Git*). This often requires setting up an access control mechanism and deciding on the permission structure; see *Chapter 11, Git Administration* on how one can set up this.

You would also need to decide how to structure your branches; see *Chapter 6, Advanced Branching Techniques,* for possible solutions. This decision doesn't need to be cast in stone; as your project and your team experience grows, you might want to consider changing the branching model, for example, from the plain branch-per-feature model to full Gitflow, or to GitHub-flow, or any of the other derivatives.

The decision about licensing, the collaboration structure, and the branching model should all be stated explicitly in the developer documentation (at minimum, including the README and LICENSE/COPYRIGHT files). You need to remember that if the way in which the project is developed changes, which can happen, for example, because the project has grown beyond its initial stage, this documentation would need to be kept up to date.

Choosing which files to keep under version control

In most cases, you should not include any of the *generated files* in the version control system (though there are some very rare exceptions). Track only the sources (the original resources); Git works best if these sources are plain text files, but it works well also with binary files.

To avoid accidentally including unwanted files in a repository, you should use the **gitignore patterns**. These ignore patterns that are specific to a project (for example, results and by-products of a build system) should go into the `.gitignore` file in the project tree; those specific to the developer (for example, backup files created by the editor one uses or the operating system-specific helper files) should go into his or her per-user `core.excludesFile` (which, in modern Git, is the `~/.config/git/ignore` file), or into a local configuration of the specific clone of the repository, that is, `.git/info/excludes`. See *Chapter 4, Managing Your Worktree* for details.

A good start for ignore patters is the `https://www.gitignore.io` trailing slash is not necessary; choose whichever looks better. Website with the `.gitignore` templates for various operating systems, IDEs, and programming languages.

Another important rule is to not add to be tracked by Git the configuration files that might change from environment to environment (for example, being different for MS Windows and for Linux).

Working on a project

Here are some guidelines on how to create changes and develop new revisions. These guidelines can be used either for your own work on your own project, or to help contribute your code to the project maintained by somebody else.

Different projects can use different development workflows; therefore, some of the recommendations presented here might not make sense, depending on the workflow that is used for a given project.

Working on a topic branch

Branching in Git has two functions (*Chapter 6, Advanced Branching Techniques*): as a mediator for the code contributed by developers keeping to the specified level of code stability and maturity (long-running public branches), and as a sandbox for the development of a new idea (short-lived private branches).

The ability to sandbox changes is why it is considered a good practice to create a separate branch for each new task you work on. Such a branch is called a **topic branch** or a **feature branch**. Using separate branches makes it possible to switch between tasks easily, and to keep disparate work in progress from interfering with each other.

You should choose short and descriptive names for branches. There are different naming conventions for topic branches; the convention your project uses should be specified in the developer documentation. In general, branches are usually named after a summary of a topic they host, usually all lower-case and with spaces between words replaced by hyphens or underscores (see the `git-check-ref-format(1)` manpage to know what is forbidden in branch names). Branch names can include slash (be hierarchical).

If you are using an issue tracker, then the branch which fixes a bug, or implements an issue, can have its name prefixed with the identifier (the number) of the ticket describing the issue, for example, `1234-doc_spellcheck`. On the other hand, the maintainer, while gathering submissions from other developers, could put these submissions in topic branches named after the initials of the developer and the name of the topic, for example, `ad/whitespace-cleanup` (this is an example of **hierarchical branch name**).

It is considered a good practice to delete your branch from your local repository, and also from the upstream repository after you are done with the branch in question to reduce clutter.

Deciding what to base your work on

As a developer, you would be usually working at a given time on some specific topic, be it a bug fix, enhancement or correction to some topic, or a new feature.

Decision about where to start your work on a given topic, and what branch to base your work on, depends on the branching workflow chosen for a project (see *Chapter 6, Advanced Branching Techniques* for a selection of branchy workflows). This decision also depends on the type of the work you do.

For a topic branch workflow (or a branch-per-feature workflow), you would want to base your work on the oldest and most stable long-running branch that your change is relevant to, and for which you plan to have your changes merged into. This is because, as described in *Chapter 6, Advanced Branching Techniques*, you should never merge a less stable branch into a more stable branch. The reason behind this best practice rule is to not destabilize branch, as merges bring all the changes.

Different types of changes require a different long-lived branch to be used as a base for a topic branch with those changes, or to put those changes onto. In general, to help developers working on a project, this information should be described in the developer documentation; not everybody needs to be knowledgeable about the branching workflow used by the project.

The following describes what is usually used as a base branch, depending on purpose of changes:

- **Bugfix**: In this case the topic branch (the bugfix branch) should be based on the oldest and the most stable branch in which the bug is present. This means, in general, starting with the maintenance branch. If the bug is not present in the maintenance branch, then base the bugfix branch on the stable branch. For a bug that is not present in the stable branch, find the topic branch that introduced it and base your work on top of that topic branch.

- **New feature**: In this case the topic branch (the feature branch) should be based on the stable branch, if possible. If the new feature depends on some topic that is not ready for the stable branch, then base your work on that topic (from a topic branch).

- **Corrections and enhancements**: To a topic that didn't get merged into the stable branch should be based on the tip of the topic branch being corrected. If the topic in question is not considered published, it's all right to make changes to the steps of the topic, squashing minor corrections in the series (see the section about rewriting history in *Chapter 8, Keeping History Clean*).

If the project you are contributing to is large enough to have dedicated maintainers for selected parts (subsystems) of the system, you first need to decide which repository and which fork (sometimes named "a tree") to base your work on.

Splitting changes into logically separate steps

Unless your work is really simple and it can be done in a single step (a single commit) — like many of the bug fixes — you should make separate commits for the logically separate changes, one commit per single step. Those commits should be ordered logically.

Following a good practice for a commit message (with an explanation of what you have done — see the next section) could help in deciding when to commit. If your description gets too long and you begin to see that you have two independent changes squished together, that's a sign that you probably need to split your commit to finer grained pieces and use smaller steps.

Remember, however, that it is a matter of balance, of the project conventions, and of the development workflow chosen. Changes should, at minimum, stand on their own. At each step (at each commit) of the implementation of a feature, the code compiles and the program passes the test suite. You should commit early and often. Smaller self-contained revisions are easier to review, and with smaller but complete changes, it is easier to find regression bugs with `git bisect` (which is described in *Chapter 2, Exploring Project History*).

Note that you don't necessarily need to come up with the perfect sequence of steps from the start. In the case when you notice that you have entangled the work directory's state, you can make use of the staging area, using an interactive add to disentangle it (this is described in *Chapter 3, Developing with Git* and *Chapter 4, Managing Your Worktree*). You can also use an interactive rebase or similar techniques, as shown in *Chapter 8, Keeping History Clean*, to curate commits into an easy-to-read (and easy-to-bisect) history before publishing.

You should remember that a commit is a place to record your result (or a particular step towards the result), not a place to save the temporary state of your work. If you need to temporarily save the current state before going back to it, use `git stash`.

Writing a good commit message

A good commit message should include an explanation for change that is detailed enough, so that other developers on the team (including reviewers and the maintainer) can judge if it is a good idea to include the change in the codebase. This *good or not* decision should not require them to read actual changes to find out what the commit intends to do.

The first line of the commit message should be a short, terse description (around from 50 to 72 characters) with the summary of changes. It should be separated by an empty line from the rest of the commit message, if there is one. This is partially because, in many places, such as in the `git log --oneline` command output, in the graphical history viewer like `gitk`, or in the instruction sheet of `git rebase --interactive`, you would see only this one line of the commit message and you would have to decide about the action with respect to that commit on the basis of this one line. If you have trouble with coming up with a good summary of changes, this might mean that these changes need to be split into smaller steps.

There are various conventions for this summary line of changes. One convention is to prefix the first summary line with `area:`, where area is an identifier for the general area of the code being modified: a name of the subsystem, of an affected subdirectory, or a filename of a file being changed. If the development is managed via an issue tracker, this summary line can start with something like the `[#1234]` prefix, where `1234` is the identifier of an issue or a task implemented in the commit. In general, when not sure about what information to include in the commit message, refer to the development documentation, or fall back to the current convention used by other commits in the history.

> If you are using Agile development methods, you can look for especially good commit messages during retrospectives, and add them as examples in the developer documentation for the future.

For all but trivial changes, there should be a longer meaningful description, the body of the commit message. There is something that people coming from other version control systems might need to unlearn: namely, not writing a commit message at all or writing it all in one long line. Note that Git would not allow to create a commit with an empty commit message unless forced to with `--allow-empty`.

The commit message should:

- Include the rationale for the commit, explain the problem that the commit tries to solve, the **why**: in other words, it should include description of what is wrong with the current code or the current behavior of the project without the change; this should be self-contained, but it can refer to other sources like the issue tracker (the bug tracker), or other external documents such as articles, wikis, or Common Vulnerabilities and Exposures (CVE).

- Include a quick summary. In most cases, it should also explain (the **how**) and justify the way the commit solves the problem. In other words, it should describe why do you think the result with the change is better; this part of the description does not need to explain what the code does, that is largely a task for the code comments.

- If there was more than one possible solution, include a description of the alternate solutions that were considered but were ultimately discarded, perhaps with links to the discussion or review(s).

It's a good idea to try to make sure that your explanation for changes can be understood without access to any external resources (that is, without an access to the issue tracker, to the Internet, or to the mailing list archive). Instead of just referring to the discussion, or in addition to giving a URL or an issue number, write a summary of the relevant points in the commit message.

One of the possible recommendations to write the commit message is to describe changes in the imperative mood, for example, `make foo do bar`, as if you are giving orders to the codebase to change its behavior, instead of writing `This commit makes ...` or `[I] changed ...`.

Here, `commit.template` and commit message hooks can help in following these practices. See *Chapter 10, Customizing and Extending Git*, for details (and *Chapter 11, Git Administration*, for a description of the way to enforce this recommendation).

Preparing changes for submission

Consider rebasing the branch to be submitted on top of the current tip of the base branch. This should make it easier to integrate changes in the future. If your topic branch was based on the development version, or on the other in-flight topic branch (perhaps because it depended on some specific feature), and the branch it was based on got merged into a stable line of development, you should rebase your changes on top of the stable integration branch instead.

The time of rebase is also a chance for a final clean-up of the history; the chance to make submitted changes easier to review. Simply run an interactive rebase, or a patch management tool if you prefer it (see *Chapter 8, Keeping History Clean*). One caveat: *do not rewrite the published history*.

Consider testing that your changes merge cleanly, and fix it if they don't, if the fix is possible. Make sure that they would cleanly apply, or cleanly merge into the appropriate integration branch.

Take a last look at your commits to be submitted. Make sure that your changes do not add the commented out (or the `ifdef-ed out`) code, and it does not include any extra files not related to the purpose of the patch (for example, that they do not include the changes from the next new feature). Review your commit series before submission to ensure accuracy.

Integrating changes

The exact details on how to submit changes for merging depends, of course, on the development workflow that the project is using. Various classes of possible workflows are described in *Chapter 5, Collaborative Development with Git*.

Submitting and describing changes

If the project has a dedicated maintainer or, at least, if it has someone responsible to merge the proposed changes into the official version, you would need also to describe submitted changes as a whole (in addition to describing each commit in the series). This can be done in the form of a cover letter for the patch series while sending changes as patches via e-mail; or it can be comments in the pull request while using collocated contributor repositories model; or it can be the description in an e-mail with a pull request, which already includes the URL and the branch in your public repository with changes (generated with `git request-pull`).

This cover letter or a pull request should include the description of the purpose of the patch series or the pull request. Consider providing there an overview of why the work is taking place (with any relevant links and a summary of the discussion). Be explicit with stating that it is a work in progress, saying this in the description of changes.

In the dispersed contributor model, where changes are submitted for review as patches or patch series, usually to the mailing list, you should use Git-based tools such as `git format-patch` and, if possible, `git send-email`. Multiple related patches should be grouped together, for example, in their own e-mail thread. The convention is to send them as replies to an additional cover letter message, which should describe the feature as a whole.

If the changes are sent to the mailing list, it is a common convention to prefix your subject line with `[PATCH]` or with `[PATCH m/n]` (where m is the patch number in the series of the n patches). This lets people easily distinguish patch submissions from other e-mails. This part can be done with `git format-patch`. What you need to decide yourself is to whether to use additional markers after PATCH to mark the nature of the series, for example, PATCH/RFC (RFC means here Request for Comments, that is an idea for a feature with an example of its implementation; such patch series should be examined if the idea is worthy; it is not ready to be applied/merged but provided only for the discussion among developers).

In the collocated contributor repositories model, where all the developers use the same Git hosting website or software (for example, GitHub, Bitbucket, GitLab, or a private instance of it, and so on), you would push changes to your own public repository, a *fork* of the official version. Then, you would create a *merge request* or a *pull request*, usually via a web interface of the hosting service, again describing the changes as a whole there.

In the case of using the central repository (perhaps, in a shared maintenance model), you would push changes to a separate and possibly new branch in the integration repository, and then send an announcement to the maintainer so that he or she would be able to find where the changes to merge are. The details of this step depends on the exact setup; sending announcement might be done via e-mail, via some kind of internal messaging mechanism, or even via tickets (or via the comments in the tickets).

The development documentation might include rules specifying to where and to what place to send announcements and/or changes to. It is considered a courtesy to notify the people who are involved in the area of code you are touching about the new changes (here you can use `git blame` and `git shortlog` to identify these people; see *Chapter 2, Exploring Project History*). These people are important; they can write a comment about the change and help reviewing it.

Crediting people and signing your work

Some open source projects, in order to improve the tracking provenance of the code, use the sign-off procedure borrowed from the Linux kernel called Digital Certificate of Origin. The sign-off is a simple line at the end of the commit message, saying for example:

```
Signed-off-by: Random Developer <rdeveloper@company.
com>
```

By adding this line, you certify that the contribution is either created as a whole or in part by you, or is based on the previous work, or was provided directly to you, and that everybody in the chain have the right to submit it under appropriate license. If your work is based on the work by somebody else, or if you are just passing somebody's work, then there can be multiple sign-off lines, forming a chain of provenance.

In order to credit people who helped with creating the commit, you can append to the commit message other trailers, such as `Reported-by:`, `Reviewed-by:`, `Acked-by:` (this one states that it was liked by the person responsible for the area covered by the change), or `Tested-by:`.

The art of the change review

Completing a peer review of changes is time-consuming (but so is using version control), but the benefits are huge: better code quality, reducing the time needed for quality assurance testing, transfer of knowledge, and so on. The change can be reviewed by a peer developer, or reviewed by a community (requiring consensus), or reviewed by the maintainer or one of his/her lieutenants.

Before beginning the code review process, you should read through the description of the proposed changes to discover why the change was proposed, and decide whether you are the correct person to perform the review (that is one of reasons why good commit messages are so important). You need to understand the problem that the change tries to solve. You should familiarize yourself with the context of the issue, and with the code in the area of changes.

The first step is to reproduce the state before the change and check whether the program works as described (for example, that the bug in a bugfix can be reproduced). Then, you need to check out the topic branch with proposed changes and verify that the result works correctly. If it works, review the proposed changes, creating a comprehensive list of everything wrong (though if there are errors early in the process, it might be unnecessary to go deeper), as follows:

- Are the commit messages descriptive enough? Is the code easily understood?
- Is the contribution architected correctly? Is it architecturally sound?
- Does the code comply with project's coding standards and with the agreed upon coding conventions?
- Are the changes limited to the scope described in the commit message?
- Does the code follow the industry's best practices? Is it safe and efficient?
- Is there any redundant or duplicate code? Is the code as modular as possible?
- Does the code introduce any regressions in the test suite? If it is a new feature, does the change include the tests for the new feature, both positive and negative?
- Is the new code as performing the way it did before the change (within the project's tolerances)?
- Are all the words spelled correctly, and does the new version follow the formatting guidelines for the content?

This is only one possible proposal for such code review checklist. Depending on the specifics of the project, there might be more questions that need to be asked as a part of the review; make the team write your own checklist. You can find good examples online, such as Fog Creek's Code Review Checklist.

Divide the problems that you have found during reviews into the following categories:

- **Wrong problem**: This feature does not lie within the scope of project. It is used sometimes for the bug that cannot be reproduced. Is the idea behind the contribution sound? If so, eject changes with or without prejudice, do not continue the analysis for the review.

- **Does not work**: This does not compile, introduces a regression, doesn't pass the test suite, doesn't fix the bug, and so on. These problems absolutely must be fixed.

- **Fails best practices**: This does not follow the industry guidelines or the project's coding conventions. Is the contribution polished? These are pretty important to fix, but there might be some nuances on why it is written the way it is.

- Does not match **reviewer preferences**. Suggest modifications but do not require changes, or alternatively ask for a clarification.

Minor problems, for example, typo fixes or spelling errors, can be fixed immediately by the reviewer. If the exact problem repeats, however, consider asking the original author for the fix and resubmissions; this is done to spread knowledge. You should not be making any substantive edits in the review process (barring extenuating circumstances).

Ask, don't tell. Explain your reasoning about why the code should be changed. Offer ways to improve the code. Distinguish between facts and opinions. Be aware of negative bias with the online documentation.

Responding to reviews and comments

Not always are the changes accepted on the first try. You can and will get suggestions for improvement (and other comments) from the maintainer, from the code reviewer, and from other developers. You might even get these comments in the patch form, or in a fixup commit form.

First, consider leading your response with an expression of appreciation to take time to perform a review. If anything in the review is unclear, do ask for clarification; and if there is a lack of understanding between you and the reviewer, offer clarification.

In such case, the next step is often to polish and refine changes. Then, you should resubmit them (perhaps, marking them as v2). You should respond to the review for each commit and for the whole series.

If you are responding to the comments in a pull request, reply in the same way. In the case of patch submissions via e-mail, you can put the comments for a new version (with a response to the review, or a description of the difference from the previous attempt), either between three dashes - - - and the diffstat, or at the top of an e-mail separated from what is to be in the commit message by the "scissors" line, for example, - - - - - - - >8 - - - - - - -. An explanation of the changes that stays constant between iterations, but nevertheless should be not included in the commit message, can be kept in the `git notes` (see *Chapter 8, Keeping History Clean*) and inserted automatically via `git format-patch --notes`.

Depending on the project's governance structure, you would have to wait for the changes to be considered good and ready for the inclusion. This can be the decision of a benevolent dictator for life in open-source projects, or the decision of the team leader, a committee, or a consensus. It is considered a good practice to summarize the discussion while submitting a final version of a feature.

Note that the changes that got accepted might nevertheless go through few more stages, before finally graduating to the stable branch and be present in the project.

Other recommendations

In this section, you would find the best practices and recommendations that do not fit cleanly in one of the areas described before, namely starting a project, working on a project, and integrating changes.

Don't panic, recovery is almost always possible

As long as you have committed your work, storing your changes in the repository, it will not be lost. It would only perhaps be misplaced. Git also tries to preserve your current un-committed (unsaved) work, but it cannot distinguish for example between the accidental and the conscious removing of all the changes to the working directory with `git reset --hard`. Therefore, you'd better commit or stash your current work before trying to recover lost commits.

Thanks to the reflog (both for the specific branch and for the HEAD ref), it is easy to undo most operations. Then, there is the list of stashed changes (see *Chapter 4, Managing Your Worktree*), where your changes might hide. And there is `git fsck` as the last resort. See *Chapter 11, Git Administration* for some further information about data recovery.

If the problem is the mess you have made of the working directory, stop and think. Do not drop your changes needlessly. With the help of interactive add, interactive reset (the `--patch` option), and interactive checkout (the same), you can usually disentangle the mess.

Running `git status` and carefully reading its output helps in many cases where you are stuck after doing some lesser-known Git operation.

If you have a problem with the rebase or merge, and you cannot pass the responsibility to another developer, there is always the third-party `git-imerge` tool.

Don't change the published history

Once you have made your changes public, you should ideally consider those revisions etched in stone, immutable and unchanging. If you find problems with commits, create a fix (perhaps, by undoing the effect of the changes with `git revert`). This is all described in *Chapter 8*, *Keeping History Clean*.

That is, unless it is stated explicitly in the development documentation that these specific branches can be rewritten or redone; but it is nevertheless better to avoid creating such branches.

In some rare cases, you might really need to change history: remove a file, clean up a unencrypted stored password, remove accidentally added large files, and so on. If you need to do it, notify all the developers of the fact.

Numbering and tagging releases

Before you release a new version of your project, mark the version to be released with a signed tag. This ensures integrity of the just created revision.

There are various conventions on naming the release tags and on release numbering. One of more common ones is tagging releases by using, for example, `1.0.2` or `v1.0.2` as a tag name.

> If the integrity of the project is important, consider using signed merges for integration (that is, merging signed tags), see *Chapter 5*, *Collaborative Development with Git*, and signed pushes, see *Chapter 11*, *Git Administration*.

There are different conventions on naming releases. For example, with time-based releases, there is a convention of naming releases after dates, such as `2015.04` (or `15.04`). Then, there is a common convention of **semantic versioning** (`http://semver.org/`) with the `MAJOR.MINOR.PATCH` numbering, where `PATCH` increases when you are making backward-compatible bug fixes, `MINOR` is increased while adding a functionality that is backward compatible, and the `MAJOR` version is increased while making incompatible API changes. Even when not using a full semantic versioning, it is common to add a third number for maintenance releases, for example, `v1.0` and `v1.0.3`.

Automate what is possible

You should not only have the coding standards written down in the development documentation, but you also need to enforce them. Following these standards can be facilitated with client-side hooks (*Chapter 10, Customizing and Extending Git*), and it can be enforced with server-side hooks (*Chapter 11, Git Administration*).

Hooks can also help with automatically managing tickets in the issue tracker, selecting an operation based on given triggers (patterns) in the commit message. Hooks can also be used to protect against rewriting history.

Consider using third-party solutions, such as Gitolite or GitLab, to enforce rules for access control. If you need code review, use appropriate tools such as Gerrit or the pull requests of GitHub, Bitbucket, or GitLab.

Summary

These recommendations, based on the best practices of using Git as a version control system, can really help your development and your team. You have learned the steps on the road, starting from an idea, all the way ending with the changes being integrated into the project. These checklists should help you develop better code.

Index

Symbols

3-way merge
  performing 102
34ac2 branching point 29
.gitignore templates
  reference link 93

A

advanced branching techniques 165
ancestry references 33
annotated tags 12, 28, 158
anonymous Git protocol 361, 362
attribute macros
  defining 107
author
  mapping 57
  versus committer 54

B

bare repositories 126
binary files
  identifying 97, 98
blame command 48, 50
Blob object 225
branches
  about 27, 166
  anonymous branches 82
  branch name, changing 87
  changes, discarding 111
  creating 19, 20
  deleting 86
  Git checkout DWIM-mery 83
  listing 83

long-lived branches 167
merging 20, 21
new branch, creating 80
obstacles, switching to 81
orphan branches, creating 80
purposes 166
release engineering 173
resetting 84, 85
rewinding 84, 85, 111
selecting 81
short-lived branches 171
switching 81
types 166
unpublished merge, undoing 21
workflows 173
working with 79
branches, interacting in remote repositories
  about 183
  automatic tag following 189
  current branches, fetching 186
  current branches, pushing in nonbare
      remote repository 187
  current branches, updating 186
  default fetch refspec 187
  downstream 183
  fetching and pulling, versus pushing 186
  fetching branches 189
  fetching tags 188-190
  pushing branches 190
  pushing tags 190
  push modes 187, 190
  refspec 184-186
  remote-tracking branches 184, 185
  upstream 184
branches list, tracked by node
  modifying 136

contents, matching 43
creating 62
DAG view 62, 63
faulty merge, reverting 253-255
index 63, 64
moving, to feature branch 111
removing 108
reverted merges, recovering 256-259
reverting 252, 253
selective commit 74
splitting, with reset command 110
squashing, with reset command 109
commit-msg hook 338
commit object 224, 225
commit parents 43
commit process hooks
about 337
commit-msg hook 338
post-commit hook 338
pre-commit hook 337
prepare-commit-msg hook 337, 338
committer
versus author 54
commit tools 319
commit walker downloader 139
content-addressed storage 157
contributions
summarizing 56, 57
credentials 150
credentials/password management
about 150
asking for password 150
credential helpers 152
public key authentication, for SSH 151
current push mode 194

D

data recovery
about 349
lost commit, recovering 349, 350
default branch
setting, of remote 136
detached HEAD situation 27
development workflows
augmenting 367, 368

diff
revision range notation, using in 41
diff configuration 99
diffing binary files 99, 100
diff output
configuring 101
Directed Acyclic Graph (DAG) 23, 24
directed edges 25
directed graph 24
directories
examining 118, 119
distributed version control systems (DVCS) 25
double dot notation 37, 38
dumb protocols 363, 364

E

Easy Git (eg) 318
end-of-line conversions
identifying 97, 98
end of line (eol) characters 97
environment variables
affecting committing 230, 231
affecting global behavior 228
affecting repository locations 229, 230
external tools
for large-scale history rewriting 247

F

failed merges
conflict markers, in worktree 212, 213
differences, examining 214, 215
examining 211
git log 216
three stages, in index 213
feature branch
about 371
commits, moving to 111
file attributes 96, 97
file contents
searching 119
file history
about 46
path limiting 46
simplification 48

I

IDE integration 320
ignored files
  examining 94-96
ignore patterns 17
index
  about 63
  about 90
  resetting 109
information
  updating, of remotes 135
integration branches 174
integration manager workflow
  about 130
  advantages 130
  disadvantages 131
interactive rebase
  about 77, 109, 232, 233
  commits, fixing 233-236
  commits, removing 233-236
  commits, reordering 233-236
  commits, splitting 237-239
  commits, squashing 236, 237
  rebased commit, testing 239

K

keyword expansion 105, 106
keyword substitution 105, 106

L

leaf nodes 25
lieutenants 131
lightweight tag 158
line-ending 330
local protocol 360
local transport 138, 139
long-lived branches
  automation branches 169
  graduation 167, 168
  hotfix branches 169
  integration 167
  mob branches, for anonymous
      push access 170
  orphan branch trick 170

per-customer branches 169
per-deployment branches 169
per-release branches 168
per-release maintenance 168
progressive-stability 167, 168

M

maint branch 29
master branch 29
matching push mode 191
merge
  undoing 112
merge commits 29
merge configuration 99
merge conflict, resolving
  about 14-17
  file changes, undoing 18
  files, adding in bulk 17
  files, removing 17
merge conflicts
  about 210
  avoiding 216
  dealing with 218
  failed merges, examining 211
  files, marking as resolved 219
  git-imerge 220
  graphical merge tools, using 219
  manual file remerging 218
  merge, aborting 218
  merge options 216
  merges, finalizing 219
  rebase conflicts, resolving 220
  rerere (reuse recorded resolutions) 217
  resolving 210
  scriptable fixes 218
  three-way merge 210, 211
  version, selecting 218
mixed reset 109
multiple working directories 123

N

native Git protocol 140
nodes, DAG
  leaf nodes 25
  root nodes 25

triple-dot notation 39, 40
troubleshooting, Git 349, 351
trunk 173
trunk branches workflow 173

U

update hook 354
upstream push mode 192, 193
user-defined revision formats 53, 54

V

version control system (VCS) 24

W

web interfaces 365
whitespace 330, 331
whole-tree commits 26
WIP commit
  state, restoring with 110
  state, saving with 110
workflows, branches
  Git-flow 181
  graduation branches workflow 174, 175
  progressive-stability branches
      workflow 174, 175
  release branches workflow 173
  security issue, fixing 182, 183
  topic branches workflow 176
  trunk branches workflow 173, 174
working area
  cleaning 122
worktrees
  about 90
  managing 118

www.ingramcontent.com/pod-product-compliance
Lightning Source LLC
Chambersburg PA
CBHW081503050326
40690CB00015B/2910